DATE DUE

MAR 29 '91		
4/16		
MAY 04 '91		
ILL		
SWIFT		
#1625742		
#1625740		
FCI-Florence		
9-15-03		

DEMCO 38-297

THE
BORGIAS

THE
BORGIAS

IVAN CLOULAS

Translated by Gilda Roberts

FRANKLIN WATTS

1989

New York • Toronto

Excerpts from *The Prince* by Machiavelli, translated by Harvey C. Mansfield, copyright © 1985 by The University of Chicago, are reprinted by permission of the publisher, the University of Chicago Press.

First published in France in 1987 by Librairie Arthème Fayard

Copyright © 1987 by Librairie Arthème Fayard

Translation copyright © 1989 by Franklin Watts, Inc.,
387 Park Avenue South, New York, NY 10016

6   5   4   3   2   1

Design by Tere LoPrete

Library of Congress Cataloging-in-Publication Data

Cloulas, Ivan.
   [Borgia. English]
   The Borgias / by Ivan Cloulas ; translated by Gilda Roberts.
   p. cm.
   Translation of: Les Borgia.
   Bibliography: p.
   Includes index.
   ISBN 0-531-15101-8
   1. Borgia family. 2. Italy—History—15th century. 3. Italy—
History—1492–1559. 4. Italy—Nobility—Biography. I. Title.
DG463.8.B7C5613 1989
945'.06'0922—dc19
[B]   88-34560
                                      CIP

CONTENTS

PROLOGUE

The Borgias and Our Time

The Borgias . . . the very name conjures up a violent, blood-red world, a world of luxury, sensuality, and death, where poison and the dagger rule. The characters loom up before us, their names ringing out like a fanfare of trumpets. Cesare Borgia, Lucrezia Borgia stand arrayed in silks and gold. . . . Incest and murder blacken the name of the Vatican. . . . The forces of evil drag the head of God's Church to the very abyss of hell. . . .

This caricature is the result of centuries of hostile writings. Paradoxically, this biased view has actually been reinforced by certain clumsy attempts to whitewash the Borgia name. Scholars refute these attempts, arguing that the evils associated with the family were real, hardly mitigated by extenuating circumstances. The case seems closed. But anyone examining the mountain of records built up over the centuries will see that some allegations lose their scandalous hue when subjected to rigorous criticism. Put into historical perspective, the so-called heinous crimes can be explained quite naturally. Thus it is evident that much new light still needs to be shed on a long family history.

The greatness of the Borgias is, in fact, the result of a concerted family effort stretching over hundreds of years. Their story begins in the late fourteenth century. A quirk of fate gave a handful of modest Spanish landowners their chance when the Great Schism tore Western Christendom apart.

One of the actors in the drama is Alonso Borgia. A simple cleric from the kingdom of Valencia, he rose to the papacy and, gathering his family around the throne of St. Peter, founded a dynasty of priests.

Fifty years later, this family held sway over Rome and many parts of Italy, France, and Spain. Pope Alexander VI and his children, Cesare, Juan, Lucrezia, and Jofré, were no different from such dynastic figures of the age as the Riarios, Medicis, Sforzas, Estes, and Gonzagas. But the Borgias remained outsiders, they loathed hypocrisy, and their genius inspired Machiavelli. This is what their enemies have held against them, branding them with the mark of infamy.

Yet Providence keeps watch: a half-century later a scandalous Borgia pope's sins are redeemed by the merits of his descendant, a genuine saint.

When examined in detail, the Borgias' story is an extraordinary one, full of dramatic twists. Closely linked to the crises tearing Europe apart, the family's saga provides the human counterpoint. We learn about the customs, ways of thinking, the arts and technology prevailing in the Renaissance courts and the camps of the great condottieri.

Yet our interest in the Borgias is not confined to the picturesque or the bright colors of a painting. We feel a strange, personal involvement in this period. Licentiousness, cruelty, and violence are with us today just as in the time of the Borgias and, in their portrait, we see a reflection of ourselves.

PART ONE

*The Rise
of the Borgia Family*

1

Valencia and Aragon: The Borgias' Roots in Spain

Sons of conquerors

The House of Borgia traces its roots back to Spain, to Játiva, a little town on the slopes of the Sierra de las Agujas at the southern tip of the Valencia *huerta*, its lush lowlands.

After Valencia had been reconquered from the Moors in 1238, soldiers of Jaime the Fortunate, king of Aragon, stormed the citadel of Medina Xatibea, as Játiva used to be called. Perched high among jagged rocks, the walled city, built on the ruins of the ancient Saetabis, was the second largest in the kingdom of Valencia. It was a bustling place, noted for the manufacture of paper. For the Moorish nobility, however, Játiva had served mainly as a delightful resort. Springwater splashed into three hundred basins, and in their midst a magnificent fountain sent spray gushing from a score of jets. Below, sheltered from the winds, lay the richly irrigated plain, its groves of palm and orange trees and pale rice fields contrasting refreshingly with the starkness of the sierra.

Storming the citadel of Játiva was an easy matter after Valencia, and King Jaime divided up the land with his knights. Among these men were Estebán de Borja and eight of his relatives. They came from a village of the same name far to the north in the Ebro Valley, 37 miles from Saragossa. The Borja family had been living there for a hundred years, ever since the village, reconquered from the Arabs in 1120, had been granted to their ancestor, Count Pedro de Atares, an illegitimate son of Don Ramiro Sánchez, king of Aragon. Their coat of arms showed a grazing bull on a field gules, or red ground; representing the Borjas' pastoral origins, the animal was symbolic of the fierce courage of their warrior clan. In the fourteenth century the senior branch of the family migrated to the kingdom of Naples while the junior branches, which stayed on in Spain, became closer-knit through matrimonial alliances. At the same time these marriages kept intact their lands, expertly tended by Moorish farmers. After Islam came the Mozarabic period, a fine reminder of which was the superb Gothic chapel of San Feliu, set halfway up the mountainside below the castle, where it nestled among cypress and locust trees.

Birth of Alonso de Borja
Prophecy of St. Vincent Ferrer

As the years went by, fine manor houses, or *solares*, sprang up in Játiva. One of them, a rich-looking dwelling at the corner of the calle de Ventres, was the home of Rodrigo Gil de Borja and his wife, Sibila de Oms, who came from one of the leading families of Aragon. In the calle de la Triaca other Borjas occupied the Palau, once a Muslim monastery where the *alfaquis*, or fakirs, were housed. Farther on, toward the collegiate church, is an aristocratic-looking street called the calle de Moncada. There, a vaulted doorway surmounted by the family crest leads to a flower-filled courtyard with palm trees and a central fountain—purportedly the home of Juan Domingo de Borja of Canals and his wife, Doña Francisca Martí (or Martinez) of Valencia. The couple also had a fortified manor in the village of Canals called La Torreta, where their son Alonso was born on December 31, 1378. He had several sisters, who married into the local gentry. The eldest girl, Catalina, was wedded to Don Juan de Mila, the baron of Mazalanes. Another sister, Isabel, married her cousin Jofré de Borja y Oms, the son of Rodrigo Gil de Borja and Sibila de Oms. Two other sisters, Juana and Francisca, made similar matches.

In those waning years of the fourteenth century, resonances of the tumult shaking world history were felt in Játiva. Young Alonso's birth coincided with the outbreak of the Great Western Schism, an event seen as catastrophic by the faithful. On September 20, 1378, the cardinals, in revolt against Urban VI, elected a rival pope, Robert of Geneva. He assumed the name of Clement VII and declared the seat of the papacy once again to be Avignon, abandoned shortly before by the popes after a seventy-year stay. Christendom was split asunder.

Rome and Avignon quarreled over the allegiance of the states. As the scandal reverberated, people worried about the legitimacy of one or the other pope. Through the votes of its *jurados* the city of Valencia attempted to impose neutrality, which was the choice of its king, Pedro IV, the Ceremonious, of Aragon. Pedro commanded obedience and inspired fear in his subjects. The pope of Avignon, unlike his rival, was backed by loyal partisans who spared no effort to rally the people to his side.

The most energetic of his henchmen was a fifty-year-old Spanish cardinal, Pedro Martinez de Luna. He was linked to the royal family, the Infante Don Martí having married one of his cousins. The cardinal put his wide knowledge of the law at the service of his monarch. For a long time he had been provost of the cathedral chapter of Valencia as well as archdeacon of Saragossa; now the Avignon pope, Clement VII, appointed de Luna legate on Spanish soil. Aiding him was the prior of the Dominican monastery of Valencia, one Vicente Ferrer, known to posterity as St. Vincent Ferrer. This thirty-year-old cleric showed in debate the same keen mind he had displayed not long before when teaching logic at his order's monastery in Lérida, seat of the University of Aragon. Pedro de Luna ordained him priest in 1378. Vincent, who was exceptionally eloquent, immediately demonstrated his ability. For ten years he went around preaching in every parish of Valencia, moving people to tears as he exhorted them to ponder the Day of Judgment.

Vincent was convinced that the legitimate Pastor of the Church was in Avignon. Preaching in Játiva, he was struck by the fervor of young Alonso de Borja. "My son," he told him, full of prophetic inspiration, "I commend you. Remember that you are called to become one day the ornament of your house and of your country. You will be invested with the highest dignity that can fall to the lot of man. After my death, I myself shall be, through you, the object of a very special veneration. Strive to persevere in virtue." Alonso never forgot this combined compliment and prophecy, which encouraged his parents to send him away to study in Lérida, where Vincent Ferrer had begun his career.

The jurist of Lérida and the Aragonese pope

Two hundred and eighty miles to the north of Játiva, Lérida lies halfway between the Aragonese capital of Saragossa, 93 miles to the west, and

Barcelona, the great Catalan port and political center, roughly 100 miles to the east. The city was a major crossroads, having witnessed the momentous days when Alonso de Borja's forbears set forth to fight the Infidel. The Church of San Lorenzo had once been a mosque, which in turn had been built on the ruins of a Roman temple. In the twelfth century the Moorish castle had become a palace of the counts of Barcelona. There were also the imposing Old Cathedral with its magnificent Romanesque ornamentation and the *casas consistoriales*, or town-hall buildings, which had been reconstructed and given Gothic windows. In this monumental setting the Cortes, the parliament shared by Catalonia and Aragon, met from time to time. It is hard to imagine a finer place for young Alonso's university education than Lérida, heady with memories of the glorious history of Aragon.

Alonso plunged enthusiastically into the study of law. While he was working toward his degree of doctor in civil and canon law, Cardinal Pedro de Luna and Vincent Ferrer were campaigning indefatigably for the Avignon pope throughout the length and breadth of the Spanish peninsula. The king of Aragon, Pedro IV, still refused to give up the neutral position he had taken with regard to the two popes, but when he died in 1387, his son Juan I pledged absolute allegiance to the Avignon pope. In 1394 the architect of this bond with Aragon, Cardinal de Luna, was elected by the Avignon cardinals to succeed Clement, becoming Pope Benedict XIII. In Aragon the news was hailed with jubilation.

Favors were showered upon the Aragonese in the early days of Benedict's reign. Alonso de Borja became canon of the venerable Lérida cathedral. But Benedict's future was far from certain, since he had promised to come to an agreement with his rival in Rome to put an end to the Schism. As it turned out, his negotiations with Urban VI's successors were to fail. Nor was there any way to heal the breach by force. The champion of the Avignon papacy, Louis I of Anjou, had been crowned king of Naples by Clement VII; but he was defeated by the champion of the Roman pope, his rival Charles of Durazzo.

Misfortunes of Benedict XIII

In 1398 the new king of Aragon, Martin I, learned to his consternation that Pope Benedict was being besieged in his Avignon palace by the

French king, who had withdrawn his allegiance. When Martin asked for money to help save the pope, Barcelona merchants, together with the clergy, raised funds to cover the costs of an expedition to Provence. Unfortunately, however, the fleet carrying Martin's troops was scattered by the French.

Alonso de Borja was by now reunited with the fiery Vincent Ferrer and his brother Boniface, prior of the Grande Chartreuse monastery, both of whom championed the cause of the captive pope. To their satisfaction they learned that the pope had escaped from his palace in disguise and found refuge in friendly Provence. Over the next five years, Benedict regained the upper hand, even winning back the allegiance of the French. Now, more than ever, people saw the need to work for the unity of the Church, which was being threatened by two heresies. One came from England, where John Wycliffe talked about predestination, portraying the pope as an Antichrist and rejecting most of the sacraments. The other, springing from Wycliffe's ideas, was gaining a large following in Bohemia behind Jan Hus. Like the Englishman, Hus rejected the sacraments and the hierarchy, claiming for his followers alone the right to possess land and hold any kind of office. A religious and social revolution seemed to be afoot.

Even this danger could not bring the rivals together, and the many negotiations between the courts of Rome and Avignon met with failure. Meanwhile monks, clerics, and learned men of each camp struggled to find a solution. The University of Lérida was canvassed like the others, but the discussions were fruitless.

There was no option other than to use force and once again it was France that took the initiative. A council held in Paris at the king's behest stated that Benedict XIII had not kept his promise to come to an agreement with his rival in Rome, and condemned him as a schismatic and heretic. The sentence, however, had not the slightest effect: Benedict placed himself under the direct protection of King Martin of Aragon, who offered him sanctuary in his castle in Perpignan. There the pope convened another council and proclaimed his legitimacy. In mid-1409 another conclave, called at Pisa by cardinals of both Avignon and Rome, threw out the claims of both Benedict and the Roman pope. A new pope, Alexander V, was elected. He died shortly afterward and was at once replaced by another, who took the name John XXIII. All this was the height of confusion; even a learned jurist like Alonso de Borja was hard put to decide which side was in the right. He had spent a good half of his forty years working in vain to bring about reconciliation between the rival pontiffs.

Next, King Martin dreamed up a new plan to support his pope. Believing that Sicily, whose throne he had held before that of Aragon, might serve as a base from which to attack Ladislas, king of Naples, who supported the Roman pope, he decided to forge an alliance with a rival of the king's, Louis II of Anjou. The campaign had to be halted, however, when Martin died in 1410. Meanwhile, Louis's fleet was scattered and the French king defeated at the Battle of Garigliano.

These repeated blows of fate did not succeed in discouraging Benedict, who still commanded the obedience of many states. The death, without issue, of King Martin forced him to try to settle the Aragonese succession. The first order of business was to have a prince elected who would be his ally and give him the sanctuary he needed. To choose a new king, the parliaments of Catalonia, Valencia, and Aragon named a committee of nine wise men, among them Vincent Ferrer and his brother Boniface, both loyal supporters of Benedict. After endless discussion the candidate favored by Benedict was chosen— Fernando of Castile, grandson of Pedro III of Aragon. Fernando pledged his support to the exiled pope and looked with favor on the clerics and jurists who had got him elected. From now on, Alonso de Borja would have entree to the court of Aragon.

Bolstered by the new king's support, Benedict refused the summons of the emperor Sigismund, who had ordered him to appear before the ecumenical Council of Constance, and remained on his papal throne while his rivals were forced to step down. Sigismund himself traveled to Perpignan in an attempt to make Benedict change his mind, but could get nothing from him and had to leave after three months of vain palavering.

Despite Sigismund's assurances, Benedict thought it wise to flee to a safer place, and, with the four cardinals who had stayed loyal to him, he shut himself up in the rock-fortress of Peñiscola on the Aragonese coast. Here bad news reached him: not only had Aragon withdrawn its allegiance, but he had been condemned by the Council of Constance, and a new pope, Martin V, had been elected. The new king of Aragon, Alfonso V, pleaded with Benedict to retire, but, magnificently detached from worldly affairs, the old man loftily excommunicated Martin V along with those of his own cardinals who had rallied to the new pope's side. For six years he defied the world from his rocky perch.

In Peñiscola, a primitive refuge in an extraordinary setting, the dethroned pope was completely out of enemy reach. The way to the rock led south from Castellón de la Plana—first across a narrow plain squeezed between the sierras and the sea, then along paths that wound through a forbidding mountainous area bristling with watchtowers. No army of any size could make its way along this perilous route. After 60 miles or so a fortress came into view, marking the coastal road, and from here the path led down to Peñiscola. The island was linked to the shore by a sandspit, completely under water in stormy weather. Houses were piled up the rock slopes to the castle at its peak, which the Knights Templar had built over Phoenician and Greek ruins.

Benedict made considerable improvements in his rocky home. He inspected the ramparts and had them buttressed, determined to go on guiding Christendom and guarding her against all comers. Yet he had lost the support of his most loyal followers, such as Vincent Ferrer, who had retired to Brittany, where he died in 1419. The Aragonese clergy were shunning him. Only one Christian territory remained faithful, Armagnac, in southern France. In 1422 he appointed new cardinals, two Frenchmen and two Aragonese, the latter being sworn to name a successor after his death.

Alfonso V of Aragon continued, officially, to demand the resignation of the aging pope, but he was playing a double game: it was in his own interest to keep open the rift between the popes since the Schism could help him realize a dream, the conquest of Naples. In 1421 Queen Joanna of Naples chose Alfonso as her heir, then brushed him aside in favor of Louis III of Anjou. As Louis was supported by the Roman pope, Martin V, Alfonso took pains to avoid disturbing the rebel pontiff.

Alonso de Borja, victor of the Great Schism

On May 23, 1423, the stubborn old Benedict XIII gave up the ghost in his fortress-palace. Not losing an instant, three of his recently named cardinals held a conclave and elected as pope Gil Sánchez Muñoz, the provost of Valencia, henceforth known as Clement VIII. Since King Alfonso was away fighting Castile, his consort, Queen Maria, ordered all Muñoz's assets to be confiscated and blockaded the island of Peñiscola. On hearing of this, Alfonso promptly canceled his wife's measures, a reaction that people ascribed to a royal domestic quarrel. Around this time, Alfonso had been publicly carrying on a love affair with the beautiful Margarita de Hijar, and the queen had her strangled. It may have been this mistress or, more likely, an obscure Castilian woman, Carlina Villardona, who bore the king a bastard son, whom he named Fernando—or Ferrante—after his own father.

Yet the king's behavior was dictated even more by foreign-policy considerations. He wanted to use the new antipope to put pressure on the Roman pope, Martin V, who was supporting his rival in the kingdom of Naples. When, however, the Aragonese forces were defeated in 1424 beneath the walls of L'Aquila, Alfonso lost all interest in backing the puppet pope and instructed Alonso de Borja, now his private secretary, to find an honorable way out of the situation. This had in fact begun to smack of farce: Benedict XIII's fourth cardinal, Jean Carrier, on his return to Peñiscola had single-handedly elected a new antipope, Bernard Garnier, who became Benedict XIV.

After the L'Aquila defeat, fresh negotiations were entered into with Rome. Alfonso V insisted on receiving assurances that Martin V would be on his side. Up to now he had left the antipope, Clement VIII, free to act out a pontifical life in miniature on his rock and in 1426 have himself crowned pope amidst a court of twenty-two dignitaries. No sooner had Alfonso come to an agreement with Rome, however, than he put an end to such make-believe and dispatched Alonso de Borja to Peñiscola to demand that the pseudo-pontiff abdicate.

Clement's response was to stage an extremely dignified ceremony. Sitting on his throne in pontifical splendor, he solemnly revoked the excommunication that he and his predecessor had pronounced on the Roman pope and declared his intent to divest himself, of his own free will, of papal dignity. He cast off his papal robes and put on those of a secular doctor of learning. Then, at his request, the last of his supporters held a conclave and elected Cardinal Otto Colonna—that is, the Roman pope, Martin V, who had in fact been pope for a dozen years.

Two weeks later the antipope bowed to the papal legate Pierre de Foix and was reconciled with the Church, receiving in recompense the bishopric of Mallorca. As for the successful negotiator of the end of the Schism, Alonso de Borja, he was given a sumptuous reward: on August 20, 1429, Pope Martin V, in agreement with King Alfonso, raised him to the wealthy episcopal see of Valencia, which had been vacant for two years.

The bishop of Valencia and Aragon's conquest of Naples

At fifty, Alonso Borja had the satisfaction of returning as pastor to the diocese of his birth. His new, exalted rank brought him close to King Alfonso V, who engaged him not only as private secretary but also as tutor of his illegitimate son, Ferrante. He also turned to him constantly for advice in the disputes between Aragon and Castile.

Between his stays at court, Alonso journeyed to Játiva, where he saw his family increasing in size. On January 1, 1432, his nephew Rodrigo was born to Alonso's sister Isabel and Jofré de Borja y Oms in their house in the calle de Ventres. The bishop of Valencia was very fond of this little family, which included at least five children destined to make their mark in the world. Besides Rodrigo—the future Pope Alexander VI—the eldest child, Pedro Luís, would become duke of Spoleto and prefect of Rome, while the daughters would make good matches among the nobility.

Another child, Francisco de Borja, was born ten years after Rodrigo and raised in the countryside around Valencia, where he was known as the "Borja bastard." Kept somewhat in the background, he did not make his mark until much later, becoming bishop in 1495 and cardinal in 1500. One historian refers to him as the bishop of Valencia's illegitimate son, but this is unproven, although such a thing would be quite normal, given the mores of the time.

Alonso's work was not restricted to Spanish internal affairs. His employer brought him into a new plan to seize Naples. Louis III of Anjou had died in 1434, and Queen Joanna had just had time to appoint René, the Angevin pretender's brother, as heir before she herself died. René was then being held prisoner by the duke of Burgundy, so it was left to his wife, Isabelle, to confront Alfonso V. She did so, valiantly, with the aid of the duke of Milan, Filippo Maria Visconti, and won. Alfonso suffered a crippling naval defeat on August 5, 1435, and was taken prisoner in Milan. On being released—he had managed to charm the jailer, who became his friend—he was free once more to take up his fight against the kingdom of Naples.

The bishop of Valencia was unstinting in his efforts to aid the king's great Neapolitan venture. This soon came to resemble a colonial expedition involving a whole people. In one campaign after another,

Alfonso threw his nobles into the attack, promising them rich domains as a reward. He also relied on great local landowners who were opposed to the pretender of Anjou, as well as descendants of Catalan families that had settled in Naples a hundred years before—such as the senior branch of the Borjas. Finally, on June 12, 1442, the capital fell into Alfonso's hands. The next year he made his solemn entrance into Naples in a golden chariot drawn by four white horses, and paraded through streets strewn with flowers amidst allegorical scenes showing Fortune, the Virtues, and Caesar crushing the face of the world beneath his feet.

Now, Alfonso set about organizing his kingdom. Anarchy was rampant. Rather than restore the old freedoms, the king centralized power on the advice of his jurists. The councils and magistratures were put in the hands of Catalan and Aragonese families. The bishop of Valencia was the prime mover of this reorganization, which culminated in the setting up of the Sacro Consiglio, a supreme court to which all the tribunals under Alfonso's domain—Aragon, Catalonia, the Balearics, Sardinia, Sicily, and, of course, the kingdom of Naples—had to appeal.

Alonso, the first Borgia cardinal

The king of Aragon and Naples could now, if he chose, have his revenge on Eugenius IV, the active supporter of René of Anjou. The pope had been the target of hostility from the Council of Basel, which deposed him and set up another antipope, Felix X, in his place. But, as in the days of the Peñiscola antipopes, Alfonso had not taken sides. Nevertheless, after his Neapolitan triumph he hesitated no longer. An alliance with Rome, which would end the continual warring between Naples and Rome, struck him as the wiser course. The envoy he chose to carry his peace proposals to Eugenius IV was Alonso de Borja.

On June 14, 1443, in the Eternal City, the bishop of Valencia scored a resounding success. He agreed in his employer's name to accept Eugenius as the sole legitimate pope, to respect the liberties of the Church, to outfit ships for the war against the Turks threatening Christendom in the East, and lastly to raise an army of 5,000 men to drive the condottiere Francesco Sforza out of the Ancona Marches, the important papal territory on the Adriatic coast.

For his part, the pope recognized the legitimacy of Queen Joanna's adoption of Alfonso as her heir and granted him investiture of the kingdom of Naples and the right to the papal lands of Benevento and Terracina. The following year the skilful mediator Alonso de Borja was received into the purple and named cardinal-presbyter of the Quattro Santi Coronati, or Four Crowned Saints. The pope authorized him to remain bishop of Valencia. Not long afterward, Eugenius acknowledged the right of King Alfonso's illegitimate son, Ferrante, to succeed his father in the kingdom of Naples. The new cardinal was flattered by this move honoring the young prince who had been his pupil.

While the thorny Naples question was being settled, the recent Schism was collapsing. The antipope was losing support. Another distinguished career opened up before the sixty-year-old cardinal-bishop of Valencia. He took leave of his employer in Naples. He now had a wealth of human and political experience behind him; he would use it to serve the Holy See and to enhance his family's greatness.

CHAPTER

2

The Borgias Arrive in Rome: Pontificate of Calixtus III

The Quattro Santi Coronati

Alonso Borgia's appointment as cardinal was intended both to reward him for his services and to further the interests of his master, the king of Naples. With his former secretary as cardinal of Valencia, the king now had a first-class representative at the Holy See.

The new cardinal arrived in a Rome to which Pope Eugenius IV had just returned from a nine-year banishment. It was a Rome that had been fought over endlessly by the great families, chief among them the Orsinis and the Colonnas, and ravaged in bloody revolts ruthlessly suppressed by the rival clans' condottieri. To stem further outbreaks and ensure the pope's temporal power, the Orsini and Colonna barons had to be held in check. The cardinals were encouraged to do their part by taking over their titular churches within the vast wasteland bounded by Rome's ancient walls. Soon, next to his sanctuary every "prince of the church" had a palace, which in many cases was fortified.

Alonso Borgia's church was dedicated to the Quattro Santi Coronati, or Four Crowned Saints. It stood—and still stands today—on the Coelian Hill, one of the seven hills of Rome. His palace nearby was a fortified observation post dominating the overgrown Forum and facing the Colosseum, which at that time was a fortress topped by feudal towers. At the foot of the Coelian Hill was the Via Labicana, from which a steep path climbed to a crenellated wall, its gate capped with a bell tower. Alonso's church had two courtyards, the first containing the early Chapel of San Silvestro. The second led to the church itself, with its marble mosaics and delightful cloister. In this peaceful haven Cardinal Borgia (as he was known in Italy) used his diplomatic talents to bring about a reconciliation between the Church and the difficult Alfonso V of Naples.

Family concerns

Even though the cardinal's time was so largely taken up with politics, he never forgot his homeland. Játiva was always close to his heart; indeed, one of Alonso's first acts on being received into the purple had been to commission a painting for the collegiate church where he was baptized. An Aragonese artist called Jacomart Baço, who was court painter to the king of Naples, painted a triptych. One of the side panels shows a saint, St. Idelfonsus, at whose feet Alonso kneels devoutly in scarlet cappa magna and cardinal's hat. His expression is solemn, as befits a painting intended for a funeral chapel. But pious works were not his only concern: he devoted an amazing amount of energy to promoting the worldly interests of his relatives, especially those of his nephews, the legitimate heirs of the Borgia clan. At the same time he kept a discreet eye on the education of Francisco, the mysterious bastard some claimed he had fathered.

Catalina, the cardinal's elder sister, now had two sons, Pedro and Luís de Mila. The younger boy had entered holy orders. Thanks to his uncle, he quickly moved up the ecclesiastical ladder, becoming in 1453 bishop of Segorbe in the kingdom of Valencia.

Alonso's second sister, who married Jofré de Borja y Oms, also had two sons, Pedro Luís and Rodrigo. At their father's death, in 1441, Alonso became the boys' tutor. Rodrigo was a bright, good-looking youth who loved pleasure and was known for his passionate, violent nature: rumor had it that at twelve he had stabbed to death a boy of his own age who was "of lower birth." Turning a deaf ear to such gossip, his uncle launched him on an ecclesiastical career, as he had his cousin Mila. Lucrative offices came his way. Soon he was appointed sacristan in the Cathedral of Valencia. As such, he was steward of the cathedral chapter and keeper of the precious ornaments and holy vessels.

The power of the Roman humanists

In Alonso's mind, moving up the ranks of the Church was a way to gain position in society and attract the notice of important people. An ecclesiastical career also provided a youth with the means to get a sound education. In those days, a man without culture had no way to penetrate the narrow circle of those who counseled the rulers of the world and shaped policy.

The papal court abounded in success stories. It swarmed with scholars—the humanists—who were brought together by a common love of antiquity. King Alfonso of Aragon, convinced of the authority they conferred, had become one of their protectors, and Cardinal Borgia had seen them flock to Naples. Once, during the siege of Gaeta in 1435, Alfonso took time out to have passages of Livy read and explained to him by the Sicilian scholar Panormita.

In Rome, the Curia had its share of humanists from Pope Martin V's time—Antonio Loschi, Poggio Bracciolini, Cencio de Rustici, and others. These dignified drafters of papal bulls and briefs flaunted a freethinking philosophy and loose morals. Their ideals are reflected in the *Facetie* of Poggio, a work that is a mine of information on the seamy side of Roman life at that time.

A friend of Poggio's who wanted a position befitting his status was hurt to find himself passed over by others who were his inferiors in knowledge and virtue. Nothing surprising in that, observes the writer: "In the Roman Curia it is always chance that carries the day, and there is seldom room for talent or virtue. Everything is won by intrigue or luck, not to speak of money, which is the true ruler of the world." Disillusioned, the worthy man told a cardinal of the pains he had taken to become a learned man. He received the following reply, astonishing from a man of the cloth: "Here, knowledge and merit count for nothing. But don't lose heart. Spend some time unlearning what you know and learning the vices you don't know, if you wish to get in the pope's good graces."

The picture of contemporary Rome is hardly an edifying one. Poggio's behind-the-scenes sketches of life in the papal palace and the Holy City paint a parade of dissolute monks, licentious young girls, hordes of prostitutes—and their clients, Poggio's colleagues at the Curia.

The popes were blind to all this, merely exploiting the learning of these men. After all they wrote the purest Latin, and Latin was the working language of the Holy See.

The troubled conclave of 1447

The pope, now Christendom's sole mouthpiece, had constantly to make decisions—not decisions about averting conciliar rebellion or uprisings in Rome, which recent popes had had to face, but about other perils just as great. The gravest menace to Christianity came from the East. The alarm had been sounded fifteen years before. John Palaeologus, the Byzantine emperor, had visited Florence in 1439, seeking aid from the pope and the Western states against the rising tide of Ottoman power. The Greeks agreed to unite the two churches, Orthodox and Catholic, but once they were back in Byzantium their fellow-countrymen rejected the agreement. Result: the Council of Florence failed to raise any effective help among the Western rulers. For their part, the Turks, now straddling the Bosporus, were pressing inexorably against the last bastions of the Byzantine Empire.

In Italy, the papacy's temporal power faced immediate danger. The condottiere Francesco Sforza was carving out a principality for himself in Italy's north and center. This was dangerously close to the Papal States—that large chunk of Italy that belonged to the papacy, stretching from the Tyrrhenian Sea to the west to the Adriatic, and from around Bologna in the north to Terracina, south of Rome. One of the points in Alonso Borgia's 1443 agreement with the Holy See was aimed at preventing such a move: Alonso was to ensure that the States were protected from Sforza's incursions. He had the satisfaction of seeing the alliance between Pope Eugenius and Naples gain new members, such as Sigismonda Malatesta, the lord of Rimini. Meanwhile, however, Francesco Sforza was rallying Florence and Venice, the duke of Urbino, and others against the Rome-Naples league. The fight looked as if it would be a close one.

King Alfonso of Naples sent 4,000 to 5,000 men to Rome in early 1447, planning to march them against Sforza's ally, Florence, in the dry season. Pope Eugenius died, however, before they had even set out. With this army the king might have been able to put pressure on the conclave to elect the candidate of his choice. However, he was not interested in antagonizing the other states, and doubtless Cardinal

Borgia had advised him to keep strictly neutral. The conclave therefore was held in highly regular fashion. The Orsini-Colonna rivalry brought about a stalemate, and on March 6, 1447, the cardinals elected a man of learning who was above both parties: Tommaso Parentucelli da Sarzana, who became Nicholas V.

Nicholas V, restorer of papal powers

The new pope was a friend of the humanists, and he gave them free rein at the Vatican. The library of the Vatican palace became one of the greatest in the world. Although no one knows precisely how many books Nicholas collected, the catalogue of Latin manuscripts lists 842—as many as the finest Florentine collection and only slightly fewer than the rich library at the castle of Pavia. There were an equivalent number of Greek manuscripts, as well as works in the vernacular, and as many profane literary works as sacred ones. Nicholas had the manuscripts richly bound, a work supervised by his friend Tortello. Bisticci, a bookseller and scholar, was another intimate friend. Poggio and many other learned men had easier access to the pope than did the prelates representing the great nation-states.

Nicholas set about rebuilding the old palace, against the north side of St. Peter's Basilica, which his earlier namesake, Nicholas III, had put up in the thirteenth century. He erected a new building opening on the Cortile del Pappagallo. The whole complex was protected by a thick wall and battlemented towers. Fra Angelico was engaged to decorate the palace, and soon Nicholas's study—known today as the Chapel of Nicholas V—was adorned with wonderful frescoes depicting the lives of the Virgin, St. Lawrence, and St. Stephen. Nicholas also planned the rebuilding of the early St. Peter's, which was close to ruin. In 1452 he had Bernardo Rossellino lay out plans for a church in the form of a Latin cross.

While the papal city was being transformed, the papacy saw its reputation enhanced. Several important events marked the new pope's reign: the pope's 1450 Jubilee drew swarms of pilgrims to the Holy City; St. Bernard of Siena was canonized, the process of rehabilitation of Joan of Arc was begun, and a renewed attempt at Church reform was carried out all over the empire by Nicholas da Cusa and Giovanni Capestrano. In a few years the papacy had regained the prestige it had enjoyed before the Great Schism.

In the political field, the year 1452 saw Frederick III, the Holy Roman emperor, travel south to Italy to receive the imperial crown from the pope's hands and a blessing on his marriage to Leonora of Portugal. Alonso Borgia and other members of the Sacred College witnessed the extraordinary spectacle of the emperor offering the pope his horse and holding the stirrup for him when they left St. Peter's. The symbolic gesture, not seen for centuries, confirmed the preeminence of spiritual over temporal power.

Still, to maintain power in Italy the emperor had to cement good relations with the princes—in particular, the powerful King Alfonso. With Rome behind him, Frederick made for Naples, where the king entertained him with a dizzy whirl of stage spectacles, hunts, banquets, and balls. Alonso Borgia saw this Neapolitan triumph as the crowning of an endeavor he had long pursued. But he also witnessed terrible events that weakened the papacy and Christendom, in rapid succession, during 1453: the foiled plot of the ardent republican idealist Stefano Porcari and the fall of Constantinople to Mahomet II.

Disaster: the Turkish conquest of Byzantium

The end of the Western empire had long seemed inevitable. Any hope of seeing the Christians of the West halt the Turkish menace had evaporated when Ladislas of Hungary was defeated at Varna, in Bulgaria, on November 10, 1444. Four years later this disaster was followed by an even greater one in the Serbian town of Kosovo: Mahomet II crushed a vast Christian force of Hungarians, Bohemians, and Germans led by the Hungarian hero John Hunyadi.

In Byzantium itself, Constantine XII, emperor since 1448, was proving unequal to the task of organizing his capital's defense. Sultan Mahomet II had blockaded the city by erecting the formidable fortress of Roumeli Hissar on the Bosporus. Genoa and Venice deployed naval support at the last moment, and the papacy sent galleys, but in vain: the Turkish force, 160,000 strong, vastly outnumbered the opposing army of 7,000 men. On May 29, 1453, Mahomet stormed Constantinople. The emperor was slaughtered, thousands of inhabitants massacred, and others led off into slavery.

As soon as he learned of the catastrophe, Nicholas made another effort to mobilize the Christians, but failed. Venice had signed a separate treaty with the sultan to keep hold of its possessions. Genoa had done the same: the Bank of St. George, which managed the Eastern territories, had become a tributary of the sultan. As for the king of Naples, he haughtily refused to hear of a pact with the other Italian states.

This pact which the pope had failed to restore did, however, come about in 1454 when a treaty was signed between Milan and Venice. The Holy See acceded to it at once, as did Naples and Florence, and the next year, in Rome, Nicholas solemnly announced that the Italian states had formed a league for twenty-five years to ensure "the peace and repose of Italy and the defense of the Christian faith." This was to be Pope Nicholas's last act.

The conclave of 1455
Accession of Calixtus III

The events in the East had sorely tested the pope's health, and Nicholas, who had been ailing for a long time, died during the night of March 24, 1455. On April 4 the conclave duly met to name his successor.

At that time the Sacred College had twenty members, but five were absent: two Frenchmen, two Germans, and a Hungarian. Of the fifteen voters, seven were Italian: cardinals Fieschi, Scarampo, Capranica, Calandrini, and Barbo as well as two members of the leading Roman families, Prospero Colonna and Latino Orsini. Two more were from the Eastern empire—Bessarion and Isidore—while two others were Frenchmen—de Coëtivy and d'Estaing. Four were from Spain—Torquemada, Carvajal, Antonio de la Cerda, and Alonso Borgia.

As usual, sparks flew between the Colonna and Orsini partisans. Cardinal Orsini could count on the votes of the Spaniards whom King Alfonso had asked to vote for him, but it was clear even before the conclave met that this support was not enough. It was whispered that the next pope would be the Venetian Pietro Barbo, nephew of Eugenius IV; then it looked as though Capranica had the advantage—but he was a Roman and a friend of the Colonnas.

Nothing would suffice but to choose a neutral candidate. The Greek Bessarion seemed to be well qualified, and eight cardinals declared for him. But there were fears public opinion would be shocked if the Roman Church were headed by an Eastern churchman who had only just abandoned the Schism. At long last—after a session said to have

been held at night in the latrines—the majority decided to nominate
a "transition pope."

During the morning of April 8 the cardinals chose Alonso Borgia
"by accession." Doubtless it was his age—seventy-seven—that swung
their vote. The cardinal of Valencia accepted, declaring that he would
take the name Calixtus III.

Only one of the conclavists was not surprised by the result—Alonso.
Deep down he had always been certain that Vincent Ferrer's prediction
would one day come true. In a desire to thank the famous Dominican
preacher and fulfill his prophecy to the letter, Alonso lost no time in
canonizing him, on June 29.

Not long before that Calixtus carried out his predecessor's instructions and ordered a revision of the trial of Joan of Arc. On July 7,
1456, judgment was passed quashing the sentence passed on Joan and
solemnly rehabilitating her.

Opinions on the new pope

Smoothing the way for the pope's election had been the prestige and
political weight of Alfonso, king of Aragon and Naples. Alfonso's glory
was at its height. All Italy now recognized his power. To eclipse the
memory of the Anjou rulers before him he had erected a huge triumphal arch on the austere facade of the Castel Nuovo in Naples on
which were carved, in marble and bronze, episodes of his conquest
of the kingdom and triumphant entry of 1443.

Alfonso's power behind the new pontiff was therefore palpable,
and it aroused great concern. A general apprehension can be felt in
the words of St. Anthony, the archbishop of Florence: "At first, the
election of Calixtus III pleased the Italians but little, for two reasons.
First, since he was a native of Valencia, or Catalonia, they feared that
he might one day think of moving the pontifical court to a foreign
land. Second, they were afraid that he would give the strongholds of
the Papal States to Catalans and that later, in some cases, it might be
difficult to retrieve these places from their hands." But at the same
time Anthony recognized the pope's reputation for wisdom and integ-
rity. He was deeply touched by the solemn declaration Calixtus made
just after his election, thousands of copies of which were distributed
throughout Christendom:

"I, Calixtus III, pope, do promise and swear, were it to cost me my own blood, to do, so far as my strength allows and with the help of my venerable brothers, all in my power to recover Constantinople, which has been seized and destroyed by the enemy of the crucified Savior, the son of Satan, Mahomet, prince of the Turks, for the punishment of men's sins; to deliver the Christians languishing in slavery; to restore the true faith and exterminate in the East the diabolical sect of the infamous and treacherous Mahomet. . . . If I forget thee, O Jerusalem, let my right hand forget her cunning; let my tongue cleave to the roof of my mouth if I forget thee, O Jerusalem, if I prefer thee not above my chief joy. God be my aid, and His holy gospel, Amen."

Behind this passionate determination to bring the Crusade to a triumphant end there burned the same zeal that drove the aging pope's forbears to do battle with the Moors. Calixtus still cherished the memory of his native land where Islam had left so many visible traces—in Játiva, Valencia, Lérida. Providence, he felt, had singled him out to carry on the great work the kings of Aragon had begun.

Taking possession of the Holy See

In many ways the seat of the papacy had a military look befitting the capital of the Holy War. With its ramparts and the advance-fortress of the Castel Sant'Angelo, the Vatican palace and the so-called Borgo area surrounding it were rather like an armed camp. This was the "Leonine City," named after Pope Leo IV, who had built it in the mid-ninth century. The palace wing that Nicholas rebuilt looked austere from the outside, but inside it resembled one of those pleasure domes that feudal kings and princes built throughout Europe behind their castle walls. Ranged around the wing were the various pontifical offices and an audience chamber—a large chapel foreshadowing the present Sistine Chapel. An inner corridor led to the atrium of St. Peter's, a huge cloister with a fountain in the middle and monuments of former popes around the sides. One of these sides was the basilica facade. Opposite was a tall campanile, next to which stood the Pavilion of the Benediction with its elegantly arcaded loggia. The monumental gateway alongside the pavilion had three entrances for pilgrims. Eugenius IV had decorated these with magnificent carved bronze panels by Filareto showing Christ and the Virgin in Majesty, St. Peter, and St. Paul, as well as the chief events in the pope's reign, especially the

Council of Florence and the meeting of the Greek and Roman churches just before the Crusade.

On April 20, Calixtus threaded his way through his palace corridors to St. Peter's. When the pope entered the church, a cleric set fire to a bundle of tow in front of him, a symbol of the ephemeral grandeur of the papacy: "Pater Sanctissime, sic transit gloria mundi!" The pope stepped up to the high altar where he celebrated Mass, assisted by cardinals Barbo and Colonna. Then a procession formed and he was led to the square in front of the basilica for his coronation. Watched by a crowd of the faithful, the dean of cardinals, Prospero Colonna, placed on Calixtus's head the tiara, the conical bonnet with its white peacock feathers and three diadems of gold. Then he pronounced the ritual formula: "Receive the tiara adorned with three crowns and know that thou art the father of princes and kings, the rector of the universe, the vicar of Our Savior Jesus Christ, to Whom be honor and glory from century to century. Amen."

When the ceremony was over, pope and cardinals mounted their horses. Another cortege formed, consisting of eighty white-robed bishops, the Roman barons, and the municipal corps of conservatori, or councillors. Calixtus was about to take possession of his episcopal seat at the Cathedral of St. John Lateran. All the streets were festooned. On the Piazza Monte Giordano the Jews, following tradition, presented him with the Book of the Law from their synagogue. To this the pope replied, "We recognize the Law, but we condemn your interpretation, for He Who you say will come has come, and that is Our Lord Jesus Christ, as the Church teaches and preaches." The gold-encrusted Book of the Law aroused the crowd's greed and the pope was jostled, the Jews managing to slip away. But later, at the Lateran, the populace shattered the pope's dais as they tried to grab the rich decorations.

Hard on the heels of these popular disturbances, a violent dispute arose over the county of Tagliacozzo between Count Everso of Anguillara and Napoleone Orsini, whose servant had been murdered. The city seemed engulfed in a civil war. While Orsini sacked the count's home in the Campo dei Fiori, an army of 3,000 armed men shouting "Orsini to the rescue!" assembled on the Monte Giordano and made ready to march against the Colonnas, who were Count Everso's protectors. After strenuous effort the papal envoys, Cardinal Orsini and Francesco Orsini, the prefect of Rome, managed to prevent bloodshed, and order was gradually restored.

A case of political nepotism

After his terrifying investiture day, Calixtus urged Cardinal Barbo to arrange an armistice between the two sides. To prevent any further riots he decided to follow his predecessors' example and put power in his relatives' hands. His nephews were summoned to Rome and were promptly given the rank of princes. They were not to be promoted all at once, however. Calixtus had in fact promised the Sacred College that he would not advance his relations to positions of power. Thus, a week after Rodrigo's arrival in Rome, the pope contented himself with making him apostolic notary, later adding the deanery of Santa Maria de Játiva together with substantial revenues from parishes in the diocese of Valencia. Rodrigo's cousin Luís de Mila was made governor of Bologna, chief city of the Papal States.

The two young men left for Bologna. Rodrigo, traveling with the humanist Gaspare da Verona, was to study law. Instead of the usual five-year course, it took him only sixteen months of mingled study and pleasure to gain his doctorate in October 1456. While they were away the pope managed to disarm the Sacred College's opposition by making both nephews cardinals.

The cardinals held their peace, hoping that death would overtake the aging pope before the promotions were made public. But Calixtus cheated them of their expectations. Taking advantage of the cardinals' absence from Rome—they had fled the city to escape the heat and the threat of epidemic—he published the recent appointments on September 17, and his young nephews made their solemn entrance into the city as cardinals. Two months later their uncle crowned them with cardinals' hats and symbolically opened their mouths—a ceremony signifying that they would always be faithful spokesmen of the Holy See. Luís de Mila received his uncle's old title, that of the Quattro Santi Coronati, while Rodrigo became cardinal-deacon of San Nicola in Carcere Tulliano. The choice of this little church was significant, standing as it does in a central spot opposite the Capitol, close by the Theater of Marcellus, which the Orsinis had made into a fortress. Built over the ancient Roman herb market, the venerable church had jurisdiction over all the city prisons, giving the young cardinal authority over law and order.

The key to the control of Rome, however, and the real papal fortress, was the Vatican and its advance-post, the Castel Sant'Angelo. In 1455 Rodrigo's brother Pedro Luís, seven years his senior, had been named captain general of the Church. Now the twenty-five-year-old young man became governor of the Castel Sant'Angelo, the emperor Hadrian's ancient mausoleum. Refortified when the popes returned to Rome, the massive round fort not only protected the side of the Vatican facing the city but also provided the pope with a convenient hiding place. It was reached by a corridor atop the wall leading from the Vatican. Ignoring the Roman barons' protests, Calixtus handed the castle over to his nephew in March 1456. That autumn he rained other titles on him, making him governor of Terni, Narni, Todi, Rieti, Orvieto, Spoleto, Foligno, Nocera, Assisi, Amelia, Città Castellana, and Nepi and, shortly afterward, governor of the Patrimony of St. Peter.

Lest such favoritism discredit the papacy in the eyes of the Christian rulers, Calixtus proceeded to nominate six cardinals representing the leading European powers. That done, he returned to the business of advancing his family. In December young Cardinal Rodrigo was appointed legate of the March of Ancona, on the Adriatic coast, leaving for his post in early 1457. Cardinal Luís, already governor of Bologna, became its legate.

The pope conferred rich benefices on the two young men to allow them to maintain their rank. The highest and most lucrative post in the Curia was that of vice-chancellor, who handed out favors and collected huge taxes for the papal coffers. Since the death of Eugenius IV's nephew in 1453, the post had been vacant. The French cardinal d'Estouteville was angling for it. Nevertheless, in 1457 it was entrusted to Rodrigo Borgia, who that December was also made general in chief and commissioner of all the papal troops in Italy.

Rome under the Catalans' thumb

So outrageous was this promotion that Cardinal Capranica, who had been grand penitentiary under Nicholas V, raised his voice in protest— a brave gesture that earned him the hatred of the Borgia clan. They did not, however, succeed in ousting him from Rome. In fact, the opposition of a highly placed Church official counted for little, since the Borgias had allies who were important in other ways. They were on excellent terms with the Colonnas, for instance. In the summer of 1457 rumor spread abroad that Pedro Luís was about to marry a member of the Colonna clan. Now, friendship with the Colonnas had as its counterpoint the enmity of the Orsinis. So when the pope sent Pedro Luís to seize a few Orsini castles, hatred turned into open warfare and Cardinal Orsini swept out of Rome. Most of the cardinals sided with the Colonnas and approved Pedro Luís's promotion to the post of prefect of Rome, the highest lay office.

The nomination took place on August 19. Later in the day the conservatori and leading citizens of Rome came to the Vatican and congratulated the pope on his choice. In reply, Calixtus declared that Pedro Luís was Italian both in thinking and behavior. He assured them that his nephew wanted to live and die a Roman citizen. One of the conservatori expressed the hope that he would soon see the new prefect crowned king of Rome; then he begged the pope to give Pedro Luís the castles that had, from time immemorial, belonged to the prefect's fiefdom. Next came deputies who obsequiously presented their compliments to Pedro Luís.

He smiled, but was not fooled by their flattery. He knew full well he was not liked by the Italians any more than he liked them. The pope's nephew, in fact, treated the Italians with an insufferable arrogance—an attitude that aroused the hatred of the Romans. They detested these swarms of Borgia relations or cronies who flocked in from all over Spain. In the city streets, as in the Papal States, people saw and heard only them. Pedro Luís surrounded himself with a staff made up of Spanish adventurers of every sort. Some came from Naples, others from Aragon, but all were known simply as "the Catalans," just as all the pope's relatives were called "Borgia," whatever the father's name. In no time, Rome and the Church came to resemble colonies of this foreign power.

When the newcomers invaded the Curia, many Frenchmen and Germans lost all hope of pursuing their careers and resigned their offices—which, of course, were immediately snapped up by Catalans. Ordinary people were affected just as much as nobles and prelates for, with the military and police under their thumb, the Catalans used them to suit their fancy. Brawls and murders became more frequent every day. Recurring epidemics created further chaos. In June 1458 the plague raged so virulently that everyone who could took off. While the cardinals abandoned the city, the pope remained stoically at his post and busied himself with the fate of the plague's victims. He turned one of the buildings of his former cardinal's palace of the Quattro Santi Coronati into a hospice, donating more than 5,000 ducats for

its upkeep. He also showered benefits on the Hospital of the Holy
Spirit.

Stripping the library and archaeological collections to benefit the Crusade

This charitable devotion, however, did not detract Calixtus from his
main concern: to save Christendom from the peril of Islam. On a visit
to the rich Vatican library just before his coronation, he had ordered
some manuscripts to be stripped of their gold and silver bindings to
help finance the Holy War. Some of the humanists of the Curia cried
shame and claimed that Calixtus wanted to break up the collections
so painstakingly built up by his predecessors. They accused him of
handing over books to the bishop of Vich, his datary, as well as to
Catalan barons. All this was obviously exaggerated. Only four books
apparently were given away, including two that went to the king of
Naples. Gifts of that kind were common in Italian courts in Renaissance times. Moreover, other humanists were on excellent terms with
the pope and made no complaints.

True, Calixtus did not share his predecessors' passion for antiquity,
as he proved in 1458 when an archaeological discovery was made in
the Church of Sta. Petronilla, adjoining St. Peter's. An enormous
marble sarcophagus had been found containing two cypress caskets,
one made for an adult and the other for a child; they were so heavy
that six men could hardly carry them. The corpses, which crumbled
to dust on exposure to the air, were wrapped in magnificent shrouds
of gold brocade. The caskets were lined with silver. The richness of
the tomb suggested a royal burial, possibly that of the emperor Constantine and his son. But Calixtus refused to be impressed. He gave
orders for the gold and silver to be melted down, and a thousand ducats
went into the Crusade fund.

When addressing the ambassadors who came to swear obedience to
him, the pope never failed to speak about the Crusade fund—to the
Florentines, the Venetians, the Imperials from Emperor Maximilian.
On May 15, 1455, he published the Crusade Bull, setting the date of
departure for the Holy Land at March 1 the next year. The graces and
indulgences announced earlier by Nicholas were confirmed, and tithes
raised throughout Christendom for the war against the Infidel.

In September, Calixtus sent his men out to preach the Crusade in every land. The cardinals set the example: de Coëtivy in France, Szechy in Hungary, Carvajal in Germany, da Cusa in England. Archbishop Urrea of Tarragona traveled all over Spain. Aiding these prelates were fiery orators such as Capestrano and Montefalcone, and the Dominican Heinrich Kalteisen. The general and provincials of the Augustine order were told to use all their friars in the preaching campaign, on pain of excommunication.

The operation was carried out with extraordinary attention to detail. According to one chronicle, "On September 8, a Franciscan monk opened the preaching of the Crusade on the great square, standing next to the fountain; first, he ordered a roll of drums accompanied by pipes, then he had a silver-gilt cross set up, bearing a Christ; that done, he drew the papal bull from his bosom and gave detailed explanations of its contents." In every city of the Papal States, scribes took down contributors' names and the amounts given, in huge registers. Anyone refusing to donate was sentenced to the harshest ecclesiastical penalty by the papal delegates, who could also call in the secular authorities if further pressure was needed.

Funds also poured in from the sale of pontifical jewels. Calixtus sold many pieces of gold and silver to Alfonso of Naples: silver-gilt vases, a carved tabernacle, chalices, paxes, and, more prosaically, a wine-cooling vat and a preserves dish made of silver. He also sold off a number of papal lands and castles, such as Giulianello, Vullerano, and Carbognano, which fetched 12,000 gold florins.

Pacification of Italy

While amassing this war chest for the Crusade, the pope was striving to stop the Christian states from fighting each other so that they could all pull their weight in the holy enterprise. In July 1455 he ratified a treaty between warring France and Burgundy. In Italy he had his hands full. The unruly condottiere Giacomo Piccinino, who had been driven out from the Milanese, had invaded Sienese territory. Against him the pope dispatched the army he had raised to fight the Turks. Serving the Sicilian commander were both Stevano Colonna and Napoleone Orsini as well as the two sons of his old adversary, Everso d'Anguillara. Venice, Florence, and Milan all pledged their support. A united front had formed against Piccinino.

Only Alfonso of Naples refused to come out against the condottiere, which made people suspect a conspiracy between the two. In a skirmish on the shores of Lake Trasimene, Alfonso showed his colors and came to Piccinino's aid. The latter boldly tried to set fire to Calixtus's ships in the port of Civitavecchia, then seized the Sienese port of Orbitello and sacked it. In despair, the Sienese begged the king of Naples to intercede with Piccinino, but to no avail. Calixtus acted by promulgating the bull *in Coena Domini,* in which, following custom, he excommunicated all those who laid hands on Church possessions and went against the pope's wishes. Piccinino and Alfonso were worried, and for good reason. The king of Naples, threatening to banish all the pope's relations from his lands, took his time about reopening the dialogue with him. As a sign of goodwill, Alfonso did bring about Piccinino's withdrawal from Siena, in return for a large indemnity, but he never forgot the incident, which pitted him against his former protégé.

Operations of the pope's fleet in the Levant

With peace restored in Italy, Calixtus gave the signal for the opening of the Crusade. Pedro Urrea, archbishop of Tarragona, had outfitted ships with the monies he had raised as a legate in Spain. The pope put him in command of the vessels that were to free the Greek islands from Turkish blockade. Unfortunately, instead of setting sail for Greece, the archbishop joined Alfonso's fleet, which was about to ravage the Genoa coast. Seeing that he had once more been duped by his former protector, Calixtus dismissed Urrea and his cohorts and named Cardinal Luigi Scarampo captain-general and admiral of the fleet, giving him legate's powers in Sicily, Dalmatia, Macedonia, Greece, and all the islands and provinces of Asia. Scarampo was responsible for governing all the lands he subdued. In a yard set up in Rome at Ripa Grande, on the Tiber, the new admiral rebuilt the Crusade fleet.

Finally, on May 31, 1456, the Feast of Sta. Petronilla, the pope himself bound a cross to the cardinal-admiral's shoulder and Scarampo sailed down the Tiber toward Ostia with the twenty-five ships built in the Roman yard. On board were 1,000 sailors and 500 soldiers, and 300 cannons. The fleet got under way near Naples, whose monarch had promised fifteen galleys as a gesture of reconciliation with the pope.

That summer the papal fleet was to aid the Greek islands by driving out the Turkish garrisons. But could the pope carry on the enterprise unaided? None of the European powers had kept its promise. The French king, Charles VII, for one, had pledged thirty vessels and armed them, but had ended up using them against England and Naples. The other leaders had acted in similar fashion, save for a few small states like Mantua. It was enough to dampen even the boldest spirit. But Calixtus refused to lose heart. He went on selling the papal artworks and treasures. One day, noticing some saltcellars of silver gilt and other precious objects on his table, he cried, "Take it away, take it all away for the Turks. Earthenware is quite good enough for me!" He made do with a linen miter. Neither setbacks nor age had cooled his ardor. "Only cowards fear danger," he declared. "Only on the battlefield can one win the palm of glory!"

Crusade in Central Europe
The heroic Skanderberg

Eastern Europe offered the Christians many an opportunity to win glory in the service of the faith. In 1456 Mahomet II ringed Belgrade with a force of 150,000 men, supported by 300 artillery pieces. Opposing him were John Hunyadi, the doughty Hungarian chieftain, and Calixtus's two envoys, Fra Capestrano and Cardinal Carvajal. Hunyadi managed to break the blockade, force his way into the city square, and, a week later, compel Mahomet to lift the siege. This victory was, sadly, followed by the deaths, of disease, of both Hunyadi and the papal legate Capestrano.

That autumn the king of Hungary got ready to resume the campaign. A German contingent under Count Ulric de Cilly joined his army in Belgrade, but a skirmish broke out between Cilly's German soldiers and the Hungarians under Ladislas Corvinus, Hunyadi's son. The Hungarian king avenged Cilly's death by having Corvinus beheaded. The crisis put an end to the Crusade, and Cardinal Carvajal sent the Crusaders home.

Fortunately, while prospects for the Crusade looked bleak up north in Germany, some notable successes were being scored in other areas. The Albanian national hero, Skanderberg—whom Calixtus dubbed the "athlete of Christ"—destroyed the Turkish army at Tomornitza in July 1457. A month later Scarampo and the papal fleet routed the Turkish navy at Metelin, seizing twenty-five ships.

Conflict with the crown of Naples and Aragon

With his old protector, Alfonso of Aragon, Calixtus still had thorny relations. After the incident of the bull *in Coena Domini*, relations between the two rapidly soured. In 1457 conflict flared up afresh over the question of episcopal appointments, and the pope threatened to excommunicate the king and depose him—but Naples was still indispensable for his Crusade.

He tried compromise. When the fair Lucrezia d'Alagno, Alfonso's mistress, came to Rome in October, the pope—perhaps prodded by Cardinal Rodrigo, who was trying to bring the two courts together—received her with honors. Yet the king adamantly refused to think of reconciliation. Exasperated, Calixtus excoriated him publicly: "Since the day that Alfonso took possession of Naples, the Church has had no rest. He has continually caused torment to my predecessors and to myself. Hence I am resolved, if he should die, to deliver my successors out of this servitude. I shall do all in my power to prevent his natural son Ferrante from inheriting his crown."

Alfonso fell gravely ill—at the same time as the pope—early the next summer, and died on June 27. As soon as he heard the news, Calixtus got down to settling all the questions outstanding between Rome and Naples. As pope, he had retained the bishopric of Valencia with its revenues of 18,000 ducats. Now, he handed over its administration to his nephew, Cardinal Rodrigo, raising it to an archbishopric. Other Aragonese benefices were conferred on his datary, Cosimo da Monserrato, and to members of the Borgia family. Meanwhile, Alfonso's illegitimate son, Ferrante, was denied the crown. If it were proved that Naples belonged by right to René d'Anjou, then the pope would give it to him; if not, he would give it in fief to whoever seemed best qualified to rule. There were rumors that Calixtus wanted to hand over Naples to his nephew Don Pedro, before making him emperor of the East, or at least king of Cyprus. True or not, he declared in a bull that the kingdom of Naples was in escheat. The Neapolitans were forbidden to swear loyalty to anyone whatsoever.

The bull spread panic throughout Christendom. In Rome it produced a huge rise in the price of wheat. One of the conservatori said that Romans would be forced to choose between the pope and King Ferrante. Calixtus refused to budge. He gave orders to Don Pedro to prepare a military campaign against Ferrante, whom he called "little bastard, son of an unknown father." "This whippersnapper who amounts to nothing," he told the Milanese ambassador, "claims the throne without our permission. Naples belongs to the Church: it is the property of St. Peter. Alfonso would not claim the throne without the consent of the Holy See, and We, who were his counselor at that time, supported him in this view. . . . Let Ferrante give up his usurped claim, let him leave the matter to Our judgment and We will treat him as we do Our nephews."

Ferrante, of course, refused to comply. The messenger who had brought the July 14 bull to Naples was caned. Summoning parliament, he called on the barons to help him fight the pope's evil claims. At the same time he lodged an appeal against the papal declaration. Just when rupture was complete, the pope was struck down by an exceptionally violent attack of gout. Recovering a little, he again took up the question of dividing the benefices of the kingdom of Naples among his kith and kin. Terracina and Benevente went to his elder nephew Pedro Luís, the archbishopric of Naples to Cardinal Tebando, his physician's brother. His nephew Luís Juan received the wealthy Lérida see and Rodrigo, the vice-chancellory of the Roman Church.

Calixtus's illness and death
Election of Pope Pius II

In the summer of 1458, at the news of the pope's illness there were rumblings of opposition in the Curia and confusion reigned in Rome. A committee of cardinals had the Capitol seized by a force of 200 men under the archbishop of Ragusa. Pedro Luís Borgia was stripped of his authority. It was clearly risky for him to stay on in Rome, where the Orsinis were very likely poised for revenge. He therefore handed over to the cardinals all the strongholds under his sway, including the Castel Sant'Angelo. He also gave them the Church treasury, some 120,000 ducats. In exchange he received 22,000 ducats, a legacy Calixtus had set up for him.

At dawn on August 6 Pedro Luís left the Castel Sant'Angelo on horseback, heavily disguised, together with a disguised Rodrigo and

Cardinal Pietro Barbo, who had given him an escort of 300 horse and 200 foot soldiers. The group reached the Porta San Paolo. Once outside the city walls, Rodrigo and Barbo took leave of Pedro Luís, having first ordered the soldiers to escort him to the Roman port of Ostia. But the promised galley failed to appear, and Don Pedro was forced to take a fishing boat to Civitavecchia, where he died shortly after, in mysterious circumstances.

Cardinal Rodrigo returned to Rome to find his palace sacked by a populace gone berserk. He witnessed the protracted agony of his uncle, who died on the feast day of the Transfiguration, which he himself had instituted. As word of the pope's death leaked out, confusion redoubled. The Borgias' enemies, especially the Orsinis, made no secret of their jubilation. Meanwhile most of the Catalans had followed Pedro Luís's example and fled. Those still left had to lie low to escape violence. The cities of the Papal States were in revolt. Piccinino seized several of them, notably Assisi, and in cahoots with Ferrante of Aragon, laid siege to Foligno.

The leading question now was to ensure the pontifical succession. On August 16 at the Vatican, eighteen cardinals met in conclave—eight Italians, five Spaniards, two Frenchmen, two Greeks, and one Portuguese. The majority wanted to stop the election of a foreigner. At this juncture the cardinal of Siena, Aeneas Silvius Piccolomini, was backed by Francesco Sforza, the duke of Milan, and Ferrante, who despite Alfonso's efforts later became the king of Naples. It was Piccolomini who, on the third day of voting, was elected by the so-called accession procedure. He gained nine votes; the Frenchman d'Estouteville, just six. A long silence fell on the St. Nicholas gallery where the conclave was being held, a silence broken by the voice of Rodrigo Borgia: "I accede to the cardinal of Siena." There was a pause; then one by one the cardinals declared themselves for Piccolomini. That humanist, emperor's spokesman, and shrewd diplomat became Pope Pius II. Clearly, what the Borgia clan must do in the new pope's reign was preserve all it had won in the reign just ended.

3

Cardinal Rodrigo's
Charmed Career

The vice-chancellor's newfound favor

Rodrigo Borgia's star was in the ascendant now that he was a protégé
of the new pope. In earlier years Pius II had been an epicurean prelate,
dashing diplomat, celebrated author of erotica, and hero of countless
amorous adventures. Once energetic and robust, he now looked like
an old man rather than one in his fifties. He still retained his enthusiasm, but chronic attacks of gout sapped his strength. His career as
imperial orator, bishop of Siena, and then cardinal had given him an
excellent knowledge of politics and religion. He knew how to handle
people, in particular how to rely on ambitious young men who reminded him of his own youth. With his courage and dynamism Cardinal Borgia was just such a man. At twenty-seven he dreamed of
making his mark in the world, and he had the means to fulfill his
dream.

Rodrigo was now administrator of the see of Valencia, which gave
him an income of 18,000 ducats. Besides that, the pontifical chancellory, which brought in 70,000 ducats a year to the papal treasury,
provided him with an allowance of 8,000 ducats. That was just the
beginning of a fortune that was to swell to huge proportions in the
years to come. The vice-chancellorship gave him a privileged position
that was the envy of the inner circles of the Curia.

Gregory VIII had scrapped the post of chancellor in 1187 to make
it quite clear that the pope alone had the right to certify documents
emanating from the Holy See. However, over the years the vice-

chancellor, who was chief of the chancellory, had regained his privileges, if not his title, to the point of becoming the second most important figure in the Church. Under him were a hundred pontifical agents. The chief clerks, or "abbreviators of the great office," decided on requests for pardon. Next came the "abbreviators of the little office," who drew up the deeds signed by the chancellory regent and vicechancellor. Affixing the leaden seal, or bulla, gave the deed legal validity. An extremely elaborate tax system made it possible to line the papal coffers and at the same time dole out handsome sums to the chancellory staff. The system applied equally to the bulls of canonization and to those granting dispensations or pardons in a whole gamut of cases, from marriage within the prohibited degrees and legitimation to bigamy, incest, and sordid or unnatural crimes.

Pius left Rodrigo free to enjoy the delicate, lucrative position his uncle Calixtus had given him. In other matters, however, his policies ran quite counter to the former pope's. For example, he dismissed, with a purse of coins, the Catalan governors Calixtus had set up in the Papal States. Pedro Luís, Rodrigo's late brother, was replaced by Pius's nephew, Antonio Piccolomini. A friend of the pope's, Antonio Colonna, became prefect of Rome. The difference in the papacy's relations with Naples was like night and day. On October 17, 1458, an agreement was sealed with Ferrante recognizing papal suzerainty and accepting the payment of a tribute. In return Pius published a bull granting Ferrante the investiture of Naples.

This political about-face was not without strings. The pope needed peace in Italy so as to launch another Crusade against the Turks. He called a meeting of the Christian princes in Mantua to discuss resuming the Holy War. He himself left for the north in January 1459, ordering the eleven cardinals residing in Rome to go with him, among them Rodrigo Borgia and his cousin Luís Juan de Mila. Everywhere they went in the Papal States, the cities hailed the splendid cavalcade.

Portrait of Rodrigo Borgia

Amid all the panoply of the Roman prelates, the vice-chancellor stood out with his magnificent retinue and unique presence. Rodrigo was unusually handsome; tall and dark, by turns animated and nonchalant, always smiling, he left no one indifferent. Women easily fell under his spell. His tutor, Gaspare da Verona, had already noted his extraordinary charm. "He has a honeyed eloquence," he wrote. "He speaks with warmth and gentleness at the same time. He has magnificent dark eyes. His conversation excites the weaker sex in a strange manner, more powerfully than iron is drawn to a magnet. Yet he skilfully hides his conquests, so that no one knows how many have succumbed to him."

Another witness, Jason Naimus of Milan, praised "the vice-chancellor's elegant bearing and matchless physique" and admired his "calm forehead, regal brows, his face which bears the imprint of liberality and majesty, his genius, and the harmonious and heroic proportion of all his limbs."

The cardinal did not make a secret of his amorous adventures, but no one would have dreamed of taking offense, since the vow of celibacy was openly flouted every day. When in orders, Pope Piccolomini himself had fathered illegitimate children, and he had been heard to cast doubt on the virtues of celibacy for priests. Once raised to the papacy, however, he was circumspect and grateful to his clerics for their discretion.

Scandal in Siena

To encourage loyalty in his dynamic young protégé, Pius entrusted him with a confidential mission during his long stay in Siena, from February 28 to April 23, 1459. The pope had decided to make his native village, Corsignano, a bishopric under the name Pienza. Rodrigo was to act as foreman, supervising the building of a cathedral and the Piccolomini palace in the heart of the new city. The job was certainly not taxing enough to absorb all the young vice-chancellor's energy. The ladies of Siena, like their Roman sisters, fell for his charms. When the gossip reached Pius's ears—he had gone to the Petriolo baths for his gout—he called Borgia to order on June 11:

"We have learned that, three days ago, a number of Sienese ladies met in the gardens of Giovanni Bichi and that, with little regard for the dignity of your office, you spent the afternoon with them from one until six o'clock and that you had as companion a cardinal whose age, in the absence of respect for the Apostolic See, should have reminded him of his duty. We have learned that the most wanton dances were performed, that no amorous allurement was wanting, and that you behaved like a young man of the laity.

"Shame forbids mention of all that took place, for the very name of the acts are unworthy of your position. In order to give free rein to your lusts, the husbands, fathers, brothers, and other kinsmen of the young women were not admitted. Only you and a number of servants were present, arranging and taking part in the dances. It is said that today in Siena there is talk of nothing but this matter, and that your frivolity is the subject of universal ridicule.

"We leave it to you to judge whether you can court women, give them presents of fruit and wine, indulge yourself in every kind of amusement all day long and, finally, send the husbands away so that you can be free to pursue your pleasures—whether you can do all these things without surrendering your position. On your account people blame us, and the memory of your uncle Calixtus, for having heaped upon you so many responsibilities and honors. Remember the dignity of your office and do not try to win a reputation among the young as a ladies' man. Here, where there are many members of the Church and the laity, you have become a laughingstock."

Pius had just settled a ticklish question of internal Sienese politics. He had persuaded the state to let the nobles once again stand for public office. In this way he hoped to do away with a major cause of local unrest. Cardinal Borgia's behavior, however, ran counter to his aims and threatened to bring back a state of tension, one that could undermine the authority of the Holy See and the results Pius had so painfully achieved.

Although Pius took care not to have the incident bruited abroad, diplomats gossiped about it in their courts. A letter from Bartolomeo Bonatto to his prince, the marquess of Mantua, gives more details of the orgy: "I can find nothing to write about to your lordship save that a baptism took place today, at the invitation of a gentleman of this city, at which the Monsignor of Rouen [the licentious Guillaume d'Estouteville, then in his forties] and the vice-chancellor were godfathers. They were assembled in the garden of one of the godfathers and a child was brought in. The food and drink were lavish and the fete magnificent, but there was not one present who was not in holy orders. . . . A facetious Sienese who was not admitted, along with many others, said, 'By Our Lady! If those born one year hence come into the world dressed like their fathers, they will all be priests and cardinals!' "

Rodrigo was shrewd enough to convince the pope that gossipers had maliciously twisted the facts. He proved it was only a question of a peccadillo, and Pius forgave him: "What you did is assuredly not blameless, but perhaps far less reprehensible than I have been told." He advised him to behave more prudently in the future.

Pius's indulgence toward his vice-chancellor knew no bounds. He had just learned that one of the chancellory abbreviators, Giovanni de Volterra, had sold a papal bull for 24,000 gold ducats when Calixtus III was pope. This was a bull authorizing the French count Jean d'Armagnac to have carnal relations with his own sister. The clerk had simply erased the words "fourth degree," replacing them with "first degree" in the wording of the dispensation. The vice-chancellor, like the abbreviator, had pocketed a large percentage of the commission. Then the covetous de Volterra had returned to the charge and claimed a further 4,000 ducats from the count. D'Armagnac lodged a protest with Pius II, who had found out about the swindle. In consistory court Pius denounced the grave abuse committed in the chancellory but cleared Cardinal Rodrigo of any wrongdoing. The inquest showed that although he was paid a sizable commission, the vice-chancellor knew nothing of the fraud. Both the Siena and chancellory scandals, though muted by the pope's benevolence, served as a useful lesson for the young cardinal.

Finally, the pope and his cardinals left Siena. Their progress through the state was one of Siena's most memorable ceremonial occasions, figuring later in the cathedral Libreria, in a fresco by Pinturicchio. On April 25 it was Florence's turn. That city welcomed the papal cortege with a parade of honor attended by two young princes, Galeazzo Maria, the son of Duke Francesco Sforza of Milan, and Lorenzo de' Medici, the ten-year-old heir of the powerful merchant Como, who ruled the state. The superb celebrations staged in Florence— hunts, jousts, animal fights, theatrical displays, banquets, and balls— hailed not only the pope's arrival but also the triumph of the merchant dynasty of the Medicis. The stopover here was important, since it proved the papacy could count on the credit of the most powerful bank in Western Christendom.

A brief stay in Bologna followed, where Cardinal Borgia retraced his happy days at the university; then, on May 17, the procession made a triumphal entry into Ferrara. The pope was carried in his chair beneath a golden canopy. The streets were strewn with branches, the palaces and houses hung with gorgeous tapestries and garlands of flowers. Choirs greeted the procession as it wended its way through the city. Borso d'Este, the duke of Modena, wanted to impress the pope and his cardinals no matter what the cost, and he succeeded perfectly.

The Congress of Mantua

Shortly thereafter, Pius reached Mantua, where Marquess Ludovico da Gonzaga managed to outshine the splendors of Ferrara. He presented the pope with the keys to the city. The streets were richly carpeted, the facades covered over with flowers, while young gallants and ladies were to be seen at every window and rooftop. The marquess welcomed the pope and the cardinals to his palace, and the stage was set for the arrival of the temporal rulers. But hours went by and no one showed up.

After offering this image of earthly paradise, Mantua grew empty once again. Daily life resumed and the city drooped in the deadening heat of summer, while noxious miasmas wafted up from the Mincio. The older cardinals blamed the pope for cooping everyone up in an unhealthy, fever-ridden place in the vain hope of mobilizing the West against the invincible Turks. Rodrigo Borgia, for his part, chose to amuse himself by arranging boat parties with his friends cardinals de Coëtivy and Colonna and a few fair companions.

Months went by. In mid-August the duke of Burgundy's ambassador appeared, in mid-September the duke of Milan, then one by one the representatives of the other Italian states and lastly, in October and November, the French and German delegates. But by now all enthusiasm had faded. The ambassadors of the French King, Charles VII, and of René d'Anjou just wanted to present their claims to the kingdom of Naples—at the very moment when René's son Jean, duke of Calabria, was launching his galleys against Ferrante of Naples, ships that had been paid for out of Crusade funds.

The political comedy played out at Mantua mirrored the worldly comedy that Rodrigo Borgia was involved in day and night. The Congress of Mantua gave him a chance to study the forces driving men's passions. Pius II grew desperate and published a Crusade bull calling on Christians to take up arms against the Turks for three years. At the same time he ordered taxes to be levied as a war chest for the Christian forces. The clergy, including the cardinals, would pay one-tenth of their revenues, the laity one-thirtieth and the Jews, one-twentieth. That done, Pius left Mantua at the head of the pontifical cortege.

Great disappointment awaited him in the Papal States. Confusion had engulfed Rome during his absence. Barons Savelli, Anguillara, and Colonna had struck up an alliance with the redoubtable condottiere Piccinino, and eighteen months would go by before a semblance of peace could be restored.

Dazzling receptions of the Eastern princes

Back in Rome once more, Cardinal Borgia was immediately caught up in worldly ceremony. With his taste for aristocratic display, he enhanced the brilliant occasions when the pope received the Greek princes fleeing Turkish rule. Before that, when he was returning from Siena, Pius had received a so-called archdeacon of Antioch who had come to petition the pope in the name of the Greek patriarchs of Jerusalem, Antioch, Alexandria, as well as Ibrahim Bey, the prince of Karamania, and other Eastern rulers. In December 1460, Rome had witnessed an exotic procession made up of the ambassadors of the emperor of Trebizond, the king of Persia, and the prince of Georgia, among others. The appearance of the Persian and Mesopotamian ambassadors created a sensation, the latter wearing a tonsure like a monk's, with a small circlet of hair but with a tuft of hair sticking up from the top of his head.

On March 7, 1461, a descendant of the Greek Paleologus emperors, Thomas of Morea, showed up. A handsome, solemn man of fifty-six, he paid his respects to the Vatican in a long black robe and tall white velvet hat. His escort included seventy horses, only three of which were his. This sumptuous retinue hid real poverty and represented the last pathetic appeal of Eastern Christendom. On his way to Rome the emperor left a remarkable relic, the head of St. Andrew, in the fortress of Narni. The pope made Cardinal Borgia responsible for installing his visitor in the palace of the Quattro Santi Coronati, left vacant when Cardinal Luís Juan de Mila left for Lérida. The Sacred College raised funds so that the emperor could receive an annual income of 6,000 ducats.

The St. Andrew relic and the alum miracle

Happy as he was to help welcome these exotic rulers, Cardinal Rodrigo found an even better way to show off his love of splendor. In Rome in 1462 Pius II received the head of St. Andrew, which was moved to the Vatican on April 13. The relic was greeted by an enormous crowd bearing 30,000 candles. Altars smoky with incense were erected all along the procession route, while gorgeously dressed women crowded at the windows of the houses, also richly decorated. But even the most sumptuous decorations, those of the proud Roman nobles, were outdone by the vice-chancellor's, whose house in the heart of the capital near the Zecca, or Treasury House, was hung from top to bottom with rich stuffs. With tapestries suspended over the street and the houses magnificently adorned, this section of the city was transformed into a theater full of music and chanting. Whether or not Providence heard these prayers, a miracle did occur—while the fund-gathering for the Crusade went on and on and the rulers of Europe were slinking away—which, for the pope, was like manna from heaven.

Giovanni de Castro, a jurist's son from Padua, had fled Constantinople when it was sacked by the Turks. In Byzantium he had run a large dyeing works that used alum, a mineral that was a vital element in the industries of the time, dyeing, glaziery, and armory. With the Turkish conquest the West had been cut off from the alum produced in Byzantine mines and forced to become dependent on the Infidel. Castro discovered no less than seven mountains rich in the purest alum at a spot called La Tolfa, in the Papal States near Civitavecchia. He proudly informed the pope of his find: "I bring you victory over the Turk, for every year he extorts from the Christians more than 300,000 ducats for the alum he provides." It was a windfall. Pius II lost no time in ordering the mines worked, and by 1463, 8,000 men were digging at La Tolfa. The papal coffers suddenly showed a surplus of 100,000 ducats.

Even this was not enough to finance a Holy War. The pope, thinking up expedients of every kind, set a ceiling of seventy for the total number of abbreviators in the chancellory, of which only twelve would be appointed by the vice-chancellor, with the rest buying their posts. Vice-Chancellor Rodrigo Borgia had to stand by while his whole staff was reshuffled. The existing members were let go while new men, most of them from Siena, entered the chancellory.

Death of Pius II
Election of Paul II

Years went by while the pope waited in vain for the European princes to show their support; the French and Burgundian leaders were notably unforthcoming. At last he decided not to delay the Crusade any longer. After taking the waters once more at Petriolo, he made ready to leave for Ancona in the spring of 1464. Venice had promised enough ships to carry 5,000 Crusaders in conjunction with the papal galleys. The plan was to cross the Adriatic to Ragusa, where the fleet would join forces with Mathias Corvinus, king of Hungary, and the Albanian Skanderberg. Only cardinals who were old or infirm were excused from following the pope.

At Terni, in Umbria, Cardinal Borgia joined the procession accompanying Pius II—now suffering excruciating pain—on its way to Ancona. All along their route were signs of the plague. The plague had in fact reached Ancona, where the papal retinue arrived in July. Rodrigo Borgia seemed to take it all quite lightly. The vice-chancellor does not sleep alone, wrote the ambassador of Mantua. He did fall sick, but people blamed that on his loose living.

Meanwhile, on the other side of the Adriatic, Ragusa was being blockaded by a vast Turkish army. Pius ordered a landing of troops. The Venetian ships, however, had failed to join the papal fleet, and by the time they finally showed up, many soldiers had deserted. The whole operation was gravely compromised; some thought the disaster was a "death blow" for the pope, who was in fact racked with pain. On August 15, he received the last sacraments and expired. Pius's death sounded the knell of the Holy War. The troops disbanded and the cardinals wended their way back to Rome, where they held a conclave. Shortly after, the election was settled, and Rodrigo's close friend the Venetian cardinal Pietro Barbo became Pope Paul II.

Rodrigo Borgia very soon became a habitué of the Vatican, for the two men shared the same love of luxury and show. Borgia had watched wide-eyed as Cardinal Pietro Barbo's sumptuous new home went up beside his titular church of San Marco. Standing at the foot of the Capitol, the Palazzo Venezia (to use its modern name) today is one of the most striking monuments in Rome. Marking the transition from medieval castle to grand Renaissance residence, it has a magnificent unfinished courtyard with a double arcade. A majestic arch links the palace with the Church of San Marco. Inside, the halls are filled with art.

Paul moved out of the Vatican, which he found uncomfortable and too near the insalubrious Tiber, preferring to entertain his friends in his new home. The Apostolic Treasury was transferred there, and the palace became the center of Roman life. Here festivals took place at Carnival time. Instead of the Piazza Navona or Monte Testaccio, they now were held on the long artery that cut through the old quarter of the city and ended at the Palazzo Venezia. Under Paul, the street, which became known as the Corso, served as a racecourse not only for donkeys, buffalos, and unbridled horses—called Barberi, after the pope—but for young and old, Christians and Jews (who had to wear heavy woolen garments stuffed up to the neck with cakes). Huge feasts were held for the people on the Piazza San Marco, which the pope watched from his palace window, tossing coins down to the frenzied crowd. Other spectacles—reenactments of ancient Roman triumphs—brought festivity and color to the various quarters of the city. On these occasions the pope himself appeared, borne on a gilded *sedia*, or litter, worth the price of a castle, and wearing his new sapphire-studded tiara which had cost 200,000 gold florins. Surrounding him were the members of the Sacred College of Cardinals, who now had to appear in public robed in purple and wearing either the red beretta or a large miter of damask silk embroidered with pearls, a privilege that hitherto had been the pope's alone.

A luxurious court

Rodrigo Borgia felt perfectly at home at the Venetian pope's luxurious court, where he himself lived like a prince of the time, surrounded by courtiers and paramours. One of the latter gave birth in 1467 or 1468 to a son, Pedro Luís; Rodrigo immediately declared himself to be the child's father, legitimizing him some fourteen years later. Next came Gerolama, then Isabella, who was born around 1470. According to their marriage contracts, they were the daughters of Cardinal Borgia and an unwed mother.

At the Curia, Rodrigo once again had important duties to perform. In an effort to undo what his predecessor had done about nominations to the chancellory, Paul II got rid of the Sienese appointees, reimbursing them the money they had spent on buying their positions.

This step immediately sparked rebellion among the fired clerks, one of whom, Bartolomeo Sacchi de Piadena, called Platina, addressed a pamphlet to the pope. He threatened to urge the Christian princes to call a council and summon the pope to appear before it. Although the imprudent Platina was denounced, tortured, and clapped into jail at the Castel Sant'Angelo, the rebellion caught on. Pomponius Laetus, a teacher at the University of Rome, took the lead, gathering together all the freethinkers of Rome, who were utterly opposed to papal centralism. Their grumblings developed into a plot to murder the pope and his retinue, which was foiled in the nick of time in February 1468. As a result, Paul and Cardinal Borgia became even more distrustful of the Curia humanists, and of dissidents and heretics as well. Bulls of condemnation fulminated against the "little friars" of Assisi who denounced the luxurious ways of the pope and his cardinals.

The net result of this harshness was by no means negative. Paul's repressive policy together with the worldly brilliance of the throne of St. Peter gave Western Christendom and its leader an impressive image of strength. People praised the spectacular welcome Paul gave in December 1466 to the Albanian hero Skanderberg and Emperor Frederick III, who made a pilgrimage to Rome—both men destined to march in the vanguard against the Infidel. The pomp and ceremony showed that the papacy had the temporal power necessary to mount another Crusade. With their luxurious way of life, Rodrigo and the other worldly cardinals were the best proof of this power. Nor did this pomp count for nothing in the matter of alliances with the East: because of it, good relations were formed with Ouzoun Hassan, the prince of Turkmenistan, and preparations made to hoodwink the Turkish sultan. A treaty was just about to be signed in July 1471, but fate decreed otherwise: on the 26th the pope suddenly died of apoplexy.

Once again Rodrigo Borgia sat in conclave, and once again he was shrewd and farsighted enough not only to pinpoint the candidate with the best chances of winning but to give him his vote and his friends' at precisely the right moment.

Election of Sixtus IV
Rodrigo Borgia as Spanish legate

On August 9, the Franciscan cardinal Francesco della Rovere became pope. As Sixtus IV, he rewarded the cardinals who had got him elected;

thus Orsini was appointed cardinal *camerlingo*, or administrator of temporal affairs at the Holy See, and Borgia was endowed with the rich Benedictine abbey church of Subiaco, held for him *in commendam*.

On August 22, Rodrigo Borgia crowned the new pontiff—his first duty as dean of cardinal-deacons. Shortly afterward, he was promoted to the rank of cardinal-bishop of Albano, one of the seven suffragan sees of Rome; before receiving the order, however, he had to be ordained. He resigned himself to taking the vow of chastity and celibacy out of the corner of his mouth, which did not prevent him from starting a liaison of many years with Vannozza Cattanei, a rich Roman beauty and owner of a number of inns.

Having reorganized the Curia, Pope Sixtus threw himself wholeheartedly into the great plan his predecessors had been so devoted to: the war against the Turks. In just one year he spent 144,000 gold ducats—derived in part from the sale of alum from the Tolfa mines, which produced more than 1,500 tons a year—on fitting out a fleet of twenty-four galleys and an expeditionary force 4,000 strong. Venice and Naples pledged to send larger forces. On December 23, five legates *a latere* were appointed to get help from the other Christian rulers. Rodrigo Borgia, one of the five, was told to scour the kingdoms of Aragon and Castile. It was both an honor and a delicate mission for him. What he had to do, in effect, was to persuade both sovereigns to establish peace in their lands and devote all their energies to the Crusade. However, Spain, and especially Castile, felt that its mission against the Infidel should be targeted specifically at the kingdom of Granada, the last vestige of Islamic rule. But Rodrigo, who was born in that eastern part of Spain abounding in descendants of the Moors, did not lack arguments to prove that the Crusade was indivisible and that the Spaniards must play their part, at least financially, in the Holy War.

The cardinal had just been given a new title, that of *camerlingo*, or treasurer, of the Sacred College of Cardinals. When he left, on May 15, 1472, Rodrigo handed his chamberlain's seal to Cardinal d'Estouteville, who was to replace him during his absence. A procession of cardinals saw him to the gates of Rome, then, after a banquet in the d'Estouteville vineyard, he went on to the Roman port of Ostia. Along the way he saluted the Crusade vessels drawn up on the Tiber under Cardinal Carafa's command: soon they would be setting sail for Karamania, on the Turkish coast, where they would disembark.

The crossing was a short one. In June, Rodrigo Borgia reached Valencia, his episcopal see, where a royal reception awaited him. Mounted on a magnificent horse, the cardinal was greeted by dignitaries at the Serranos gate, which was draped in satin, and paraded through the streets with a canopy over his head. Trumpets and kettledrums, singing and cheers hailed the city's native son. But the crowds' enthusiasm was even greater when Rodrigo entered his birthplace, Játiva. The cardinal's stay in Aragon went a long way toward bringing peace to the region, thanks to a reconciliation arranged between the king and his rebellious subjects in Barcelona.

Rodrigo's next step was Castile. Its king, Enrico IV, nicknamed the Impotent, the husband of Juana of Portugal, had as heir Juana, who was born in 1462. Public gossip, poking fun at the king's puny physique, had it that the child had been fathered by a favorite of the royal household, Beltran de la Cueva; hence the ignominious nickname la Beltraneja that was tagged onto the unhappy Juana's Christian name. Now, the princess's supposed bastardy gave the barons revolting against Enrico an excuse to claim that his sister, Isabella, was the rightful heir to the crown. To strengthen her position, Isabella had married her cousin Ferdinand, heir to the Aragonese throne, in 1469, when they were both minors. Enrico refused to recognize the marriage, which had been contracted without his consent, and publicly called it incestuous since it united, without papal dispensation, two people who were related "to a prohibited degree." By the time Rodrigo reached Castile there were rumblings of civil war. He got involved in long, complex bargainings, aided by the archbishop of Toledo, Alonso Carrillo, an eccentric character given to magic, luxury, and good living, and by the wily political prelate Gonzalez de Mendoza. Meanwhile every Castilian city blazed with fetes and fashionable gatherings, and the gallant cardinal stole favors of beauties who were only too ready to comply.

In Madrid, King Enrico was asserting his daughter's claim to the throne. Rodrigo, however, had met the ambitious Isabella and Ferdinand, come to an agreement with them, and now counseled the pope to regularize their marriage. He even offered to serve as godfather to the couple's firstborn, thus providing Isabella with decisive support against la Beltraneja.

In the kingdom of Valencia he was tempted by a fief near Játiva; this was Gandia, a little town nestled in a fertile valley on the other side of the Agujas Mountains near the seacoast and the capital of a duchy created in 1399 by King Martin for his nephew Alfonso of Aragon. Its handsome castle went back to Moorish times and sported the shields of Aragon and Sicily alternating with Kufic monograms. This fief would round out the cardinal of Valencia's domains very handily, besides making an ideal principality in ancestral lands for his eldest son, Pedro Luís. No doubt Rodrigo set his heart on this duchy from the very beginning of the legation. He would gain it in 1485, when Ferdinand became king of Aragon and Pedro Luís was made duke of Gandia.

Rodrigo Borgia managed to persuade Enrico that his sister Isabella recognized Juana la Beltrancja's rights. As a reward, the king showered him with Spanish benefices and ecclesiastical pensions, while Rodrigo, in turn, had Rome provide his accomplice Mendoza with a cardinal's hat. Later, when the legation had left Spain, Enrico received Ferdinand and Isabella in Segovia, but the feast of reconciliation proved his undoing, for he supposedly was poisoned by Ferdinand. At her father's death in 1474, the unfortunate la Beltraneja had to enter a convent to leave the coast clear for Isabella. The loyal Castilians laid the responsibility for the disaster squarely at the door of the Aragonese legate, the treacherous Borgia, whose name they publicly cursed. Rodrigo, however, was by then miles away from the scene. Rome had pronounced his mission a success, and he was praised for having reconciled Castile and Aragon and made both kingdoms contribute funds for the Crusade.

Borgia's return trip was marked by disaster. In September 1473 he loaded his coffers and large retinue on two Venetian galleys. As they crossed the Gulf of Savona they were hit by a frightful storm, and one of the ships foundered. One hundred ninety-two souls drowned, among them three bishops, and the cargo that sank included coffers containing 30,000 gold ducats. Yet the tragedy served to enhance the public image of Cardinal Borgia's admirable composure in the face of danger. On October 24 members of the Sacred College went to welcome him back at the Porta del Popolo, and the next day the pope received him in a public consistory and congratulated him on his courage and the fruits of his mission.

Thanks to Rodrigo, the Holy See had gained prestige and financial resources; yet because of the deteriorating situation in the East it could not make use of them as it hoped. After a promising start, naval operations off the Turkish coast yielded disappointing results. Ouzoun Hassan, the Turkmenian chief, was beaten by the sultan, a defeat that deprived the West of the diversionary force it needed. Discouraged, the pope abandoned the Crusade so as to devote himself to temporal matters in Italy, especially his family's fortunes.

Flagrant nepotism of Pope Sixtus

Sixtus IV's two nephews Piero Riario and Giuliano della Rovere were made cardinals in 1471, when they were twenty-five and twenty-eight respectively. The former received the title of St. Sixtus, the latter that of San Pietro in Vincoli, a title that Sixtus himself had held before becoming pope.

Their uncle saw to it that his nephews were showered with favor after favor. Giuliano della Rovere received the archbishoprics of Avignon and Bologna, the episcopal sees of Lausanne, Coutances, Viviers, Mende, Ostia, and Velletri, and the abbeys of Nonantola and Grottaferrata. His cousin Piero Riario was even better provided for: archbishop of Florence, patriarch of Constantinople, abbot of St. Ambrose of Milan, he was given a host of bishoprics. His annual revenues exceeded 60,000 ducats—barely enough, however, to cover his expenses. Piero Riario flaunted his wealth in the celebrations he arranged in June 1473 for Eleonora of Naples when she passed through Rome to join her husband, Ercole d'Este, at Ferrara. In front of his residence near the Basilica of SS. Apostoli he had a wooden palace erected. It was hung with tapestries and cloth of gold and boasted priceless furniture and utensils—even the chamber pots were silver gilt. People were still talking about this extraordinary celebration when Rodrigo Borgia came back to Rome.

Favors were also heaped on the pope's lay nephews. Sixtus married Leonardo della Rovere, the prefect of Rome, to an illegitimate daughter of Ferrante of Naples. Giovanni della Rovere was wed to Giovanna de Montefeltro, the family thus acquiring the inheritance of the duchy of Urbino. Girolamo Riario, Piero's brother, was married to Caterina Sforza, the great-niece of the duke of Milan, and was given the fief of Bosco, which the pope had bought for 40,000 ducats. To this Sixtus wanted to add the lands of Imola, held by Galeazzo Maria Sforza, at a cost to the pope of 40,000 ducats. The plan aroused the displeasure of Lorenzo the Magnificent, who feared, rightly, that a powerful domain would be built up on the Tuscan border. The Medici bank that handled the papal finances therefore refused to advance the money, but its rivals, the Pazzi bankers, laid out the necessary funds.

This rush to reap honors and profits began again with renewed vigor after Cardinal Piero Riario disappeared from the scene. He died of excess at the age of twenty-eight in 1474, his brother, Girolamo, taking his place in Sixtus's favor. Girolamo was obsessed with enlarging his principality, following the example of Pedro Luís, Cardinal Borgia's late brother. To please him, the pope formed an alliance with Venice so as to oust the duke of Ferrara, but once again, Lorenzo the Magnificent foiled the scheme. Enraged, Girolamo Riario determined to have both Lorenzo and his brother Giuliano murdered, acting in collusion with the Pazzi bankers. The conspiracy cost Giuliano his life but failed to rally Florence—a failure that served to increase Lorenzo's power. Vexed by his nephew's lack of success, the pope along with his ally King Ferrante of Naples would spend two years trying, in vain, to subdue Florence.

Amid these turbulent events, Christendom's cause seemed decidedly abandoned. More and more, the Papal States came to resemble a principality like all the others that squabbled for their material interests alone. The only difference between it and the petty Italian tyrannies was in the way power was passed on—by election, not inheritance. Still, the pope's cardinal nephews believed they held a prior right to the succession. Piero Riario had put in his claim to be the rightful heir. Now it was his cousin Giuliano della Rovere's turn. Blocking his ambitious path, however, was the vice-chancellor, Rodrigo Borgia. A ferocious rivalry, barely veiled beneath pomp and ceremony, pitted the two men one against the other, each being backed by a devoted following.

Rodrigo Borgia's life of luxury

Under Sixtus, as under the popes before him, Rodrigo was riding the twin steeds of political intrigue and love. This prompted a rebuke from the cardinal of Pavia, who wished to lead Rodrigo into the strait and narrow: "You must put off the old Adam: this is essential not only for the cardinalate but for Christianity. Those who take pleasure in studying our faults will cease their laughter, and those who bear us hatred or envy will cease to rejoice. May your lordship have the piety to forget the past, to change your way of life. I have confidence that thanks to your wisdom and goodness you will accomplish this transformation. Keep this letter, place it in your bed so that you may reread it often."

Both admonition and counsel were useless. Rodrigo's way of life hardly lent itself to devotional practices. He lived surrounded by luxury. Since 1470 his palace had stood midway between the Ponte Sant'Angelo and the Campo dei Fiori: a section of it survived the building of the Corso Vittorio Emanuele in the nineteenth century and can be found in the Palazzo Sforza Cesarini. In time past the palace had an imposing facade decorated with the cardinal's coat of arms, half Borgia, half Oms from his mother's side: on one half the Borgia bull, on the other three bands of blue decorated with gold palm leaves, all on a gold ground.

One visitor, Cardinal Ascanio Sforza, even though accustomed to the luxurious apartments of the duke of Milan, was extremely impressed with the rich furnishings in Rodrigo's palace. Sforza visited it together with Giuliano della Rovere and two other cardinals who were invited to dinner. The entrance hall was hung with tapestries of historical subjects. In the middle of the reception room was a canopied daybed of crimson satin, draped with fine hangings; superb gold and silver plate gleamed on a dresser. More beautiful tapestries and carpets were to be found in the next room, which had a ceremonial divan with a blue-velvet canopy. Another even more luxurious room contained a daybed of gold brocade, canopied in black-striped gold cloth fringed with gold, and a table covered in blue velvet with delicately carved stools around it.

Giacomo di Volterra also sang the praises of Rodrigo's home. The cardinal, he wrote, "has a palace as handsome as it is conveniently disposed. . . . He possesses vast revenues, which derive from many ecclesiastical benefices as well as a great number of Italian and Spanish abbeys and three sees, those of Valencia (18,000 ducats), Porto (1,200 ducats) and Cartagena (7,000 ducats). The office of vice-chancellor alone brings in 8,000 ducats a year. He has a huge quantity of silverware, pearls, church tapestries and ornaments embroidered in gold and silk, as well as books on every branch of knowledge—all this of a richness worthy of a king or pope. I have not mentioned the countless jewels adorning his beds, nor his horses, nor all the gold, silver and silken articles in his possession, nor his wardrobe, both elegant and costly, nor the piles of gold in his treasury."

The cardinal's revenues amounted to more than 80,000 ducats, and his wealth steadily increased over the years between the return of the Spanish legation in 1473 and the death of Pope Sixtus IV in 1484.

Vannozza, best-loved mistress

Successful in his actions as a prince of the Church, Rodrigo also enjoyed a happy private life. This is the period of his love affair with Vannozza Cattanei, the longest-loved of his mistresses. Born in 1442, the young woman was at least twelve years his junior, having first met him possibly in 1460, at the Congress of Mantua, when she was eighteen. According to some historians, Vannozza bore the cardinal's first three children, Pedro Luís, Gerolama, and Isabella: no mother or mothers are named in the registries. As Vannozza's epitaph in the church of Sta. Maria del Popolo in Rome does not give the children's names, it is likely they had already died or were without issue at the time their mother passed away in 1518. In any case, Rodrigo's liaison with Vannozza had become public knowledge by the time the cardinal was in his forties and Vannozza was thirty.

The cardinal's mistress, if a portrait in Rome's Congregazione della Carità is to be trusted, was a handsome, robustly built, fair-haired woman with limpid eyes. Her straight brows and the purposeful set of her lips bespeak energy and good sense. From her, her daughter Lucrezia would inherit her blond tresses and light-green eyes, and her sons their light-brown or red hair, while Rodrigo would give them his fascinating dark eyes, at once dreamy and full of life.

On his return from his triumphal Spanish mission, the vice-chancellor established Vannozza in a house she owned on the Piazza Pizzo di Merlo, quite near his own palace. That same year he presented her with a husband of a respectable age, one Domenico d'Arignano, an officer of the Church; it was a marriage of convenience that made for easy encounters between the cardinal and Vannozza.

In the early summer the cardinal and his intimates made their way to Subiaco. The strong-walled double monastery that Rodrigo held *in commendam* was situated in the Apennines, 50 miles east of Rome. It was a pleasant place, famous for its pure mountain air. Overnight the austere retreat was transformed. Nobles and their ladies swarmed over the huge abbey palace, now completely refurbished. Everywhere—in the cloisters with their picturesque antique tombs and carvings from the ruins of Nero's villa nearby, in the passageways decorated with frescoes and mosaics, in the fountain-filled gardens, the chapels and churches, the mountain grottoes—the air rang with laughter and music of a decidedly nonreligious nature. For those seeking more scholarly pursuits, there was a superb library filled with illuminated manuscripts and a large collection of incunabula printed at Subiaco itself.

Cardinal Borgia's children

In this aristocratic, bucolic setting Vannozza gave birth to Cesare, in 1475. The child was thought to be legitimate, but Rodrigo Borgia lost no time in acknowledging himself as the father. Another son, Giovanni, was born the next year, by which time Vannozza was widowed; then it was Lucrezia's turn: she came into the world in April 1480 in the abbey castle of Subiaco. At this point Cardinal Borgia decided to regularize his mistress's position once again, and in 1480 arranged for her to marry a Milanese, Giorgio di Croce, who was secretary to Sixtus IV. A wealthy man, Croce had an estate on the Esquiline Hill—a country house with a vineyard and orchard near San Pietro in Vincoli, where the children would enjoy family reunions. Their mother later inherited the property from her second husband, when it became known as the Borgia Vineyard. Most of the time Vannozza and her husband lived in Rome itself, in a house in the Piazza Branchis with a beautiful garden, which was Vannozza's own property.

In 1482 Rodrigo declared himself the father of the last of his sons, Jofré (or Gioffre), then his relationship with his mistress cooled. Vannozza had another, legitimate, son, Ottavio, whom she lost immediately. Her second husband died in 1486. She promptly remarried a Mantuan, Carlo Canale, bringing with her a dowry of 1,000 florins. Canale was a man of letters of some repute—the young Florentine poet Poliziano had submitted his *Orfeo* to him—and had been the cardinal of Gonzaga's chamberlain. Extremely proud of his union with the cardinal vice-chancellor's mistress, he had his coat of arms quartered showing the Borgia arms with his own and threw his weight around with the marquess of Mantua, the head of his former protector's family.

As he mellowed into his fifties Rodrigo watched over his children's interests assiduously. In 1482 he married his eldest daughter, Gerolama, to a Roman noble called Gian Andrea Cesarini; she died the

year after. The year 1483 saw the betrothal of Isabella to the nobleman
Pier Giovanni Matuzzi. Pedro Luís went off to Spain to join the
campaign against the Muslim kingdom of Granada. After he had
distinguished himself at the siege of Ronda, in May 1485, Ferdinand
of Aragon made him duke of Gandia and promised him the hand of
Doña Maria Enriquez, the king's niece. Pedro Luís died, however,
shortly afterward at Civitavecchia. Showering his affection afresh on
Vannozza's children, Rodrigo made his sons princes. His daughter
Lucrezia was entrusted to his cousin Adriana da Mila, the widow of
Baron Ludovico Orsini and mother of young Orso (who gossip had it
was yet another bastard son of Cardinal Borgia's).

Rodrigo became a frequent visitor at the Orsinis' Roman palace at
Monte Giordano. His position at the Curia, his aspirations, and native
charm made him an indulged guest. As usual, he seduced the ladies
there, in particular a young girl by the name of Giulia Farnese. The
daughter of provincial nobility, she was engaged to Orso Orsini—
whom she later married in 1489—and assisted Adriana da Mila, her
mother-in-law to be, in her role as female head of the household.
Thus she lavished attention on Lucrezia from her earliest childhood.
When Adriana brought the young girl to the Convent of St. Sixtus on
the Via Appia to complete her education, the cardinal continued his
frequent visits to the Orsini palace, to his cousin and the fair Giulia
Farnese.

Rodrigo had been appointed dean of the Sacred College, receiving
the title of cardinal-bishop of Porto. Once again he was made legate,
in 1477, when he was sent to Naples to crown King Ferrante's new
bride, Juana of Aragon; she was the daughter of King Juan II and sister
of Ferdinand, the prince Rodrigo had got to know so well in Spain.
A cortege of cardinals accompanied him as he left Rome and welcomed
him home. This popularity, which was to grow and grow in the turbulent years when Sixtus fought Florence, became an important base
of support.

Death of Sixtus IV
Election of Innocent VIII

When Sixtus died on August 12, 1484, the Romans rose up in revolt
against the late pope's nephews and their circle of profiteers. Heading
the revolt were the Colonnas; against them Virginio Orsini, lord of

Bracciano, led his partisans. Who would be the ideal candidate to restore order and curb the excesses of the Riario–della Rovere clan but Rodrigo Borgia, friend of the Orsinis and the Aragonese of Naples?

In fact, at the conclave the cardinals unanimously denounced the nepotism of the last pontiff's reign. Each cardinal pledged, if he were elected, not to appoint "any cardinal over the age of thirty or any who is not a doctor of theology or of one or the other law or, if he is a king's son or nephew, has not been suitably educated. He shall appoint only one cardinal of his family or blood, who must meet the above conditions. He shall not wage war against any king, duke, prince, noble, or community outside his jurisdiction and shall not join any league to wage war against another without the consent of two-thirds of the most reverend cardinals.

"He shall not entrust the care of the fortresses of Sant'Angelo, Civitavecchia, Tibur, Spoleto, Fano, or Cesena to any members of his family, whether clergy or laymen. . . . The governors of the chief cities, such as Spoleto, shall be chosen from among the prelates. The pope shall not appoint either a nephew or any member of his family as captain-general of the Church. . . ."

Rodrigo took his oath along with the other members of the conclave. What would he not do to win the election! At fifty-three he considered himself supremely eligible. He therefore began to scatter rewards and promises profusely in order to win over his colleagues. To Cardinal Juan of Aragon he offered his vice-chancellorship and his palace; to Cardinal Colonna, 25,000 ducats and the abbey of Subiaco; Cardinal Savelli was promised rich benefices. He also won over Ascanio Sforza and the chamberlain Rafaello Riario Sansoni, the late pope's nephew.

Despite such largesse, he failed to gain the two-thirds majority he needed to carry the vote. Cardinal della Rovere, who was in the same situation, caught his rival unawares. Using Rodrigo's tactic at Pius II's election, he and the cardinals on his side threw themselves behind the candidacy of the Genoese cardinal, Giovanni Battista Cibo, who had a substantial lead over his rivals. Forced to give in, Rodrigo also announced his support.

The new pope, Innocent VIII, had much in common with Rodrigo Borgia. He was almost the same age—fifty-two—and, like him, lived surrounded by his illegitimate children. He was rumored to have a dozen but recognized only two, Teodorina and Francesco. Even had Innocent wanted to favor them, as seems likely, the oath sworn at the conclave was too recent to be broken. This meant that the offices handed out at the beginning of each reign were fair game for whoever asked for them. Giuliano della Rovere spoke up, having been instrumental in getting the pope elected, and from then on those of Sixtus's nephews who were of the della Rovere branch started their climb to power. Giovanni, the cardinal's brother, an ally of the duke of Urbino, became captain general of the Church, while another brother, Bartolomeo, was named governor of the Castel Sant'Angelo, or protector of the Vatican and the pope's person. Giuliano moved into the papal palace. Beside the pusillanimous Innocent VIII he would now wield more power than he ever did when his uncle Sixtus was alive. "He is pope and even more than pope," wrote the Florentine envoy to Lorenzo the Magnificent.

The inauguration was celebrated with the usual pomp and splendor. Rome witnessed first the pope's coronation and installation at the Lateran, then the embassies of obedience. It is all written up in the diary of the master of ceremonies, the Alsatian Johann Burckard, an extremely detailed chronicle begun in 1483 and continued up to his death in 1506. During four papacies, this privileged witness noted every event, big or small, that passed before his eyes. Far from trying to hide scandals behind a veil, he reports them with a sort of bitter glee.

War between Rome and Naples

Events then turned on the struggle between Ferrante of Naples and the Holy See. At that time the Aragonese king was at the height of his power. The last of his Angevin opponents, Charles of Maine, had bequeathed his rights to the French crown, but the young King Charles VIII, who was under the guardianship of his sister Anne de Beaujeu, was not powerful enough to claim the Naples inheritance. Ferrante took advantage of the situation to make those barons who had usurped royal prerogatives cough up their gains. Forced to give up their tolls and the duty they raised on merchandise, the nobles revolted from one end of the country to the other and appealed to the kingdom's sovereign, the pope.

Innocent was infuriated by Ferrante, who defied him by sending him a white palfrey instead of the yearly tribute he owed the Holy See. He therefore consulted with his cardinals over the attitude he should adopt toward the king of Naples. Rodrigo Borgia was for temporizing, while Giuliano della Rovere and the French king's representative, Cardinal Balue, favored a stern condemnation. Together they persuaded the pope to enter into war with Ferrante.

The king of Naples's forces were quickly mobilized under the command of Alfonso of Calabria, Ferrante's elder brother. Next in command was Virginio Orsini, former accomplice and ally of Girolamo Riario. Opposing a Neapolitan invasion of the Papal States, the pope had the condottiere Roberto San Severino, prince of Salerno, one of the nobles in revolt against Ferrante. Alongside the military operations a propaganda war was being waged, designed to demoralize the enemy. Virginio Orsini announced that he would ride to Rome at the head of Ferrante's armies and have Cardinal della Rovere decapitated, his head paraded around the streets on a pike, and the pope tossed into the Tiber. San Severino responded with a crime in the fashion of the day. When Cardinal Giovanni of Aragon, Ferrante's son, was visiting the castle of Salerno, San Severino seized his escort, killed its members and, the story goes, forced the cardinal to drink a slow and deadly poison.

Internationally, the king of Naples had the advantage of support from many quarters: not only did his son-in-law Mathias Corvinus, king of Hungary, favor him, but also Venice and Florence. After the first failures in the field, Cardinal Borgia pointed out that the pope's troops were incapable of defeating the Neapolitans. In full consistory he solemnly called on the pope to refuse French help against Naples. Astonished, Cardinal Balue protested vigorously. Voices were raised, and the two cardinals started to hurl insults at each other. Rodrigo Borgia, who was celebrated for his courtesy, forgot himself so far as to drown the Frenchman in abuse, calling him a madman and a drunkard. Beside himself with rage, Balue called Borgia a "Jew, Moor, Marrano, whore's son." The two adversaries came to blows. Innocent VIII was furious and tried to put an end to the consistory. But Borgia's argument had impressed him, and he signed the peace treaty with Naples on August 11, 1486. Ferrante undertook to pay the vassal's tribute money and pardon his rebellious barons. However, he signed the treaty only to stop the French army, which the pope had summoned to the rescue. As soon as danger seemed to pass, in September, he hounded the papal troops out of the mountain stronghold of L'Aquila, in the Abruzzi, and had the governor the papacy had appointed there put to death. In Naples he ruthlessly wreaked vengeance on his barons by summoning the ringleaders to a banquet at the Castel Nuovo and having them murdered. To keep the memory of this lofty deed alive he had the bodies stuffed and arranged around the walls of his dining hall. Ferrante also persecuted the condemned men's families, threw their wives and children into prison, and confiscated their possessions. To top it all, he refused to pay the tribute money promised to Rome and disposed of the ecclesiastical benefices as he saw fit.

Family union with Florence
The pope buys the Turkish hostage Djem

Innocent VIII could not leave the insult unanswered, and promptly assured himself of Venice's support; more important, he formed an alliance with Florence. In March 1487 his pact with Lorenzo the Magnificent was sealed by the marriage of his son, Francesco Cibo, by then in his forties, and Maddalena, Lorenzo's second daughter, who was not quite fourteen. The pope promised the cardinal's hat to the second Medici heir, Giovanni, then twelve years old, but to avoid canonical obstacles he kept the appointment secret. When Maddalena's marriage contract was signed in Rome, it created a great scandal. This was the first time a pope had been known to arrange the marriage of one he acknowledged officially as his own flesh and blood.

It was not too much to pay for the alliance with the Medicis. This bond not only assured the pope of military and financial aid from Florence but also the goodwill of the Orsini clan; Lorenzo's wife Claricia was, in fact, sister to Virginio Orsini, the condottiere who had gone over to the Neapolitan side. This happy collusion of interests allowed Innocent to stand up to the king of Naples and quell the riots raging in the Romagna—at Forlì, Ancona, Faenza, Perugia, and Foligno. Freed from the Neapolitan threat, the pope hoped to be able to resume the Crusade.

The signs had never looked so favorable. Sultan Bayezid II's brother and rival, Prince Djem, had in 1482 taken refuge with Pierre d'Aubusson, grand master of the Order of Rhodes, who was keeping him as a captive guest. Djem received an annual pension of 40,000 ducats from the sultan, who wanted to keep his brother far removed from Turkey. In 1489 Innocent had the prince brought to him by the grand master and on March 13, under the gaze of the cardinals, Djem entered the Eternal City. Like his colleagues, Rodrigo Borgia was fascinated by this tall, exotic prince with the enigmatic expression who held in his hands the future of the Crusade. In June 1490 the pope unveiled his plans to the Sacred College. Djem would be put at the head of the Crusaders' army so that, at the sight of him, the people and even the soldiers guarding the Turkish empire would surrender. The contributions raised in Christendom would make it possible to muster large forces—15,000 cavalrymen and 80,000 footsoldiers—but a commander in chief still had to be found. Mathias Corvinus, king of Hungary, who had been hinted at, had been mortally stricken by apoplexy at the age of forty-seven.

Rodrigo Borgia celebrates the capture of Granada
Future of the cardinal's children in Spain

The project for the grand Crusade marked time as the candidates—in particular the emperor Maximilian and Charles VIII of France—argued over its organization. Fortunately for Christendom, on January 2, 1492, Granada, the capital of the last Muslim kingdom in Spain, capitulated to Ferdinand of Aragon and Isabella of Castile. When the news reached Rome, Cardinal Borgia was overjoyed. He felt he had contributed to the victory, his eldest son Pedro Luís having distinguished himself brilliantly in the Granada campaign at the siege of Ronda. He and his whole family shared in the favors being meted out by the pope.

Rodrigo's two sons were beginning to attract notice. The cardinal had promised Giovanni, sixteen, and Cesare, seventeen, a grand fortune on Spanish soil. The death of his elder brother, Pedro Luís, decided Giovanni's career: he must succeed him in the duchy of Gandia. Cesare had by now made some progress in his ecclesiastical career and it fell to him, according to his father's plans, to strengthen his family's hold on the Church.

In April 1480 a bull of Sixtus IV had dispensed Cesare from having to prove that he was of legitimate birth—even though he was the "natural son of a cardinal-bishop and a married woman"—so that he could receive benefices. The Aragonese king had recognized his legitimation, naming him a subject of the kingdoms of Aragon and Valencia. Then Sixtus had conferred on him a prebend of the cathedral chapter of Valencia, in 1482, when Cesare was only seven. Soon after, he had been appointed apostolic protonotary, or dignitary of the papal chancellory. In 1483 he received another Valencian canonry together with the title of rector of Gandia and archdeacon of Játiva. The next year he became provost of Albar, then of Játiva, then treasurer of Cartagena—this when he was barely nine years old. All these benefices granted Cesare by Sixtus came in fact from his father Rodrigo, who siphoned them off from the ecclesiastical properties in Valencia. Each time, the king of Aragon confirmed the appointment, so that, around the lay principality of Gandia, the ecclesiastical principality the Borgias had held in the kingdom of Valencia since Calixtus III's time was perpetuated.

Cesare had had a very carefully planned education. Brought up in Rome until the age of twelve, he had left for Perugia with his tutor and lifelong friend, Juan Vera, a Valencian, who later became archbishop of Salerno and cardinal. At the university of La Sapienza he had studied law but had also received training in the humanities under Spanish scholars. One of these was Francisco Remolines de Ilerda, later governor of Rome and cardinal. Another, Paolo Pompilio, had dedicated his treatise on verse-writing, the *Syllabica*, to "Cesare Borgia, protonotary of the Apostolic See."

During his stay in Perugia, Cesare had a number of amorous adventures and was present at a sort of mysticism contest. At the invitation of the Dominican prior Fra Sebastiano d'Angelo, he witnessed the ecstasies of a young nun called Sister Colomba. Perhaps the prior doubted the authenticity of these manifestations, but he did nothing about it: they attracted people to his church. The Franciscan community had counterattacked by displaying a young girl who showed the signs of the stigmata, Sister Lucia de Narni. Later, in 1495, when Rodrigo, now pope, wished, skeptically, to study the merits of the two candidates for sainthood, Cesare would testify to Sister Colomba's sincerity.

From Perugia young Borgia went on to the University of Pisa, where he attended Filippo Decio's theological courses. He met young Cardinal Giovanni de' Medici, just completing his studies. And he learned that Pope Innocent had granted him the bishopric of Pamplona, in Spain. At once he appointed Martin Zapata, canon and treasurer of Toledo, as administrator of his diocese.

Thus, like his brother the new duke of Gandia, Cesare had close ties with his family's motherland. Around that time, too, their sister Lucrezia was promised in marriage to a Spaniard, at her father's wish. On February 26, 1491, when she was in her eleventh year, a marriage contract had been drawn up between her and Cherubino Don Juan de Centelles, lord of Val d'Agora in Valencia. Lucrezia was to go to Valencia sometime that year and marry within six months. Her dowry was 100,000 Valencian florins, made up partly of ornaments and jewels, partly of silver and including the 11,000 florins left her by her brother Pedro Luís. For reasons unknown, two months later the contract was annulled. A new betrothal was arranged with a youth of fifteen, Don Gaspare, the son of a Count Aversa in the kingdom of Naples. Gaspare, too, was a Spaniard, living in Valencia.

With such strong ties to Spain, it is natural that the Borgias saw the capture of Granada as an event of close personal concern. On February 1, 1492, Rome was illuminated and a huge thank-offering procession made its way, despite wind and driving rain, to the Church of San Giacomo degli Spagnoli, on the Piazza Navona. A few days later, Cardinal Rodrigo took over the job of organizing festivals. He put on five bullfights, the first in Rome. Among the family spectators the young golden-haired Lucrezia stood out, flanked by Adriana da Mila and Giulia Farnese.

Family ceremonies and archaeological discoveries in Rome

The festivals in honor of Granada were followed by others in March, when young Cardinal Giovanni de' Medici came to Rome. In May the city was decorated for the visit of Ferrantino, prince of Capua. This grandson of King Ferrante of Naples brought with him the king's promise to pay his yearly tribute of 36,000 ducats or 2,000 cavalry and five triremes. As a tangible sign of union, a great wedding celebration was held in the Vatican when Louis of Aragon, Ferrante's grandson, was married to Innocent's granddaughter Battistina. On June 4 a secret consistory was held in which the pope announced that Ferrante's son Alfonso of Calabria was the rightful heir to the Neapolitan crown. This outraged Charles VIII of France. He feared that France's recovery of the crown and the Crusade he wanted to head from the kingdom of Naples would both be compromised. Besides, the pope seemed to be on excellent terms with Turkey. Had not Sultan Bayezid just sent him the Holy Spear that the Roman soldier Longinus had used to pierce Christ's side on the cross?

The ambiguous relations between the pope and the sultan—founded on a kind of mutual respect between rivals—no longer raised any eyebrows. Moreover, the paganism of the ancient world was now being treated with the same respect. Thanks to humanism and archaeology, paganism was, in the strangest of ways, here and there being revived. A marvelous statue of Apollo had been discovered at the Porto d'Anzo, and the pope had at once had the pagan god brought into the Cortile del Belvedere at the Vatican, quite unconcerned at this apparent homage to one of the idols on whose account the first Christians had been persecuted. Amazing finds happened one after the other. One day some Lombard masons working near the cloister of Sta. Maria Nuova just off the Via Appia had opened a sarcophagus and found the body of a young Roman woman of about fifteen, so well preserved that it seemed alive. A crowd had gathered around and admired the girl's rosy skin, her half-open lips revealing very white teeth, her ears, her black lashes, dark, wide-open eyes, and beautiful hair, done in a knot. When the tomb was moved to the Capitol, a crowd double the size came to stare at this extraordinary creature, who was now pronounced to be Cicero's daughter. To prevent anyone from proclaiming that the body was that of a saint, Innocent had the corpse removed at night and buried. Only the marble sarcophagus was left in the courtyard of the conservators' palace to mark the discovery.

Forgers and peddlers of the papal court

In this Rome of the popes, so easily excited over ancient pagan remains, no one was shocked by anything, be it priestly immorality or scandals in the Curia. One night the pontifical police arrested six people for producing and selling forged bulls. The seller, Francesco Maldente, was a canon of Forlì; the forger, Dominico Gentile di Viterbo, a papal scrivener and son of one of the pope's doctors. Their method was simple: first they placed a valid document in a bath to wash the ink away, then they added in the body of the letter the name of the "client" and the total of the tax. The system had been used over and over again. Because of it, a priest in Rouen had been allowed to keep the woman with whom he cohabited, some mendicant monks had got rich, and a Norwegian group was permitted to say Mass without serving wine. The forgers had made a lot of money, from 100 to 2,000 ducats for each bull. In the end the men were condemned to death, both being hanged and then burnt on the Campo dei Fiori; their accomplices also received severe penalties.

Even though it served as a warning, this crime was no isolated case. People peddled everything; even the pope, always short of funds, did likewise in his own court. He taxed his secretaries, to the tune of 62,400 crowns. Since Sixtus IV's time, the courtesans of Rome had had to pay an annual tax of 20,000 ducats. Thus, authorized by the Vatican, prostitution flourished and the priests patronized it quite openly. In 1490, under Innocent VIII, one of the papal vicars had seen fit to order all priests and laymen living in Rome to get rid of their "public or secret concubines" on pain of excommunication. However, the pope had disclaimed the order, arguing that canon law called for no such thing. Besides, the "respectable" courtesans added to the magnificence of the cardinals' courts, where they held salons and enhanced the splendor of the ceremonies with their sumptuous gowns and jewels.

The pope was in no position to give lectures on morality. His son, Francesco Cibo, whose infant daughter had been baptized by Rodrigo Borgia, neglected and deceived his wife, Maddalena de' Medici, with loose women. At night he could be seen roaming the unsavory areas of the city with Girolamo Tuttavilla, the bastard son of Cardinal d'Estouteville. The two raped women, broke into houses, and ruined themselves gambling: in just one night, Francesco lost 14,000 ducats. Appointments to the cardinalate were always tainted with simony. The Romans were by now unshockable. According to Gregorovius, the German historian: "[The cardinals] appeared in public, on foot or on horseback, with a costly sword at their side. Each one had a staff of several hundred servants in his palace who summoned at will those mercenaries known as *bravi*. Furthermore, they had a circle of dependents, men of the people, whom they entertained at their expense. Almost all had their particular faction, and they vied with each other in pomp, especially at times of cavalcades or carnivals, when chariots bearing masked men, troupes of singers or players, costumed at their expense, rode through the city. The cardinals outdid the old Roman barons."

Of all these princes of the Church, the most dashing was without question Rodrigo Borgia. Giacomo Volterra described him as "a man with a mind apt for all things, of great intelligence; he is an eloquent speaker and well read in a general way. He is shrewd and wonderfully skilled in the conduct of affairs. He is known to be immensely wealthy and is in great favor with many kings and princes."

The prophetic voice of Savonarola

Rodrigo's morals were hardly any different from those of most members of the Sacred College. Yet such practices, long accepted as normal by the princes of the Church, were now beginning to be frowned on by an ever larger number of believers. The most censorious voice at that time was being heard in Florence. In sermons and poetry, Girolamo Savonarola bitterly denounced Church corruption and prophesied terrible divine retribution. In 1492, in the middle of his Advent sermon, he revealed that he had seen a hand in the heavens, holding a sword around which blazed an inscription: *Gladius Domini super terram cito et velociter* (The sword of God is about to strike the earth). Voices promised mercy for the just and punishment for the wicked, and foretold the coming of divine wrath. Then, suddenly, the sword point headed down to earth, the sky grew dark, and a shower of swords, arrows, and fire descended, while awesome thunderclaps rang out and the scourges of war, famine, and pestilence were unleashed.

In other parts of Italy, similar predictions spread abroad. Prophets arose in many places. In 1491 one such appeared in Rome, a preacher dressed in rags and carrying a small wooden cross. An eloquent and erudite speaker, he harangued the crowd clustered around him in the marketplace: "Romans, before the year is ended you will shed many tears and dire happenings will befall you. Next year these disasters will spread throughout all Italy, but in 1493 will appear the angelic Shepherd, He Who, devoid of temporal power, will seek only the salvation of souls."

In this apocalyptic atmosphere, Innocent VIII felt himself nearing death in the summer of 1492. His doctors had tried every remedy, even attempting to revive him by using the blood of three young boys, who were paid one ducat each and died as a result of the experiment. After five days' agony the pope expired, on July 2, while around his bed ambitions took wing. Rodrigo's were the most fervent: he was determined to do all in his power to crown his career with the highest dignity on earth, that of Vicar of Christ.

PART TWO

The Reign of Alexander VI

CHAPTER

1

On Olympian Heights

The conclave's favorites

Even before Innocent's death, the conclavists squabbled over who should succeed him. Naples and Milan confronted each other in the persons of Giuliano della Rovere and Ascanio Sforza. King Ferrante of Naples promised Giuliano the aid of his condottieri, Virginio Orsini and Fabrizio and Prospero Colonna, while the French king, Charles VIII, who also favored him, sent him 200,000 ducats. The republic of Genoa offered him 100,000 ducats. With these gifts, Giuliano was in a position to buy the six votes he lacked; on top of the nine he already had, this would give him the two-thirds majority he needed to win.

The Milanese party, headed by Ascanio Sforza, held seven votes at the outset. It might win four more, but it put forward no single candidate. Among those it supported were the Portuguese Jorge Costa, the Neapolitan Oliviero Carafa, the archbishop of Naples who had broken with Ferrante, Ardicino della Porta, Francesco Piccolomini, Ascanio Sforza himself, and lastly Rodrigo Borgia. The electoral maneuvering went on as a muted backdrop to the grandiose ceremonies marking the pope's funeral. The vacancy at the seat of power aroused passions. Before order was eventually restored, 220 murders were said to have been committed in the capital in twelve days.

Finally, on August 6, everything was ready for the cardinals to hold their conclave at the Vatican. That morning a procession of voters and conclavists was climbing the steps of St. Peter's when an extraordinary phenomenon occurred. The astonished Romans saw three identical suns appear in the eastern sky. This rare accident of refraction was immediately interpreted as a sign that in the next pope's reign the three powers of the papacy—temporal, spiritual, and heavenly—would be kept perfectly under control. In the evening, people looked up and saw sixteen torches burning high up in one of the towers of Cardinal Giuliano della Rovere's palace, where no one was allowed; the torches lit up spontaneously, then went out one after the other, except one which burned all night long. The news was skillfully broadcast by Giuliano's champions. The people, eagerly watching for signs emanating from the Vatican, found these omens disturbing.

Elevation of Rodrigo Borgia

Shut up in the Sistine Chapel, the princes of the Church heard the opening homily given by the Spanish bishop Bernardino Lopez de Carvajal. It was a pious invitation to choose the candidate most likely to cure the Church's vices, especially the trading in sacred possessions. His words, however, fell on deaf ears. The successive ballots—three were counted up to August 10—were preceded by shameless bargainings as the candidates tried to win votes by making all sorts of tempting promises. The Milan faction managed to garner fourteen votes—just one more was needed to reach the fateful number that would win the day. But none of its candidates commanded unanimity. The man with the best chances, however, seemed to be Rodrigo Borgia, who spared no effort in trying to win the necessary votes. Young Giovanni de' Medici, cardinals Giovanni-Battista Zeno, Lorenzo Cibo, Carafa, Costa, and Piccolomini refused to have any part in the bargaining. But the aged Maffeo Gherardo, the Venetian patriarch who, at ninety-five, no longer had all his faculties, let himself be won around and, offered a rich reward, cast his ballot for Borgia in the night of August 10–11, 1492.

At daybreak the windows of the conclave were thrown open, the cross appeared, and a voice announced the election of Rodrigo Borgia, Pope Alexander VI. The new pope wanted to recall Alexander III, the twelfth-century pontiff who had dared to confront Frederick Barbarossa. But this was also the name of Alexander the Great, the fabulous conqueror of the ancient world. There were murmurings that the new pope wanted to make his pontificate a universal reign where all nations would be subject to him, as would the heavenly powers, through the power Christ had granted St. Peter to bind and unbind all things on earth and in heaven.

On August 12 a torchlit procession of 800 Roman notables came to pay homage to the new sovereign, while the people rushed, as they always did, to pillage the house of the new pope. The enthronement took place at midday on Sunday, August 26, a month after the previous pope's death. In a ceremony of unprecedented grandeur, Alexander VI was crowned on the steps of St. Peter's Basilica in the presence of the ambassadors of the Italian states, who showered him with compliments. Next came the cardinals, who had already paid him homage in the cathedral. Each one was accompanied by a dozen squires in tunics of their particular colors—rose, silver, green, white, and black— and, with their white miters on their heads, rode richly caparisoned horses. A cortege formed to take possession of the Lateran. Thirteen companies of men-at-arms marched in front followed by the members of the pope's household, the orators of the various states, prelates, bishops, and, lastly, the cardinals.

The lords of the cities and castles of the Church dependencies— the Baglionis of Perugia, the Varanos of Camerino, and others— crowded around Count Antonio della Mirandola, who held aloft the papal standard, the first time it had been carried through Rome. On one side was the Borgia bull, passant gules on field vert, and on the other three black bands on a gold ground, the whole surmounted by the tiara and the keys of St. Peter. Next came the prelates carrying the Holy Sacrament, which was preceded by a lantern and escorted by Count Niccolò Orsini of Pitigliano, captain general of the Church, armed and helmeted. Behind the Sacrament rode the pope, mounted on a hackney. On his head was the tiara, and protecting him from the sun was a golden canopy with yellow and red stripes. Cardinals Piccolomini and Riario held the ends of his cloak. Crowds of prelates from the Curia and members of the various religious orders and brotherhoods brought up the rear of the procession, which was numbered at more than 10,000. At the pope's bidding, coins were thrown into the crowd—carlinos of silver and even, at certain squares, golden ducats.

Over the streets, which were hung with iridescent fabrics, silks and velvet, towered triumphal arches, one of them representing the Arch of Constantine. Young girls recited verses in honor of Alexander VI.

There were live tableaux symbolizing the pope's triumph and inscriptions that sang his praises, comparing him to Alexander the Great and Caesar. One banner proudly proclaimed: "Rome was great under Caesar. Now she is even greater. Caesar was a man. Alexander is a God!"

Cardinal Barbo had put up a statue of a bull, like the Borgia emblem, that gushed water from its mouth and nostrils. The Capitol was magnificently decorated, as was the Castel Sant'Angelo, which had soldiers posted on its walls. Cannons fired salvos of honor. At the top of the central tower flew a standard, 40 feet wide, splendidly decorated with the pope's arms and flanked by two banners showing the emblems of the Church and the Roman people.

The Jews were waiting for the pontiff at the foot of the castle to present him with the Book of the Law, which was placed on a lectern with candles all around. Following tradition, Alexander approved their Law but blamed their interpretation of it, then gave them authority to continue living amidst the Christians of Rome.

Interrupted at every turn, the procession took several hours to wend its way from St. Peter's to the Lateran, exhausting those who took part. Just as the pope was about to receive the homage of the Lateran chapter, he fainted, falling into Cardinal Riario's arms. Those near him had to throw water onto his face to revive him.

According to Bernardino Corio, the orator of Ferrara, Alexander next submitted to the examination "instituted, so they said, after the scandal of the election of Pope Joan"—the verification of his male sex, for which he obliged by lying down on a low seat. But this story of a test applied to as prolific a father as Alexander VI was merely intended to amuse the duke when he read his ambassador's letter. The symbolic ceremony, described mischievously by Corio, in fact represented the elevation of the pontiff by his rise from the low seat, called the *sedes stercoraria*, to the glorious throne of St. Peter.

Immediately after the ceremonial "taking possession" of the Lateran, messengers were sent out north, south, east, and west to announce the happy advent of Alexander VI. Each man was given 350 ducats for his travel expenses. One messenger reached Valencia in eighteen days, so delighting the inhabitants that they gave him a suit of scarlet and enough money to marry off two of his daughters. Everywhere, in this cradle of the Borgia family, there was rejoicing. Processions were held, the Te Deum was sung, and everyone came to kiss the hands of the pope's sister, Doña Beatrice, the wife of Jimen Perez de Arenas.

There was similar joy in Játiva. The *jurados* of Valencia sent the pope a letter complimenting him in Latin and Catalan.

Price of the election

In Rome, Alexander set about making good his promises. Burckard, the pope's master of ceremonies, writes that on August 31 a consistory was held at which he "distributed his goods and gave them to the poor." These "poor" were none other than his electors, already abundantly provided with material wealth, though forever insatiable. The manna divided among them was particularly rich: more than 80,000 ducats in the form of bishoprics, abbeys, many ecclesiastical benefices, and a large number of fiefs, towns, and castles. The accusation of simony that the pope's enemies were later to hold against him would be based on the fact that he had formally promised the rewards, before his election, to those who would vote for him. Nevertheless, such practices had become common over the years in the conclaves. It seemed quite normal for the pope, who had everything, to leave the revenues from his cardinalate to his former colleagues.

First in line was Cardinal Sforza, the leading voter for the pope, who became vice-chancellor. He was given the castle of Nepi, the bishopric of Erlau in Hungary, Rodrigo's annuities from the bishoprics, monasteries, and churches of Sevilla and Cádiz, and the legations of Bologna, the Romagna, and the exarchate of Ravenna. Before the election, four mules laden with sacks of silver had been seen wending their way from the Borgia palace toward Sforza's home on the Piazza Navona. However, rather than a gift, this most likely represented a deposit, made as a safety measure, in light of the popular custom of pillaging a cardinal's house after he had been made pope.

Cardinal Orsini received the cities of Monticelli and Soriano, the legation of the Marches and bishopric of Cartagena, valued at 7,000 ducats, as well as a bonus of 20,000 ducats. For his part, Cardinal Colonna was given the abbey of Subiaco with the twenty-two castles belonging to it, and an income of 2,000 ducats, to which the pope added a bonus of 15,000 ducats. Cardinal Savelli received Città Castellana and the bishopric of Mallorca, worth 6,000 ducats, together with a bonus of 30,000 ducats.

Cardinal Pallavicini was granted the bishopric of Pamplona, vacant since Cesare Borgia had been transferred to the archbishopric of Valencia. He also received a Benedictine monastery in the Nocera diocese, the Castle of Cellano, and a large pension.

Cardinal Ardicino della Porta, the bishop of Aleria, was given the abbey of San Lorenzo in Rome; Cardinal San Severino, the priory of the Sta. Trinità of Modena and several benefices in the dioceses of Reggio, Messina, and Bourges; Cardinal Conti, 3,000 gold ducats and 2,200 pounds of silver; Cardinal Michieli, the bishopric of Porto, worth 1,200 ducats, as well as benefices in the dioceses of Florence, Lucca, and Aqui; Cardinal Campofregoso, the legation of the Roman Campagna, the *commendam* of Petervorodino in Hungary, several other benefices, and 4,000 ducats; Cardinal Domenico della Rovere, the fief of Acquapendente and several abbeys and prebends in the Amelia and Turin dioceses; Cardinal Raffaello Riario, prebends and pensions in Spain worth 4,000 a year, as well as the house on the Piazza Navona recently confiscated from the heirs of Girolamo Riario; Cardinal Lorenzo Cibo, a monastery at Huesca; and finally old Cardinal Gherardo, who cast the deciding vote for Rodrigo, 6,000 ducats.

Among the cardinals who had not supported Rodrigo, Giovanni de' Medici was granted the legateship of the Patrimony of St. Peter as well as the Fortress of Viterbo; Alexander hoped thus to get into the good graces of Giovanni's brother Pietro de' Medici, the Master of Florence. Cardinals Costa, Zeno, Piccolomini, Girolamo Basso della Rovere, and Carafa received only slight gratuities, which kept them free of the so-called sin of simony of which the conclave would later be accused. Their reputations were not blameless, however. Even Giuliano della Rovere, forced to bend to the will of the majority, got a reward; the legateship of Avignon, the fortress of Ostia, of which he was bishop, the Ronciglione castle, and other benefices, including a canonry of Florence, were all confirmed or granted to him.

Nor was the pope's family forgotten. Cesare, his son, received the archbishopric of Valencia and the Cistercian abbey of Valdigna nearby, providing him with 18,000 and 2,000 ducats respectively. And the pope's nephew, Giovanni, the archbishop of Monreale in Sicily, was named cardinal of the titular Church of Sta. Susanna.

Portrait of Alexander VI

The Romans applauded these favors; since they were the cardinals' clients, they looked to profit substantially from their patrons' wealth.

In these early days of the new pope's reign, there was general agreement on the favorable impression he inspired in his subjects. Sigismondo de Conti spoke of the pope's wisdom: he had reached his sixties, "the age," Conti noted, "as Aristotle says, when men are wisest." The chronicler describes Alexander as a large, robust man, praises his sharp gaze, his amiability, and "wonderful skill in money matters." Bishop Carvajal dwelt on his handsome appearance. Hieronimo Porzio also admired his tall figure, his florid complexion, dark eyes, and rather full mouth. The pope enjoyed excellent health, he wrote, had exceptional stamina and great eloquence. The portraits of the pope, the medals with his likeness, and Pinturicchio's fresco of the Resurrection in the Borgia apartments all show his features to the life—the broad forehead beneath the bald crown, the hooked nose, fearless gaze, sensual lips, and fleshy chin bespeak his intelligence and love of pleasure. The overriding impression is one of haughty geniality. Alexander was, in truth, an opportunist and bon vivant. Not bothered by scruples, he always chose the most pragmatic path. He was also frugal in his personal needs: his monthly housekeeping bill was no more than 700 ducats, and his meals usually included only one dish—which explains the lack of enthusiasm with which his friend Ascanio Sforza or his own children came to dine with him. True, this simplicity went by the board whenever he received princes or ambassadors— lavish occasions that upheld his reputation as a supremely generous host.

Alexander had got into the habit many years before of flattering those around him, and after his accession he showered spiritual favors on his friends. The domestic prelates, as Burckard testifies, were allowed to pick a confessor who would be able to absolve them of all crimes, even the most heinous—which in fact only the pope himself had the right to do. Yet it would be a mistake to take this as a sign of laxity on the pope's part. Common criminals and delinquents were subject to extremely harsh penalties, as witness the sensational punishment of a murderer executed in September 1492 with his brother on the Campo dei Fiori. The pope, however, sought to encourage prevention rather than repression. He set up four magistratures to end disputes before they came to court. The bearing of arms was put under control of the police, who were to ensure that no blade was poisoned. The municipal *conservatori* were responsible for dispensing justice at the Capitol each morning. Alexander himself held audience every Tuesday.

Alliance with Milan and Lucrezia Borgia's first marriage

It was a peaceful Rome that, in the autumn of 1492, watched as the whole world came to swear allegiance to the Borgia pope. Contrary to expectations, Siena, Lucca, Venice, Mantua, and Florence, which had been rather reserved during the conclave, now fell over each other in their attentions to the Holy See. Pietro de' Medici headed the magnificent delegation from Florence; Milan sent a sumptuous embassy. Even far-off countries presented tokens of obedience, with the Swedish regent sending gifts of furs and horses.

Unanimity, however, was far from complete. If the French and Genoese seemed to be making the best of the failure of their candidate for the papacy, King Ferrante of Naples appeared not at all resigned. It was a worrying situation for Alexander. Troops of the Neapolitan armies were always camped menacingly near the boundary of the Papal States. He therefore took the precaution of sealing the alliance that had linked him to the Milanese faction during the conclave. The way to do this was by joining the two families, the Borgias and Sforzas. The instrument of this union would be his daughter, Lucrezia, then age twelve.

A citizen of Parma, Niccolò Cagnolo, had observed the young girl when she first appeared on the political stage: "She is of medium height and slender," he wrote; "her face is long, her nose well cut; she has golden hair, light-blue eyes, a somewhat full mouth, very white teeth, and a bosom white and shapely." Lucrezia had been betrothed a year before, first to Don Juan of Centelles, then to Don Gaspare d'Aversa, both nobles of Aragonese stock. As soon as he became pope, however, Alexander went back on his word. Cardinal Ascanio Sforza suggested a husband from his family—his cousin Giovanni Sforza, the bastard son of Costanzo Sforza, count of Cotignola and lord of Pesaro, a papal fief near the border of the Romagna and the Marches. The future bridegroom, a conceited young man of twenty-six, cut a good figure and had received a fine education, which had not, however, muted his violent temper. He was the widower of the duchess of Urbino's sister, Maddalena da Gonzaga, who had died in childbirth. Decidedly interested, Giovanni was called to Rome, arriving incognito in mid-October, 1492. Warned of this dangerous rival, Don Gaspare d'Aversa rushed with his father to plead with the pope the validity of the marriage contract between himself and Lucrezia, returning with an indemnity of 3,000 gold ducats. After the preliminary talks, Giovanni Sforza went back to Pesaro, leaving behind a proxy, Niccolò da Saiano, a doctor of law, to put the finishing touches to his contract. As the pope's daughter's husband-to-be, he saw his situation change overnight: his cousins in Milan presented him with a lucrative command in their army. All that remained was to get ready for the wedding ceremony. From her father, Lucrezia received jewels and sumptuous robes, including one dress that cost 15,000 ducats. To make a good appearance, young Sforza borrowed a gold chain from the marquess of Mantua, his late wife's brother.

After her proxy marriage, on February 2, 1493, Lucrezia hardly left the house she shared with Adriana da Mila and Giulia Farnese, whose husband, Orso Orsini, Adriana's son, was away from Rome in the pope's service. The three women, together with their train of ladies-in-waiting and servant girls, lived in a handsome palace next door to the Vatican. It had been built by Giovanni-Battista Zeno, the cardinal of Sta. Maria in Portico. The house was close to the entrance to the pope's palace and had a private chapel opening on St. Peter's. That meant the young women could slip unnoticed into the Sistine Chapel and the pope's private apartments, while Alexander could easily come and visit them.

The palace of Sta. Maria in Portico was now bubbling with worldly animation as ambassadors and fashionable ladies thronged in, and the air was filled with gay chatter and laughter. Adriana da Mila welcomed Andrea Bocciaccio, bishop of Modena, who conveyed to Lucrezia the duke and duchess of Ferrara's congratulations. In turn, the pope's cousin promised to have the Holy Father bestow the cardinal's hat on Ippolito, the duke's younger son.

Giovanni Sforza made his official entrance into Rome on June 2, 1493. His brothers-in-law, Juan of Gandia and Cesare, came to meet him at the city gates. Then the cavalcade trotted past the loggia of the palace of Sta. Maria in Portico where Lucrezia sat, splendidly gowned and with jewels in her hair that sparkled in the sunlight.

The wedding ceremony had been set for ten days later, June 12. On that day the duke of Gandia, who was acting as master of ceremonies, escorted his sister into the papal apartments. He wore a Turkish-style costume, similar to the one Pinturicchio painted him in in his fresco of St. Catherine: a white tunic embroidered with gold thread, a collar of rubies and pearls, a bronze-colored cloak, and a large turban with a jewel. This exotic mode of dress had been the rage at the papal court ever since Prince Djem first came to Rome.

Lucrezia was brought to her father, who greeted her with smiles, surrounded by ten cardinals and a throng of bishops and notables. The thirteen-year-old bride had a long train, held by a young Moorish maid-in-waiting, and a retinue of 500 ladies headed by Giulia Farnese and Battistina, Pope Innocent VIII's granddaughter. Then it was the groom's turn. He entered accompanied by two of the pope's sons. Like the duke of Gandia, he wore a Turkish costume of gold cloth. The two young lords' elegant dress made Cesare's episcopal purple look lackluster indeed, and perhaps the glaring contrast aroused bitter thoughts in the young man's breast.

Meanwhile, Lucrezia and Giovanni knelt before the pope on golden hassocks and exchanged their vows. Among the crowd of relations and friends of the Borgias and Sforzas, was the well-built, dark-haired Alfonso d'Este, son of the duke of Ferrara, Ercole I, and the youthful husband of Anna Sforza. Little could he know that destiny would one day link his life with the young bride's.

Finally the bishop of Concordia slipped the wedding rings on the young people's fingers and Niccolò Orsini, as captain general of the Church, raised his sword above their heads. The secular festivities could begin.

The guests took their seats around the pope's throne in the first room of the Borgia apartments to watch the entertainment—first, a pastoral poem, then Plautus's comedy the *Menaechmi*, performed by young actors dressed in animal skins. The entertainment was a new one, very popular at the papal court. The humanist scholar Pomponius Laetus, who may have been one of Lucrezia's teachers, had made a specialty of putting on Plautus's plays. The pope applauded this picture of the mores of classical times, so close to those of papal Rome with its buffoonlike fathers, its libertines, voracious mistresses, parasites, and pimps. But the eclogue, by Serafino Aquilino, was more to his taste.

After the play the young couple received gifts. Lucrezia's brothers, her cousin the cardinal of Monreale, the pope's intimates, and the protonotaries Cesarini and Lunati all presented jewels, precious stuffs, and objects of gold and silver. Ludovico il Moro brought five lengths of gold brocade and two rings, one a diamond, the other a ruby; his brother Ascanio presented a complete table setting of solid gold. At the lively banquet that followed, 200 goblets and silver cups filled with sweetmeats, marzipans, fruit, and wine were passed around among the guests, while leftover cakes were scattered out of the window to the crowd on the square below. Another chronicler, the maliciously gossipy Infessura, whose word must be taken with a grain of salt, says that the pope and eminent prelates amused themselves by throwing sweets into the low-cut bodices of the ladies' gowns. Later, a more intimate meal was offered the young pair in the Sala dei Pontifici. The pope and four of his cardinals attended it before accompanying the couple to their marriage chamber in the palace of Sta. Maria in Portico.

Cesare and the Aragonese alliance

If Alexander's enemies later vied with each other in denouncing Lucrezia's wedding celebrations as an orgy designed to appeal to the basest instincts of the pope and those around him, such scenes were actually far from exceptional in Renaissance times. Justifying all the expense and show was the need to give the Rome-Milan agreement the greatest possible publicity. By June 1493, however, this agreement was beginning to lose importance in the pope's eyes. Another political union was looming as more desirable, one that would set the Borgias' seal even more surely on the world and assure the future of Alexander's sons. It concerned the house of Aragon.

At the beginning of his father's reign, Cesare Borgia, archbishop of Valencia since the age of seventeen, had resolved to use the prestigious post as a stepping-stone for his personal fortune as both his father and great-uncle had done before him. To do so, however, he had to serve the interests of the king of Aragon, Ferdinand the Catholic. He saw nothing shocking in that.

The duke of Ferrara's chargé d'affaires, Andrea Bocciaccio, bishop of Modena, described Cesare in March 1493 as a highly intelligent young man who had already chosen his own way of life and course of action. "The other day," he writes, "I went to see Cesare in his home in the Trastevere; he was about to go hunting and was dressed in an altogether worldly manner. He wore silk, with his weapon at his side: a small circle in his hair was the only sign of a tonsure. We rode side by side, conversing. When others came up he treated me with great familiarity. He has a fine, remarkable mind and exquisite character; his manners are those of a potentate's son, his mood serene and full of gaiety; he radiates joy. He has great modesty, his demeanor being far preferable and superior to that of his brother the duke of Gandia, who, however, has many good qualities. The archbishop of

Valencia has never had any liking for an ecclesiastical career, but one must recall that his benefice brings him more than 16,000 ducats."

It was plain for all to see that Cesare had his eyes on the Spanish royal house. Around him swarmed advisers and servants, all totally devoted to him, almost all of whom hailed from Aragon or Catalonia. Alongside the prelates who had known him since his student days were some disturbing characters, such as the Valencian Miguel Corella, known as Michelotto—a thug ready to do anything for his master. As the bishop of Modena noted, Cesare stuck to his ecclesiastical post only for the money it brought him. No doubt he was not overjoyed to see himself overtaken by his brother Juan, who was a year younger than himself. But being a realist, he recognized that his family had to keep its hands on the duchy of Gandia. That meant that Juan must succeed his elder brother, Pedro Luís, not only as duke but as husband of the princess marked out for him, Maria Enriquez, cousin of Ferdinand of Aragon.

Alexander and the Catholic kings
The dividing up of America and expulsion of the Jews from Spain

This was the ideal time to bring about such a dynastic alliance between the Borgias and the royal house of Spain. Before Alexander became pope, the capture of Granada had given Christendom mastery over the last Islamic possession in the Iberian peninsula. As Cardinal Borgia, he had celebrated this victory to the fullest, and the Spanish kings were grateful. One of his first acts as pontiff would now be to extol Spain's extraordinary venture into the unknown lands where, thanks to her, Christianity would be able to take root.

In March 1493 Christopher Columbus returned from the New World he had just discovered. The triumph brought an unexpected adornment to the crown of Castile, and briefly that of Aragon, since Ferdinand shared power with his wife, Isabella. On May 4, 1493, to make the discovery official and prevent rival claims, Alexander solemnly published a bull marking the boundaries of the territories of the Spanish and Portuguese, who had been vying with each other for years to find a western route to the Indies. "In these unknown lands where Christopher Columbus has stepped," he wrote, "lives a people, naked, vegetarian, who believe in one God and ask but to be taught to believe in Jesus Christ. All these islands and territories, abounding in gold, spices and treasure, situated west and south of a line that runs from the North to the South Pole, a hundred leagues west of the Isles of the Azores and Cape Verde, are allocated to the Catholic Kings, on condition that they were not discovered before the preceding Christmas by another Christian prince. This act is established by virtue of the authority of Almighty God bestowed on the blessed Peter and the right of the Vicariate of Jesus Christ which the pontiff exercises upon earth." A papal brief noted that this concession was granted for the propagation of the faith. Another one granted Spain privileges similar to those the Portuguese held with regard to Africa. Offenders were subject to severe penalties. If a ruler, even an emperor or king, allowed his subjects to enter the demarcated areas, whether for trade or any other reason, without the permission of the Catholic Kings, he would be excommunicated on the spot.

Thanks to the Borgia pope, Ferdinand and Isabella now had their right to the Americas. In 1494 the brief would receive just one modification: the line of demarcation would be moved 270 leagues to the west by the Treaty of Tordesillas.

The Spaniards had the best possible insurance for the future of their conquest. Yet they were loath to let the Holy See meddle in their internal affairs. Alexander VI found this out when the Catholic Kings were persecuting the Jews in their kingdom. By the edict of March 31, 1492, all observers of Jewish law, both acknowledged and secret— the Marranos—were forced to convert to Christianity and to practice it or to emigrate. If they emigrated, they were forbidden to take any gold or silver with them. In the months that followed, hundreds of thousands of Jews chose to leave for Italy, North Africa, or Portugal. Unlike the Jews, the Moors were protected by agreements made at the surrender of Granada. However, some Moors fled too, fearing they would soon be subjected to the same kind of persecution as the Jews.

In this huge exodus, Jews and Marranos took refuge in Rome, where they were traditionally made welcome. A forest of tents sprang up along the Appian Way near the Tomb of Cecilia Metella. That the pope consented to this charitable treatment of misbelievers aroused the Catholic Kings' indignation, despite the fact that he recognized their dominance over the New World. They dispatched an ambassador, Diego Lopez de Haro, to Rome, who denounced the hateful practice in no uncertain terms. But he had another mission. His masters, he told the pope, noted the expenses incurred by the conversion of infidels both in Spain and in the New World and begged permission to tax the assets of the churches in their kingdoms. Such a request was not unusual, and Alexander readily granted it. But he refused to go back on his protection of the Jews and Marranos; he insisted on maintaining the liberal traditions of the Holy See and the promises he had made to the Jewish community when he rode through Rome at his coronation.

Ferdinand and Isabella had received too many favors at the pope's hands to be ungrateful, so the ambassador confirmed in their name the granting of the duchy of Gandia to Juan de Borgia and their consent to the union of the new duke and Princess Maria Enriquez.

The new duke of Gandia: Juan de Borgia

After Lopez de Haro's audience with the pope, Juan de Borgia could not wait to go to Spain, and left Rome with a large retinue. The pope had given him the archbishop of Oristano in Sardinia, Jaime Serra (soon to be cardinal), as chief adviser; Genis Fira, canon of Cartagena, acted as his secretary, and Jaime de Pertusa, his treasurer. All three were subjects of the king of Aragon. Besides magnificent presents for his future daughter-in-law, Alexander had given his son huge sums of money in coins and bills of exchange drawn on the Spannochi bank in Catalonia. With that he could buy new lands and fiefs near Gandia and Lombay.

Juan made a triumphal entry into Barcelona on August 24, 1493. The heir to the Aragonese throne, the Infante Don Juan, and all the Enriquez family greeted the pope's son enthusiastically. Not long after, however, a shadow was cast on the brilliant spectacle as young Borgia— who was not yet eighteen—started to sow his wild oats and, rather than settle down to married life after the wedding ceremony, plunged into the pleasures of low society. The news reached Rome. Cesare, who had been raised to the purple on September 20, took up his pen to chastise his younger brother: "I have less joy in my promotion to the cardinalate than sorrow in learning, through a report addressed to the pope, of your wicked behavior in Barcelona. You are spending your nights roaming the streets, killing dogs and cats, frequenting the brothels, and gambling for high stakes, instead of obeying your father-in-law and paying the homage due to Doña Maria." This stern warning hit home. Don Juan left Barcelona and its temptations for Valencia, where the viceroy received him and the *jurados* paid him homage.

The couple settled in Gandia, rarely leaving the castle. The money the pope had provided quickly vanished. Acting on a report from the archbishop of Oristano, Alexander gave orders for a cashier accused of embezzlement to be sent back to Rome. But the newlyweds continued in their frivolous ways. Alexander had to remind his son to thank Alfonso II of Naples for presenting him with the principality of Tricarico and the *contados* of Chiaramonte and Lauria. In fact, as time went on, Juan began to feel more Spanish than Italian.

Stormy relations with Ferrante of Naples

In the person of the duke of Gandia, a very close link had been forged between the Borgias and the House of Aragon. The tempting idea of strengthening it by a similar link with the Aragonese dynasty in Naples had occurred to both the pope and Cesare when Alexander first took office. But the recent alliance with Milan made any rapprochement with Naples hard to achieve. Ludovico il Moro wanted to be sure of the pope's help should Ferrante try to restore Gian Galeazzo Sforza, Ludovico's young nephew and ward, as the legitimate duke of Milan. With his title of duke of Bari, Ludovico, and his young wife, Beatrice d'Este, totally eclipsed Gian Galeazzo and his wife, Isabella of Aragon, the granddaughter of the king of Naples. He therefore had good reason to fear reprisals from Ferrante. But if worst came to worst, the Papal States would act as a barrier to stop, or at least slow down, the Neapolitan army's northward march.

Ferrante hit on a way to clear his soldiers' path. In the autumn of 1492 his condottiere Virginio Orsini, who was captain general of the kingdom of Naples, purchased the papal fiefs of Cerveteri and Anguillara in the Roman Campagna; Francesco Cibo, Innocent VIII's son, had put them up for sale. The castles, which lined the road to friendly Tuscany, would assure passage toward the Milanese. This acquisition, which was made behind the pope's back, placed Rome under the threat of Naples. On hearing about it, Alexander at once ordered the purchase repealed. Adding to his irritation, at that time the king of Naples was pressuring him exasperatingly about a private matter concerning his illegitimate daughter Beatrice, the widow of King Mathias Corvinus of Hungary. Beatrice had now married the new king of Hungary, Ladislas of Bohemia. She proved sterile, and

Ladislas asked Rome for an annulment. Ferrante wanted it rejected, but Alexander was prepared to accept it.

These differences provided grounds for negotiation. In December 1492 Federigo d'Altamura, Ferrante's second son, turned up at the Vatican. He was the guest of Alexander's enemy, Cardinal Giuliano della Rovere, who advised him to be adamant in his dealings with the pope, and so the talks came to naught. On January 10, 1493, d'Altamura withdrew to Ostia. Cardinal della Rovere had just taken refuge there after quarreling with Ascanio Sforza, who reproached him for siding with Naples. From his impregnable castle at the mouth of the Tiber, the cardinal kept Rome at a respectful distance. A frightened Alexander now found himself threatened in the hinterland and blocked from the sea. One day when he was at the papal villa of La Magliana, near Ostia, the garrison fired a salvo of honor, which made him suspect an ambush. Without taking time to eat he at once returned to the Vatican, with his courtiers and clergy fuming over the enforced fast. Feverishly, he ordered the fortification of Civitavecchia and decided to follow the advice of Ascanio Sforza and Ludovico il Moro and join them in a league with Venice.

As soon as Ferrante learned of this, he determined to put a stop to such a nefarious alliance and made some concessions. He sent the abbot Rugio to Rome to settle amicably the question of Cerveteri and Anguillara. He suggested tokens of goodwill, offering to arrange a marriage between a princess of his family and Cesare Borgia if his father wanted him to abandon his ecclesiastical career. Another royal princess could wed Jofré, then eleven and the pope's youngest son. But when the negotiator reached Rome, the pope's discussions with the northern states had already resulted in an alliance and the treaty had been published in Rome. On April 25, 1493, Siena, Ferrara, and Mantua joined Milan and Venice in the League. These states would give Alexander the troops he needed to hound Virginio Orsini out of papal territory. Confrontation between Rome and Naples seemed inescapable.

The Neapolitan faction then launched a vigorous propaganda campaign against the pope. Word had leaked out that Alexander was about to reward his new allies by making them cardinals. Giuliano della Rovere urged those cardinals still on his side to oppose the move firmly. Ferrante himself denounced the plan in the foreign courts, particularly in Spain, where his ambassador Antonio d'Alessandro spoke up against the pope for thinking of selling cardinalates in exchange for money with which to fight Naples. King Ferrante condemned this immoral conduct, he said. "Alexander," cried the ambassador, "leads a life that is the object of general execration. He has no thought for the seat he occupies. By fair means or foul he seeks only the aggrandizement of his children. He is now preparing to go to war against the kingdom of Naples. Rome is swarming with soldiers, who outnumber the priests. The pope's counselors—the Sforzas—seek only to tyrannize the papacy so they may use it to their own ends after this pope's death. Then Rome will become a Milanese camp."

Threat of French invasion

It was against this backdrop of tension that Lucrezia and Giovanni Sforza's wedding took place on June 12. On the 19th, the ambassador of Ferdinand and Isabella of Spain had an audience with the pope. Primed about all the grudges of the Neapolitan court, Diego Lopez de Haro expressed regrets concerning Rome's hostile attitude toward Ferrante, his monarch's cousin, but his concern was really with other, more important things. He stated, simply, that the king of Naples could not count on the aid of the Spanish monarchy. Meanwhile, he pointed out, Ferrante's situation was rapidly deteriorating in the international field.

The news from France was disturbing: on the advice of some refugee Neapolitan nobles, Charles VIII had just raised a sizable army to march on Naples. The king claimed that he wanted to recover his legitimate inheritance and use it as a springboard for a future Crusade. To protect France from external threat during his absence, Charles had made peace with all her neighbors: with Henry VII of England at Etaples in 1492; with Ferdinand and Isabella at Barcelona; and with Maximilian of Austria at Senlis in 1493. He expected the pope, as suzerain, to give him the patrimony of the former Angevin dynasty in the kingdom of Naples, and to recognize his rights and investiture. Such a menace did not brook any beating about the bush. Ferrante had decided on reconciliation with the Borgia pope, at any price.

In late June Federigo d'Altamura was sent to Rome once more to iron out the dispute concerning Virginio Orsini and demand that the pope quit the Lombardy-Venice League. He pointed out the threat represented by the opposing cardinals and his elder brother Alfonso of Calabria, who could well invade the Papal States with the troops he had marshaled on the frontier. On learning that the French king had sent his ambassador, Perron de Baschi, to Italy to announce the French march on Naples, Federigo dropped his uncompromising attitude and the dispute was settled on the spot. The pope was satisfied with Orsini's assurances of nonbelligerence. He would let him keep the castles of Cerveteri and Anguillara against a payment of 35,000 ducats. Jofré Borgia, who was now twelve, would wed the sixteen-year-old Sancia of Aragon, the illegitimate daughter of Alfonso of Calabria. He would receive the principality of Squillace and the contado of Cariati. But as Jofré was not yet of marriageable age, the wedding would not be announced until Christmas. A rider to the document foresaw the reconciliation of Giuliano della Rovere with Alexander VI.

On July 24, to everyone's astonishment—so secret were the negotiations—Virginio Orsini and Cardinal Giuliano came to Rome and dined with the pope. Federigo of Altamura officially announced to his father, King Ferrante, on August 1, that the pope had signed the agreed-on articles. Just as this pact with the court of Naples was completed, the duke of Gandia left for Spain where he joined the other court, that of Aragon. So it was clear that there had been a complete reversal in the papal alliances: Alexander was deliberately abandoning the camp of Ludovico Sforza and Charles VIII. When the roving French ambassador de Baschi visited Rome a few days later and asked the pope to give Charles VIII title to Naples, Alexander palmed him off with dilatory talk and the Frenchman left empty-handed.

Ferrante was jubilant; he was convinced that this refusal meant the dreaded invasion would not take place. One act after another proved that the pope had rallied to his cause. On the very day that de Baschi left Rome, marriage vows were exchanged, by proxy, between Jofré and Sancia of Aragon. A week later the censures pronounced on Virginio Orsini were lifted. Then Alexander, who had not broken with Ludovico il Moro, handed him the terms of the compromise he had agreed to regarding Cerveteri and Anguillara. The remarkable result of these dealings was that now the pope was reconciled with all his enemies. An account sent from Rome to Milan on August 13 is full of his praise:

"Many believe the pope has lost his wits since his elevation. It seems that quite the contrary is the case. He has negotiated a League which made the king of Naples groan; he has married his daughter to a member of the house of Sforza who has, besides his pension from the duchy of Milan, a yearly income of 12,000 ducats; he has obliged

Virginio Orsini to pay 35,000 ducats and forced him to obey his will;
and he has used the threat of the League to bring the king of Naples
into a family connection with himself. These are not the actions of a
man who has lost his intellect: he can now enjoy his papacy in peace
and quiet."

Shrewd promotions to the cardinalate

In creating new cardinals on September 20, 1493, Alexander showed
that he was keeping an equal balance between Milan and Naples.
None of Ferrante's subjects figured among the twelve new promotions.
Cesare Borgia was named cardinal-deacon of Sta. Maria Nuova; Alessandro Farnese, the treasurer general of the Holy See, became cardinal-
deacon of SS. Cosma e Damiano. As he owed his promotion to the
fact that his sister, the beautiful Giulia Farnese, was the pope's mistress,
Alessandro was nicknamed the "petticoat cardinal" and even, in a
salacious play on the term for coitus, *cardinale fregnese*. Giuliano
Cesarini, another new *purpurato*, belonged to a great Roman family
connected to Alexander through his daughter Geronima. Most of the
other nominations were aimed at pleasing the powerful rulers of Milan,
Venice, Ferrara, England, Germany, France, Spain, Hungary, and
Poland. The sole exception was Gian Antonio di San Giorgio, bishop
of Alessandria, who was elevated in reward for his personal qualities
as an eminent jurist and irreproachable priest.

With these appointments to the Sacred College, so shrewdly meted
out, the first year of Alexander's reign came to a masterly close. From
now on, none of the pope's enemies would be able to put pressure on
the great powers to have his election annulled, since, by papal decree,
every state was now represented in the Sacred College. The cardinals
opposed to him—Giuliano della Rovere, Carafa, Costa, Fregoso,
Conti, and Piccolomini—would have to keep on the defensive far from
Rome. No longer could they count on King Ferrante's support now
that the alliance had been worked out between Naples and Rome.
Moreover, Ferrante had died on January 25, 1494, and his son Alfonso
de Calabria, whose daughter Sancia was betrothed to the pope's son,
was now on the Neapolitan throne. To the indignation of Charles VIII
of France, Alexander immediately recognized him as the legitimate
king. Giuliano della Rovere then was brazen enough to change sides

and, with Alfonso of Naples and the Borgia pope now friends, rallied to the side of the French king.

Plans for the Crusade
Prince Djem at the Vatican

News came that huge concentrations of troops were being built up in France. A worried Alexander tried to flatter Charles by approving his plan for a Crusade. He suggested the French king should aim for Croatia, which the Ottomans had just invaded. On March 9, 1494, he sent a Golden Rose, reminding Charles that he himself had the Holy War constantly in mind. The Vatican had in fact been sheltering the hostage prince Djem, Sultan Bayezid II's brother, ever since Innocent VIII had had him transferred from Rhodes. Assured that his brother would not be set free, the sultan paid the papacy a yearly allowance of 40,000 ducats. He wanted to prevent the Christians from invading his empire on the pretext of restoring the rightful heir to the throne. But if a Crusade was started, it was pointed out in Rome, there would be nothing to stop them.

Yet the way Alexander and his children treated the Turkish prince raised not a few doubts about their dedication to the idea of Holy War. In May 1493, not long after Alexander became pope, a cavalcade had made its way to St. John Lateran, giving the Romans a clear view of Djem and Juan of Gandia, both in Turkish dress, riding in front of the cross. In the basilica the two men walked around studying the monuments and tombs while the pope inspected the roof. Later one of Bayezid's ambassadors came to Rome to pay Djem's allowance. At the pope's orders, the prelates and ambassadors waited for him at the Porta del Popolo and accompanied him home. The Count of Pitigliano, captain of the Church, and Rodrigo Borgia, captain of the palace, escorted him with their men-at-arms. On June 12 the ambassador was led into the pope's presence in a secret consistory. Burckard describes the ceremony: the interpreter, one Giorgio Buzardo, translated the Turk's affable words and the beneficiary Demetrius read Bayezid's letters, which were in Greek, and translated them into Latin. It was learned that the sultan rejoiced greatly at the elevation of Alexander VI and was sending him several gifts, in particular brocades, velvets, and taffetas of various colors.

These good relations with the Turkish empire were well known in

France. Still, encouraged by the pope's gift of the Golden Rose, Charles VIII was setting himself up as a potential leader of the Crusade. With the death of Mathias Corvinus of Hungary, Charles thought himself even better fitted than Maximilian of Austria to head the army of Christian rulers marching against the Turks. This was one reason he persisted in his plan to head the Crusade and claim the throne of Naples, which had been linked with the throne of Jerusalem since the thirteenth century.

Alliance of Alexander VI and Alfonso II of Naples
Marriage of Jofré Borgia and Sancia of Aragon

Rome was in no mood to favor the French king. In March 1494, a Neapolitan embassy came to Rome to swear obedience in the name of the new king, Alfonso II, and show that the barons of Naples agreed on the legitimacy of the Aragonese line. The ceremony took place on the 20th; and two days later the pope had a declaration read in consistory in favor of the house of Aragon. In it he confirmed the investiture that Innocent VIII had granted Alfonso when he was duke of Calabria. On April 18 Giovanni Borgia, the cardinal of Monreale, was appointed legate to Naples for Alfonso's coronation. When it learned that Alfonso had been crowned by the legate, on May 2, 1494, the French court was enraged.

Even more than the coronation, the marriage between Jofré and Sancia stood as a symbol of the alliance between the papacy and the kingdom of Aragon and Naples. After the exchange of vows came the presentation of gifts to the Aragonese princess—pearl necklaces, rubies, diamonds, turquoises, pieces of gold brocade, silk, and velvet. Then King Alfonso presented his gifts to the pope's sons: Jofré received the principality of Squillace and the contado of Cariati. His brother, the duke of Gandia, was named prince of Tricarico and count of Chiaramonte and Laura. Finally, on May 11, the religious ceremony was held in the chapel of the Castel Nuovo, with the bishop of Gravina officiating.

Burckard, the papal master of ceremonies, was present at all the festivities and could testify that all was carried out to the last detail: "After the banquet, the bride was taken by the legate and the king, her father, to the palace. The bridegroom and the rest of the entourage went on ahead. The young couple entered the bedchamber, where

the bed was prepared. The maids of honor and serving women un-
dressed them both and placed them in the bed, the husband to his
wife's right side. When they were thus naked beneath the sheet and
coverlet, the legate and the king came in. In their presence, the young
people were uncovered down to the navel, or thereabouts, and the
bridegroom embraced the bride freely. Meanwhile the legate and the
king stayed there and conversed for about a half-hour, after which they
left the pair and went their way."

Sancia had already been betrothed seven years before that to a
Neapolitan nobleman, Onorato Gaetani. The engagement had been
annulled in September 1493. Hotheaded and temperamental, as she
was to show later on, the sixteen-year-old girl must have had nothing
but scorn for this simulation of the marriage consummation. But it
had been duly noted according to the rules, which made her marriage
indissoluble. Thus a perfect union was made between the house of
Borgia and the two branches—Spanish and Neapolitan—of the royal
dynasty of Aragon.

Lucrezia and Giovanni Sforza married

There remained the thorny problem of the Milanese alliance, sealed
somewhat hastily by Lucrezia's marriage to Giovanni Sforza. From
one day to the next the pope's son-in-law grew more and more anxious
over the Vatican intrigues. On the pretext of escaping the plague then
raging in Rome, he had taken off for his fief in Pesaro, where he had
spent the summer and autumn of 1493. He did not come back until
November, seduced by the prospect of Lucrezia's dowry—30,000 ducats—but was loath to linger in the Eternal City. In April 1494 he
even dared to complain to Alexander about the new treaty with Naples:
"I who am in the service of Your Holiness, would be forced to serve
Naples against Milan. . . . I beg Your Holiness not to oblige me to
become the enemy of my own blood and break the ties by which I
am bound to Your Holiness and the Milanese state." To this the pope
had answered: "You meddle too much in my affairs. Stay in the pay
of both!" Giovanni thought it best to warn his uncle Ludovico il Moro
of this disturbing reply.

Alexander had no desire to see his son-in-law and daughter leave
Rome. He had grown accustomed to Lucrezia's soothing presence a
stone's throw away from the Vatican. She shared the Palace of Sta.

Maria in Portico with the women the pope loved, Adriana da Mila, and especially his mistress, Giulia Farnese. He had sent away Giulia's husband, Orso Orsini, Adriana's son, to his fief of Bassanello to raise troops to join the Naples army. Giulia had just given birth in the winter of 1493 to a little girl, Laura, who gossip had it was fathered by the pope.

The warm, intimate atmosphere of the palace is conveyed in a letter written by a close relative of Giulia's who had come to visit her in Rome, Lorenzo Pucci. The Florentine prelate came to see the ladies on December 24. He found them sitting beside the fire, busy with their toilet. Fresh and graceful, Lucrezia had the piquant beauty of her fourteen years. She wore a felt-lined gown, in the Neapolitan fashion, which she got up to change. When she returned she had on a long dress of violet-colored satin. Meanwhile Giulia had been showing her relative the newborn baby. "Oh," exclaimed Lorenzo, "she is the living image of the pope! The child must surely be his!" He noticed that Giulia had put on a little weight, which suited her admirably. She then washed her hair and a chambermaid dried and combed it: the wavy tresses reached down to her feet. "I have never seen anything like it," the Florentine wrote. After dressing Giulia's hair, the maid placed on her head a veil of white lawn, then over that a snood of gold threads that was as light as a cloud and sparkled like the sun.

Transformation of the Vatican
Pinturicchio and the Borgia Apartment

While the Palace of Sta. Maria in Portico was a perfect setting for family life, Alexander preferred the official papal residence nearby— the Vatican. Determined from the beginning to turn it into a royal palace, he had a new apartment added. Entrance was by way of an antechamber on the second story of Nicholas III's old palace. Three reception rooms followed, in the north wing of Nicholas V's palace, between the Cortile del Pappagallo and the present Cortile del Belvedere, leading to two more rooms in the massive Borgia Tower the pope had built at the northeast corner of the wall facing the Sistine Chapel, overlooking a small courtyard. Corridors and closets led out from these main rooms to the bedrooms and servants' quarters on the floors above. The first floor had, since Sixtus IV's time, housed the library and archives. The apartment windows had a view, to the north, of a hill with gardens and vineyards. Here Innocent VIII had built the Belvedere, an elegant summer residence with bedchambers and a chapel and a panorama of the whole of Rome and the Campagna as far as Mt. Soracte. The Belvedere had been decorated by a Perugian painter who worked on the Sistine Chapel—Bernardino di Betti, known as Pinturicchio, a highly imaginative artist. Alexander appreciated his work and decided to hire him to decorate his apartments.

For two years, starting in November 1492, Pinturicchio and his assistants worked on a design illustrating, in allegorical style, the Borgias' beliefs and aspirations. The huge, 2,300-square-foot antechamber, with its two bays overlooking the Cortile del Belvedere, is known as the Sala dei Pontifici. The theme is the primacy of the Roman see, illustrated with portraits of ten famous popes. Among them: Stephen II, being honored by Pepin the Short, king of the Franks; Leo III, crowning Charlemagne; Urban II, the first preacher of the Crusade; Gregory XI, restorer of the Roman papacy; and Nicholas III, founder of the Vatican palace. Sadly, nothing remains of Pinturicchio's painted ceiling, which collapsed in 1500 during a storm.

A narrow marble doorway with a crest above it showing the keys of St. Peter and the arms of Nicholas V leads to a suite of three reception rooms giving onto the Cortile del Belvedere. The walls are not parallel, and the majolica flooring is uneven, each room being a step lower than the one before. But all this is forgotten as one admires the rooms, which are some 100 square yards each. On the floor above the apartment are three of the Raphael Stanze—the Eliodoro, Segnatura, and Incendio. Julius II, Alexander's successor, moved the papal apartments to this upper story because of his intense hatred of his predecessor.

One comes into the first of the Borgia rooms, the Sala dei Misteri della Fede, with a thrill of pleasure. The delicate harmony of the gilded stuccowork with its blue background enhances the richness of the murals. Joyous scenes from the New Testament representing the mysteries of the faith are framed in gold arabesques set against a pale-green ground. The walls depict six scenes: the Annunciation, Nativity, Epiphany, Resurrection, Assumption and Pentecost.

In the scene of the Resurrection, Alexander is portrayed kneeling in front of Christ's tomb, from which the Savior ascends to heaven. Wearing his ceremonial jewel-studded cope, the pope has placed his golden tiara on the ground beside him. He is shown receiving the blessing of the resurrected Christ. The pope's calm, majestic air is in striking contrast to the agitation or torpor of the soldiers around the tomb. The observant artist makes no effort to conceal his sitter's sensuality, which is very evident in his features. Yet the message Alexander wanted to convey comes across very strongly: the pope appears as the Vicar of Christ. Through the bond between himself and the living God, he alone has the right to transmit God's will to mankind.

In the same room Alexander paid discreet homage to the memory of his uncle Calixtus III. A red-robed figure kneeling in the "Assumption" painting represents Calixtus's bastard son, Francesco Borgia: just a chamberlain when Alexander became pope, he was soon made cardinal. The Borgia family is in fact present everywhere in the ceiling decoration above the figures of the prophets, where the bull alternates with a gold crown shooting three or five rays to earth.

The next room contains scenes from the lives of the saints. Six frescoes fill the lunettes formed by the vault; above them is a marble cornice carved with the bull motif. On the rear wall, St. Catherine of Alexandria faces fifty opponents as Maximian challenges her to refute the pagan beliefs; Lucrezia was the obvious sitter for the saint, her youthful face, slender figure, and golden hair matching the descriptions we have of her at the time of her marriage to Giovanni Sforza. The emperor, sitting on his throne with a gold canopy over his head, is generally identified as Cesare Borgia. The man in Turkish dress standing to the left of the throne is most likely Prince Djem; his tunic has a stylized flower design often found in Ottoman art. The other figure, standing to the right of the throne in a pink cloak and red cap, is thought to be Andrew Palaeologus, son of Thomas, the despot of Morea and a descendant of the early Eastern emperors. The man on horseback in oriental dress arriving with his dogs to the right of the fresco is said to be Duke Juan of Gandia; he was fond of copying Prince Djem and dressing in Turkish costume. Pinturicchio also included himself in the picture as well as the architect of the papal apartments; they stand behind the despot of Morea.

The grouping of the figures in this "family portrait" is pleasant and serene—a far cry from the bitter, impassioned "dispute" of St. Catherine depicted in the *Golden Legend* of Jacobus da Voragine. The composition is, in fact, reminiscent of those brilliant parties so dear to Alexander and his family. The atmosphere is that of a bucolic fete against the backdrop of a triumphal arch, like the arch of Constantine, erected to honor the pope—as witness the Borgia bull and the inscription, *Pacis cultori*, "To him who brings peace."

The next scenes have a similarly naturalistic, lifelike quality. The visit of St. Anthony, Abbot, to St. Paul the Hermit takes place in a desert with touches of a flower-filled paradise. The Visitation of Mary by St. Elizabeth serves as an excuse to show children at play and young girls spinning and sewing. In the scene of the Martyrdom of St. Barbara, the figure of the saint, with her disheveled golden hair and panic-stricken eyes, is one of the most exquisite female portraits Pinturicchio painted; it may have been taken from one of the ladies of the court. The episode of Susanna and the Elders is set in a lush garden, with a rose hedge around it, full of animals of various kinds—stags, does, rabbits, even a monkey on a gold chain. In the middle there is a magnificent hexagonal fountain with two basins; the lower one is carved with two stucco genies, while the upper one has a cupid. The last fresco, the Martyrdom of St. Sebastian, shows archers, soldiers, and horsemen moving forward against a backdrop of the Palatine Hill and the Colosseum—a reminder of the fortification work the Borgia pope carried out in the Holy City.

There is a round stucco frame, or *tondo*, above the entrance to this room. It shows the Virgin, surrounded by six seraphim, teaching the infant Jesus to read from a volume which she points out to him with her right hand. Some critics see it as the counterpart of a painting that Cardinal Rodrigo had executed for the collegiate church of Játiva, to thank the Virgin for the special protection she had given him in his childhood in Spain. Others identify the fresco as the one Vasari speaks of in his *Lives of the Artists*: "Over the door of one of the rooms, Pinturicchio portrayed Giulia Farnese as the Madonna." But Vasari adds that the same painting showed "the head of Pope Alexander VI adoring her." This detail is missing in the tondo seen here.

If these frescoes are easy to interpret, the ceiling frescoes are complicated, because they were done for the initiated. They tell the story of Isis and Osiris and reveal Alexander's fondness for the esoteric: in this choice of theme, the head of the Church proclaims that ancient mythology foreshadows Christian dogma. At the same time he glorifies his dynastic pride. The legend of Osiris, brother and husband of Isis, who was transformed after death into a sacred animal—the bull Apis—served to give pride of place to the Borgias' animal emblem. A sort of genealogical link, or rather a link of a totemic type, is established between the pope and the ancient Egyptian god. That is the explanation suggested in a recent work on the Vatican. However, in Alexander's day, if the humanists grasped the allusion, most of the faithful were shocked to see ancient pagan gods depicted in the residence of the Supreme Head of Christendom.

The five octagonal panels of the great arcade in this room tell the first part of the story of Isis. Io, changed into a heifer, is placed under the care of Argus, whose body is studded with eyes. The king of the gods, who is in love with Io, sends Mercury, who plays his pipe and hoodwinks Io's guardian. Mercury slays Argus and brings the heifer Io to Zeus, who then entrusts the heifer to Hera and brings her to Egypt where, changed into a beautiful young woman, she is proclaimed queen under the name Isis.

The story is continued in the painted medallions of the ceiling. Isis weds her brother, the king Osiris, elder son of Heaven and Earth, who teaches men to plow and plant vines and fruit trees. This good work arouses the jealousy of his brother Set (or Typhon), god of the abyss and fire, and he kills Osiris and cuts up his body. Grief-stricken, Isis puts the scattered pieces of her husband's body together again. Osiris comes to life once more for a moment and with Isis conceives a son, Horus, who will succeed him on the throne of Egypt when he reaches the heavenly kingdom and lives forever, in the form of the bull Apis, adored by all generations.

At Alexander's request, the humanist Pomponius Laetus wrote a commentary on the frescoes to dispel any ambiguity and show that the story represented the mystery of death and resurrection. By escaping the wiles of the devil—the wicked Typhon—man could, like Osiris, be reborn for eternity. Osiris, Isis, and Horus prefigure the Trinity of Christianity, with this difference: one of these persons, Isis, was female, a woman at once respectful of religion and passionate, the kind of woman Pope Alexander liked.

In the next room the decoration changes completely. This is a large study brightened with frescoes representing the liberal arts and sciences. Beautiful young women sit on marble thrones, while around them are the principal scholars in each branch of knowledge. The female figures represent grammar, rhetoric, and dialectic (the arts of the first cycle of education, or *trivium*), next, music, astronomy, geometry, and arithmetic (the second cycle, or *quadrivium*). With a little study one can make out portraits of several members of the pope's court. For instance, the painting of Rhetoric, which bears Pinturicchio's signature, shows a chamberlain whose secret job was to guard the little door leading from this Sala della Scienze e delle Arti Liberali to the pope's sleeping quarters. On the vault are allegories of Justice together with biblical scenes from the stories of Lot and Jacob. Here, too, are the Borgia symbols—the bull and the crown with its rays.

From the study one moves on to the Borgia Tower, which was built in 1494. The vast, 1,000-square-foot Sala del Credo served for receptions. Lit by three windows, it has twelve frescoes showing, alternately, an apostle and a prophet. Each apostle holds a scroll containing an article of the Creed, in accordance with the story that the text of Christian beliefs was composed by the apostles before they left Jerusalem. Finally the Sala delle Sibille, a little over 700 square feet, depicts twelve sibyls, each accompanied by a prophet. The ceiling recalls the myth of Osiris and the pagan gods. Again, the frescoes are meant to show the unbroken continuity of God's revelations, from pagan antiquity to the Christian era.

Closed since the papacy of Julius II (1503–1513), then restored and reopened to the public in 1897 by Leo XIII, the Borgia Apartment is one of the jewels of the Roman Renaissance. The British historian Evelyn March Phillipps, who first saw the rooms when they were reopened, perfectly conveys the strong impact they still make on the visitor:

"There is perhaps hardly a place in Rome where you feel so transported into the heart of that old life of the Renaissance as you do in the Borgia Apartment. After midday it is almost empty of sightseers; and in the long rooms, where the silence is only broken by the splash of the fountain in the quiet, grassy court outside, you realise the setting of the passionate lives that once ran their course here. Here the light caught Lucretia's golden hair, here the famous pontiff rustled in his brocaded robes, and Cesare Borgia strode in gilded armor."

The work of decoration was carried out, remarkably quickly, in the presence of the pope and his family. Pinturicchio's magic brush had, in some strange way, given his models immortality.

Lucrezia's stay in Pesaro

Intimate correspondence between the pope and Giulia Farnese

In the spring of 1494 Lucrezia left the glittering world of the Roman court. The pope had sent his son-in-law Giovanni Sforza to Pesaro to prepare to fight in the Romagna, alongside the Neapolitans, against the dreaded French invaders. Lucrezia left Rome amid pomp, a long cortege of lords and ladies accompanying her from Sta. Maria in Portico. She and Giulia, her lady-in-waiting, each rode a fine hackney. Behind them came litters bearing Adriana da Mila and Juana Moncada, two of the pope's nieces. A confidential agent, the canon Francesco Gacet, had joined the group; he was in charge of keeping in touch with the Vatican.

Their arrival in Pesaro was greeted by a torrential downpour that ripped down the garlands of flowers and overturned the triumphal arches put up in their honor. In the days following, Lucrezia explored her principality—a little valley, ringed with green hills, through which the River Foglia babbled before reaching the sea. The city itself was laid out on a grid plan, with convents and churches lining its straight streets. The castle, with its four bastions, stood at the corner of the ramparts overlooking the Adriatic. In midsummer the place became stiflingly hot, but happily a half-hour away from the Pesaro road was the Villa Imperiale with its large halls and refreshing gardens; it had been built in 1464 when Frederick III passed through the state.

Between the castle and the countryside Lucrezia led a peaceful existence, sometimes enlivened by small-scale festivities. Some family letters, fortunately preserved in the archives of the Castel Sant'Angelo, mention Lucrezia's stay in Pesaro. Their special interest, however, is in what they convey of the affectionate relations between the pope, his daughter, and his mistress. We see Lucrezia marrying off the papal datary's daughter, Lucrezia Lopez, one of her ladies-in-waiting, to Gian Francesco Ardizio, a physician to the lord of Pesaro. Next, the little court got ready to receive a neighbor, Caterina da Gonzaga, the wife of Count Ottaviano di Montevecchio. One of the amusements organized on this occasion was a beauty contest between Caterina da Gonzaga and Giulia Farnese. The pope, in Rome, was to be judge. Adriana da Mila, Juana Moncada, Canon Gacet, Giulia herself, and Lucrezia all sent him their opinions, Lucrezia's being particularly biting.

"I shall describe Caterina Gonzaga's beauty to Your Holiness who, for sure, are not unaware of its renown. She is taller than Signora Giulia by six inches, is becomingly plump, has white skin and beautiful hands; she is pretty but she has a disagreeable mouth with bad teeth, also huge pale eyes and a rather ugly nose; her hair is a nasty color, her face long and somewhat masculine." For Lucrezia there was no question that her father's mistress, her friend Giulia, was the fairest.

Caterina da Gonzaga also carefully observed her rival, and a prelate in her retinue, Giacomo Dragazzo, sent his opinion to Cesare Borgia. He thought that Giulia, with her olive skin, dark eyes, round face, and passionate expression was the complete counterpoint to Caterina, whose white skin, blue eyes, and proud bearing perfectly met the standards of heavenly beauty.

Amusements of this kind, which were common in Renaissance courts, were a welcome break from the boredom of the stay in Pesaro. No sooner had Giulia arrived, in fact, than she complained to her "one and only lord": "Your Holiness is absent from me, and since all my well-being and happiness depends on you, I can find no pleasure or satisfaction in tasting such pleasures, for where my treasure is, there my heart is also." In the contest with Caterina da Gonzaga she had taken her rival's side and, out of coquetterie, exalted her merits far above her own. The sixty-two-year-old pope seized his pen and sent back a passionate letter to his mistress:

"In your willingness to describe the beauties of this person who is not worthy to unlace your shoes, we see that you have behaved with great modesty and we know why you did so: you know well that everyone who has written to us assures us that beside you she is like a lantern compared to the sun. When you describe her as very beautiful, it is so that we may understand your own perfection, which indeed we have never doubted. Just as we know this to be true, we would wish you to be attached totally and undividedly to the one who loves you more than any other in the world. And when you have made up your mind about this, if you have not done so already, we shall know that you are as wise as you are perfect."

Most historians have seen this letter, which is certainly authentic, as a passionate declaration of love. Others (such as Giovanni Soranzo), for whom Pope Alexander must be above all suspicion, find it disturbing and interpret it, paradoxically, as an invitation to respect marriage vows. According to them, the person whom the pope describes as loving Giulia "more than any other in the world" would be none other than her husband, Orso Orsini, who was banished at the time, far from his wife, in the fortress of Bassanello. The suggestion would be interesting if the other letters in the correspondence did not give evidence of the passionate nature of Alexander's feelings with regard to Giulia.

The French invasion and capture of the pope's mistress

The atmosphere at Pesaro changed for the worse in the summer of 1494. Lucrezia fell rather seriously ill. Giovanni Sforza had grave doubts about the part he should play in face of the inevitable French invasion. Once more he approached his uncle, Ludovico il Moro, while Alexander deliberately chose to join the Neapolitans in resisting the French. On July 14, 1494, at Vicovaro, he studied Alfonso II's battle plans. It was a meeting of commanders in chief: the king had brought 1,000 cavalrymen, the pope, 500 together with a large force of footsoldiers. The allies exchanged gifts, Alexander receiving a gold goblet and several precious objects worth 4,000 ducats. It took them two days to put the finishing touches to the plan for cutting off the Romagna. Alexander, who knew nothing of Giovanni Sforza's dealings with his uncle, believed Lucrezia and Giulia would be out of harm's way in Pesaro, a defended spot on the papal and Neapolitan front, and advised them to stay put during the coming hostilities. Lucrezia obeyed her father—being sick, she could not leave in any case—but Giulia was called back by her family. With anxiety Alexander learned that she had left for Bolsena with Adriana, and from there would go to Capodimonte to see her elder brother, Angelo, who was gravely ill.

Angelo died shortly afterward, and Giulia decided to stay a few days with her mother and another brother, Cardinal Alessandro. At that point she received some imperious letters from Orso Orsini demanding that she return to Bassanello. Giulia told the pope, who ordered her to refuse and come to Rome immediately. Hesitating between the two commands, to gain time Giulia wrote to the pope that before she obeyed him she had to obtain her husband's consent. Alexander took this very badly: "Thankless and perfidious Giulia. . . . Although we judged your soul, and that of him who advised you, to be wicked, we could not know that you would act with such treachery and ingratitude when, so many times, you had sworn you would be faithful to our commandments and never go near Orsini. Now you want to do the opposite and go to Bassanello at the risk of your life. . . . In brief, we hope that both you and the ungrateful Adriana will acknowledge your error and do the appropriate penitence. Finally, by this letter, on pain of excommunication and eternal damnation, we order you not to leave Capodimonte or Marta and, even more, not to go to Bassanello."

In fact, this was hardly a good time to travel along the Italian roads. News came, like a thunderbolt, that Charles VIII had crossed the Alps on September 2 and marched across the Milanese aided by Ludovico il Moro. In late October the Neapolitan army beat a retreat and petered out of the Romagna. Piero de' Medici handed over to the king the forts guarding Tuscany. Pisa rose up in favor of the French in early November. Charles entered Florence and the Medicis' rule was toppled. The Dominican preacher Girolamo Savonarola recalled his vision of the sword of God striking Florence: this sword was none other than the king of France, come to wreak vengeance on the sins of the Florentines. Alexander found this collusion of mysticism and politics exasperating in the extreme. He also was to suffer its consequences.

On November 22, Charles VIII solemnly announced that the object of his expedition to Naples was to prepare for the destruction of Turkish power and liberation of the Holy Land. He demanded that the pope grant him free passage through the papal territories.

Alexander was in a bad position to reply. An embarrassing incident at that time seemed to put him beyond the pale of Christendom. A papal envoy, Giorgio Buzardo, had just been captured at Sinigaglia, on the Adriatic coast: he was on his way back from Istanbul, bearing letters from Bayezid II assuring Rome of his support against the French. The revelation of an alliance between the Vicar of Christ and that of Mahomet created an enormous scandal. Giovanni della Rovere, Cardinal Giuliano's brother, pocketed Djem's allowance of 40,000 ducats, which a Turkish ambassador who accompanied Buzardo was bringing to Rome. He dispatched Buzardo to Florence together with the seized letters, one of which offered the pope 300,000 ducats if he had Prince Djem put to death. Public indignation was even greater when it was learned that Turkish ambassadors had come to Naples to form an alliance with Alfonso, the pope's friend and ally, and help him fight the French.

This moral defeat followed hard on defeat in the field. The Orsinis covering the frontiers of the Papal States changed sides as Virginio Orsini, the king of Naples's condottiere, handed over his strongholds of Anguillara and Bracciano to the French.

Central Italy was now in enemy hands. Anguished over Giulia's fate—he feared she would be captured by soldiers during a movement of troops—Alexander sent an envoy to her husband. On November 28, in exchange for a promise of a huge sum of money, Orso agreed not to insist on his wife's joining him in Bassanello. Instead, she could take the quickest way to Rome along with Adriana da Mila and her sister, Girolama Farnese Pucci. On the 29th the ladies left Capodimonte with a mounted escort of thirty men. When they were nearing Montefiascone the pope's fears were realized and soldiers of the French advance guard under Yves d'Alègre surprised the travelers, captured them, and set a price on their heads of 3,000 crowns.

The pope's feelings when he heard the news can readily be imagined. He at once dispatched a chamberlain to bring Giulia the ransom money and urged Galeazzo San Severino, the brother of Cardinal San Severino, to intervene with the French king to secure the ladies' immediate release. In gentlemanly fashion, Charles gave the necessary order and had the ladies escorted to Rome by a detachment of honor.

Relieved and joyful beyond measure, Alexander went to greet his mistress dressed like a cavalier. He wore a doublet of black velvet edged with gold brocade, a crossbelt in the Spanish style, fine boots from Valencia, and a velvet cap. In his belt he had stuck a sword and dagger. The well-informed Ludovico il Moro passed on these details to Giacomo Trotti, the ambassador of the duke of Ferrara, a champion of the French. However, he may have embroidered the facts to discredit the pope, whom he now treated as an enemy like the king of Naples. For the ambassador's benefit, Ludovico added that he had been told Alexander was sleeping at the Vatican with three women, a former nun from Valencia, a Castilian lady, and a young bride of fifteen or sixteen. As a finishing touch to his slander, he told Trotti that he expected any hour to hear that the despicable pontiff had been arrested and decapitated.

Back in Rome, Giulia grew anxious seeing the pope's apprehensiveness. The Vatican was on the alert. The silver and tapestries had been packed up ready to be taken to the Castel Sant'Angelo. Alexander had been toying with the idea of going to the kingdom of Naples, where Alfonso had offered him asylum in Gaeta, but under Giulia's influence—and perhaps out of a desire to impress her—he found renewed courage and resolved to stay in the capital. On reflection, his great fear was that his enemies, especially Giuliano della Rovere, would take advantage of his departure to arraign him and remove him from office by having his election annulled.

After showing how brave she could be, Giulia suddenly lost her nerve. The fear she had felt when she was captured returned when she heard that the Orsinis, her husband's relations, had invited the French to use their fortresses. In mid-December her brother, Cardinal Farnese, accused the bishop of Alatri of spiriting her out of Rome behind the pope's back. (Later Alexander punished the cardinal by imprisoning him in the Castel Sant'Angelo.) The young woman fled under the protection of the condottiere Mariano Savelli, who with other members of his family and the Colonnas was fighting along with the French. Giulia could thus be said to have gone over to the enemy's side. The pope's passionate idyll was over. His beautiful mistress would not return to the Vatican until much later, in 1505, to see her daughter Laura wedded to Niccolò della Rovere, the nephew of Julius II, who was then pope.

In that discontented winter of 1494 there seemed a whole world between the petty Roman sovereign, reduced to the defensive, and the Vicar of Christ, the link between heaven and earth, posing as a mythic descendant of the heroes of Egypt and Greece. Yet all the gains Alexander had achieved so far—his efforts to unite the Borgia family with the Sforzas and with Aragon, his flattery of powerful rulers, the money he had poured into the pouches of clerics and soldiers—constituted the best of ammunition. He had only to use it astutely—and he did not lack cunning—and the situation would be turned around.

2

The Weapon of Ruse

For years, Alexander had known the French would invade Rome. When he first become pope he had had Rome's fortifications reinforced. In February 1493 he reviewed 114 footsoldiers and 80 light horse—but they were barely sufficient to man the ramparts of the Castel Sant'Angelo and the Borgo, the area around St. Peter's. He therefore recruited mercenaries to form a regular army. They would be led by Niccolò Orsini, count of Pitigliano, a captain general of the Church, and able commanders such as Giulio Orsini and Niccolò Gaetani. The pope's son-in-law, Giovanni Sforza, was also part of this command. Soldiers and artillery were deployed at the city gates and on the banks of the Tiber near the Via Salaria bridge. No sooner had the camp been set up, however, than it was destroyed by a terrible summer storm that caused the river to flood over, carrying off horses, arms, and munitions in the swirling waters. As soon as he could regroup his forces, Pitigliano led them in a parade in front of the Vatican to show them off to the foreign ambassadors. This army was in fact about to join the duke of Calabria's forces in an attempt to halt the French on the northern boundary of the Papal States.

Rome herself would not be left defenseless. While his troops were massing in Rome, the pope gave orders for the walls of the Borgo and the Castel Sant'Angelo to be repaired. Soon the massive squat tower of Hadrian's mausoleum sprouted a crenellated brick wall, complete with machicolations. Inside this extra top story was a cistern and five vast storerooms capable of holding large quantities of oil and over 3,000 quintals of grain. With these provisions and a huge arsenal of weapons, the Vatican could withstand the longest siege. The fortress, which had five windowless dungeons, served as a barracks and prison as well. But there were also pleasant lodgings and reception rooms for visiting dignitaries. Off the Borgia Court, or Cortile del Teatro, was an open walkway that ran halfway around the upper platform, protected by the crenellated wall.

The area around the castle was cleared, the nearby houses razed, ditches redug. The 300-foot-square outer wall of the Borgo was fortified with bastions, and a sturdy tower put up to bar the entrance to the Sant'Angelo Bridge. Linking the castle to the Vatican was a raised passageway that ran along the top of the wall from the fortress to the papal palace. This work of extension and reinforcement was carried out by the governor, Juan di Castro, bishop of Agrigente, in whom the pope placed absolute trust.

When Alexander learned that the French king had left Viterbo in December 1494, he moved all the treasures of the Holy See to the Castel Sant'Angelo for safekeeping—the gold tiaras, papal jewels, and relics. Beds and chests, tapestries and precious carpets were set up in the staterooms around the Borgia Court. Even though Alexander was not about to hole up there for the time being—he still hoped the duke of Calabria and the papal army would slow the invaders—it was clear nothing would stop a swift advance by the French forces.

These were divided into three armies. The first, with 7,000 infantrymen and 2,400 horse provided by Ludovico il Moro of Milan, was driving back the Neapolitan-papal forces north of Rome, in the Romagna. The second army, led by Charles, with 6,000 footsoldiers and 4,000 cavalry, was making ready to join the first before the gates of Rome. The third, with 5,000 footsoldiers and over 2,000 horse, transported by ship, was due to disembark just south of Rome at Nettuno, the plan being that it would link up with members of the Colonna family, who were opposed to Alexander and were occupying the fortress port of Ostia in collusion with Cardinal Giuliano della Rovere. Thus the disposition of French troops was aimed at capturing Rome in a pincer movement.

Forced to retreat, Duke Ferrantino of Calabria went to Rome to draw up a new plan of action with Pitigliano. The two men decided to use the various Roman forts to resist the invasion. The north gate, where the Viterbo road ended, was bricked up and cannons placed on the top story of the Castel Sant'Angelo. These warlike signals gave the pope and his court fresh optimism and courage. Charles VIII noticed this from the cavalier way his ambassadors extraordinary were received in Rome. Louis de la Trémoille, chamberlain, Jean de Ganay, president of the Paris Parliament, and Denis de Bidault, chief of finance, had come to ask for free passage on papal territory, also that the Turkish prince, Djem, be handed over to the French in light of the Crusade, and the pope's recognition of Charles's rights to the throne of Naples.

Feeling emboldened with the duke of Calabria at his side, the pope threw out the Frenchmen's demands. Those cardinals that had sided with Milan and France—Ascanio Sforza, Savelli, San Severino, as well as laymen like Fabrizio Colonna—he ordered to be thrown into jail and taken hostage. The Roman people, however, were not in a mood to go along with these bellicose gestures. Since the Colonnas seized Ostia, the Roman port, the supply routes had been cut off and food shortages were rife. The countryside swarmed with deserters and bandits, while the few merchants that dared come to Rome were forced to form armed caravans.

Diplomatic passages at arms

By mid-December Charles had moved dangerously close to Rome. At Nepi the fortress of Bracciano, which belonged to the pope's allies the Orsinis, fell to him. Realizing that armed resistance was useless, Alexander considered fleeing to Gaeta, the stout stronghold on the coast between Rome and Naples. His bags were buckled and his horses harnessed when he suddenly made a volte-face. The Venetian and Spanish ambassadors had pointed out that he ran the risk of being deposed if he left the Holy See vacant. He therefore tried diplomacy, dispatching to Charles three prelates—Lionello Chieregato, bishop of Concordia, Juan Fuentes Salida, bishop of Terni, and Graziano da Villanova, his confessor—followed soon afterward by Cardinal San Severino, who had been released from prison to show that the pope harbored no ill feelings toward the friends of France.

The prelates begged Charles to give up his expedition. They assured him the pope would make the king of Naples pay a tribute in recognition of France's rights. He would then call a council of the Christian rulers, who would give Charles military and financial aid for the Crusade. Thus could the king have his foreign expedition and at the same time avoid the risks of trying to conquer Naples.

But none of these arguments swayed Charles. He merely repeated his previous demands. Far from capitulating, Alexander thought up a maneuver that he hoped would weaken the French and force Charles to beat a retreat. He freed Prospero Colonna, promising him such plums as a lucrative military command, then sent him to Ostia to rally to the papal side his brother Fabrizio, who was holding the fort with some Swiss and French soldiers. But as soon as Prospero was out of the pope's reach he spat on the promises extorted from him and rejoined his brother's army. Thus Ostia remained both a barrier, capable of preventing the Romans from getting food, and a bridgehead for the Borgia pope's enemies.

Meanwhile the French continued their inexorable southward march. The important fort of Monterotondo was seized by the marshall of Rieux, whose 5,000 men crossed the Tiber and invaded Latium. The cities of Corneto and Civitavecchia fell. Soon Burckard saw French scouts making their way from the Monte Mario to the banks of the Tiber.

Cardinal Raymond Péraud, who had gone over to Charles's side, tried to seize one of the gates of Rome, the Porta San Paolo. He appealed to the inhabitants of the Papal States to welcome the French. "He exalted to the heavens," wrote Burckard, "the loyalty and fairness both of the king and his men. According to Péraud, the French would not lay their hands on a hen or an egg or anything even of minute worth, without paying full price for it."

In particular, Péraud strove to win over the German colony. He offered himself to Burckard's compatriots as a friend, reminding them that he had been raised to the purple on the German emperor's recommendation: "I impressed on His Most Christian Majesty [i.e., Charles]," he wrote, "that his soldiers should not wrong those members of the court remaining in the city, or any others, provided they were not found bearing arms against His Majesty and his troops."

Charles confirmed Péraud's promises. In a letter to the Roman municipal police he guaranteed the safety of Roman citizens. The *conservatori* brought the letter to the Vatican. Alexander had just seen proof that the king was disposed toward peace in the order given two French captains to avoid all skirmishes with Ferrantino of Calabria's Neapolitan-papal army. Such a confrontation, if it occurred, would receive no support from the Romans. The Romans were in fact torn between their trust in the king's indulgence and sheer panic: had they not just seen the city wall crumble where the French were expected to attack? Seeing his subjects' defeatism, the pope made a reasonable decision and sent the duke of Calabria away to Naples. On Christmas

Day after High Mass the duke was received at the Vatican in combat dress, wearing his breastplate, sword, and dagger. Alexander talked with him for a long time, then dismissed him with his blessing. It was agreed that the pope could at any time take refuge in the kingdom of Naples, where he would receive an allowance of 50,000 ducats as well as the castle of Gaeta and a further 10,000 ducats to ensure the safety of Prince Djem.

Ferrantino of Calabria left the same day. He made for Tivoli, destroying everything as he went so that the French, if they came after him, would find nothing but scorched earth. Accompanying him to the gates was a delegation of cardinals including Ascanio Sforza, fresh out of prison. As a friend of the French king, he brought with him the assurance that Charles would live up to his promise and would not harry the Aragonese. Juan Borgia, the cardinal of Monreale, another member of the delegation, bade the duke farewell at the Porta di San Lorenzo before he went north to Bracciano, where he was to discuss with Charles the conditions of his entry into the capital.

Charles VIII's victorious entry into Rome

Events now proceeded in a headlong rush. In the evening of December 25, Charles appointed three ambassadors—Pierre de Rohan, Jean de Ganay, and Etienne de Vesc—to convey his wishes to the pope. Next morning the three Frenchmen were conducted into the Sistine Chapel, where they had to attend the High Mass of St. Stephen in the pope's presence, and quite shamelessly took over the seats reserved for the prelates. Burckard, the papal master of ceremonies, was horrified: "I made them leave . . . ," he wrote, "but the pope called me and told me in an irritated tone that I was upsetting his plan and that the French had to be allowed to sit wherever they wished. I replied to His Holiness . . . that . . . I would say nothing more to them and they would sit where they liked."

The pope agreed to let 1,500 French soldiers camp on the right bank of the Tiber. On December 30 the count of Montpensier commandeered some palaces in which to billet French officers. That afternoon a delegation of Roman notables went to see the king. Among them the pope had appointed his secretary, the auditor of the Rota, a consistorial lawyer, and Burckard. The city of Rome was represented by a few patricians. All in all it was a meager delegation, hardly befitting the dignity of the Most Christian King.

While the party was en route the winter weather broke out in torrential rains, leaving the roads so sodden that the papal envoys hardly dared alight from their carriages when they reached Galera, where the king was encamped. With cardinals Savelli, Péraud, and della Rovere clustered around him, Charles lingered just long enough to be greeted by the papal delegates. Briefly, he told them he intended to enter Rome that very evening, without any ceremony whatsoever. Earlier discussions had fixed the day as January 1, but on his astrologers' advice Charles had decided to put it back a day to the Feast of St. Sylvester. According to legend, Pope Sylvester had received Rome as a gift from the emperor Constantine. He was the very image of a pope as the king imagined him—conciliatory, tractable with regard to civic power but jealous of his spiritual independence. Having announced his plans, Charles was amiable and relaxed. "Along the way," wrote Burckard, "for some four miles, he spoke with me continually, asking me questions about ceremonial, the pope's health, about the cardinal of Valencia's rank, and so many other subjects that I was hard put to answer them well."

Night had fallen by the time the cortege, which now included the Venetian ambassadors and Cardinal Ascanio Sforza, reached the Porta del Popolo. The king crossed the city and arrived at the Palazzo di San Marco (now Venezia), where he was to stay. In spite of the storm, the Romans lit up the street with thousands of torches, and a huge crowd cheered the sovereign and his allies: "Francia! Francia! Colonna! Colonna! Vincula! Vincula [short for San Pietro in Vincoli, Giuliano della Rovere's church]!" The welcome seemed to turn Charles's improvised entry into a show of hostility toward the pope.

Representatives of the people had given Pierre de Rohan, one of the king's marshalls, the heavy keys of the city, and all night long the gates stayed open. The various contingents of the French army made their way into the city in orderly fashion—the Swiss with their fearsome-looking pikes more than 10 feet long, the Germans with their axes and halberds, the Gascons with their crossbows and harquebuses. Then the cavalry trotted up: first the light horse, then the men-at-arms carrying their unwieldy maces, swords, and spears, the manes and ears of their great horses cut in such a way as to strike terror in the enemy. In their wake rumbled a formidable array of artillery—thirty-six bronze cannons, each 3 yards long, trundled in wagons, and a host of small culverins, falconets, and even the ancestor of the machine gun, carried on the soldiers' backs.

The pope against the barbarians

In the Palazzo di San Marco, now turned into an entrenched camp, most of the members of the Sacred College gathered to pay homage to Charles VIII. Cesare Borgia came on January 1, but could not get near the king as he was attending Mass. Burckard noted with horror the free-and-easy way in which the French had taken over the palace. The rooms were littered with straw, which served as bedding and was never changed. Dripping candles stained the marble fireplaces and the lintels of the fine marquetry doors. Looting and stealing were rife, with the Italian soldiers of the Colonnas taking an active part. "To find lodging, the Frenchmen force open houses, enter them, drive out the inhabitants, horses and so on; then they burn the wood and eat and drink everything they can find without paying a penny," wrote Burckard, who, with other notables, was one of the victims. Vannozza Cattanei's houses, as well as those of several city dignitaries and Jews, were ransacked. Malipiero, a Venetian, lost an estimated 40,000 ducats' worth of goods. Forced to take harsh measures, the king at one fell swoop had five looters hanged, ordered a curfew, and organized night patrols. The Jews could obtain special protection by wearing a white cross on the shoulder for identification. Finally Charles gave orders for the stolen goods to be brought back to their owners. To the Romans' astonishment, quite a lot were in fact restored.

In the face of this human scourge now striking the city, the important thing was to keep a cool head and avoid panic. Although no longer in control of the situation, Alexander displayed remarkable composure. He received the French nobles, who tramped noisily into the Vatican, and granted them the rare privilege of kissing his feet for the Feast of Epiphany. But on the same day he rejected the king's three demands, refusing to give the Castel Sant'Angelo to the French, hand over Djem, or give up Cesare as a hostage. In compensation, he proposed handing over the city of Civitavecchia as a pledge.

On hearing this, Charles was stupefied. "My barons will make known my wishes to the king!" he cried. Alexander's enemies—della

Rovere, Sforza, Colonna, and Savelli—advised the king to depose the pope, pointing out that his election was tainted with simony. Taking the threat seriously, the pope slipped away to the Castel Sant'Angelo along his secret corridor together with six cardinals, including his nephew Juan Borgia and Cesare. Shortly after they got there, however, a section of the rampart near the secret corridor collapsed, leaving a huge gap and carrying off three guards in the rubble. This accident, so reminiscent of the wall that had crumbled just before Charles's arrival, struck many people as yet another sign from heaven that the pope should capitulate. But Alexander, refusing to believe omens, had the breach repaired and aimed his artillery at the French. Juan di Castro, the governor of the fortress, gave orders for the 400 Spaniards of the garrison to take up their positions on the rampart walk. But he used something else to defend the Castel Sant'Angelo: Rome's most precious relics, which were stored there. Twice, when the enemy troops approached, the shrines containing the heads of SS. Peter and Paul and the veil of St. Veronica were displayed on top of the ramparts. The French withdrew, disconcerted. After that came a shuttling back and forth of emissaries between the king and the pope. Convinced that Alexander was about to yield, the king left his delegates to argue over the fine points and went off to visit the city's churches and ancient monuments.

Alexander capitulates

On January 15 the ink was dry on the text of the agreement between Rome and France. The first clause stated that "Our Holy Father shall remain the king's good father, and the king shall remain a good and devoted son of Our Holy Father." The pope would hand Cesare over to Charles—the pope's son would accompany the king on his expedition for four months—as well as Prince Djem, who would be held in the fortress of Terracina "for his own safety and to prevent the Turks from entering Italy." As security for the prince's person, Charles would leave behind certain nobles and prelates who would deposit 500,000 ducats in the Apostolic Treasury. The pope was to keep the 40,000-ducat allowance that Sultan Bayezid paid each year for his brother.

During the Naples expedition, the king could use the city of Civitavecchia "to obtain any provisions, men, and articles that he may need." The French, however, would ensure that merchants and their goods moved freely in Civitavecchia as in Ostia and other places in the Papal States. Only the Neapolitan merchants would have to show a pass from the pope. Alexander would provide the French army with "provisions and free passage" in all the Papal States cities; the French were to pay "reasonably, however, for the said provisions." The cardinals and nobles who handed over their fortresses to Charles would not incur any penalty. The pope would post friends of the king's as lieutenants in the Papal States castles and legations. Cardinal della Rovere would be given back his Avignon legation and all his possessions. Cardinal Péraud would be compensated as if he had stayed on in the Sacred College, and the pope would grant him the sees of Metz and Besançon. Those cardinals friendly to the king would be able to leave Rome and go where they pleased without the pope's permission.

In return for these major concessions, the pope wanted only the king's formal assurance: "The king shall pay homage to Our Holy Father in person before his departure from Rome . . . ; he shall promise not to offend him; and the cardinals . . . shall give neither aid nor favor to his enemies in the form of soldiers, money or in whatever fashion."

This apparent capitulation on the pope's part aroused a host of contrary reactions. Charles was pleased and relieved at having won the pope's cooperation without having to use force. The rebellious cardinals, on the other hand, mistrusted the pope's sudden reversal and saw the agreement as a piece of double-dealing. The Romans, for their part, could hardly contain their glee seeing that the French would be leaving, they could have their houses back once more, and there would be no more shortages with the end of the Tiber blockade. Alexander beamed most of all. By making the minutest concessions he had won the naive Charles to his side, and from now on he was certain he would not be deposed. To keep the king in a good mood, he decided to exploit to the fullest the matchless ceremonial of the Eternal City.

The day after the signing Charles went to St. Peter's Basilica, attended Mass in the French chapel of Sta. Petronilla, then lunched at the Vatican, which the pope had put at his disposal. That afternoon he went to meet Alexander as he left the Castel Sant'Angelo in his sedia gestatoria. The king devoutly made the ritual genuflections as the pope descended from his litter, but Alexander took no notice. Only when the spindly young king was making his third sweeping bow did the pope turn to greet him. Raising him to his feet, he bared his head at the same time as Charles, and embraced him warmly.

For his first favor, Charles requested that his favorite, the bishop of St. Malo, be raised to the purple, and Alexander readily agreed. But when Charles demanded that the ceremony take place immediately, the pope tried to hide his displeasure by pretending to faint. Patiently, Charles waited until he came around, and Alexander finally had to give way. At a consistory held in the Vatican's Cortile del Pappagallo, St. Malo was proclaimed cardinal. Cesare Borgia let him borrow his cardinal's cape, and Burckard scrounged a red hat from one of the cardinals' chambers. A satisfied Charles retired to his apartments, having first satisfied himself that men of his Scots guard were posted at all the Vatican doors.

Comedy of the oath of obedience

Charles was eager to discuss his two major demands: his investiture as king of Naples, and his appointment as leader of the Crusade. Alexander hinted that before anything else Charles should swear obedience to him. After much bargaining a decision was reached as to the form the oath should take. The pope would be acknowledged as the "true Vicar of Christ and successor to St. Peter." This produced a counter-demand from Charles, that the number of French nobles held as surety for Djem be reduced to ten (the pope was insisting on forty). After three hours of parlaying, a compromise text was finally agreed on and read out by two notaries, in both Latin and French. Then, exhausted, the two sides retired.

Next day, Charles and his entourage awoke with the unpleasant sensation of having been swindled. He was determined to give the pope a piece of his mind. That morning, when Alexander came into the consistory chamber, there was no sign of the king, so he sent the bishop of Concordia and Burckard to find him. The papal master of ceremonies noted: "We found him in his room by the fire, in his shirt and without his shoes." Unfazed, Charles slowly finished dressing, went to the Basilica to hear Mass, and came back to the Vatican to eat. An hour went by, and still the king had not shown up. Alexander decided to sit in state, and went to the Sala del Pappagallo, where he put on full pontifical regalia—the rich, seamless red cape made for

Innocent VII, the heavy gold miter that had belonged to Paul II. Thus arrayed, he took his place on his throne—but still no Charles. He removed his heavy miter and put on a light one. Once more Burckard was dispatched to find the king, this time with four cardinals and six bishops. Charles was still eating and made them wait one half-hour then, after a confab with his counselors about the oath of obedience, another half-hour. Finally he set off for the consistory.

Alexander was ready for him, wearing once again the priceless heavy miter. With satisfaction he watched as the king made the three ritual obeisances and kissed his right hand. In his master's name, the envoy Jean de Ganay beseeched the pope to grant three graces "as vassals ask a boon before they swear obedience." The first: that the pope confirm all the privileges traditionally granted the Most Christian King and his family; secondly, that Charles be given the investiture of Naples; thirdly, that the pope repudiate the guarantees agreed on concerning Prince Djem. Although agreeing to the first request, Alexander said he would have to discuss the other two with his cardinals. In spite of this evasive answer Charles could scarcely refuse the pope his obedience, and he uttered the brief formula: "Holy Father, I have come to swear obedience and reverence to Your Holiness in the manner of my predecessors, the kings of France." Jean de Ganay then elaborated on his king's words: "He acknowledges you, blessed Father, as the sovereign pontiff of the Christians, the true Vicar of Christ, the successor of the apostles Peter and Paul. He pays you the filial, obligatory homage that his predecessors, the kings of the French, rendered the sovereign pontiffs. He offers himself, and everything that belongs to him, to Your Holiness and the Holy See." Alexander had got what he wanted— recognition that his election to the papacy was legitimate—but without giving up anything in exchange. He had not granted Charles the investiture of Naples. All Charles's public sulking had been in vain.

High Mass and indulgences

At the very least, Charles hoped to come away with the pope's blessing on his expedition, which he presented as another Crusade. It was agreed that he would receive it during a High Mass to be celebrated on January 20, the Feast of SS. Fabian and Sebastian. That morning twenty cardinals joined the pope in the Sala del Pappagallo and the procession made its way to the high altar of St. Peter's. The king was not in his place of honor, however; he was attending a private Mass in the Chapel of Sta. Petronilla, at the other end of the basilica. After Mass, he went to have something to eat in a nearby canon's residence. Pots, jugs, and dishes laden with food were brought to him from the Vatican, borne across the cathedral in front of Alexander's nose while he waited patiently at the foot of the high altar. Finally, after a quarter of an hour, Charles arrived and took his place on the pope's right. Burckard suggested that the king hand the pope the ablution water, which he agreed to do "if that is the custom for kings." Then followed the full papal ceremonial—the reading of the epistle and gospel in Greek and Latin, communion in both kinds, monstrance of the Veil of St. Veronica and exposition of the Holy Lance, solemn benediction, proclamation of plenary indulgences—all of which satisfied Charles's curiosity but brought him no nearer to being confirmed as leader of the Crusade. Alexander was extremely wary of making a pronouncement on the subject, having given Charles a figurative pat on the head by promoting his cousin, the bishop of Le Mans, to the cardinalate.

Meanwhile the prolonged garrisoning of troops in Rome was causing riots. The Swiss soldiers of the French army and the Catalans of the garrison of the Castel Sant'Angelo were at each other's throats. And once more, the disgust of the opposition cardinals came to the surface. Cardinal Péraud, one of those who had received the pope's pardon, could not help venting his bitterness: "He denounced the pope for his crimes," wrote Burckard, "his simony, his carnal sins, his relations with the sultan and the collusion between them. If what I heard is true, he declared that the pope was a great hypocrite, a veritable scoundrel."

Alexander was not about to be swayed either by riots on the public squares or angry outbursts in the very heart of the Curia. He had resolved to humor the king by flattering him, yet without letting him have anything he wanted. Next Sunday, the Feast of the Conversion of St. Paul, he invited Charles to accompany him in the traditional procession to the Cathedral of San Paolo fuori le Mura. As usual, the French created supreme confusion in the sanctuary, but Alexander feigned not to notice. He even offered Charles another unexpected honor, making him kneel on the same prie-dieu as himself at the moment of granting the faithful a hundred years of plenary indulgence. If this meant a shorter stay in Purgatory, was it not a greater favor than the promise of an earthly kingdom?

Charles VIII departs
Escape of Cesare Borgia

Despite this papal trickery, Charles had essentially got what he wanted, namely to travel to Naples accompanied by Cesare Borgia. The pope's son had a legate's powers and would crown Charles when he had defeated the Aragonese king. Alexander also fulfilled another promise in his treaty with Charles—the handing over of Djem. The unfortunate Turkish hostage was duly escorted from the Castel Sant'Angelo to the Palazzo di San Marco, where the king was once more staying.

Charles took his leave, with Alexander—who was overjoyed to see the last of him—clasping him to his heart. From the top of the Loggia of the Benediction the pope watched as the procession filed past, the cardinal legate, Cesare Borgia, riding at the head along with his colleagues cardinals della Rovere, Savelli, and Colonna. Later, Pinturicchio would paint this episode as well as other memorable moments of Charles's visit in the apartments of the Castel Sant'Angelo, portraying them as glorious evidence of the Borgia pope's preeminence over the greatest king in Christendom.

No sooner were the Frenchmen's backs turned than songs making fun of Charles were heard all over Rome. They praised young Ferrantino, Ferrante's son, who had just assumed power in the kingdom of Naples. "Long live Ferrantino . . . and death to the King of France . . . !" Alexander did nothing to stop the songs, even though they smacked of revenge. He congratulated the governor of the Castel Sant'Angelo, Juan di Castro, for his stern handling of the French and promised him the purple hat. The pope was preparing his revenge. The first act of the drama would be played by his son, Cesare.

On January 29 the royal cortege reached Velletri, where both Cesare and the king lodged in the bishop's palace. Cesare had left Rome with nineteen richly caparisoned mules laden with his belongings. He had opened the chests carried by two of the animals to show the French their contents—sumptuous clothes, vessels of silver and gold. Unfortunately, the two animals lost their way. Early in the morning of January 30 Cesare was looked for everywhere, but in vain. Aided and abetted by one of his relatives in Velletri, he had escaped in the dead of night, disguised as a stable boy. Charles at once had the remaining chests opened: they were filled with rocks. Not long after, news came that Cesare had taken refuge in Rome with Antonio Flores, the auditor of the Rota, before fleeing to Spoleto.

Charles immediately sniffed a plot and cried, "Lombard riffraff!—the pope most of all!" He dispatched two heralds to complain to the pope and the Roman people about the cardinal of Valencia's behavior, and demanded the fugitive's return. But the pope had a surprise up his sleeve. He sent Charles his apologies via his secretary, the bishop of Nepi. Meanwhile the Romans were begging Charles not to punish Rome for Cesare's escape. Next the king's uncle, Philippe de Bresse, asked for another legate, but Alexander received his plea with olympian calm. "He knew," wrote the Florentine historian Guicciardini, "that the French are used to accepting faits accomplis."

Rather than turn back to punish the Borgias, Charles was in fact continuing on his way to Naples. The frontier forts yielded to him under threat of force. On February 18 he entered Capua. Rumor had it in Rome—as Burckard noted in his diary—that during the night the royal standard with the inscription *Missus a Deo* (I am the envoy of God) was seen flying on top of a chest while a terrible voice reminded Charles that he should pursue his mission until he had conquered the Holy Land and the Tomb of Christ. In rapid succession, Alexander learned of this so-called divine message and the news—more significant for him—that Djem had fallen dangerously ill.

Illness and death of Prince Djem

As the king entered Capua, the sultan's brother rode at Charles's side, but he could barely stay on his horse because of violent pains in his head and throat. Over the next few days the pain struck his chest, and Djem had to be carried by litter into Aversa, then into Naples. The king's doctors could do nothing about the mysterious disease, and three days later the twenty-five-year-old prince died, doubtless of pneumonia caused by bronchitis.

As often happened when someone of royal blood died suddenly, there were rumors of poison. According to Burckard, Djem had swallowed "a food or beverage that did not suit his stomach and which he was not used to." This was the discreet formula for a suspected poisoning. The Venetian chronicler Marino Sanudo felt sure that the corpse showed unmistakable signs of death by this means. Repeating the current rumors, he wrote, "The pope handed over the poisoned prince to the king," but added at once that this was an "accusation which it is wrong to trust, since the pope would have been the first to suffer from it." Obviously, Djem's death was hardly to Alexander's advantage: he lost the 40,000-ducat annual income that Bayezid provided for his brother's upkeep. Yet Alexander's enemies were quick to recall that in his letters to the pope, which were seized in 1494, the sultan had offered him 300,000 ducats in exchange for Djem's suppression. Even if there is no trace of such a payment being made, the fact that later Alexander would try to hand over the body to Bayezid in exchange for money is disturbing, to say the least. The Turks themselves believed in the poisoning theory. The chronicler Sanudo imagined that a barber had injected the pope's poison with a razor.

Thus, from all sides a campaign arose to smear the Borgia name. Whispered by contemporaries, the accusation would be shouted more and more stridently by later generations. In the next century the Italian historian Paolo Giovio came out for the poisoning theory: "It is widely held that the pope, out of hatred for the French king and in order to obtain the reward promised by the sultan, had a deadly poison mixed with the sugar that Djem added to everything he drank. It was an extremely white powder, not unpleasant to the taste, which did not destroy the vital spirits like the poisons of today, but flowed little by little into the veins, gradually causing death." Guicciardini repeated the accusation, adding that the pope's nefarious nature made such a crime likely. The poison used was said to be either arsenic or cantharidine powder, obtained from tiny dead beetles. Taken in small doses, cantharides has an aphrodisiac effect, while medium doses produce internal lesions capable of causing death. The legend of the slow poison of the Borgias would burgeon into a rich literary fortune from these few hypotheses.

Not wanting to spoil his relations with the Holy See, Charles VIII opted for the theory of a natural death. He had the corpse embalmed and kept in the castle of Gaeta. The unfortunate prince's remains would not be repatriated until four years later, in 1499, when they were interred in his ancestral burial ground at Bursa in Anatolia.

Clearly, Djem's death worked indirectly to the advantage of the pope and all those in Italy who now declared themselves anti-France. With Djem dead, Charles lost the trump card he had hoped to use for the Crusade after conquering Naples. Now that the king's religious motivation had vanished, Alexander could strike an alliance with Venice and Milan and trap Charles by cutting off his links with the duke of Orléans, who had stayed behind in the Piedmont, and with France.

The Pope unmasks himself

The situation became worrisome for the French in Naples, where they faced not only scattered rebellions but also the hitherto unknown disease syphilis. Some Swiss mercenaries were granted leave to go home to their country. On their way through Rome, fifteen of them, including one woman, were murdered and robbed to the tune of 500 or 600 crowns. Word spread that the ambush had been masterminded by Cardinal Cesare Borgia in revenge for the looting of his mother's house when the French first passed through Rome. Similar attacks occurred all over Italy. In one case, Cardinal St. Malo's son was assassinated near Isola, a few leagues north of Rome, and the 3,000 crowns he had on him were stolen.

Behind the violence was a radical change of mentality. From now on, no one was afraid to confront those who just three months before had marched as conquerors into the Eternal City. Except for Tuscany, all Italy was rising up against the invaders. On the very day the Swiss were attacked in Rome, a so-called defensive League was being formed in Venice that in fact was aimed against France. Made up of the pope, the emperor, the Spanish kings, Milan, and Venice, the League was intended to ensure "the maintenance of peace in Italy, the salvation of Christendom, the defense of the honor due the Holy See and of the rights to the Roman Empire." Alexander promised to furnish 4,000 horse and 2,000 footsoldiers who would join the allied contingents to form an army of 36,000 horse and 18,000 infantry. French diplomats kept Charles informed of the pope's about-face, but he already knew he could not expect Alexander to recognize him as king of Naples. In March he had asked Rome to send a legate to Naples so that Charles could be crowned king. In reply, Alexander had pointed out that Charles must first prove his rights in law. A later mission had also failed. Alexander had turned on the sentiment: his youngest son, Jofré, was being held hostage in Spain by partisans of Ferrantino, and another son, Juan of Gandia, was also in Spain, in the power of Ferdinand of Aragon. He regretted that he could not give Charles the bull of investiture he so craved, even in return for 100,000 ducats and an annual income of 50,000. From now on he was too involved with Venice and Milan and, besides, the huge levies of coalition troops made it likely the French would suffer a bloody defeat on their homeward march.

The Borgias versus the king-Antichrist
The stampede against France

Charles VIII's retreat was quickly prepared. One week after the coronation cavalcade, the king left Naples with 10,000 men laden with booty and dragging heavy cannons after them. Although diminished, his army was still capable of inflicting losses on the Papal States, since the pope had not yet raised mercenaries as he told the League he would. For his own safety, therefore, Alexander decided to get out of Rome. When Charles reached the city gates the pope was far away, having left for Orvieto under a Milanese-Venetian escort. In Orvieto he announced that he had ordered Viterbo and Montefiascone to supply him with all their available artillery to harass the French. However, he advised the Romans to give the king a good welcome so as to avoid reprisals.

Charles reached Rome the same day, to be greeted amicably by the city dignitaries and by the pope's representative, Cardinal Pallavicini. Offered the use of the papal apartments, the king refused and stayed instead in Cardinal Domenico della Rovere's house in the Borgo. He distrusted the pope's excessive politeness as much as the Romans distrusted him.

The French army was still formidable. The Spanish had all gone so there were no more provocateurs left; nevertheless, the king insisted on strict discipline for his men. "You would have thought they were monks," wrote the Venetian Guidiccioni. The Swiss, with their reputation for vindictiveness, had been billeted on the Testaccio Hill, once a Roman dumping ground. As a token of goodwill, the king sent his counselor, Perron de Baschi, to Orvieto to ask for an interview with the pope, but rather than meet the king, Alexander was making ready to go on to Ancona and from there to Venice, if he had to. Charles did not insist but left Rome in early June.

With relief Alexander returned to his capital just as Charles crossed the Apennines at the Tuscany border. The battle of Fornova, on July 6, did not stop the French, who were far from annihilated, though the people of Venice and Rome hailed it as a victory and believed the invaders were gone forever. Around this time there was an explosion of polemical writings, ridiculing the French king and his soldiers. They were accused of bringing about all the evils besetting Italy, including the terrible venereal disease which they had contracted mainly in Naples.

With the invaders departed, Alexander had the satisfaction of announcing that the French king was now the Antichrist. He profited from the situation by setting himself up as Italy's moral defender against the vile invader. As the latter was now too far away to do him any harm, the pope vented all his spleen against him. He forbade the Swiss, on pain of excommunication, to send troops to Charles or the duke of Orléans, then encamped in the Piedmont. At Venice's request, he published a letter threatening Charles with excommunication. He sanctimoniously renewed friendship with Ferrantino of Naples, sending him the cardinal of Monreale to set him up fully in power. He enticed Prospero and Fabrizio Colonna away from the French side and urged Ludovico il Moro and his brother Ascanio to send 500 men-at-arms and a troupe of infantrymen to Ferrantino to bring down the French viceroy, Montpensier. Similarly, he asked Emperor Maximilian to come south, in person, to rid the peninsula of France's allies. Finally, on hearing that Charles had crossed the Alps, Alexander sent Ferrantino his contribution to the war effort—a troop of 500 footsoldiers, 100 light horse, and 100 mounted bowmen. Transported to Naples, the papal artillery went into action against the Castel Nuovo, forcing it to capitulate, and the Castello del'Uovo.

Yet in spite of their enemy's unprecedented military effort, the French—now encamped in Calabria, the Abruzzi, and the Terra di Lavoro—again had the advantage. In early 1496 ships came to Gaeta bringing provisions, ammunition, and 2,000 troop reinforcements. The French were now joined by Virginio Orsini and his relatives—a move prompted by their hatred of the Colonnas, whom the pope had just brought around to Ferrantino's side. Nevertheless, Alexander assessed the situation shrewdly. Believing that, in spite of appearances, the French had lost the game, he strengthened his ties to the members of the coalition. In Rome he received the captain general of the League, Francesco da Gonzaga, who was leaving to campaign in Naples. The reception was planned on a lavish scale and, despite torrential rain, the Roman crowds swarmed around the procession. When Gonzaga crossed the Sant'Angelo Bridge he received a cannon-fire salute from the castle. At the Vatican the pope greeted him wearing, curiously, black and green robes that had belonged to Pope Boniface IX at the beginning of the century. Perhaps he wanted to show the continuity of the papal function—he was putting his temporal and spiritual authority in the service of the sacred cause of freeing Italy from the Barbarians.

The next day, Palm Sunday, Gonzaga occupied the place of honor during the four-hour service. The pope gave him the first blessed palm as well as the Golden Rose—a sign that he enjoyed the exceptional favor of the Holy See. Next, Alexander granted him a special audience so as to hear a firsthand account of the Battle of Fornova, where the marquess claimed to have defeated Charles of France. Then Gonzaga left for Naples, where Cesare Borgia had already gone as papal legate. In March the cardinal of Valencia publicly proclaimed the close ties linking the Borgias and the Aragonese by riding in the streets of the capital with his brother Jofré and his brother-in-law, Alfonso of Aragon, the bastard son of Alfonso II.

The new campaign against the French met with resounding success. The League forces, reinforced by Guidobaldo of Urbino's army, compelled the duke of Montpensier to retreat to Atella, where he capitulated on July 20, 1496. His ally Virginio Orsini also surrendered and, to please the pope, was imprisoned in the Castello del'Uovo. A week later the archbishop of Naples gave orders for victory to be celebrated with processions and Te Deums. Naples was lit up and people danced in the streets and squares. There was even more jubilation when it was learned, shortly after, that the last of the French partisans had been captured in the Abruzzi, among them Virginio Orsini's son Giangiordano.

That summer Alexander invited the European powers to play their part in this hounding of France. England, hitherto neutral, joined the League of Venice, and Maximilian of Austria came down to Lombardy with 4,000 men. Alexander also tried to persuade the doge to aid the emperor in his enterprise: "It is mistaken to think that we must not fight the French because, for the moment, they are not doing battle with us. They are determined to keep a foothold in the kingdom of Naples, and they are still holding Ostia. Every day they send troops and weapons to Italy. Armed ships are continually heading for Gaeta. Their every action can be construed as open warfare. . . ."

The pope himself was not able to help the emperor financially, Charles having deprived him of some of his most reliable sources of income—the dues paid for appointments to ecclesiastical benefices in

France. Meanwhile the subsidies promised Maximilian by Venice and Milan were not forthcoming. So, after a vain attempt to seize Livorno from the Florentines, who were on the French side, Maximilian headed back through the Tyrol. This melancholy expedition proved to Alexander that he had to rely on his own strength to fend off the threats and possible reprisals of the French.

Lesson of terrible times

Charles's campaign had shown the pope that he had to consolidate his power as temporal ruler. The Papal States had witnessed disaster after disaster as armies crisscrossed the territory. Harvests had been spoiled; shortages and excessively high prices of goods had hit the poor just when syphilis was spreading like a terrible scourge. Catastrophic floods came in the wake of an exceptionally cold spell in December 1495. With hundreds of houses destroyed in the Tiber valley and in Rome itself and with inhabitants of the low-lying sections of the city drowned, foodstuffs destroyed, and cattle carried off in the waters, Rome was in some parts the very picture of desolation. Rumors spread of extraordinary sights, which many took as evidence of divine wrath. One such was a strange monster found stranded on the banks of the Tiber after the floods had receded. No doubt the "monster" was merely an animal's decomposed remains, but it was described to the Venetian ambassadors as being in the shape of a woman, with one right arm ending in an elephant's trunk, with a bearded posterior, a serpent's tail, one right foot with claws and the left foot cloven like a bull's, and with scaly legs.

The horrors of that winter, heightened by similar nightmarish tales, frightened the people. Their mystical fears were fed by sermons from the pulpits. In Florence, Savonarola's doom-laden eloquence rang out even more insistently as he declared that Charles VIII had been punished because he had not reformed the Church or dismissed disreputable priests when he was in Rome. At Christmas 1495, he had a decree promulgated by the Grand Council proclaiming Jesus Christ king of the Florentine people. In Lent the next year Savonarola conjured up an awesome vision before his congregation:

"I tell you that Italy will be shaken to her foundations. The first will be last. Unhappy Italy! . . . There shall be the abomination of war upon war. . . . The law of the priesthood shall perish and priests shall be stripped of their place. Princes shall wear haircloth and the people be crushed by tribulation."

It was a meeting of two worlds, one a world of spoils and worldly pleasure, the other of austerity and fanaticism. Taking advantage of the foreign invasion and the social disorder of the times, Savonarola was determined to hold high the cross as a symbol of unification, and to root out evil by penitence. But the Borgia pope and his sons had a different vision of the future. Charles VIII had failed in his venture, and they had labored hard to see him fail. They saw no trace of divine intervention in these events. Contrary to Savonarola's designs, they wanted to build a strong empire upon the ruins. The ruined structures and demoralized populace gave them a golden opportunity to realize their dreams. Henceforth they were resolved to stop at nothing in order to succeed. If the French invasion had not fazed them, they would not allow themselves to be distracted by the fanatical preacher of the City of God.

3

The Enfants Terribles

The family reunited at the Vatican

In those fine spring days of 1496, untouched by the sufferings of the people and the prophecies of doom, the Vatican was an oasis of peace and harmony. Here Alexander VI, a beaming pater familias, gathered his offspring around him.

Lucrezia had joined her father at Perugia when he was fleeing from the advancing French, then in the autumn of 1495 came back to Rome and settled in the Palace of Sta. Maria in Portico with her husband, Giovanni Sforza. That winter she played hostess at several elegant parties.

At sixteen, the young countess of Pesaro had become expert at court life. In March she received the four prelates her father had just raised to the cardinalate. They were Spaniards from Valencia, trusted cohorts who would conveniently swell the ranks of the pope's followers in the Sacred College: Bartolomeo Martini was pontifical majordomo, Juan di Castro, governor of the Castel Sant'Angelo, and Juan Lopez, datary. The fourth was Juan Borgia the younger, Alexander's grand-nephew. Lucrezia also welcomed Francesco da Gonzaga, general in chief of the anti-France League, an arresting figure both physically and because of the name he had made for himself in the war against Charles VIII.

The pope made good use of Lucrezia's social talents when he wanted to show off his court. One occasion was the reception held for his youngest son, Jofré, and his wife, the fascinating Princess Sancia of Aragon. At noon on May 20 the area around the Porta Laterana was abuzz with animation. Lucrezia left the city on a mule with black-silk trappings, together with twenty richly attired ladies. Before her rode two pages, one horse caparisoned in gold brocade, the other in crimson velvet. The pope's daughter drew up to face 200 men-at-arms of the papal guard standing at attention on the square. Around them thronged members of the cardinals' families, chaplains, and squires. The envoys of the Catholic Kings of Spain were there, also those of the king of Naples.

Soon the Neapolitan party showed up, and a lively, glittering escort of nobles, ladies, and jesters gathered around the young couple. Sancia, a young woman of twenty in the full bloom of her youth, was the cynosure of all eyes. The fair-haired Lucrezia observed with curiosity—and maybe a little resentment—this dark, blue-eyed beauty, who wore a black, long-sleeved gown and rode a gray Spanish horse with black velvet and satin trappings. Six ladies of honor walked alongside her. Her brother-in-law, Cesare, already knew the princess of Naples's charm at firsthand, and no doubt the Mantuan ambassador, who was present, had him in mind when he wrote, "By her gestures and appearance, the sheep will surrender readily to the wolf's desire." As for Sancia's ladies: "They are in no way inferior to their mistress; thus they say publicly it will be a fine flock."

Jofré was riding ahead of Sancia, flanked by the senator of Rome and the envoy of the Holy Roman emperor. A lively youth of fifteen with an olive complexion, he was dressed elegantly in black. Auburn curls peeped out from under the brim of his black-velvet cap. In spite of his proud, insolent air he looked, when compared to his wife, more like a page than a prince.

Lucrezia welcomed the pair affectionately and accompanied them to the Basilica for a brief thanksgiving service. Then, again on horseback, the cortege made its way to the Vatican, passing the Colosseum and the ruins of the Forum and weaving through the narrow medieval streets until it reached the Castel Sant'Angelo.

Alexander awaited his children's arrival impatiently. According to Burckard, he peeped down at the procession from behind a half-open window in one of the bedchambers of the Borgia apartments. When the advance guard trotted up, he hurried to the Sala dei Pontifici and installed himself on his throne, with eleven cardinals in scarlet standing around him. In front of his footstool were two crimson-velvet cushions. Here Lucrezia and Sancia sat, having first, like Jofré, kissed the pope's right foot and hand and received a fatherly embrace from him and the cardinals. After a few words of welcome, the pope interrupted the audience's solemn mood and joked with the girls, making them collapse with giggles, while Jofré talked gravely with the cardinals and his brother Cesare.

Finally everyone took leave of the pope, and the young couple were conducted to Cardinal della Porta's palace, where they were to stay and where, for two days, they were entertained by the wives of Roman nobles.

Sunday, May 22, the Feast of Pentecost, saw the pope's family once again gathered in St. Peter's Basilica. The preacher was a Spaniard, and his sermon was inordinately long. The pope was the first to show signs of boredom. Sancia and Lucrezia, for their part, grew more and more restless. In the end, Christianity's foremost sanctuary witnessed the unheard-of spectacle of two young women in their gorgeous gowns climbing up to the cathedral stalls and making themselves at home in the marble pulpit where the epistle and gospel were chanted. Their maids-in-waiting clambered after them and sat down in the canon's stalls. Burckard called the episode "a great dishonor, a shame and a scandal for the clergy and the people," but the pope merely laughed it off, happy to see the youthful conspiracy of his daughter and daughter-in-law.

Juan of Gandia, general in chief of the Holy See
Campaign against the Orsinis and expedition from Ostia

Jofré had been too young to serve in the Holy League army when it attacked Charles VIII's last strongholds in the kingdom of Naples. But another one of the Borgia offspring had taken part—Juan of Gandia. His father had visions of him treading in the glorious footsteps of his dead brother, the first duke of Gandia. During the French invasion, King Ferdinand had forbidden Juan to leave Spain, but now that the king had broken the Treaty of Barcelona, which he had signed with Charles, he had nothing against Juan's going to Italy.

In late July, Juan said goodbye to his wife, Duchess Maria Enriquez Borgia, who was pregnant, leaving her and his heir, little Juan II, in the fortified castle of Gandia. On August 10 he reached Rome, where the cardinals' families, and Cesare himself, awaited him at the Porta Portese. Juan rode a bay horse with cloth of gold trappings and harness edged with tiny bells. In his brown-velvet suit studded with pearls and precious stones, he outshone the more sober richness of Cesare's retinue.

The pope was planning to give Juan some land seized from the Orsinis. He had decided to punish that family for forsaking the king of Naples's side and leaving the way open for the French to push into Italy. Virginio, chief of the clan, was declared a rebel, but he was impossible to catch while under French protection. As soon as this was eased, Virginio and his family were excommunicated and told in no uncertain terms that their possessions would be confiscated and their vassals released from their oath of obedience.

Thus by the time Juan of Gandia showed up, the decks were cleared. By moving against the Orsinis, France's allies, the pope's son would be carrying out the orders of the Holy See as well as those of his Spanish suzerain, Ferdinand. He also stood to benefit himself, since the conquered lands would fall to him. The venture was made all the easier because when the French surrendered at Atella, Virginio Orsini had been taken prisoner together with his son Giangiordano. Locked up in the Castello d'Uovo, Virginio died soon afterward, very conveniently for the pope—whom gossip would later accuse of poisoning his enemy.

Alexander did not wait until the leading Orsini was out of the way to announce his plans for his son Juan. During the August feast days, the duke took his place on the topmost step of the pope's throne—an honor granted only to sovereigns. The next month he received the legation of the Patrimony of St. Peter, which meant he was now governor of the large area stretching north and east of Rome, to the borders of Tuscany and Umbria, that contained the fiefs of the Orsinis. The pope created a completely new army for him by hiring hundreds of mercenaries. Once all this was done, Juan was named gonfalonier of the Church—a huge honor—in a magnificent ceremony at St. Peter's. He also was invested with standard and baton as captain general of the papal army. His bearing, magnificent clothes, and the jewels his father had given him won universal admiration. Duke Guidobaldo of Urbino, a papal vassal who took part in the ceremony, also received a commander's baton. The pope wanted him to lead the campaign against the Orsinis, Juan being totally inexperienced in the art of war. He handed both men the banners of the expedition, one bearing the arms of the Church, the other the Borgia bull. Cardinal Lunati, who was to function as legate, was given papal powers throughout the campaign. His specific duty would be to pronounce excommunication and interdict on the Orsini partisans.

The attack on the Orsini castles led to ten fortresses' being seized in swift succession: Scrofano, Galera, Formello, and Campagnano surrendered, while Anguillara voluntarily flung open its gates. Finally the papal forces reached the castle of Bracciano, the chief Orsini stronghold. With its five massive towers rising up at the lake's edge, the fort enjoyed an almost impregnable position. Virginio Orsini's brother-in-law, Bartolomeo Alviano, a young condottiere who was ugly and misshapen but the bravest in all Italy, had overseen its defense, piled up weapons and ammunition, and hoisted the French flag atop the towers. War cries of "Francia!" greeted the pope's soldiers. Bracciano was besieged at the same time as Trevignano and Isola, on the other side of Lake Bracciano.

In the course of the engagement, the duke of Urbino was wounded and left the field. The duke of Gandia had no idea what orders to give. He ended up asking his father to have the king of Naples's siege artillery trundled to the battle site, but the cannons did not arrive until late November. Unlike Trevignano and Isola, which surrendered, Bracciano held out. The attackers shivered in their quarters while the besieged made one sortie after another, even in some cases to the gates of Rome. Cesare Borgia, out hunting near Rome's Tre Fontane, came across a detachment and only just escaped it.

Meanwhile, Juan's conspicuous lack of success was upsetting the pope, who collapsed and was unable to celebrate Christmas Mass. He reinforced the blockade of Bracciano, hoping to starve it into submission, but Bartolomeo Alviano had enough provisions to hold out for a long siege. In January Alviano drove back the papal soldiers who had swarmed into the fort through a breach in the wall, and sent out a donkey with a large sign that read, "Let me pass: I am sent as an ambassador to the duke of Gandia." There was even a letter from Alviano fastened under the animal's tail. Alviano offered those of his soldiers who had deserted the Orsini side double the pay Gandia was giving them for being turncoats, on condition that they returned to Bracciano.

The Orsini faction did not in fact lack troops. Carlo Orsini and his cousin Giulio had the support of Vitellozzo Vitelli, the lord of Città di Castello, who had returned from France with a lot of money from Charles VIII to recruit fresh troops. Giovanni della Rovere, the prefect

of Rome, had raised cavalry. The new army was concentrated at Soriano, east of Viterbo, where the papal troops marched to meet it in
order to divert it from Bracciano. The two sides clashed. The 500
Swiss of the pope's army were routed by Vitellozzo's troops, who
brandished pikes even longer than those of the Swiss. The duke of
Urbino was taken prisoner, Gandia was lightly wounded, and Cardinal
Lunati nearly died of fright. Once again, the barons opposed to the
pope were masters of the Roman Campagna.

Alexander was impatient to make peace. By early February the
Orsinis had recovered all their castles except for Anguillara and Cerveteri. They had had to fork over 50,000 golden ducats to the papal
treasury, but they recouped that sum by setting an equivalent ransom
on the head of their prisoner, the duke of Urbino. They had got out
of the campaign lightly: their possessions were recognized by the pope,
those of their relatives still held in Naples were freed, and they were
allowed to go on serving the French king. Extremely displeased, Alexander laid the responsibility for this defeat not on his son Juan but on
the luckless duke of Urbino. He gave Guidobaldo's family sole responsibility for paying his ransom and planned, as a punishment, to
set up one of his own sons—perhaps Cesare—as the duke's successor,
in the absence of a direct heir.

Happily, a chance came up to erase the duke of Gandia's humiliation. The pope sent him off to join Gonsalvo de Cordoba, the general
whom the Catholic Kings had dispatched to Italy to chase the French
out of Naples. On February 21, having left Rome with 600 men-at-
arms and 1,000 footsoldiers, Gonsalvo laid siege to Ostia, which Cardinal della Rovere had turned over to the French. It was a brief
campaign, and soon Gonsalvo was back in Rome, dragging behind
him the chief of the Ostia garrison whom he had forced to surrender.
The duke of Gandia and his brother-in-law Giovanni da Pesaro were
given places of honor in the march-past of the victorious troops. In
full agreement with his father, Juan took precedence over Gonsalvo,
so much so that on Palm Sunday the proud Spaniard refused to take
the seat offered him, which was a step lower than Juan's on the papal
throne. He also refused to take the palm, blessed by the pope,
after Juan. Alexander had to settle the difference diplomatically by
offering Gonsalvo the Golden Rose, the supreme reward of Christian
princes.

Scandal at the Vatican
Flight of Giovanni Sforza
Cesare's jealousy

An atmosphere of oppression hung over Rome. With the fighting against the Orsinis and della Roveres at an end, the city was swarming with unruly soldiers. Crime and extortion were rife. On Good Friday, 1497, a crowd flocked to the Campo dei Fiori and demanded that the Spaniards be stoned. Gonsalvo of Cordoba, who was growing more and more exasperated, held the Borgias responsible for these public displays of hatred. Without mincing his words he remonstrated with the pope, reproaching him for leading a dissolute life. In fact, rumor had it that Alexander had just had a child by a married woman, whose husband had taken revenge by stabbing his father-in-law, who had served as a go-between. Tongues also wagged about Sancia, Jofré's wife, who was said to be leading a life of debauchery behind the Vatican walls.

The Holy See, it seemed, had no self-respect, nor did it respect other people's honor. Lucrezia's husband, Giovanni Sforza, was floundering in this court where his presence now meant nothing, for the Borgias no longer needed the Sforzas, and Giovanni found the arrogance of his brothers-in-law harder and harder to bear. On Easter morning, piqued beyond endurance, he quit Rome on the pretext of making a pilgrimage to the Church of San Onofrio fuori le Mura. Here he leaped on an Arab horse that had secretly been made ready for him and galloped off at full tilt, covering the nearly distance between Rome and Pesaro in twenty-four hours. When he reached the city gates the horse dropped dead.

The pope and his sons pretended to be surprised at Giovanni's sudden disappearance, but they were actually very relieved. Lucrezia was tired of her husband, whom she complained of neglecting her. According to confidential information given by one of Giovanni's chamberlains, Cesare had come to see his sister shortly before the incident. Lucrezia had made the chamberlain hide behind a tapestry, from where he overheard Cesare warn his sister that orders had been given for her husband's murder. When Cesare left, Lucrezia told the youth to run and tell his master what he had just heard. Once warned, Giovanni had immediately fled the coop. Was Lucrezia acting in cahoots with her brother, putting on a show to get rid of an undesirable husband, or, on the other hand, had she warned him out of some remnant of affection in order to save his life? She knew he was painfully jealous of her two brothers, Juan and Cesare, who not only were sharing the favors of Sancia, Jofré's spirited young wife, around this time, but also were excessively fond of their sister. In any event, it may have been because she felt like a prisoner in the Vatican palace that Lucrezia followed a convention of the time, which said that a married woman deprived of her husband should withdrew from society, and sought refuge in the Convent of San Sisto, near the Via Appia.

Lucrezia's flight brought Cesare's hatred of his brother Juan to the point of paroxysm. He held him responsible, and this fresh grudge was now piled on the contempt he felt for his brother on account of his failures in the field. Cesare hoped that, having proved Juan was a good-for-nothing, he would be packed off to Spain by his father after the parody of a triumph that had so annoyed Gonsalvo of Cordoba. Cesare could then take his place and win the title of prince that had eluded Juan. But he was forgetting the pope's doting, obsessive love for his son. Far from giving up his dream, Alexander was plotting to realize it by carving the papal fiefs inside the kingdom of Naples into a principality.

In early June 1497 a secret consistory was held, and three cities of the Campagna, south of Rome—Benevente, Terracina, and Pontecorvo—were made into a duchy. The new fief was conferred on the duke of Gandia, who would have the right of succession for his legitimate issue. Only Cardinal Piccolomino of Siena—the future Pope Pius III—dared protest against this alienation of Church possessions. In Alexander's mind the measure was a first step toward elevating his son to the throne of Naples. He considered King Federigo of Naples too much under the thumb of Venice and Spain to thwart Juan's ambition. The duke of Gandia therefore stood a good chance of succeeding him. To soothe the king's feelings, Alexander suggested that the tribute Naples paid the Holy See each year be canceled.

Cesare, who was present at the consistory and heard these extraordinary proposals, said not a word, though he voted for them with most of the other cardinals. Yet it is easy to imagine Cesare's fury at seeing his brother rewarded in such a way when he had no talent and his activities in Rome were confined to the boudoir. As a crowning touch of irony, on June 8 Cesare was appointed legate for the king of Naples's coronation. This meant both brothers would leave together for Naples, where Juan was to take possession of his new principality after the ceremony.

Murder of Juan of Gandia

Proud of the honors the pope had just conferred on her two sons, Vannozza Cattanei invited them to dinner on June 14 at her vineyard on the Esquiline Hill, near the Church of San Pietro in Vincoli. Banqueting tables had been set up under the vines, and all the Borgias' friends were present. Cesare arrived with his cousin Juan, cardinal-archbishop of Monreale. Vannozza, still beautiful, sumptuously gowned and bejeweled, was in high spirits as she presided graciously over the festivities. She hoped before the party was over to see her sons reconciled. During the evening a masked man showed up who whispered something to Juan, then disappeared. No one was very surprised, however, as the duke often surrounded himself with mysterious characters when he went on his assignations.

Darkness had fallen by the time the two brothers and Cardinal Juan Borgia headed back on their mules to the Vatican. They had left the Campo dei Fiori and were approaching the Sant'Angelo Bridge when they separated, Juan of Gandia telling his brother and cousin that he wanted to take the air alone. He and his groom disappeared down a narrow lane leading to the Piazza Guidea, in the ghetto. There the masked man from the party was waiting for him. He mounted behind Juan. The duke left the groom to keep watch on the square, telling him to return to the Vatican alone if he had not returned within the hour.

The next day, the duke's servants noticed that their master had not come home the night before. They told the pope, who felt sure, like them, that Juan must have visited some courtesan and not wanted to leave the place in broad daylight lest his father hear of it. Hours went by. When night fell and the duke still had not returned, the pope grew extremely perturbed. "Distraught to his very bowels," as Burckard described him, he ordered the police to search high and low. Meanwhile news of Juan's mysterious disappearance spread like wildfire throughout Rome. The burghers barricaded their doors as word went around that the Borgias' enemies had committed the crime. Spanish troops ran through the streets with their swords drawn. The Orsinis and Colonnas took up arms. In the meantime the police had found the duke's young squire, gravely wounded and hardly able to speak. Next they caught Juan's mule. Its stirrups were buckled as though they had been violently wrenched.

Finally, in the afternoon, an important witness, one Giorgio Schiavino, came to see the police. He had spent the night in a fishing boat moored to the bank of the Tiber near the hospital of San Girolamo degli Schiavoni, keeping watch over a cargo of timber. Around five o'clock in the morning Schiavino had seen two men coming out of the street alongside the hospital. They looked about them warily, then vanished. Two others appeared a little later. After observing their surroundings in the same way, they gave a signal, and a man on a white horse emerged from the narrow street. Across the saddle was thrown a man's body, its head and arms dangling on one side and the legs on the other. On reaching the riverbank, near the place where carts dumped refuse, the two men on foot grabbed the body and threw it with all their might into the river. When the rider asked them if the corpse had sunk, they replied, "Yes, my lord." The rider had then come up closer, seen that the dead man's cloak was floating, and ordered the others to throw rocks to sink it. Then they all left, including the two men who had stood watch during the sinking of the corpse.

Why had he not spoken up before? the boatman was asked when his statement had been taken down. He answered that he must have seen a hundred bodies thrown into the river at night, but no one ever made a fuss about it. He treated this incident as he did the others.

Details like these made people immediately suspect they were on an important trail, and a reward of 10 ducats was promised any fisherman or swimmer who recovered the body. Three hundred men showed up. Some dived into the river, while others dragged the bottom with nets. Toward vespers a body was fished out of the water. It was obviously the duke: he was still wearing his velvet cloak, his hose and doublet; his spurs were still attached to his boots, and his gloves and dagger were still at his belt. There were 30 ducats in his purse, which ruled out robbery as a motive for the murder. It was clear he had been stabbed by several hands. In all, nine dagger blows were counted— eight in the body and legs, and a single, deadly stab in the throat.

The body was taken by boat to the Castel Sant'Angelo, where Burckard's colleague, Bernardino Guttieri, washed it and dressed it in the full regalia of captain general of the Church. When the pope, who had rushed up to the fortress, saw the body he broke into sobs so violent that his cries could be heard on the Sant'Angelo Bridge. He lamented all the more, wrote Burckard, knowing that his beloved son had been tossed into the river along with the city's filth. In the Vatican he shut himself in his room, refusing to see anyone, and fasted for three days.

The Borgias' enemies gloated to see the Father of Christianity weeping over his son. Sannazar's cruel verses went the rounds of society:

> *It's easy to believe, Sixtus,*
> *That you're a fisher of men,*
> *Since out of the waters*
> *You've fished your own son!*

In spite of his grief, Alexander gave orders for the funeral arrangements to proceed with due solemnity. The same evening on which the body was found, it was laid on a bier and carried, uncovered, beside the river to the Church of Sta. Maria del Popolo. A cortege lit by nearly 200 torches accompanied it—an extraordinary honor, since most funerals had only about twenty. All the palace prelates and the pope's chamberlains and squires joined in the straggling procession, lamenting loudly. The common people pressed close, curious to catch a glimpse of the young prince who seemed in the flickering torchlight to be asleep rather than dead. A guard of Spanish soldiers, their swords unsheathed, lined the route where, either as a sign of mourning or out of fear, the shopkeepers had closed their shutters. Finally, the body was buried in the Chapel of Sta. Lucia, which Vannozza, intending it as her own tomb, had had Pinturicchio decorate with frescoes.

A delicate inquest

While the pope was burying himself in his grief, an extremely close investigation was afoot to find the murderers. But although the chief of police ordered a search of all the houses the duke frequented, no clues turned up.

Everyone had a different theory. Some accused the Orsinis. The murder had in fact been committed in a section of Rome where their dependents lived, and the victim's mule had been found there as well. The Orsinis also had a motive, namely to avenge the death of Virginio, the head of their clan. Another malcontent who might also have had a hand in the assassination was Guidobaldo of Urbino; he had borne the Borgias a grudge since the recent campaign against the Orsinis led by Juan of Gandia. Some cardinals were also suspected: Federico San Severino and, especially, Ascanio Sforza, who had quarreled violently with Juan at a recent banquet, at which his majordomo had been killed. The Milanese cardinal might have wanted to avenge this murder and at the same time pay back the insult to his cousin Giovanni de Pesaro.

Other clues were provided by the young duke's amorous exploits. He had provoked not a few fathers and husbands, among them Antonio Maria della Mirandola, who was humiliated through his daughter; Jofré of Squillace, through his wife, Sancia; and Giovanni de Pesaro himself, through Lucrezia. Yet no one dared mention the name of Cesare Borgia, even though his intense jealousy of Juan was known to everyone.

When Alexander finally emerged from his anguish, he called a meeting of his cardinals and ambassadors where he spoke touchingly of his grief. Never, he said, would he feel so piercing a sorrow, so great was his love for his son. From now on the pontificate mattered nothing to him, or anything else on earth. If he had seven thrones, he would gladly give them all for the young duke's life. As for the murderer, he did not know who was guilty but he exonerated the duke of Urbino as well as Jofré of Squillace and Giovanni of Pesaro, his son-in-law. Conscious of having offended heaven by his wicked reputation and that of his family, he declared that he wished to make amends and atone for his conduct by reforming the Church.

The Spanish ambassador, Garcilaso de la Vega, answered this dignified speech by expressing his sympathy for the pope. He then made excuses for Ascanio Sforza, who had not dared attend the consistory. He himself gave his word that the prelate had not been involved in the murder or plotted with the Orsinis. One by one, the other ambassadors offered their condolences, and the meeting ended in tears.

That day the pope wrote to the Christian rulers informing them of the tragedy. He had vowed, he said, to reform the Church and the Vatican after receiving this cruel warning from Providence. Even his enemies seemed convinced by his pious resolve. Cardinal Giuliano della Rovere wrote to Alexander from Avignon that Juan's death had grieved him as much as if it had been his own son's. The Holy See also witnessed a touching reconciliation, directly due to Juan of Gandia's death: Savonarola, who had been excommunicated for more than seven months, sent a letter of condolence, thus making a truce with

Rome after a particularly bitter crisis. Such a rapprochement had seemed inconceivable, so far had relations between the monk and the pope deteriorated.

Alexander VI and Savonarola
Reconciliation on the basis of reform

Toward the end of 1496 the Holy See had launched a brutal offensive against Savonarola, the prior of Florence's monastery of San Marco. At that time Florence was taken up with the approach of Maximilian of Austria's army, and the government had grown somewhat lax in its efforts to defend Savonarola against the papacy. Meanwhile the monk had strengthened his hold on the city's Dominican monasteries by joining the Lombard Congregation, which was independent of the Holy See. The simplest way for the pope to bring him back into line was to dissolve this affiliation and create a new community directly under Rome's thumb. In this way Savonarola would cease to be vicar of the community, becoming instead simply a member of his order.

The new Tuscan-Roman congregation was accordingly set up by a brief of November 7, 1496. Savonarola rejected it and was promptly excommunicated, although he went on preaching. His hold over the Florentines was such that on February 7, 1497, on the Piazza della Signoria, he set up the famous "bonfire of the vanities," on which lascivious paintings, obscene books, lutes, pommades, perfumes, mirrors, dolls, playing cards, gaming tables, and scores of other articles were confined to the flames. During his Lenten sermons he had called the Roman Church a harlot and, more vehemently than ever, denounced the pope's debauchery. In Rome, before the consistory, Savonarola's implacable enemy, Fra Mariano, urged Alexander to "root out this monster from the Church of God," and Cardinal Carafa, who had until recently been Savonarola's protector, withdrew his support.

After the duke of Gandia's death, this ruthless struggle seemed to give way to mutual understanding. Savonarola exhorted the pope to stick to his good intentions and get down to the task of Church reform. At the same time he begged him to look favorably on his work and lift the ill-deserved excommunication. A changed Alexander received these words with complete equanimity. Every day at the Vatican he presided over the reform commission he had convened on June 19, which was made up of six cardinals. After consulting previous popes' plans for reform, the committee drew up a bull reorganizing the liturgy, curbing simony and the transfer of Church possessions, and regulating the conferring of bishoprics.

No cardinal should have more than one diocese, or an income of more than 6,000 ducats; no one should serve as legate for more than two years. The princes of the Church should not take part in worldly entertainments—plays, tournaments, or carnivals. Their servants should be limited to eighty at the maximum, and they should have no more than thirty horses. They should not receive jugglers, jesters, or musicians, nor should they employ young boys or adolescents as valets. They should reside at the Curia. And they would not be allowed to spend more than 1,500 ducats on their funerals or burials.

The venality of Curia offices would be abolished. Whatever their rank, the clergy would have to give up entertaining concubines in the ten days after the publication of a bull, offenders being liable to lose their benefices within a month. Oaths taken by children would be declared worthless. A range of abuses in the transfer of ecclesiastical possessions and the overtaxing of acts of chancellory would be severely repressed.

This remarkable text reflected the personal experience of a pope who had, as vice-chancellor, meted out dispensation after dispensation for a wide range of faults that he was now determined to root out completely. Unfortunately for pious souls, the bull did not see the light. A month after setting up the commission, Alexander no longer deemed it necessary. He stopped enacting the reform measures and went back to his old ways.

A terrible suspicion

The cause of this volte-face is to be found in the pope's character, always more inclined to savor life's pleasures than to endure its woes. Once the mourning period was over, oblivion set in. In the meantime a conviction was taking hold of him and filling him with horror: he had become almost certain that his son Cesare was his brother's murderer. Although people were careful to avoid mentioning him by name, the cardinal of Valencia very soon appeared on the list of suspects. On June 23 the Florentine envoy, one Bracci, wrote to the Signoria that the pope had all the information that could be got on the murder but did not want the investigation to go on because "the culprits were persons of quality." Twenty days after the crime, Alexander ordered the police to stop their search. He had been heard to say that he knew who the murderer was, but was careful to avoid naming him. People deduced that the murderer was someone the pope did not dare punish because of the fearful scandal that would ensue. Clearly, no Roman baron or jealous husband was involved—they would have been promptly handed over to justice. The culprit must be someone close to the pope.

He was not hard to pinpoint. Everyone at the Curia knew about Cesare's contempt for his brother and his increasing frustration at seeing Juan pile up honors—honors that Cesare, even though his senior, could not claim for himself since his cardinal's rank did not allow it. Juan's death would force the pope to make Cesare a layman once again. He could then obtain a princely position quite eclipsing the one his father gave his younger brother. Cesare's destiny decreed that he should physically eliminate the duke of Gandia: no one had more interest in this elimination than he.

As time passed, Rome became a beehive of rumors. "I have once more heard it said that the duke of Gandia's death must be imputed to his brother the cardinal," Giovanni Alberto della Pigna wrote from Venice to the duke of Ferrara in February 1498. Cesare's guilt was affirmed by the historians Sanudo and Guicciardini. Later writers, depending on their view of the papacy, would either accept his guilt or cast doubts on it. The murderer had seen to it that no evidence could be adduced against him. Yet this very cautiousness points to the criminal's exceptional character. Cesare was a man of genius—there was scarcely anyone else of his stamp at the court of Rome.

Cesare's legation to Naples

The clearest sign that Alexander very soon suspected his son was that he did not attempt to see Cesare before the latter took off for Naples. Cesare left Rome on July 22, with a legate's powers, to crown Federigo at Capua. On August 7, Alexander sent Jofré and Sancia to Naples to attend the ceremony. Sancia arrived in time to nurse Cesare, who had fallen sick, and the coronation took place on the appointed day. Most of the Neapolitan nobility, except for the anti-Aragon San Severinos, were in the cortege accompanying the king as he was borne on his golden dais to the cathedral. Federigo doled out titles and favors to his partisans, in particular Prospero and Fabrizio Colonna.

The royal celebration was well timed for Jofré and Sancia, who were being mentioned embarrassingly in the inquest on Juan's murder. Meanwhile Lucrezia was still sequestered in the convent of San Sisto. The pope was not sorry his offspring were far away, and separated, since in this way they were not likely to tear each other to pieces. But the atmosphere at the Curia was a strange one. The chronicler Sanudo tells of ghosts haunting the Vatican and Castel Sant'Angelo, and of fantastic lights and otherworldly voices that terrified the pope's entourage.

Miles away from Rome, Cesare was comporting himself with admirable composure. After crowning Federigo at Capua, he accompanied him to Naples, staying at the royal residence of Castel Capuano. Coolly, he told the court that the papal enclaves had been set up as the duchy of Benevente and transferred to Juan of Gandia's son and heir—thus acting as executor of his murdered brother, to the fury of Juan's widow, Maria Enriquez, who was convinced of Cesare's guilt. He paraded in the streets of Naples at the head of 300 horsemen, proudly representing the pope, the king's suzerain, and accompanied by Sancia and her brother Alfonso of Aragon. It was a brilliant end to a stunningly successful legation, and the Sacred College paid their young colleague the compliment of going to meet him when he returned home, escorting him from the church of Sta. Maria Nuova to the Vatican. Alexander had called a consistory to welcome Cesare at the palace. He embraced his son in the traditional greeting, kissing him on the forehead, but said not a word—an uncharacteristic coldness that betrayed his deep conviction of Cesare's guilt. Indeed, because of his uneasiness, the pope left the Vatican, as though to protect himself from his son.

Evil's ceaseless round: embezzlements, debauchery, and the ravages of syphilis

Alexander moved to the Castel Sant'Angelo on October 28. By some mysterious chance, that same day the police clapped into a dungeon his former private secretary, the archbishop of Cosenza, Bartolomeo Flores, now stripped of his order. The prelate had been sentenced to life imprisonment after confessing that he and three of his employees had forged more than 3,000 bulls. One of the deeds had authorized a Portuguese woman of royal blood to doff the habit and marry the late king's illegitimate son. Another gave an ecclesiastic permission to marry without losing his position. For the most part, the bulls granted dispensations and graces for the purpose of amassing rich benefices. Charged with widespread peddling of such forgeries, Flores was imprisoned in what was once Emperor Hadrian's funerary chamber, the terrible bottlenecked dungeon of San Marocco. Here he awaited his death.

From his luxurious rooms on the upper story, the pope had given orders for Flores to be given a little bread and water every three days, as well as some oil for his lamp so that he could meditate on the Bible and his breviary. Alexander needed to keep his former amanuensis alive for some time yet. Without showing his hand, several times he sent Flores visitors such as Juan Marades, the bishop of Toul, Pedro de Solis, the archdeacon of Bavia, and others of his circle to play chess with him. They managed to make Flores own up to having sent off several briefs without the pope's knowledge, including some concessions of benefices in Spain. This confession later enabled Alexander to do Ferdinand and Isabella a favor by voiding, as false, certain authentic deeds obtained by people they disliked. Flores was promised his freedom and new responsibilities if he confessed. But when he did, his visitors vanished and he rotted miserably away in his cell until his death in 1498.

Such were the goings-on behind the scenes of the papal residence. One sign of divine wrath was seen in the terrible storm that shook the Castel Sant'Angelo. A thunderbolt fell on the powder magazine, which exploded, and blocks of stone were hurled far and wide, some landing on the other side of the Tiber and injuring more than fifteen people. The huge statue of the archangel St. Michael that topped the monument disappeared, broken into fragments—lightning had struck the point of the angel's sword, which pointed to the sky. People swore the archangel had flown away.

Evil lurked on all sides. Now that penitence was no longer the order of the day, debauchery made its brazen appearance once more in the Eternal City. Burckard writes that prostitutes and prelates' mistresses sat in the first row of the Church of San Agostino on the saint's feast day during a celebration of High Mass. Syphilis ravaged all classes of society. Two days before Flores was sent to prison, the warden of the Castel Sant'Angelo, Bartolomeo de Luna, bishop of Nicastro, perished of the "French evil." Cesare had certainly caught the disease in Naples. His private physician, Gaspare Torrella, had fortunately hit on a treatment which, combined with Sancia's nursing, enabled him to weather the attack. The practitioner later achieved notoriety by publishing his prescription in a treatise called *De Pudendagra*. Protected by his remedy, the cardinal of Valencia enjoyed the favors of the Roman courtesans, one of his mistresses being the famous Fiammetta. Cesare was also adept at dissimulation, and no one knows who were the mothers of his illegitimate children. At the most it has been suggested that one of Lucrezia's ladies-in-waiting was among them.

Lechery, encouraged by the example on high, knew no bounds. Burckard noted the most flagrant cases in the Sacred College: the cardinal of Segorbe, who was devoured by syphilis, was given a dispensation from bowing to the pope at the 1499 Easter celebration. The cardinal of Monreale, Juan Borgia, was authorized not to show up at ceremonies for two years, but was finally cured and attended Mass in December 1499. The pope's enemy Giuliano della Rovere, the future Julius II, also caught the disease. This indulgence in carnal pleasures, more visible than before because of disease, marked a mood of profound skepticism. The pope's moral abdication was indeed more obvious than ever: he even allowed scurrilous writing to circulate which denied there was a life after death. Debauchery was limited only by the needs of public health. In April 1498 the Romans witnessed a strange procession in which six peasants with tall paper "miters" on their heads were dragged along the streets, whipped by policemen. Some men suffering from syphilis had paid the peasants to be allowed to immerse themselves in barrels of oil to relieve their suffering. Once the men had bathed in the oil, the peasants had come to town to sell their oil, which they claimed was pure.

As numerous as the offenses committed for profit were those provoked by debauchery. Homosexuality was widespread, catamites being a common sight around the pope and his cardinals. In Florence, Savonarola condemned sodomy as the most criminal of practices. In Rome, on the other hand, it was tolerated except for the brief period of penitence after Juan of Gandia's murder, when Alexander considered prohibiting prelates from employing boys.

Yet this confusion of the sexes was cruelly punished when it caused a public scandal. At the beginning of April that year the Roman populace was offered another sight just as curious as the punishment of the oil sellers. A prostitute called Cursetta was led through the city together with a Moor, a homosexual transvestite. He had his hands tied behind his back and had on a dress raised to his navel so that his sexual organs were in full view. After making the rounds of the city the prostitute was released, while the Moor was sent to prison. A week later he emerged from the Tor di Nona jail chained to two brigands. In front of them was a policeman on a donkey. At the end of a stick he carried two testicles that had been cut off the body of a Jew convicted of having had carnal relations with a Christian woman. At the Campo Marzio the three prisoners were put to death, the two brigands being hanged and the Moor strangled, then burned. But, adds Burckard, because of the rain "the corpse was not consumed, only the legs which were nearest the flames being burned."

The hypocrisy of the Roman court, which punished public vice and connived at private debauchery, hardly encouraged the cardinals and others to devote themselves scrupulously to the celebration of divine office. They much preferred looking after their material interests and had become past masters at finance. Cesare was an expert like many others. When he sold off his brother's possessions, the furniture and jewels that Juan had in Italy were valued at 30,000 ducats; however, his widow insisted they be sold for 50,000 ducats. She finally got her way by an act signed at the Vatican on December 19, 1497. That same month, Cesare received from his father the benefices of the late Cardinal Sclafenati, estimated at 12,000 ducats.

Divorce of Lucrezia and Giovanni Sforza

Besides the matter of increasing their revenues, the pope and Cesare were still preoccupied with the aggrandizement of the Borgia family. They hoped to profit handsomely by arranging another marriage for Lucrezia. First of all, though, her union with Giovanni da Pesaro had to be dissolved. The duke of Gandia's murder gave them an opportunity to begin preliminary negotiations with the Sforza clan, and Alexander received Cardinal Ascanio five days after the assassination. He told him he absolved him of any guilt and took advantage of the interview to ask him to get Giovanni Sforza's consent to a divorce.

Giovanni refused to discuss the matter. He begged the head of his family, Ludovico il Moro, to help him, but Ludovico was reluctant to quarrel with the pope. He needed his help against Charles of France, fearing that if the French came down to Italy again he would lose his duchy to Louis d'Orléans. On the pretext of aiding Giovanni, therefore, he asked him to prove that the reason given for the divorce—the husband's impotence and the nonconsummation of the marriage—was false. He suggested that Giovanni meet Lucrezia at Nepi and sleep with her, under the supervision of members of the Borgia and Sforza clans. Cut to the quick by this malicious proposal, Giovanni rejected it: a public test of his virility could end up a complete fiasco. Ludovico then proposed that the test be done in Milan with another lady in the presence of one person, Juan Borgia; again Giovanni refused. He pointed out that he had already proved he was fit for marriage: had not his first wife, Maddalena da Gonzaga, died in childbirth? And the Gonzagas still respected him. Hearing of the pressure he was being subjected to, they had offered him the hand of another princess of their house in case his unhappy "papal marriage" was broken off.

Despairing of getting help from his Milanese relatives, Giovanni went back to Pesaro. Not only did he assert, over and over again, that his marriage had in fact been consummated, but he fought off Rome's accusations by going to the attack himself. If the pope wanted to break off his daughter's marriage it was because he wanted her for himself. Already, in Milan, Giovanni had made this outrageous accusation of incest in the presence of Ludovico il Moro. While it was almost certainly untrue, given the number of mistresses the pope could avail himself of at any time, Giovanni may not have conjured it up out of the blue. During his visits to Rome he could well have seen certain shows of affection—uncalled for, to say the least—between the pope and Lucrezia, and also between her brothers and their sister. Stung by the memory, he used it to hurt the Borgias as much as they had hurt him.

Instead of taking umbrage at such an accusation, Alexander wrote his fugitive son-in-law letters full of consideration. He offered him an honorable way out of his marriage: Giovanni would only have to claim a momentary physical deficiency caused by an evil spell. Or he could say the marriage was invalid since Lucrezia was already betrothed to Gaspare d'Aversa. For the sake of peace and quiet, Giovanni agreed to have this argument examined by members of the commission investigating the divorce proceedings. But one of them, an expert in canon law, declared he could find no lawful impediment in the previous betrothal since this had been broken off. This meant falling back on the only valid argument for annulment—nonconsummation.

The pope was furious. They had come back to the starting point of the case, while already preparations were under way in Naples for Lucrezia's second marriage. To put an end to Giovanni's resistance, Alexander promised to leave him all his daughter's considerable dowry. Ludovico Sforza urged his cousin to accept the pope's demands, threatening to withdraw his protection if Giovanni refused. This time Giovanni had no choice but to give way, and on November 18, 1497, in the Pesaro palace before several witnesses he signed the confession of his impotence and sent Ascanio Sforza, in Rome, the necessary letters for the annulment of his marriage.

The Perotto affair

Lucrezia awaited her divorce from the confines of the convent of San Sisto. For some time now—ever since the period just after Juan's murder when the pope seemed converted to a life of penitence—Alexander had stopped sending his daughter his usual affectionate messages. However, when he went back to his old ways he immediately began to take a lively interest once again in everything that concerned his daughter. The bargainings with Giovanni Sforza called for constant liaison with the convent. A young Spanish chamberlain, Pedro Caldes—nicknamed Perotto—whom Alexander trusted completely, acted as go-between for Lucrezia and her father. Visiting her almost every day, he quickly won the friendship and confidence of the seventeen-year-old Lucrezia, who was unhappy at being deprived of male company. This relationship between the boy and girl was to end in a drama that can be reconstructed as it very likely happened.

In the gardens of the convent, and in her large apartments, Lucrezia felt freer than she ever had in her life. Far from her father's overbearing protectiveness she could follow her own nature, which was joyous and pleasure-loving like all the Borgias'. Young Perotto profited from this, and with his charm made Lucrezia forget the precarious situation she was in. She was, after all, simply a hostage whose only function was to serve her family's ambitions. Perotto persuaded the girl to take advantage of her brief moment of freedom. Unfortunately, however, the young people were imprudent, and Lucrezia became pregnant. She managed to disguise her condition under her full skirts, helped by her servant Pentasilea, a young woman the pope had given her and who, so gossip had it, had been one of his mistresses. But in her sixth month she had to face a formidable test when, on December 22, 1497, she was forced to take part in the ceremonial annulment of her marriage.

A crowd of the curious flocked to the Vatican that day. Ambassadors and prelates scrutinized the pope's daughter as she stood before the canonical judges at the winding up of the case. The sentence was read out declaring her "*intacta*," in other words, a virgin. This was Giovanni Sforza's sworn testimony, and she herself confirmed it. Smilingly, Lucrezia thanked the court in Latin, arousing universal admiration. The Milanese orator, Stefano Taverno, wrote that she expressed herself "with such elegance and nobility that if she had been a Tullius or a Cicero she would not have been able to do so with more delicacy and grace." The text may have been dictated to her by her brother Cesare who was henceforth to be in charge of his sister's destiny.

The divorce had scarcely been pronounced when suitors for Lucrezia's hand stepped eagerly forward: Francesco Orsini, the duke of Gravina, who was keen to link his clan with the Borgias; Ottaviano Riario, a descendant of Pope Sixtus VI and of the Sforzas, through his mother, Caterina, countess of Forlì; and Antonello San Severino, son of the prince of Salerno, a Neapolitan nobleman who favored the king of France.

Lucrezia's marriage to a Neapolitan would have superbly served the purposes of the cardinal of Valencia, whose designs on the kingdom of Naples were an open secret. Everyone knew that he wanted to abandon his ecclesiastical career and marry a Neapolitan princess. There was talk that he might wed Sancia of Aragon if Jofré gave her up in exchange for a cardinal's hat. But Sancia was illegitimate, and at this time Cesare no doubt would rather have had King Federigo's legitimate daughter, Carlotta, who was reared in France at the court of Anne of Brittany. Lucrezia could clear the way for her brother's marriage if she herself took a prince of Naples as a husband. During his trips to Naples Cesare had got to know and like Sancia's brother, Alfonso of Aragon, who was not only one of the handsomest princes of the day but known for his gentle character and fine manners. Cesare thus chose Alfonso for his sister, and negotiations were soon off at a fast clip. The king of Naples proposed to give Alfonso the title of duke of Bisceglie with a large revenue, while Lucrezia would bring with her a dowry of 40,000 ducats—larger than the one her former husband was left with—and, to live in, the Roman palace of Sta. Maria in Portico.

While the negotiations were going on, Cesare found out about his sister's pregnancy and her affair with Perotto. His fury can be easily imagined. The Venetian envoy, Capello, described the drama that was played out at the Vatican at the time. One month after Lucrezia's marriage had been annulled, Cesare made a run at Perotto, his sword at the ready, and chased him all the way up to the pontifical throne where the pope sat in state. There, under the pope's nose—he was wrapping his chamberlain in the folds of his cape, as if to protect him—the cardinal of Valencia struck the young Spaniard savagely so that "the blood spurted onto the pope's face." Though not mortally wounded, Perotto, in prison, hardly had time to languish on his straw. During the night of February 8, writes Burckard, "he fell into the Tiber against his will." Six days later his body was fished out—at the same time, according to the Venetian Sanudo, as that of Lucrezia's servant, Pentasilea. These murders, which wagging tongues immediately attributed to Cesare, could not erase the scandal, and the news of Lucrezia's pregnancy buzzed from one Italian court to the next. Cristoforo Poggio, the secretary of Bentivoglio, the tyrant of Bologna, wrote to the marquess of Mantua informing him that Perotto had been imprisoned "for having made His Holiness's daughter, Lucrezia, pregnant."

Not long after that, a dispatch was sent from an agent of the duke of Este residing in Venice—where echoes from all over the world were continually received—mentioning the birth of an illegitimate child to Lucrezia. An anonymous announcement from Rome also referred to it: "It is reported that the pope's daughter has given birth to a child." Hardly any news, however, leaked out of the Vatican, where Lucrezia had fled. The Borgia family huddled around their head, giving no hint of any emotion. After Perotto's body had been found in the Tiber, the Borgia cardinals had left Rome, wearing hunting costume in the French style, for Ostia, where they had a few days' relaxation. They presented to the world a front of perfect calm, quite unaffected by the surge in violence that was encouraged by the mysterious acts of revenge at the Vatican. As a preventive measure the pope decided to ban masquerades at Carnival time, since disguises encouraged assassinations.

Papal incest
The mystery of the "infans Romanus"

Lucrezia savored the joys of motherhood in secret. There was no mention of the mysterious infant until three years later, when he was legitimized by Alexander just before Lucrezia left for Ferrara. Two bulls had to be drawn up for the purpose. In the first bull, the only one made public, the pope legitimized the child, who was called Giovanni, the "infans Romanus," and acknowledged that he was the offspring of Cesare and an unmarried woman. The use of Cesare's name allowed Alexander to get around the canonical law prohibiting him from recognizing a bastard born during his pontificate. However, it did not ensure that Giovanni would inherit the duchy of Nepi, which the pope had granted him. The second bull, which was secret, therefore acknowledged that the child was in fact the son of the pope himself. The duchy of Nepi thus became as incontestable a property as those the pope bestowed on Cesare, Lucrezia herself and, later, on her legitimate son Rodrigo, the offspring of her union with the duke of Bisceglie.

This acknowledgment of papal paternity had another effect: Cesare, whom Alexander mistrusted, would have no way of getting hold of the young child's lands. True, each of the bulls did postulate, on papal authority, a false relationship, yet it would have been impossible to legitimize a bastard of Lucrezia's. Later, the pope, his daughter, and Cesare would all three fall victim to this excessive caution, for when the two bulls came to light, people deduced that the "infans Romanus" was the son of either Cesare and Lucrezia or of Lucrezia and the pope, although there was no mention anywhere that Lucrezia was the child's mother.

From that time on, Giovanni Sforza's accusation of paternal incest was more and more widely heard, together with that of fraternal incest. The humanist Sannazar wrote an outrageous epigram against Lucrezia, in the form of a Latin epitaph:

> *Hoc tumulo dormit Lucretia nomine, sed re*
> *Thais, Alexandri filia, sponsa, nurus.*

> *Here lies Lucrezia, who was really a Thais,*
> *The daughter, wife, and daughter-in-law of Alexander.*

This charge of double incest, echoed gleefully by contemporary poets and anti-Borgia chroniclers as well as the Romantic poets, would be taken up again in the twentieth century by a writer, Giuseppe Portigliotti, who suggested that Lucrezia had insisted the two bulls be drawn up because she did not know which of her two lovers, her father or her brother, had fathered the child.

On the other hand, some historians would refuse to accept that Lucrezia was the *mulier soluta,* or unmarried woman, referred to in the bull as being the child's mother. They point out that when Alfonso d'Este welcomed young Giovanni Borgia to the Ferrara court, together with Lucrezia, he treated the child as his wife's brother, truly the son of the pope and an unknown woman. But this behavior only showed how prudent Alfonso was, how eager to save appearances. The Ferrara family was quite used to a mingling of legitimate and illegitimate children in its midst. As soon as a papal document came out attesting the origin of the "infans Romanus," appearances were saved and Lucrezia was free to keep her child with her under the pretense that he was her brother.

The child's birth did nothing to hamper the negotiations Alexander and Cesare were working out with Naples about Lucrezia's marriage to Prince Alfonso. Federigo particularly liked the idea at this time because, with the pope's help, he had just crushed his enemies, the San Severino barons, celebrating his victory by making a triumphal entry into his capital. For Alexander, a strong alliance with the House of Aragon in Naples was becoming more and more indicated. His policy was aimed at making it impossible for the French to come down to Italy—one of the reasons he hoped to have Savonarola destroyed in Florence, the Dominican preacher being Louis's staunchest partisan in all Tuscany.

The last episode in the battle against Savonarola
The prophet is put to death

Savonarola's letter consoling the pope over the loss of his son had soothed Alexander's anger for a while. But once the penitential period was over, the pope sent the Signoria of Florence new and draconian conditions that had to be met before the brief excommunicating Savonarola could be revoked. The prior of San Marco must vindicate himself in Rome, or else agree to join the Tuscan-Roman congregation as a simple monk. The ultimatum reached Florence just when the plague was raging through the city, causing many deaths. The Medici partisans took advantage of the chaos to stir up a plot. It was thwarted at the last minute and five of the conspirators were sentenced to death as an example. In this climate of civic disorder, Savonarola resolved not to add to his fellow citizens' woes by remaining obdurate and on October 13 gave in and beseeched the pope to pardon him:

"As a son, grieved by his father's anger, seeks every way to placate him and does not despair of his father's compassion, I, more afflicted at the loss of Your Holiness's good graces than at any other misfortune, unceasingly throw myself at Your Holiness's feet, begging that in the end my cry will be heard and that you will no longer suffer that I should be torn from the bosom of Holy Church."

This submission did not satisfy Alexander, who was determined to turn it to his political advantage. Before absolving Savonarola of his sin of rebellion he insisted that Florence should join the anti-France league of Venice and Rome, and so ward off the threat of another French invasion.

Aware of the stakes of the bargain, which was at the expense of the French king to whom he was still faithful, Savonarola once more brandished the sword of rebellion. He took to his pulpit again in February 1498, oblivious of canonical censure, ready to engage in a battle he hoped would be decisive. Beneath the vaults of the Duomo he solemnly called upon Jesus Christ to choose between him and the pontiff. Most of the Signoria members supported their preacher and rejected Rome's conditions. Savonarola encouraged his fellow citizens:

"The briefs from Rome call me 'the son of perdition.' O my lords, write to them this: 'He whom you call thus says that he keeps no concubines nor boys for pleasure, but devotes himself to preaching the faith of Christ, while you seek to ruin it!' "

Again he went to the attack, this time from the pulpit of the convent of San Marco. Lost in the throng was Niccolò Machiavelli, who had come out of curiosity and, for the time being, was skeptical about the outcome of the battle with the Borgia pope. In fact, in Rome at the pope's orders a preacher called Mariano de Genazzano was preparing a harsh indictment, calling Savonarola a "great drunken Jew." The pope dictated a brief laying Florence under an interdict. At the news, Savonarola wrote to all the princes of Europe asking them to convoke a council to depose the infamous pope. Retribution was swift. Alexander made his brief immediately enforceable, and solemnly promulgated the interdict. He then had the Florentine merchants living in Rome arrested and their goods seized—shrewd measures that turned the city's traders against the friar.

At the Signoria, Savonarola's enemies were gaining the upper hand. Quarrels broke out between Franciscans and Dominicans, the former siding fervently with Alexander. The friar Francesco di Puglia announced that he was ready to undergo the ordeal by fire to show that God rejected Savonarola's austere doctrines. Domenico da Pescia took up the challenge. Savonarola's enemies saw at once that this monks' dispute gave them an unhoped-for chance to get rid of Fra Girolamo.

The majority of the Signoria members agreed that the ordeal by fire should take place on April 7. The two champions, Domenico, representing Savonarola, and Giuliano Rondinelli, for the Franciscans, were to face each other on a great raised platform 90 feet long by 16 feet wide, erected on the Piazza della Signoria. Fagots of dry wood impregnated with oil, resin, and cannon powder were laid along the platform, leaving a narrow pathway barely 2 feet wide down the middle. The two monks were to enter the pathway at the same time from opposite ends, after the fagots had been set alight. Lengthy discussions about procedure delayed the start of the test. Then just when the fire was about to be lit, a providential rainstorm stopped the barbaric ceremony from proceeding.

Savonarola withdrew to San Marco with his monks. The next day, Palm Sunday, a mob attacked the convent. The Signoria let them have their way, arresting Savonarola for having thrown the city into disorder. Domenico and another monk, Silvestro, who was Savonarola's confessor, were clapped into prison with him, interrogated, and tortured. His muscles ripped by the strappado and his left arm broken, Savonarola signed what was required of him. Even though canon law did not allow anyone to try clerics without papal authorization, the pope sent Florence a congratulatory bull together with a plenary indulgence. He had just learned of the death of Charles VIII, who had long been Savonarola's protector. This meant Alexander was free to wreak his revenge on the Dominican. He ordered Savonarola to be tried in ecclesiastical court, after a civil trial, delegating as papal representatives the general of the Dominicans and the governor of Rome, both men well experienced in legal quibbling.

On May 20 the judges began their interrogations by once again torturing the monk, on their master's orders. They wanted to find out the names of the cardinals and dignitaries who had encouraged Savonarola to ask the Christian rulers to depose the pope. Seeing they were getting nowhere, they forced him to recant his prophecies. Savonarola and his companions were given one and the same sentence: they must be dismissed from their order and handed over as heretics and schismatics to the secular authorities, who had already condemned them to death.

To the anguish of their followers, the three Dominicans were led to the gallows. Their last moments were full of pathos. In front of the Signoria palace, Bishop Benedetto Pagnotti, a former monk of San Marco, denounced Savonarola with the words, "I separate you from the Church militant and the Church triumphant." This Savonarola gently corrected: "From the militant only; the other is not in your competence." Death by hanging was carried out on the three monks at ten o'clock in the morning on May 23, 1498, the eve of Ascension. The great and terrible prophet had disappeared from the pope's path at the same time as the worrisome Charles of France. From now on, the Borgias could expand their power unopposed. Without further ado, Alexander decided to seal, with due pomp and ceremony, the union of his family and the Neapolitan dynasty by marrying his daughter to Alfonso of Aragon.

Lucrezia's marriage to Alfonso of Aragon

To avoid any legal misstep in Lucrezia's new marriage, the pope annulled her previous betrothal to Gaspare d'Aversa, which was in fact still unbroken despite her union with Giovanni Sforza. Solemnly, Alexander announced that his daughter had got engaged "hastily, under the influence of a passing aberration." On June 10, 1498, she was freed and absolved of her perjury.

Alfonso of Aragon wed Lucrezia in a proxy marriage on June 29, in Naples. Next month he arrived in Rome, which put on a magnificent show of welcome for the handsome seventeen-year-old prince, and on July 21 the wedding took place, with cardinals Ascanio Sforza, Juan Borgia the younger, and Juan Lopez acting as witnesses. The Spanish captain of the papal guard, Juan Cervillon, held his unsheathed sword high over the young people's heads during the ceremony.

Next day, a joyous family gathering was held in the papal palace. Alexander was in superb form, and the banquet, which was as grand as at Lucrezia's first marriage, went on until daybreak. The beginning of the party had been spoiled somewhat by a quarrel between Cesare's entourage and Sancia's. Two bishops were knocked about, and for a moment the pope was surrounded by drawn swords. With that out of the way the entertainment, consisting of plays and masquerades, could resume. Cesare turned up disguised as a unicorn, the symbol of chastity and loyalty.

The young couple's happiness was plain for all to see. Besides her jewels, Lucrezia had received her promised dowry of 40,000 ducats, while Alfonso brought with him the Bisceglie principality and the city of Quadrata (the modern Corato). With obvious impatience, the lovers retired to the palace of Sta. Maria in Portico.

Cesare, however, was champing at the bit: his father had promised him a princely position, which was still out of his reach. Even though his son was still a cardinal, Alexander was eager to marry him to the king of Naples's legitimate daughter, Carlotta, who everyone knew would bring the wealthy city of Tarento with her as a dowry. Cesare therefore agreed to renounce his holy orders to ease the negotiations.

Cesare Borgia becomes a prince of the world

The day after the wedding celebrations, Alexander summoned the cardinals, who had fled the torrid city, back to Rome. Calling a consistory, he invited his son to take the floor. Cesare explained to his colleagues that he had never had a religious vocation, having been forced by his father into an ecclesiastical career. However, he now wished to give up his titles and marry, that being his true vocation. The cardinals agreed on the spot. Since Cesare had received only minor orders it was a simple matter to make him a layman once more.

The Spanish ambassador, Garcilasso de la Vega, who was present at the meeting, protested in no uncertain terms. He condemned the debatable process by which a cardinal could become a prince on French soil: he had learned that Cesare nursed the ambition to serve the new king of France, Louis XII, a potential enemy of the Spanish throne. But Alexander was unmoved. He replied that it was solely for the good of his soul that his son was renouncing his ecclesiastical calling. The cardinal of Valencia's amorous temperament and worldliness were causing a universal scandal. Secularization would allow him to live a layman's life without running the risk of breaking his vows, and thus he would be able to save his soul. The pope also pointed out to the ambassador that his masters stood to profit from Cesare's resignation. Several Spanish benefices, worth more than 35,000 ducats, would fall vacant and go to dependents of the Catholic Kings. The argument won the day, and the ambassador immediately gave in.

Next came the secularization ceremony. The pope released Cesare from his vows and authorized him to marry. Cesare laid down his great cardinal's cloak before the consistory and strode proudly out of the room, head high, already the conquering secular prince. That same day he was to meet an important nobleman who was entering Rome with a show of pomp by the Porta Portese. This was the French king's chamberlain, Louis de Villeneuve, baron of Trans, who had arrived in his master's name to invite Cesare Borgia to France. As a welcoming gift he brought the former cardinal of Valencia in Spain the county of Valence, in France, as well as two other fiefs, Die and Issoudun. These gifts not only made up for the loss of his ecclesiastical titles, but would allow Cesare to live in the brilliant style he craved and at the same time, with the fief of Valence, keep the name of the corner of Spain that had brought his father and great-uncle their fortunes.

All the time spent in calculation and vengeance apparently had paid off. They had surmounted obstacles, provoked and weathered terrible storms. Now the Borgias were armed and ready to face the hazards of fate in their march toward a royal dynastic future.

CHAPTER

4

The Advent of Cesare

The question of Cesare's marriage

Key to Alexander's policy was the alliance between Rome and the Naples House of Aragon, begun with the union of Jofré and Sancia and now cemented by Lucrezia's marriage to Alfonso. The policy should logically have been crowned by the marriage of Cesare to Carlotta, princess of Taranto, but Federigo had other ambitions for his daughter. Unlike Sancia and Alfonso, she was not born out of wedlock: her mother was a princess of Savoie, and she had been raised at the French court among Queen Anne of Brittany's maids-in-waiting. Her objections on hearing that the pope proposed to marry her to his bastard son were as loud as her father's—she had no desire to be known as "Signora Cardinale."

When Rome had first broached the matter, Federigo suggested that the pope change the canonical rules and allow the cardinal of Valencia to marry. This was a polite way of declining the pope's offer, but Alexander could not take no for an answer. He arranged for the Sforzas, who had become Federigo's best friends, to intervene with him. In early summer of 1498, Cardinal Ascanio went to Naples and announced that the pope was about to strip his son of his cardinal's robes, but the king still did not give in. He confided to Gonsalvo de Cordoba, the renowned army captain, that he would rather lose his kingdom or his life than consent to the marriage.

Encouraging Federigo in this attitude were the troubles now rocking the Papal States. For some months now the Roman Campagna had seen violent struggles pitting the Orsini barons and their allies the

Contis against the Colonnas. The fighting was over the possession of Tagliocozzo. In April the Orsinis had been routed at Palombara, whereupon the Colonnas had savagely seized their rivals' castles. The pope and Cesare had taken good care not to try to make peace between the two sides, since it was in their interest to bring down the great landowners.

Federigo of Naples, on the other hand, had offered to act as arbiter of the dispute, and in July, thanks to his intervention, the fighting ended and the two clans were reconciled. Not long after that a lampoon was found stuck on the entrance to the Vatican Library inviting the former rivals to "kill the bull ravaging Ausonia" and, while he descended into hell, drown his children in the Tiber. The pope suspected Federigo of having had a hand in the manifesto; yet instead of breaking off relations he tried even harder to force his son on the king. Since the princess of Naples had been brought up at the French court, he now sought an ally in the new king of France, Louis XII.

Alliance with Louis XII
The king's marriage annulled

As soon as he came to the throne on Charles's death, in April 1498, Louis had got in touch with the pope. He told Alexander that he claimed not only the Milanese, the fief of his Visconti forbears, but also the kingdom of Naples, which he had inherited from his predecessor. He needed Alexander's help to win back his Italian lands; he also relied on him to have his marriage to Jeanne of France, Louis XI's deformed daughter, annulled and to get the necessary dispensation so that he could marry Charles's widow, Anne of Brittany, without delay. In return he promised Alexander he would do what he could to promote Cesare's marriage to the princess.

His interest piqued by this overture, the pope sent an embassy to France made up of several trusted advisers: Archbishop Giovanni da Ragusa, the secretary Antonio Flores, and Ramon Centelles, the treasurer of Perugia. Officially, they were being asked to remind Louis of his duties as Most Christian King—to lead the Crusade against the Infidel and establish peace throughout Christendom. But during their secret audience they revealed the pope's intentions. Alexander had not wanted to join the anti-France league that Maximilian had tried to form in May, with Naples and Milan as chief partners. Quite the contrary, he planned to ally himself with Louis through a treaty similar to those France was just then negotiating with the king of England and the Archduke Philip, heir to Flanders and the Franche-Comté. The alliance would be sealed by Louis's divorce of Jeanne and Cesare's promised marriage to Carlotta. A new policy was being shaped, one in which Alexander had high hopes of using the king of France as a secular arm entirely at his disposal.

In July a skilled negotiator left Rome, the Portuguese Fernando de Almeida, bishop of Ceuta. Aided by a member of the French embassy in Rome, the apostolic protonotary Guillaume, he drew up a plan for the treaty. Louis XII would promise to marry the cardinal of Valencia to Federigo of Naples's elder daughter. To ensure Cesare a suitable style of living, he would give him not only the counties of Valence and Die in the Dauphiné, but other fiefs if these did not produce a revenue of more than 20,000 pounds. Valence would be made a duchy so that Cesare's title would not be inferior to his brother's and sister's. The pope's son would receive a company of 100 regimental lancers, to be increased to 200 or even 300 when the king went to Italy, and would be invested with the Order of St. Michael. As soon as Louis reached Milan he would grant him the county of Asti. Finally, as Cesare's stay in France left the pope without a protector, Alexander would receive a monthly allowance of 4,000 ducats to pay for a special guard responsible for his safety. Alexander found these terms perfectly satisfactory and accepted them, whereupon Louis ordered the baron of Trans to leave Provence with six galleys and other ships and seek out Cesare in Italy.

At the same time he was carving out the principality he wanted to bestow on the pope's son. Cesare was to receive the counties of Valence and Die together with the castellany of Issoudon in Berry, with its salt depot, the whole amounting to 20,000 pounds in revenues. The Italian princes saw this liberality as proof of a secret agreement between the French crown and the Borgias. Ludovico Sforza fully expected to suffer from it, and the king of Naples was hardly reassured. Fortunately for them, however, Louis was then immobilized in France trying to settle the tricky matter of his matrimonial situation.

According to the marriage contract between Charles VIII and Anne of Brittany, the duchess-queen could, if widowed, marry her husband's successor. This meant that Louis had to be released from his marriage bonds to Jeanne. Under canon law, the pope set up a tribunal to look into the annulment process. The judges were to go to France to hear the various parties.

The experts Alexander appointed were the bishop of Ceuta and the bishop of Albi, Louis d'Amboise. They were later joined by Cardinal Philippe of Luxembourg, the bishop of Le Mans. Long sessions were held first at Tours, then at Amboise in the Loire Valley. Among the arguments for annulment, the tribunal did not accept the "natural kinship to the fourth degree" between Louis and Jeanne, nor the "spiritual relationship" resulting from the fact that Louis XI, Jeanne's father, had been Louis XII's godfather. These impediments had been removed by a bull of Sixtus IV. The clinching argument was non-consummation. The royal proxy alleged Jeanne's deformity, and in December, prodded by the pope, Louis swore that he had never had carnal knowledge of his wife. The trial was almost at an end. The sentence of annulment was pronounced on December 17 in the Church of St.-Denis at Amboise. Jeanne was made duchess of Berry, withdrew to a convent, and founded the Order of the Annunciation, while Louis hastened to prepare for his marriage to Anne. It was then that Cesare Borgia burst on the scene, bringing to France the indispensable bull authorizing the royal union.

Cesare's voyage

For three months now the pope's son had been showing off his love of luxury as he made a sort of royal progress through France. His father had given him the means, with the money streaming in from a wide variety of sources. Alexander had been dipping into the possessions of deceased prelates of the Roman court, as was his right. For example, when Cardinal Campofregoso died, in May 1498, he had an inventory made of his silverware and furniture. Even more expedient was to take money from the living, and for this the Jewish moneylenders were first choice.

The aged bishop of Calahorra, a converted Jew previously known as Alfonso Solares, was baptized Pedro de Aranda. Alexander made him majordomo, or head of his household. The post, however, was not enough to protect him. In April 1498 he and his illegitimate son were arrested in the Vatican and accused of living as Marranos—that is, of practicing the Jewish religion in secret. Aranda's considerable fortune—20,000 ducats—was confiscated in its entirety, and he himself was dismissed and later clapped into the Castel Sant'Angelo. Here he met his death when the ceiling of his cell collapsed.

Jews expelled from Spain who had settled near the Tomb of Cecilia Metella, on the outskirts of the city, had to pay a special fine. Through denunciations and raids, 230 were rounded up, suspected because of their Spanish origins of being crypto-Christians. They were forced to do penitence in the Roman churches and walk in a candle-lit procession wearing red-and-purple robes marked with the cross to receive their pardon, not without paying substantial fines.

That summer the pope made illicit profits everywhere, from the wheat he had stockpiled, to the church benefices he meted out in exchange for money. He also got rid of the benefices Cesare had to give up when he abandoned the cardinal's habit. Everything was sold except the see of Valencia, which was conferred on Alexander's nephew, Juan de Borgia Lanzol. Two abbeys, with a revenue of 4,000 ducats, were offered to Cardinal Ascanio Sforza for a payment of 10,000 ducats.

Not surprisingly, these deals brought in a tidy sum, which went to swell Cesare's coffers. In the end he was able to take with him to France a treasury of 200,000 ducats and a fat wad of papal bulls— one of which was the dispensation Louis needed to marry his cousin's widow. Attached to it were two briefs recommending the pope's son to the king and his future queen, in which Alexander called Cesare "our beloved son, the duke of Valentinois, the one dearest to our heart in all the world, the most precious gage of the eternal bond of mutual love that unites us." Another bull gave Georges d'Amboise, the king's favorite, the cardinal's hat. A brief intended for the king's eyes said that Alexander was postponing making Amboise a papal legate.

In October, young Roman nobles, including Giangiordano Orsini, escorted the duke of Valentinois with glittering pageantry out of the gates of Rome. The hero of this pomp, resplendent with the virile good looks of his twenty-three years, had the bearing of a prince. The Mantuan envoy wrote that he wore a doublet of white damask with gold edgings, a black-velvet cloak "in the French style," and had a dashing white plume in his black-velvet cap, which sparkled with rubies. The black and white of his costume showed off his elegant pale face with its frame of auburn hair and neatly trimmed beard. Cesare's horse, which, like his companions', came from the famous Gonzaga stables in Mantua, was caparisoned in red silk and gold brocade. The bit, rings, stirrups—even, it was said, the horseshoes—were of solid silver. Following in the duke's train were 100 servants, pages, squires, armed attendants, and musicians.

Among his colorful staff were his majordomo, Ramiro de Lorca, his physician, Gaspare Torrella, and his faithful secretary, Agapito Gherardi. Men and horses boarded the vessels, and the fleet set sail from Civitavecchia in early October, arriving at Marseille. At the port Cesare was met by the archbishop of Aix and the leading nobles of Provence, together with 400 horsemen, whom Louis had ordered to give him a royal welcome.

The procession reached Avignon two weeks later, where the cardinal-legate, Giuliano della Rovere, welcomed Cesare. For over a year Giuliano had been reconciled with Alexander, the agreement being that when the cardinal returned to Italy the pope would give him back his lands—even the fortress of Ostia—in exchange for a payment of 12,000 ducats for strengthening the fortifications. Giuliano's brother, Giovanni, would again be governor of Rome, with all the privileges that entailed, and would even be allowed to keep Prince Djem's 40,000-ducat allowance, which he had appropriated three years before.

So Giuliano was all smiles as he greeted the pope's son. Writing to Alexander shortly afterward, he was unstinting in his compliments of Cesare: "I do not want to hide from Your Holiness," he said, "that the duke of Valentinois is so filled with modesty, prudence, and skill, and endowed with so many physical and moral virtues that he has captured everyone's fancy. He is in high favor at court and with the king. Everybody loves him and esteems him, and it gives me every satisfaction to be able to inform you so."

Whatever the truth of the matter, Giuliano spared neither effort nor money on Cesare's visit, forking out 7,000 ducats in gifts of silverware, in banquets, parades, and entertainment. Cesare, however, preferred to cut these festivites short, as he had just heard from Louis that his lands were being made into the duchy of Valentinois. He decided to visit his fief, even though his appearance just then was not at its best, his face having broken out in the unsightly pustules of the "French evil." In Valence, his new duchy's capital, his subjects were eager to honor him at the royal castle but, ever prudent, Cesare declined on the pretext that the letters patent concerning his duchy had not yet been registered at the Grenoble Parliament. Cesare's excessive caution even made him refuse the ribbon of the Order of St. Michael, which the royal envoy presented to him: he would only accept it from the king's own hands. This attitude, which the envoy found wounding, earned Cesare a reputation for arrogance and insolence that dogged him throughout his French trip.

From Valence the duke went on to Lyon. Here the city dignitaries served a gargantuan banquet: dishes of beef, veal, and lamb, including the highly prized tongue, were served, followed by partridge, duck, woodcock, thrushes, peacocks, and pheasants; then, after many kinds of pâté, came tarts, almond-flavored "darioles," orange cakes, sweetmeats flavored with rare spices, and exotic fruits—grapes from Corinth, dates, and pomegranates. Alternating with these feasts and receptions were entertainments like mystery plays, farces, and masked ballets.

After Lyon, Cesare continued his progress up to the Loire Valley. The French court was then ensconced in the Castle of Chinon, while Louis waited for his family home at Blois to be made into a royal palace. The pope's son was not in a hurry to join him. Louis had not yet found him a wife, and besides, the legal procedure annulling the king's marriage was not yet completed. Until it was, there was no point in handing over the dispensation. No sooner was the ink dry on the annulment parchment, however, than Cesare quickened his pace, and on December 17, the day that judgment was pronounced in Amboise, he halted at the gates of Chinon.

His arrival caused a social flutter as problems of etiquette and precedence were anxiously debated. What exactly was the rank and status of this former cardinal, the illegitimate son of a pope? The king's counselors hit on an imaginative solution: Cesare would meet Louis as though by chance, on the excuse of going hunting. This way the king could greet him as an equal, then let him make his entry into Chinon alone. The two men met according to plan, with Cesare leaving for the town after a brief interview.

At the head of the Chinon bridge were Georges d'Amboise, soon to receive his cardinal's hat from Cesare's hands, Philippe de Clèves, the lord of Ravestain, and other notables. Cesare's retinue slowly filed past the amazed townsfolk, who counted seventy mules laden with baggage. Some of them carried traveling chests painted with the duke's coat of arms, others had trappings of striped yellow satin, while the rest were draped with gold brocade. As the animals wound their way up to the castle, sixteen magnificent chargers draped in red and yellow brocade appeared on the bridge, led by squires. Behind them rode nearly a score of pages, most of whom wore crimson velvet while two were dressed in cloth of gold (gossip had it these two were the duke's favorites). Six mules with red-velvet trappings came next, followed by two more covered with brocade and with chests strapped on their backs—no doubt, the crowd fancied, these two were bringing something richer and rarer than the others, perhaps rich jewels for the duke's mistress and other ladies, or bulls and indulgences from Rome, or else some holy relics. After them came the duke's thirty gentlemen, wearing gold and silver brocade, followed by a group of twenty-four footmen in crimson velvet slashed with yellow silk. Bringing up the rear were the musicians—two drummers and a rebec player, dressed in gold brocade, and four trumpet players playing silver trumpets.

All this was a prelude to the arrival of the duke. He appeared astride a magnificent dappled gray charger caparisoned with red satin and gold brocade. At his side rode Cardinal d'Amboise. All the onlookers admired the duke's noble bearing as well as the gorgeous rubies in his biretta, his embroidered suit sparkling with jewels, the workmanship of his pearl-encrusted boots with their edgings of gold. His collar was valued at 30,000 ducats; his horse's harness, studded with gold and pearls, was also worth a fortune. Behind the charger trotted a little mule the duke would use to go about the town. Its harness was covered with tiny gold roses. At the end of the procession came twenty-four pack mules and a dozen wagons bearing the duke's furnishings and silver and gold tableware.

The king surveyed the scene from one of the chateau windows. "There is little doubt that he and his courtiers laughed at such a grand display for the petty duke of Valence," wrote the chronicler Brantôme.

But Louis had no desire to antagonize the man who was bringing him his much-desired papal dispensation. He waited for Cesare in the great hall, together with the chief nobles of the court and Giuliano della Rovere. At the entrance the duke bowed low before his new sovereign, then bowed again on reaching the middle of the hall. Louis acknowledged this homage by uncovering his head. Then, bending down close to the king, Cesare attempted to kiss his feet, following the Vatican ritual, but Louis stopped him short. He would only let him kiss his hands, thus saving him from the gibes of the French courtiers, who were only too ready to poke fun at the "vain-glory and foolish bombast" of the duke of Valence. After a brief audience, Cardinal d'Amboise conducted the pope's son to his apartments, where Louis joined him, impatient to get his hands on the dispensation. Not long afterward, Georges d'Amboise received his cardinal's hat and

Louis made ready to go to Nantes, where the wedding was soon to take place.

A good match: Charlotte d'Albret

Now that Alexander had fulfilled his part of the contract, it was up to Louis to do the same with his and arrange a marriage for Cesare. At a banquet he arranged for the duke to sit opposite Carlotta of Aragon, but it was a waste of effort. The king of Naples's daughter, who rumor had it was in love with someone else, hardly glanced at her suitor.

Next, Louis tried to interest his own niece, the daughter of Jean de Foix, but the young woman refused. Alexander, meanwhile, was driven to despair at the thought that his son would soon be the laughingstock of all Europe. Fortunately a suitable match was at hand: Alain d'Albret, called the Great, offered the hand of his daughter Charlotte. He was a man of distinction: the duke of Guyenne, count of Gaure and of Castres, while his wife, Françoise of Brittany, was a relative of Anne of Brittany and countess of Périgord, viscountess of Limoges, and lady of Avesnes. The eldest of their eight children, Jean, had been king of Navarre since 1494. As for the girl herself, she was both beautiful and intelligent, was one of the queen's ladies-in-waiting, and had been brought up at court.

Louis left his envoy to negotiate the marriage with Alain d'Albret. The negotiations were difficult and drawn out and d'Albret proved to be demanding and greedy, but finally the act of betrothal was drawn up. Ten days later the girl's father showed the document to the king. He also insisted on "seeing and touching" the papal dispensation that relieved Cesare of his vows, for he had no desire to give his daughter away to a priest who was a priest's son.

Alain d'Albret was to give Charlotte a dowry of 30,000 pounds—6,000 were to be paid at the wedding ceremony, 1,500 a year thereafter until full payment was met. Charlotte, however, would have to give up her rights to succeed her father and mother. The couple's furniture and acquests would accrue to the community. If Cesare died, his wife would receive a lifelong income of 4,000 pounds and would choose any one of Cesare's castles to live in. Having promised Cesare 100,000 pounds to augment the dowry, d'Albret asked for the money to be paid in ducats. He also demanded that his proxies ensure that the chattels Cesare held in France were actually worth 120,000 ducats, as the pope's son claimed, but this last request was rejected as excessive. Nonetheless, the king, who wanted to be done with the contract, offered the personal guaranty of the chief treasurers of France, to ensure that the 100,000 pounds were paid. He promised that d'Albret would receive the full sum within eighteen months, and Cesare himself paid half the sum in advance. In recompense, Cesare would collect the revenues of the royal seat of Issoudun and be able to sell off the salt depots there—two privileges the king had retained and which were now added to the other rights Cesare had been given. To smooth the marriage negotiations, Cesare agreed that his wife would have title to his duchy. He would also use his influence with the pope to get a cardinal's hat for one of Charlotte's brothers, Amanieu d'Albret.

At the castle of Blois, both parties signed the contract in the presence of the king, Queen Anne, Cardinal d'Amboise, and the chief nobles of the court. Cesare had as witnesses his faithful servants Agapito Gherardi and Ramiro de Lorca. Since the ultimate goal of this marriage was to ensure that the king receive the pope's help in the coming Italian wars, Louis had a clause added to the effect that the duke, together with his relations, friends, and allies, would aid him in the conquest of Naples and the duchy of Milan; in return he promised the Vatican the assistance of the royal armies if the pope requested.

On May 12 the marriage was duly solemnized and consummated. Cesare gave his father a detailed account of his wedding night in a letter, written in Spanish, where he boasted of having made "eight trips." That the claim was more than fatuous is suggested by an echo of the gossip at the French court contained in the *Memoirs* of Robert de la Marck. According to the book Cesare had asked an apothecary to make up an aphrodisiac. Whether out of mischief or by mistake, the man gave him laxative pills, "so that all night he kept going to the closet, as the ladies reported next morning."

True or not, the young bride was blissfully happy. The day after the wedding she wrote her father-in-law a charming, very respectful letter telling him that she longed to visit him at the Vatican and was delighted with her husband. King Louis, pleased at having brought about the union, also wrote the pope, congratulating him on the fact that his son's prowess was double his own. With Anne of Brittany he had "broken four lances" whereas Cesare's score was eight, two before dinner and six during the night. As a reward for his valor, Anne presented Cesare with a horse and a ring worth 400 ducats which she wanted him to wear "for her sake." For his part, Louis sent the pope

100 hogsheads of Burgundy, and at the feast of Pentecost finally conferred on Cesare the Order of St. Michael.

The French again swoop down on Italy

To celebrate the consummation of his son's marriage, Alexander ordered a huge fireworks display in the Holy City—much to the disgust of Burckard, who thought it a "disgrace and a shame to His Holiness and the Holy See." Yet these public rejoicings were intended as a clear sign, for all to see, of a political volte-face. They proclaimed that the papacy was holding to the alliance France and Venice had struck two months ago against Ludovico Sforza.

Cesare was the French king's privileged ally. As he waited till the time came to leave Italy with Louis's forces, he led a life of luxury, spending in one month all the money he had brought from Rome. Alexander had to come to the rescue, sending him 18,000, then 22,000, and finally 10,000 ducats. Cesare journeyed to his domain at Issoudun to collect some revenues, but fell ill there. As soon as he recovered he had to go back again to the French court, which was then at Romorantin, where the king had come to bid farewell to Queen Anne. Here Cesare was reunited with Charlotte for the last time. He left his young wife pregnant, but he would never see her again nor set eyes on the baby, Louise—his only legitimate child.

In the meantime, Ludovico Sforza had intercepted mail between Rome and France, and was perfectly aware of the plot being concocted against him. The pope had unmasked himself and from now on would miss no opportunity to savage Ludovico in his public utterances. On hearing that little Francesco, Ludovico's son, had bad eyes, the pope expressed glee and declared that it would be a good thing if the house of Sforza were utterly destroyed. This was too much for Cardinal Ascanio Sforza. One night in mid-July he fled Rome, reaching Milan some ten days later and was at his brother's side when the French and Venetian armies attacked.

Alexander's switch to the French side revolted France's enemies. Spain and Portugal sent envoys to Rome who decried the reversal and complained that the pope was more concerned with advancing his children than with the fate of the Church. But it was like water off a duck's back. Alexander's answer was not without a certain humor. He took Benevente away from his Spanish grandson, Juan of Gandia's orphan, and once again linked this fief to the Holy See.

His happiness, when news of the impending French invasion reached his ears, was plain for all to see. The French army—12,000 to 13,000 horse, 17,000 French and Swiss footsoldiers, and one formidable artillery park—was encamped at Asti from May to July 1499. First-class warriors constituted the still-inexperienced Cesare's staff. Venice had promised to go into action with its heavy cavalry and 4,000 Swiss, Italian, and Spanish mercenaries. Confronted with this coalition, Ludovico il Moro had no coherent force of his own and could not afford to raise mercenaries. Thus Louis calculated that the campaign against Milan would be a walkover, lasting at most two to three months.

Disgrace of the Neapolitans in Rome
Flight of Alfonso of Aragon

One man was particularly apprehensive about the new political alliance, and that was Lucrezia's husband, Alfonso of Aragon—prince of Bisceglie, a Neapolitan, and a friend of the Sforzas. But Alexander took pains to put his son-in-law at his ease. With Lucrezia, he had him attend all the Vatican ceremonies, and in January invited him with cardinals Lopez and Juan Borgia to a great hunt in the countryside around Ostia. On another occasion Lucrezia joined her husband at a rustic gathering in Cardinal Lopez's vineyard. Here, as an amusement for herself and her ladies-in-waiting, Lucrezia suggested a game of tag along the paths. The ground was sloping and slippery, however, and she stumbled and fell, knocking down a girl who was just behind her. Lucrezia fainted and was brought to her palace, where, according to Ambassador Cattaneo, "at nine o'clock at night she lost a boy or girl, one can't say which." She was, in fact, three months pregnant. Happily, two months later the anticipation of another birth erased the memory of the accident.

In the midst of all this, the news of Cesare's marriage gave Lucrezia great joy, mindful as she always was that her own happiness with her husband was her brother's doing. Alfonso and his sister Sancia, on the other hand, did not share her feelings, since from now on Cesare and his father were their enemies. In order to be able to marry, the duke of Valence had had to promise to take part in the conquest of Naples and the Milanese. Sancia found a pretext for quarreling violently with the pope when her husband, Jofré, was attacked and wounded on the Sant'Angelo Bridge one night by the commander of the papal guard. The young woman blamed the incident on the pope's hostility toward the Aragonese. Her brother Alfonso did likewise. He had been panicstricken when Cardinal Sforza fled Rome, and even Lucrezia's love had not reassured him. At dawn early in August he, too, flew from the capital and, hounded by the papal police, took refuge at Genazzano, a fief of Naples's allies, the Colonnas.

From there Alfonso wrote again and again to his wife begging her to join him, but Lucrezia, then six months pregnant, was not tempted to do anything so rash, for the pope had her palace well guarded. As soon as he heard that Alfonso had run off, he launched into a stream of invective against Federigo of Naples and his family. For vengeance's sake he ordered the ever rebellious and independent Sancia to leave for Naples on the spot, then, when the young woman refused, threatened to have her "thrown out." Furious, Sancia finally took off for Naples, leaving Jofré alone with Lucrezia.

Lucrezia, governor of Spoleto

To prevent his children from joining their spouses, Alexander hit on an ingenious and quite honorable plan. On August 8 he appointed Lucrezia, then barely nineteen, as governor of Spoleto and Foligno, an important office usually reserved for cardinals and prelates. He sent her off with her brother Jofré, who, at seventeen, knew absolutely nothing about politics.

On the day she was appointed, Lucrezia, Jofré, and her cousin by marriage, Fabio Orsini, gathered on the square in front of St. Peter's, ready to leave on their mules. Without dismounting, they bowed their heads in the direction of the pope, who beamed down on them from the Vatican loggia and gave them his blessing. Then they started off, followed by a long line of mules laden with baggage. Lucrezia sat on a riding chair, having climbed up on a silk-covered stool to reach it. As she was in an advanced state of pregnancy and the pope wanted to avoid risking another miscarriage, he had a litter arranged on another mule complete with mattresses, crimson covers embroidered with flowers, and two white-damask pillows. Over it was a beautiful canopy to shade her from the sun.

The captain of the Palatine guard, the governor of Rome, and the king of Naples's ambassador accompanied the pope's children to the Sant'Angelo Bridge, where a long cortege of Church dignitaries, walking two by two, escorted them to the Porta del Popolo together with a huge crowd. The ceremonial, which was the pope's idea, throws an interesting light on his daughter's mission. By setting his children up in Spoleto, the chief papal stronghold north of Rome, Alexander was showing that he had deliberately gone over to the side of the French king, whose army was at that very moment invading the Milanese with the active participation of Cesare Borgia. Lucrezia and her brother, linked through Cesare to the Naples dynasty, must now abandon the interests of their adopted family and hold Spoleto so as to prevent any armies that were pushing north from Naples from coming to the aid of the duke of Milan.

Slowly the procession wended its way beneath the blistering August sun. Eventually it reached Spoleto, to find its streets made magical with triumphal arches of flowers. Lucrezia acknowledged the compliments and cheers of the crowd, then crossed the town and climbed the hill to the fortress, set against the Montelucco Hill with its dark crown of oak trees. An austere place, originally built by the Lombards and restored in the previous century, the citadel dominated the little town and could easily quash any revolt that arose down below.

The Spoleto priors greeted the pope's daughter, who presented them with briefs granting her governor's powers. Alexander had given orders for Lucrezia to be paid 1,260 florins for her five-month stint as governor. Cesare was named joint governor with his sister, suggesting that she was to be his deputy. To acknowledge Cesare's preeminence, the citizens of Spoleto were to pay him 1,440 florins. The double appointment meant that the city had to pay a special contribution of 2,700 florins in all.

Lucrezia, far from being a mere figurehead, took great pains to administer the city well. At community expense she set up a corps of mounted constabulary to maintain law and order, and imposed a three-month truce between Spoleto and the rival town of Terni. While Jofré went hunting or riding in the forests, she threw herself into her task. A month after her arrival, she was rewarded by a reunion with her husband, Alfonso, whom the pope had managed to reassure with a generous gesture—he had just given the young couple the city, castle, and lands of Nepi which had been confiscated from Ascanio Sforza after his flight.

In early September, Francesco Borgia, Pope Calixtus's son, took possession of Nepi in Lucrezia's name as treasurer of the Holy See. Alexander then paid a visit to Nepi and persuaded his daughter to come back to Rome for the delivery of her child. He had already named the French cardinal, Péraud, a friend of King Louis's, legate of the region to replace Juan Borgia. Lucrezia was therefore free to leave her post as governor of Spoleto.

Lucrezia and Alfonso return to Rome
Cesare's triumphs in the Milanese
Birth and baptism of young Rodrigo

Lucrezia came back to Rome in mid-October together with her husband and Jofré, the pope's mimes and jugglers giving them a lively welcome at the city gates.

It was a glorious time for the younger Borgias. Without any risk to himself, Cesare had won a warrior's renown with the French conquest of Lombardy. From Asti, the French army had invaded the Milanese, arousing fear in people's breasts and snatching up citadel after citadel with ease. Ludovico of Milan had planned to stop Louis's army in front of Alessandria, his strongest fort, withdrawing to Pavia if need be. But he had positioned his troops in the most disorderly way. Meanwhile, the help promised by Naples and Genoa had not materialized even by the end of August, and Ludovico bankrupted himself hiring Swiss and German mercenaries. He had to face the enemy on two fronts: against the French on the one hand, and on the other Venice, which had sent a strong army from the east to take Ghiara d'Adda and Cremona.

Besieged by a force 40,000 strong, Alessandria did not hold out long, and one night in late August its garrison quit the town. Ludovico saw this as confirmation of his astrologers' solemn predictions. Discouraged, he sent his two sons and his brother, Ascanio Sforza, off to Germany. Pavia capitulated. Milan opened its gates to the French, and its castle was handed over to the governor. After that Ludovico took off for the Tyrol and the court of Maximilian, husband of his sister Bianca Maria. Nothing now stood in the way of the king's solemn entrance into Milan.

Reaching the outskirts of the city on October 5, Louis entered at six o'clock that morning. He wore a suit embroidered with golden bees and beehives, and traveled under a golden canopy, escorted by the chief French dignitaries and the allied Italian nobles. In his train were Cardinal d'Amboise and the duke of Savoie, and cardinals Giuliano della Rovere and Juan Borgia. Behind them came the Venetian envoys, then the duke of Ferrara, Ercole I d'Este, who walked at Cesare's side followed by the marquess of Mantua and the marquess of Montferrat. Once again, as when Il Valentino entered Chinon, everyone admired his baggage, which was carried on richly caparisoned mules and marked with the arms of Cesare Borgia of France—the bull and the blue bands of the Oms family united with the French fleur-de-lis. The diplomat Baldassare Castiglione expressed satisfaction that with his pomp and luxurious tastes the duke of Valence, *molto galante*, had compensated for the behavior of the French occupation troops who had turned noble dwellings and even the chateau of Chinon itself into stinking stables.

News of the Milanese triumph and his son's part in it made Alexander beam with satisfaction and pride. Soon afterward he had another pleasure, no less intense, when Lucrezia produced a baby boy. So delighted was the pope, that before daybreak he sent news of the event to every cardinal, ambassador, and friendly lord—each of whom paid the messenger at least 2 ducats, as Burckard grudgingly noted. The papal master of ceremonies was caught up in preparations for the baptism, which was to be celebrated with special solemnity. This was, after all, the pope's first legitimate grandson, who was to be named after his grandfather, Rodrigo.

The Palace of Sta. Maria in Portico had been decorated magnificently in honor of the noble Roman ladies who came to visit the young mother. The prelates and envoys were greeted in the audience chamber with its tapestry-hung walls. Lucrezia received the visitors sitting up in a bed covered with gold-embossed red satin; this was set in the middle of her bedchamber, which was hung with purple-blue velvet— the color known as "alexandrine." The whole palace—walls, inner courtyard, staircase, and all—was festooned with rich hangings and silks.

One of the doors, with gilded panels, led directly to St. Peter's and the Chapel of Sta. Maria in Portico, where six cardinals were gathered for the baptism ceremony. Since the pope himself could not officiate, he had appointed the cardinal-archbishop of Naples, Oliviero Carafa, to act for him. The procession of cardinals and envoys wound its way to the chapel with its statue and tomb of Sixtus IV. Juan Cervillon, a Catalan and former captain of the pope's guard, sported a silk gold-embroidered scarf over his right arm as he carried the baby, resplendent in a baptismal robe of gold brocade lined with ermine. On Cervillon's right was the governor of his city, to his left the envoy of Maximilian of Austria, the Holy Roman emperor. Preceded by the pope's squires and chamberlains in their rose-pink robes, he entered the chapel to the sound of flutes and tambourines—which frightened the child, who started to howl.

At the threshold of the chapel the baby was handed over to Francesco Borgia, the archbishop of Cosenza, who thereupon walked over to a huge silver-gold shell between the altar and Sixtus's tomb. Cardinal Carafa celebrated the ritual flanked by two bishops who stood as godparents. When the baptism was over, the silk scarf was given to Paolo Orsini, who took charge of young Rodrigo and brought him home to the palace. To close the festivities, next day the Sacred College sent Lucrezia "two silver bonbonnieres holding 1,200 ducats disguised as candies."

Some two weeks later Lucrezia, on the arm of a bishop, walked to St. Peter's to be churched. She spent the evening in the Vatican with her father. No doubt the main topic of conversation was the ticklish news of Cesare's extraordinary triumphs.

Il Valentino had been astute enough to profit marvelously from the situation. The French occupation of the Milanese and their Venetian allies' victory allowed him to use part of Louis's army to his own advantage. When Alexander saw Lucrezia and her husband at Nepi, he had revealed Cesare's plans to them. One plan was to take over the duchy of Ferrara. Cesare's cousin, Juan Borgia the younger, who as legate had been present when Louis entered Milan, had consulted Florence and Venice, but neither power had liked the idea of an expedition against Ercole d'Este. Nor was there any ostensible reason to act against him, since the duke was prompt in paying his vassal's tribute to the Holy See. Ercole himself, on learning of the aborted plan, had immediately learned his lesson and for his own safety formed an alliance he could trust with the French crown. That was why he figured prominently in Louis's royal procession into Milan, marching at Cesare Borgia's side.

The ruin of the Gaetanis

A far easier matter was to extend the Borgias' domain by subduing the barons in the area around Rome and in the Romagna, that large, turbulent province of the Papal States where petty tyrants had set themselves up in place of the papacy, and in the Campagna, the area around Rome. While Cesare was off fighting side by side with Louis, Alexander had begun an extraordinary campaign against the Gaetanis, who vied with the Orsinis, Colonnas, and Savellis for leadership of the Campagna. The chief of their clan, Onorato II, had died leaving three sons, Niccolò, Giacomo, and Guglielmo. Standing as the focus of Gaetani domination was the fortress of Sermoneta, high in the hills of the ancient lands of the Volscians. From Sermoneta, the Gaetanis extended their rule to the Pontine Marshes. The Appian Way was under their control, and they held large fiefs in the kingdom of Naples.

Alexander succeeded in luring to Rome one of the Gaetani family, Giacomo, the apostolic protonotary, and threw him at once into jail in the Castel Sant'Angelo. A tribunal made up of the senator and governor of the castle declared him guilty of high treason, and he died in his dungeon a year later. His mother, Caterina Orsini, later accused the pope of murder and cried for justice. While all the family's possessions were taken away from them, Giacomo's brothers had managed to escape, but later Niccolò's son was caught at Sermoneta and strangled. Guglielmo fled to Mantua, to bide his time before wreaking revenge.

Lucrezia reaped profit from the ruin of the Gaetanis, buying up the confiscated lands for 80,000 ducats in cash. Later, the "infans Romanus," Giovanni Borgia, was granted the duchy of Nepi together with several baronial lands, and little Rodrigo was invested at the age of two with the duchy of Sermoneta, to which were added twenty-one other places confiscated from the Roman lords—a risky dominion, which Julius II ended when he gave back the Gaetanis all their lands in 1504.

Downfall of the Romagnol tyrants
Cesare seizes Imola and Forlì

While the anti-Gaetani operation was going on, Alexander was busy plotting a vast expedition, to be headed by Cesare. They had failed to conquer Ferrara—now, they would try to reestablish papal power in the Romagna. Threatening bulls were sent out to the lords, or "vicars," of Rimini, Pesaro, Imola, Faenza, Forlì, Urbino, and Camerino, who were told they must forfeit their fiefs because they had not paid their annual rent to the Apostolic Chamber.

In the meantime, farther north in Milan, Cesare was busily preparing to do battle. He had borrowed 45,000 ducats from the commune of Milan to hire Italian mercenaries, led by Ercole Bentivoglio and Achille Tiberti da Cesena. Louis had let him have Yves d'Alègre, who commanded 1,800 horse—including Cesare's 100 lances—as well as Antoine de Baissey, the bailiff of Dijon, with his 4,000 Swiss and Gascon footsoldiers. In all, 16,000 perfectly trained men awaited Cesare's command, all well provided by the Holy See with money and arms.

In September the army headed south for the Romagna by way of Reggio and Modena. The troops camped beneath the walls of Bologna, where Cesare was hosted by relatives of the local lords, the Bentivoglios. To thank his hosts for a magnificent banquet he presented them with a horse, a helmet, and a huge quantity of weapons. His nearby goal was Imola, 25 miles to the west. Before laying siege to it, however, he dashed down to Rome to hold a confab with Alexander—no doubt to discuss plans for his Romagna campaign. Using the relay stops of the Knights of St. John of Jerusalem, he made the 500-mile trip from Bologna to the Vatican and back in four days.

Imola was one of the possessions of Caterina Sforza. This strong woman, whom the Italians hailed as the very incarnation of the virago, the warrior-heroine of the Renaissance, had become famous for several amazing acts. Thrice widowed, each time she had had to fight for her children's heritage. From the murderers of her first husband, the lord of Forlì—Girolamo Riario, Pope Sixtus IV's son—she extracted a cruel revenge, as she did from those who killed her second husband, her lover Feo, whom she had married in secret. Her third spouse, Giovanni de' Medici, had just died, leaving her a son who would become a famous condottiere and the ancestor of the grand-dukes of Tuscany. Warned of Cesare's plans, she prepared to resist him for the sake of her son, Ottaviano Riario.

The situation would have been delicate for the Borgias had they been normally scrupulous. When he was cardinal, Alexander had been on very good terms with Caterina and Girolamo Riario, and was in fact godfather to Ottaviano. On becoming pope, he had planned to have Lucrezia marry Ottaviano, once she was separated from Giovanni Sforza. But, past master as he was at putting family interests before those of friendship, he urged Cesare to punish Caterina. She should be the first papal vassal to suffer the consequences of rebelling against the Holy See.

As soon as he came back to Bologna, the duke of Valentinois sent his captain Tiberti—who was rumored to have been Caterina's lover—to Imola. While the city agreed to yield, the fortress put up resistance. Defending it was a noted condottiere, Dionigi di Naldo. After a heavy bombardment, he agreed to surrender if help did not arrive within three days. People were suspicious he had a secret agreement with Cesare, whom in fact he later served as one of his most trusted captains. Cardinal Juan Borgia the younger, Cesare's cousin, reached Imola on December 17 and received the city's oath of obedience to the pope. Seeing the rapid unfolding of events, the townsfolk of Forlì, which was also ruled by Caterina Sforza, surrendered in turn two days later. Cesare sent word that he accepted the surrender and continued his march, passing through Faenza, where young Astorre Manfredi, a client of Venice, received him with honors.

When Cesare's troops stormed into Forlì they wreaked havoc in the town, the Gascons especially behaving like conquerors. From the ramparts of the fortress, where she was entrenched, Caterina furiously fired down on her own subjects to punish them for giving in to the enemy. At this point, Cesare played one of those strokes of genius that would later stun Machiavelli into admiration. By punishing his undisciplined soldiers, he won the sympathy of the Forlì inhabitants. At the same time he suggested a meeting with Caterina, since he had no desire to lose time besieging the fortress if he did not have to. On December 26 he left the town, wearing armor and his famous black cap with the dashing white feathers; before him trotted a herald and a trumpeter. Just in front of the fortress, called "La Rocca," he came face to face with Caterina, who parlayed with him and slyly drew him inside. She had given orders for the drawbridge to be raised behind Cesare so as to keep him prisoner, a ruse that might have worked if Caterina's men had not raised it too soon, before he crossed. Cesare had therefore to resign himself to battering the Rocca for breaching. On January 12 he stormed the citadel. Caterina was there on the ramparts, in full armor and brandishing a sword. Seeing the game was all but lost, she ordered the ammunition to be blown up, a maneuver that created havoc among her own soldiers, one of whom hoisted a white flag. All resistance ceased. Cesare's men seized the fort, killing any of the enemy they found in their way—that night more than 400 victims were counted.

Caterina was taken prisoner by a Burgundian, who received 5,000 ducats' reward. Bringing his captive back to the town of Forlì, Cesare installed her in the same house as himself and treated her brutally, even, if the story is to be believed, forcing her to sleep with him. This scandalized the French, whose code of honor called for men to respect the fair sex, and the Burgundian demanded that Caterina be returned to his care, treating her with the courtesy due a prisoner of the king of France.

Meanwhile Cesare showed he could compromise when he did not have the upper hand. When the Swiss mercenaries mutinied for higher pay, he saw to it that they were given immediate satisfaction. The important thing in Cesare's view was to carry on the Romagna campaign.

After Imola and Forlì, Cesare made ready to attack Pesaro, his ex-brother-in-law's capital. Just then his cousin, Juan Borgia, died. The cardinal, who lived in Urbino, was about to go to Forlì to receive the homage of the newly conquered town when he caught a fever and perished after a few days' illness. His disappearance prevented the papacy from taking direct possession of Forlì, so the task was left to Cesare. At once, rumors spread that Juan Borgia had been poisoned. Tongues wagged that at Imola he had been given a dose of that slow poison known only to the Borgias—the same poison that people accused them of feeding to the unfortunate Prince Djem when Charles VIII marched down to Naples. The accusation, however, was baseless, as Cesare had always got along extremely well with his cousin.

Forced to rely on his own wits to organize and keep his hold over the city, Cesare named Don Ramiro de Lorca, his majordomo, vice-governor of Forlì and appointed the city magistrates. On January 23, 1500, he rode out of the city with Yves d'Alègre, commander in chief of the French forces. Between the two men was Caterina Sforza, riding a gray jennet and dressed in a black-satin costume "in the Turkish fashion," her head covered with a black veil. She wept, humiliated, on leaving the gates of the city she was powerless to keep. Yet her desire for revenge burned as strong as ever. Not long after that, one of her partisans sent the pope a letter impregnated with poison. The plot was uncovered, the man arrested, and he declared himself ready

to lose his life if, in killing Alexander, he could save his native city
and his princess.

The game was by no means over for Cesare Borgia: he still had to
ensure peace in his newly conquered territories and at the same time
pursue his conquests. Three days after leaving Forlì, however, he
received some bad news from Milan. Ludovico il Moro had just come
down to Lombardy from the Tyrol along with 500 men-at-arms and
8,000 Swiss, raised with Emperor Maximilian's help. To resist him,
Yves d'Alègre's forces had to be summoned back north from the Romagna. Cesare, then at Cesena, was forced to abandon his campaign.
He placed his remaining troops in the recently captured strongholds
and rushed back to Rome to get money and fresh soldiers to replace
the French.

The Holy Year of the new century

At the beginning of the year 1500, the atmosphere in the Eternal City
was one of extraordinary enthusiasm. On Christmas Eve the pope had
opened the Jubilee Door at St. Peter's, and throngs of pilgrims had
streamed through it to receive the special plenary indulgences of the
Holy Year. A new street was also opened up between the Castel
Sant'Angelo and the Vatican—the Via Alessandrina, known later as
the Borgo Nuovo—to provide a way for the pilgrims. According to
Burckard, throughout the year 200,000 souls—a huge number for the
time—came and knelt in front of the loggia of St. Peter's to receive
the papal blessing Urbi et Orbi.

Neither the plague nor dangerous roads, discomfort, nor lack of
safety kept the pilgrims from coming, and the crowds swelled from
day to day. Vassals from the Papal States, such as Elisabetta da Gonzaga, who traveled incognito, braved the dangers arising from recent
papal actions in those lands, and several princes sent envoys. Ceremonious receptions were given to Jean d'Albret, the king of Navarre
and Cesare's brother-in-law. Crowds of the faithful arrived from far-
off lands—Flanders, Hungary, Portugal. The ninety-one-year-old
duke of Sagan came all the way from Silesia. The renowned Coper-
nicus, who studied at Bologna, arrived in time to be appointed sub-
stitute professor of astronomy at La Sapienza, the pontifical university.

When not at his devotions, the twenty-seven-year-old genius spent his time observing the heavens.

Rome was not, however, the safest place to look up at the night sky. Thieves and miscreants abounded. One day, as many as eighteen of them were hanged on the Sant'Angelo Bridge. The poorly erected gallows fell down, however, and the execution had to be resumed the next day. Later a doctor from the hospital was hanged from the battlements of the Castel Sant'Angelo: he had stabbed some wealthy sick pilgrims with his lancet—they had been referred to him by the hospital confessor—and robbed them. All the roads being unsafe, a papal bull was issued making the lords responsible for robberies committed on their lands. The French envoy was burgled by a band of Corsicans between Viterbo and Montefiascone, whereupon Alexander expelled all Corsicans from papal territory.

Despite the risks, crowds still flocked in record numbers to the churches. The pope was obliged to grant plenary indulgences to people who could not get in and had to be content with praying on the cathedral steps. Processions alternated with liturgical ceremonies in a continuous pageant, both worldly and edifying. On January 1, 1500, the pope watched from the top of the Castel Sant'Angelo as Lucrezia and Alfonso rode past, followed by a glittering retinue of lords and ladies including Orso Orsini, who was married to the pope's mistress, the beautiful Giulia Farnese. The papal guard escorted the cortege, which was bound for St. John Lateran to receive major indulgences from the bishop of Rome.

Cesare's triumph
His proclamation as gonfalonier of the Church

Eclipsing the festivities at the start of the Jubilee Year were the celebrations marking Cesare's triumphant return to Rome. One day at the end of February, cardinals, ambassadors, secretaries of the Curia, and city officials trooped out to greet the duke of Valentinois at the Porta del Popolo. A hundred mules draped in black trotted ahead of the duke, who wore his distinctive black-velvet doublet, this time with the Order of St. Michael gleaming around his neck—a reminder to those who knew him as a cardinal that from now on they were dealing with a French prince, Monseigneur César Borgia of France, duke of Valentinois, relation, friend, and protégé of His Most Christian Majesty.

In front of him rode his brother Jofré of Squillace and his brother-in-law, Alfonso of Aragon, the duke of Bisceglie. From the loggia of St. Peter's the pope and five cardinals waited for the procession to wend up the new wide roadway, the Via Alessandrina. When the riders swung through the palace gates, Alexander rushed to the Sala del Pappagallo, where he sat in state to make the welcome more ceremonious. Cesare threw himself to his knees in front of his father and kissed his feet and right hand. Drawing him up, Alexander clasped him to his heart and kissed him affectionately on the lips. Then the two spoke together in Spanish—much to Burckard's irritation, since he understood not a word.

After this family reception an extraordinary ceremony was held in Cesare's honor to celebrate his victories. Eleven chariots filed past with allegorical tableaux representing the exploits of Julius Caesar. The whole event was a sixteenth-century replica of a classical Roman triumph, very likely inspired by Mantegna's famous paintings at Mantua. Proudly, the procession started out at the Piazza Navona, much to the delight of the pope, who made the chariots ride twice around the ancient Roman hippodrome. Doubtless Cesare would have liked to include the unfortunate Caterina Sforza in the procession—bound in chains like a captive—but he could not allow himself the luxury of making a spectacle of a prisoner of the king of France. She was therefore transferred to the Vatican, to be imprisoned in the Belvedere under a guard of twenty soldiers. When Caterina tried to escape she was incarcerated in much harsher conditions in the Castel Sant'Angelo.

The chariot cavalcade marked the start of the traditional Roman Carnival. For four days comic competitions took place, watched by an enormous crowd as well as the pope himself, from his loggia in St. Peter's. In one race after another, Jews, old men, bareback riders, and others mounted on three-year-old fillies, donkeys, and buffalos made the crowd roar with laughter. Bullfights were organized in the Testaccio area south of Rome, at which two bulls escaped and swam across the Tiber. They were captured with great difficulty, not before they had thrown panic among the spectators.

When Carnival was over, people once again got down to serious business. Cesare paid official visits to his former colleagues, the cardinals, and Alexander named his son vicar of Girolamo Riario's erstwhile fiefs. Cesare immediately confirmed the freedom of the city of

Imola, promising to protect his new subjects and govern them justly.

The action against Imola's former ruler, Caterina Sforza, had been only a test for greater things to come. Cesare now had to have a free hand to bring the rebellious vassals to their knees. On March 29 the pope named him captain general and gonfalonier of the Church, with the words, "Bless, Lord, our Gonfalonier here present, who, as we believe, has been appointed by Thee for the salvation of the people!" There followed the long list of the great biblical leaders in whose steps Cesare was about to follow. Then the pope got ready to invest his son with his attributes of power. The papal master of ceremonies, Burckard, promptly came forward and removed the duke's mantle, later bearing it home like a prize. On his shoulders the pope laid the gonfalonier's cloak, and on his head the crimson biretta. He handed him two standards, one bearing the Borgia arms, the other the keys of St. Peter, and finally his commander's baton. Cesare swore the oath of obedience in the colorful words taken down by the ever-watchful Burckard:

"I, Cesare Borgia of France, swear to be faithful to the See of Rome. Never shall I lay a hand on your person, Most Holy Father, or on that of your successors, in order to kill you or maim you, no matter what men may do to me. I shall never reveal your secrets!" Having sworn on the Gospel, his hands crossed on his breast, he received the Golden Rose, duly blessed by the pope: "Receive this flower," cried Alexander, "symbol of joy and crown of the saints, dearest son, you who have not only nobility but power and virtue!"

Portrait of Cesare
Threats on the pope's life

A prince of both France and Italy, solemnly invested with the temporal power of the Holy See, Cesare had now outstripped his dead brother, Juan of Gandia, in honors. What had promoted his extraordinary rise was the fierce determination that made him scorn the easy path of a Church dignitary and opt instead for the adventurous career of a conqueror. He would now show himself to the world as the complete Renaissance man. At twenty-five, he had tasted every pleasure, passed every test, used murder as a means to his desired ends. Intelligent and cunning, ambitious and totally unscrupulous, his courage and resolve were equaled only by the strength and skill he was so fond of displaying. His physical prowess aroused the jealousy of other men and the infatuation of the opposite sex. A consummate athlete, one feast day he sprang into an arena set up on St. Peter's square and took on five bulls, one after another, dispatching them all. The crowd roared when he sliced off the head of one beast with a single blow. Such feats made him a matchless hero, one whom the young men looked up to as their leader.

Cesare's bravery and vigor now presented a striking contrast to the fatigue and frailty so noticeable in his father. More and more, the pope suffered from fainting spells during the Jubilee Year ceremonies. One such attack, on the Feast of Corpus Christi, forced him to sit all through the Mass without his miter. An astrologer advised him to be extremely prudent during this Holy Year, which might be disastrous for him. In fact, an accident occurred ten days later that seemed to prove the prediction was correct. In a violent storm, one of the Vatican chimneys collapsed onto the roof. Three people were killed on the floor over the audience chamber where Alexander was sitting in state. A beam ripped the ceiling, falling on the canopy over the pope's throne, but fortunately got stuck and held the rubble in check. The pope was dragged out from under a mass of plaster. He had fainted and was hit in two places on his forehead. He was not seriously hurt, however, and soon recovered his wits, his doctors standing in surety for his life.

All this was a rude shock to Cesare. Suddenly, he had to plan against his father's sudden death. In particular, he must make sure that he could keep his hands on the huge fortune he had skillfully built up. From Venice and France he obtained assurances of support, but he could not ask for the same guarantees from the Aragonese of Naples and Spain. These two powers even had a representative—in Rome itself—poised at any moment to rise up against Cesare. This man was Alfonso of Aragon, the duke of Bisceglie, who was married to his sister Lucrezia.

Assassination of Alfonso of Aragon

On Wednesday, July 15, three hours after sundown—so goes the report of Francesco Capello, the Florentine secretary—Alfonso was crossing St. Peter's square on his way to his home at Sta. Maria in Portico. A group of armed men barred his way. The young man and his two pages fled the thugs, finding refuge in the loggia of the cathedral, but their assailants caught up with them. The young duke fell, badly wounded in the head, arms, and legs. Believing him dead, the men took to their heels and joined some forty riders who were waiting for them at one of the corners of the square. Then the whole band galloped off in the direction of the Porta Portese. Near death, the duke was carried into the papal apartments by his servants, who had escaped unscathed, and entrusted to the tender care of Lucrezia, who had come, with Sancia and Jofré, to look after her father.

Distraught, Lucrezia stayed by her husband's bedside night and day together with Sancia in the Borgia Tower. There was no doubt in the young women's minds that Cesare was the guilty one. He had good reason to hate his brother-in-law. Indeed, the two had recently quarreled violently when, according to the Venetian ambassador, Alfonso had fired his crossbow at Cesare in the Vatican gardens.

To deflect blame from himself, Cesare started a rumor that the Orsinis were responsible for starting the ambush. As captain-general of the Church, he sent out a decree forbidding the wearing of arms in the Leonine City. No one was taken in, however, least of all the two young women at Alfonso's bedside, who for his sake were taking all sorts of precautions. From the pope, still on his sickbed, they received permission for a sixteen-man guard to watch over the young duke all hours of the day and night. They had doctors come from as far away as Naples to treat him, and, terrified of poison, they themselves prepared his food.

Under his wife's loving care, the duke of Bisceglie recovered rapidly. He was almost cured when Cesare came to pay him a visit. In what looked like a gesture of reconciliation, he bent down and whispered in Alfonso's ear, "What was not done at lunch will be done at supper." The Venetian envoy, Paolo Capello, overheard these cryptic words and rushed off to tell the pope. Was this not the confession of the abortive murder and, even worse, the warning of another attempt? The pope, however, paid no attention to these insinuations, for his son had declared to his face that he had had nothing to do with the attempted assassination, and he believed him. Nevertheless he added, "If he has undertaken to punish his brother-in-law, Alfonso well deserved it!" For Alexander, right could only be on Cesare's side. He knew how impetuous his son-in-law was and censured his outbursts as severely as he did Sancia's. Moreover, like Cesare he thought the Aragonese of Naples, who were about to be chased out of their kingdom by the French, stood as an obstacle in the way of the Borgia fortune, henceforth closely linked to that of Louis of France. Assured that his father understood all, Cesare therefore prepared to do the deed once more—and this time to do it right.

On August 18 Burckard wrote soberly, "Since Don Alfonso refused to die of his wounds, he was strangled in his bed." The Venetian and Florentine envoys were somewhat less laconic. Their accounts of the events, which agree with one another, make astonishing reading. The duke of Valentinois tore into the wounded man's bedchamber toward the end of the afternoon. Ordering everyone—Lucrezia, Sancia, the servants—out of the room, he commanded his chief strong-man, the sinister Michelotto Corella, to strangle the young duke. Later, under Pope Julius II, the executioner would confess under torture that Alexander had given orders for Alfonso to be killed, but this confession, whose sole aim was to exculpate Cesare, is hard to believe.

Seeing Lucrezia and Sancia rushing into his room, the pope sent his chamberlains to try to prevent Alfonso's murder. When they got there it was already too late. "That very evening," wrote Burckard, "toward the first hour of the night, the duke of Bisceglie's body was borne into St. Peter's Basilica and placed in the Chapel of Nostra Signora della Febbre. The most reverend archbishop of Cosenza, Francesco Borgia, accompanied the body with his family. The deceased's doctors and a hunchback who tended him were arrested and taken to the Castel Sant'Angelo. Someone informed on them, but later they were released as innocent, which those who arrested them knew full well they were."

Lucrezia was grief-stricken. She was only twenty when her husband was murdered, and Alfonso was really her first great love. Yet the very excess of her grief exasperated Alexander and Cesare, who were irked to see her continually weeping and going around looking drawn. Since custom decreed that a widow had to go into heavy mourning, Alexander gave his daughter an escort of 600 horsemen and sent her off to Nepi, a forbidding castle in the Etruscan hills not far from Rome, where she was to go into retreat. Tearfully, Lucrezia left Rome on the last day of August. "The reason for this journey," wrote the skeptical Burckard, "was to find some consolation or distraction amidst the commotion that her illustrious husband's death had caused." She stayed there until November, signing her letters "La Infelicissima"— "the most unhappy of ladies."

The Crusade as diversion

At the Vatican, any mourning was the affair of the moment. Alexander gave the impression of having forced all images of the infamous crime from his mind. As a handy diversion, he turned to the preparations for a new Crusade, an idea he had put to the Christian leaders at the start of the Jubilee Year. In March one of his chaplains, the Venetian Stefano Taleazzi, had prepared an extremely detailed brief on the size of the Turkish forces, which he put at 150,000 horse and 50,000 footsoldiers. He estimated that the Christian countries could muster 80,000 infantry and 50,000 horse, which could be split into two armies. One would go by way of central Europe, the other through the Balkans up to Istanbul. Everything was planned: ships, artillery, provisions, munitions, even the guilds that would accompany the soldiers. The cost for a one-year campaign would be 3 million ducats, which would come from taxing the Christians' income 10%, that of the Jews, 20%.

The Crusade in fact provided a convenient opportunity to see exactly how much the cardinals' revenues amounted to, since the pope needed to know how much tax the revenues would bring in. Cardinal Ascanio Sforza owned up to an income of 30,000 ducats; Giuliano della Rovere, 20,000; Cardinal Zeno, 20,000; Este, 14,000; and San Severino, 13,000. Farnese claimed to have an income of no more than 2,000. In all, taxing the Sacred College would bring in 30,000 ducats; the Curia, 15,800; and the pope alone, 16,000. Including taxes on the revenues from benefices outside Rome, the total tax on the Vatican dignitaries could be 76,000 ducats. This was a far cry from the millions that had been hoped for. In September, to set an example, the pope put up 50,000 ducats at one fell swoop—a gesture in response to the fall to the Turks of Modon, an important stronghold in the Peloponnese.

The Vatican tragedies were forgotten as people threw themselves into preparations for the great overseas venture. Alexander, a past master of the dramatic gesture, decreed that church bells should ring at noon each day as a call to the faithful to say the Paternoster and the Ave Maria for the success of the Crusade. He also encouraged devotions of St. Anne and the Virgin, and confirmed Sixtus IV's bull instituting the cult of the Immaculate Conception. He started investigations into pious souls who might one day be worthy of veneration: the unfortunate Henry VI of England, and a widow, Françoise Romaine, who had given up worldly riches to devote herself to the mortification of the flesh—two absolute antitheses of the Borgias.

Suffering humanity

Between consistories, pilgrimages, and dreams of the forthcoming Crusade, the crime committed at the Vatican itself by the pope's own son vanished into oblivion. Moreover, the pilgrims fervently believed that the pope could wipe out the scandal. Had he not inherited St. Peter's power to bind and unbind sinners? The store of indulgences that could be obtained in that Jubilee Year was infinite, and with these in hand, not only the living but the dead, too, could escape Purgatory's flames.

Not a few people had come to Rome to receive pardon for exceptionally grievous sins that their usual confessors could not absolve. Burckard, always alert to other people's shortcomings, had obtained sample confessions from one of the priests of St. Peter's granting special dispensations. His account could hold its own with the raciest tales of the time. Among those listed are monks and priests who kept several concubines. Some of these Don Juans of the Church had from two to four women, often visiting simultaneously. One Strasbourg monk changed his order and his monastery, and thus his concubine, to keep from being detected. But his fourth lady friend found him out and marched up to the monastery he had just joined, demanding he be handed over to her. He managed to flee to Rome, however, and so escaped her fury. Other penitents confessed to being guilty of exhibitionism, rape, or incest. One priest revealed that he had been serving Mass for eighteen years even though he had on his conscience the murder of a child he had fathered by his niece, which he had nevertheless baptized and given a Christian burial in his stable.

To the pilgrims' psychic ills were added unexpected physical ailments. Not only syphilis but the plague swept through the Eternal City, abetted by the insalubrious summer heat. Alexander, who saw several of his servants die in the epidemic, refused to retreat into the nearby hills. He claimed he was safe, having survived a severe attack of the plague in his youth. Never, in fact, was he in better health than in that summer of 1500. "The pope is now seventy years old," wrote the envoy Capello, "and grows younger every day. His gravest anxieties do not last the night. His is a happy nature; he does only what will redound to his advantage, and his whole thought is directed to one end—the advancement of his children."

In August, amid great pomp, Cesare accompanied the handsome old man to Sta. Maria in Popolo, where they heard a Te Deum sung in thanksgiving for the pope's recovery. Alexander, who had made a vow to the Virgin while he was ill, made an offering of a golden goblet containing 300 golden ducats. The cardinal of Siena laid the coins out on the altar so that the congregation could witness this pious generosity. It was as though the pope were offering up a libation to some goddess, as the ancients did on the eve of some glorious expedition.

The Borgias had reached a decisive stage: at last they had attained the royal status they had dreamed of for so long. Ludovico il Moro's defeat at Novara and his capture by the French in April had sounded the knell of the Sforzas' power. Milan was now a French capital. And Cesare, captain general of the Church of Rome, a duke of France and noble of Venice, was the one spearheading the coalition of the three powers in the heart of Italy.

5

Royal Advance

Under Julius Caesar's sign

In September 1500, as he entered his twenty-fifth year, Cesare deliberately took as his model his illustrious namesake from the days of ancient Rome, Julius Caesar. His French marriage, the alliance with Louis XII and Venice, his campaign against Imola and Forlì in the Romagna, and investiture as captain general of the Church—all these were but a prelude to his grand design, which was to win absolute power for himself alone.

He had his magnificent parade sword engraved with episodes of Caesar's triumphs along with scenes of his own triumphant chariot procession of the previous spring. One side of the blade showed the crossing of the Rubicon and, below it, the conquered people bringing their sacrificial offerings to the Borgia bull. The other side showed the fruits of peace. In one scene, artists are busy working on a column surmounted by the imperial eagle, while in another, disarmed citizens salute the image of the Public Good: the inscription says that good faith must prevail over arms. Two cherubs stand on either side of the caduceus, the symbol of commerce and industry. Below, Julius Caesar is shown riding in a chariot as he enters Rome to the acclaim of the crowd. The allegories proclaimed Cesare's ambition to build up an empire of prosperity and peace.

The new Romagna army

Remembering Alfonso of Bisceglie's recent murder, everyone knew that to achieve his goal Cesare would not hesitate to eliminate ruthlessly anyone who stood in his way. He had formidable weapons at his disposal, not only temporal but spiritual as well, in the bulls excommunicating rebellious subjects and interdicting their cities.

Alexander lavished resources on his son. Famous condottieri were hired for huge sums: Giampaolo Baglioni, the lord of Perugia; Vitellozzo Vitelli, of Città di Castello; and the Roman baron Paolo Orsini. In late September these seasoned generals gave orders for 700 cavalry lances to line up near Rome—in all, more than 2,000 horse and 4,000 infantrymen. The latter wore iron helmets and red-and-yellow doublets bearing Cesare's coat of arms, their striking uniforms and excellent discipline contrasting markedly with the anarchy so often found in mercenaries' ranks. Trundled along with them were twenty-one large cannons. The chief of staff was Vitellozzo Vitelli, assisted by young Roman nobles, many of whom had fought under Cesare in France. The condottieri Dionigi di Naldo and Achille Tiberti, who had distinguished themselves in the first Romanga campaign, joined the army with their own companies along with some Bolognese exiles who hoped to take their revenge on the tyrant Giovanni Bentivoglio.

Contributions and borrowings
A new batch of cardinals

Alexander thought up ingenious ways to pay for all these troops. He used the donations left by the Jubilee Year pilgrims, dipped into the levies raised for the Crusade on the income of clerics and the Jews, and utilized lands confiscated from the Roman barons (in particular the Gaetanis). He also borrowed 20,000 ducats from the Genoese banker Agostini Chigi, who got a contract for the working of the Tolfa alum mines in return for a yearly rent of 15,000 ducats.

Lastly, the pope resorted to a tried and true method of raising money: creating new cardinals. In a secret consistory he suggested making a new batch of cardinals, and ten days later, on September 28, published a list of a dozen names. Each new appointee had to pay from 4,000 to 25,000 ducats for the privilege. The appointments would, the pope reckoned, bring in 150,000 to 160,000 ducats. Two of those raised to the purple were members of the Borgia family. Francesco, archbishop of Cosenza, was the illegitimate son of Calixtus III; as treasurer general of the Holy See and therefore well endowed, he was taxed for 12,000 ducats. Pier Luís, a nephew of Alexander's and a Knight of St. John of Jerusalem, had no income, having taken the vow of poverty. People imagined he would escape the tax, but since his uncle had conferred on him the wealthy see of Valencia, vacant since Giovanni Borgia died, he was in fact solvent and, according to Burckard, would fork over 10,000 ducats. Of the new cardinals who came to kiss the pope's slipper at the Vatican, pay their levies to Cesare, receive their red hats, and later dine with him, six were friends or relatives of the Borgias. The other new cardinals lived outside Italy and represented powers with whom Alexander wanted to curry favor.

Cesare's court
Priests and poets

According to a Florentine observer, Francesco Capello, Cesare's army was given its marching orders two or three days after the announcement about the new cardinals—"as soon as the astrologers told him the time was favorable." Vitellozzo Vitelli took the lead, together with Orsini and Baglioni. Cesare followed on October 2, accompanied by his advisers and complete personal staff, including three bishops, his doctor Torella, his confidential secretary, Agapito Gherardi, and Michelotto Corella, his strongman.

A number of poets also went along. One of these, Vincenzo Calmeta, had been bequeathed to Cesare by his cousin, the late Giovanni Borgia. Another writer, Pier Francesco of Spoleto, was engaged as chronicler of the duke's exploits. He was also his panegyrist, praising in fulsome Latin "the strength of his arm, the sublime glory of his noble neck, the wondrous breadth of his chest, like the statue of Hercules, and the starlike brilliance of his eyes." Two secretaries and envoys extraordinary, Battista Orfino and Francesco Sperulo, also celebrated Cesare's feats. Piero Torrigiani, the sculptor who broke Michelangelo's nose in Florence, had joined Cesare's court from Pisa.

These glittering representatives of the world of arts and letters followed in Cesare's train throughout the whole of the Romagna campaign, making the expedition a sort of pleasant movable court. Some of the poets and artists would later figure in Baldassare Castiglione's famous *Book of the Courtier*.

A special part was played by the songwriters who wrote traditional love songs to entertain the duke in the long stays in camp. One of Cesare's favorite songs was about the pain of parting:

> *Lady, against my will*
> *I must go far from you,*
> *But no matter how far I flee*
> *I shall cherish the memory of your love.*

Serafino Cimino of Aquila, known as the "divine Aquilano," improvised songs, accompanying himself on the lute. Cesare gave him the subject of the many-headed monster, the hydra:

> *Seven wonderful gifts enthrall the lover:*
> *His lady's glance, her smile, her brow, her feet and hands,*
> *Her mouth, her bosom.*
> *But these are flails and a hydra's many heads*
> *Which bite and tear the lover and devour him.*
> *Far from destroying them, passion's fire*
> *Gives life to these charms as to evil things,*
> *And at their fatal thrust, the lover meets his death.*

Capture of Pesaro and Rimini

Slowly, Cesare advanced northward along the Umbrian roads, which unremitting rain had turned into rivers of mud. At one town, Diruta, the army had to wait five days for the weather to clear because the cannons could not be wheeled through the mire. The soldiers took out their frustrations on the inhabitants, forcing Cesare to intervene in person to restore order and punish the leaders.

His objective was Rimini, where the enemies of the hated local tyrant, Pandolfo Malatesta, had appealed to him for help. Before that, however, he planned to seize Pesaro, the fief of his former brother-in-law Giovanni Sforza. Warned of his approach, the townspeople swarmed into the streets welcoming him with cries of "Il duca! Il duca!" Even by entrenching himself in the Rocca, the Pesaro fortress, Sforza had no hope of holding out long. Neither his army nor the one promised him by the marquess of Mantua, the brother of his first wife, Anna, was large enough. He therefore took the only sensible course and fled, first to Bologna then to Mantua.

On October 21, Cesare's army took Pesaro, and in the afternoon of the 27th, he made one of his usual spectacular entries, in the driving rain. He wore his customary black doublet, under a light suit of armor; his parade sword was fastened to a gold belt, and on his head was his large beret with its dashing white plume. His guards, under the sinister Michelotto, wore jerkins and short cloaks of crimson velvet embroidered with gold. Their sword scabbards and sword belts were of snakeskin, the buckle decorated with the Borgia coat of arms—the bull and seven vipers' heads with darting tongues.

Cesare settled into the palace that Lucrezia had recently lived in, still decorated with the Borgia arms quartered with those of the Sforzas. Visiting the Rocca, he found it capable of putting up some resistance as it contained seventy pieces of artillery. Meanwhile Pandolfo Collenuccio, an envoy of Ercole, duke of Este, had shown up in Pesaro. He brought friendly greetings from the duke, who was greatly impressed with Cesare's recent exploits. The envoy was lodged in an empty palace and given a barrel of wine, a sheep, eight pairs of hens and capons, and two boxes of sweetmeats, along with hay for his horses. Cesare received Collenuccio on the 29th, excusing himself for keeping him waiting on the grounds of ill health: he had an abscess, brought on by his old complaint, the "French evil." He was in low spirits, no doubt aggravated by the irregular life he was leading: he would go to bed at four or five in the morning, rise at eight in the evening and dine, then immediately get down to work, poring over files and plans for the campaign.

The envoy was impressed. "The duke is held to be a generous-hearted man," he wrote to his master, "sound and liberal. It is said that he relies on men of worth. He is also reported to be bitter in his revenge and according to many he has a vast spirit which is starved for lack of greatness and renown. He seems to be in a greater hurry to acquire states than to organize them." His master, the duke of Ferrara, got the message that Cesare was not about to limit his conquests to Pesaro.

On October 30, Cesare entered Rimini. Pandolfo Malatesta had left it to his subjects to negotiate their surrender. By previous agreement, the duke of Valentinois would receive the city and fortress as well as some other castles nearby. Pandolfo, who received 2,900 gold ducats for his cannons and munitions, withdrew to Ravenna. For two days Cesare inspected the city's defenses and attempted to pacify the city. Like Pesaro, Rimini had fallen without a shot being fired, the inhabitants coming out and surrendering to him as if he had been their savior. Yet among all these "falling cards" of cities in the Romagna, one was still holding out—Faenza. It was risky to leave this enclave alone since it could serve as a base of operations for those who resented Cesare's all too easy victories. Faenza, therefore, would be his next objective.

Setback at Faenza

Roughly equidistant from Forlì and Imola on the arrow-straight Via Emilia—and thus able to cut communications between both places—Faenza had been spared in Cesare's first Romagna campaign. Nine months before, Cesare had merely given its young lord, Astorre Manfredi, a passing greeting. The eighteen-year-old governor was beloved by his people, who appreciated his easygoing nature and exceptionally good looks. Manfredi had close ties with Venice—a Venetian dignitary lived in his household—and so Venice's protection seemed to rule out any attack on the city.

But things had been changing. By now Cesare was the doge's privileged ally. Manfredi knew he had no hope of Venice's help if Cesare Borgia attacked. Fearful, he shipped his most treasured possessions off to Ravenna and Ferrara and appealed for help to his relative, Bentivoglio of Bologna, who at once sent him 1,000 soldiers. Against his inclinations, Cesare decided to try to take Faenza and on November 10 laid siege to the city. A week later he subjected it to merciless artillery fire with his own cannons and the cannons he had seized at Pesaro. The wall was breached. Cesare's men rushed to the attack before the firing stopped. The mistaken maneuver resulted in many deaths, among them Onorio Savelli, one of Cesare's best officers. After this failure the duke of Valentinois had to resign himself to a long siege.

Winter came early to the Faenza plain where his troops camped in the cold and mud, without fuel or provisions, the Faenzans having razed the countryside before retreating behind the city walls. In late November Cesare considered halting the whole enterprise and taking to his winter quarters. For one thing, his condottiere Baglioni had withdrawn to Perugia without consulting him. Before that Cesare sent Dionigi di Naldo to the Faenza councillors to propose some kind of agreement, but nothing came of it. The other side replied that they would fight to the death.

On December 3, after publishing his father's thunderous bull announcing the interdict on the city, Cesare withdrew, placing garrisons at various points along the roads leading to Faenza to maintain the blockade. The Faenzans scoffed at these measures, however, and managed to keep huge quantities of provisions pouring in. Meanwhile the neighboring cities of Bologna and Urbino gloated over this patent setback of the papal forces.

Winter quarters at Cesena

Retreating down the Via Emilia, the duke made for Cesena, his favorite city and the capital of his new state. He entered it on December 15, attired in his duke's tunic and beret, and installed himself in the former palace of the Malatesta Novello. On his orders it was thrown open to the populace, who filed wide-eyed past the bed where their former tyrant lay in state. Cesare stayed there for three months, mingling with the people at the Christmas and Carnival festivals. Arousing universal admiration, he cut a dashing figure in processions and masquerades as well as in tournaments, where he was the first to enter the lists. He also liked to test his strength, challenging the local Romagnol athletes in wrestling matches, where he would appear dressed like his companions. He could break a rod, a horseshoe, or a piece of new rope as easily as the huskiest rival. All this made him immensely popular with his subjects. According to the poet Francesco Uberti, one day Cesare insisted that a member of his staff give his embroidered doublet to a peasant who had beaten him at wrestling.

Cesare's main concern these winter months was to administer his embryonic princedom as wisely as he could. Early in January he published an edict preventing exiled citizens from returning and stirring up trouble. At Imola he set up a charitable institution, called La Valentina, while at Forlì he paid a debt that the city owed the Ducal Chamber of the Romagna. Nevertheless, Faenza was not forgotten, and on January 21 he organized a nighttime attack. It failed, and the attackers were driven back. Even the women of Faenza helped defend the city, one of them, Diamante Jovelli, covering herself with glory.

Resuming the siege was obviously going to be anything but easy. Alexander tried to help his son on the diplomatic front, by denouncing the attitude of Faenza's ally Bentivoglio, lord of Bologna, to Louis of France. Rome's relations with the French king were excellent at this time. Alexander had given Cardinal d'Amboise a legate's powers to punish the Milanese clergy, who refused to accept French domination. Louis was now thinking of conquering Naples, and thus needed his alliance with the pope more than ever. To Cesare he sent 300 men-at-arms and 2,000 foot soldiers, under Yves d'Alègre, ordering Bentivoglio to receive them at the Castello Bolognese. In February 1501 the French troops reached the Romagna to help with the siege.

Popular festivals and amorous intrigue
The abduction of Dorotea Caracciolo

Cesare had never been as confident in his own strength or his destiny as now. His popularity and love of intrigue contributed not a little to this feeling. For most of the time he had his lust for power under control, but at times he allowed himself some high jinks, as on the occasion when he and a few young companions burst into some honest burghers' homes, splashing them with mud and spoiling their wives' gowns.

One scandal was meat for the chroniclers. It happened on February 14, 1501, when Dorotea, the wife of Giovanni Battista Caracciolo, the Venetian captain of infantry, was abducted between Porto Cesenatico and Cervia. Since the incident took place on Cesare's territory, fingers were pointed accusingly at him; and Yves d'Alègre and the French ambassador, the baron of Trans, together with the Venetian envoy Manenti called on Cesare to protest the incident in the king's name. All they got by way of reply was a prompt and clear denial of responsibility. Cesare did mention a Spaniard, Captain Diego Ramirez, who had been in his service and was now serving the duke of Urbino. He knew that Dorotea was Ramirez's mistress and he said he himself had tried in vain to discover the man's whereabouts.

This speech convinced no one. The Venetian envoy lodged a solemn protest with the Vatican, to which Alexander replied, "This action is wicked, horrible, abominable. I cannot conceive of a punishment harsh enough for the man who would offend humanity by perpetrating such a crime. If the duke is responsible, then he must have lost his wits." Louis of France reacted in similar fashion. If he had two sons, he told the envoy, and one of them had committed the crime, he would have him sentenced to death.

As it happened, Il Valentino was indeed the guilty one. This came to light later, in December 1502, when Dorotea reappeared, leaving Imola for Cesena together with Cesare. He had left the young woman in Forlì under the care of a trusted guard called Zanetto. She had certainly been Ramirez's mistress, but Cesare had made him hand her over so that he could have her for himself.

Dorotea's long detention—she was not returned to her husband until a year later in Rome, on Pope Julius's orders—seems to indicate that she was not exactly an unwilling victim. However that may be, the episode serves to show up Cesare's temperament: an unscrupulous seducer, excitable but calculating, a past master at dissimulation, eager to increase his power and dominion while maintaining good relations with Venice and France, but refusing to let anything stand in the way of his enjoyment and pleasure.

The fall of Faenza

Meanwhile, leaving his latest feminine conquest in hiding, Cesare returned to the siege of Faenza with the bulk of his troops. He received a number of newcomers to his camp, among them Leonardo da Vinci. The artist had been without a patron since Ludovico il Moro's capture by Louis XII, nor had Florence offered him any work. He therefore offered his services to Cesare, who readily took him on. His time at Cesare's side would be marked by several engineering projects, in particular plans for a canal linking Cesena to its port, Porto Cesenatico. At Faenza, however, he merely observed the siege.

Cesare launched an attack on April 15, which failed, while the defenders' bravery won universal admiration. "The people of Faenza have saved Italy's honor," Isabella d'Este wrote to her husband, the marquess of Gonzaga, whom Cesare had invited to come and watch the siege. On the 20th Cesare's men seized an outwork and set up their cannon even though burning pitch and gunfire rained down on them. The next day all his artillery concentrated on a single point in the walls, hammering away at it for seven hours on end. Next, the biggest cannon was brought to play—an enormous gun that shot balls of stone, killing one of Cesare's Condottieri, Achille Tiberti.

Many of the inhabitants lost heart, among them a certain dyer who sneaked out of the stronghold and informed the enemy that there was no food or ammunition left inside. Cesare promptly had the man hanged as a traitor to his people in front of the city walls, then awaited the proposals of the Faenza city fathers. They were not long in coming, and against the surrender he promised to safeguard the townspeople. Even though the siege had cost him dearly and he had reason to feel vindictive, he behaved with consideration, as he always did when he wanted something in return—in this case, the gratitude of his new subjects. Only the fortress would be occupied, and Cesare sent his strongman Michelotto Corella to take possession of it. The handsome prince, Astorre Manfredi, and his cousins were allowed to go where they pleased and to take their possessions with them.

Deceived by Cesare's benevolence, the young man chose not to go to his friends in Bologna or Venice but stayed on in Cesare's camp until June 15, when the duke returned to Rome. On June 26, the very day that Caterina Sforza was released from prison in the Castel Sant'Angelo, its doors clanged shut on the unfortunate Astorre Manfredi. A year later Burckard reported that his body had been fished out of the Tiber, with a stone tied around the neck.

Cesare had realized he could never rule Faenza while its lawful prince was alive. Nor could he take him on as lieutenant, for the young man would have outshone him in popularity. Like Alfonso of Bisceglie, Lucrezia's husband, Astorre Manfredi had ceased to be of use to him and might in fact be a threat. Therefore, he had to be done away with. A little later, Cesare named as vice-governor of Faenza his old tutor, Giovanni Vera, archbishop of Salerno, who had just been made cardinal.

Phony truces and compromise between Bologna and Florence

With Faenza under his thumb, Cesare's plans logically called for confrontation with the two territories adjoining the Romagna, the city of Bologna and the republic of Florence. Both places, however, were assured of French protection, since France would not let Cesare expand his domain indefinitely. Yet Louis had to agree to the annexing of a Romagnol enclave of Bologna, Castel Bolognese, and once the condottiere Vitellozzo Vitelli had beleaguered the castle, the lord of Bologna, Bentivoglio, consented to hand it over to Cesare. A treaty to that effect was duly signed. Bentivoglio even engaged the pope's son as a condottiere in his service, promising to reward him with 100 cavalry squadrons of three men each—a sizable revenue for Cesare. The treaty was signed by three of the Borgia condottieri, Giulio and Paolo Orsini and Vitelli, who were to guarantee that peace would be maintained. In the document Cesare, who was not present at the signing, was for the first time given the title his father had just bestowed on him—duke of the Romagnas.

After Bologna, Florence loomed as a tempting target. Vitellozzo Vitelli was eager to avenge his brother Paolo's death at Florentine hands. Giulio and Paolo Orsini also urged Cesare to intervene, adding their pleas to those of the exiled Medicis, Cardinal Giovanni and his brother Pietro, sons of Lorenzo the Magnificent. Florence was now weakened by struggles with Pisa, but there were hopes that the French king's protection would be enough to dissuade Cesare from sending against her the large French force he had been given—the 300 lances and 2,000 footsoldiers led by Yves d'Alègre. In fact, on May 2 Louis recalled this contingent, which was to join the forces setting out from Lombardy to march on Naples. Still, Cesare was a threatening presence. He had to cross Florentine territory on his way to Piombino, a small coastal principality which he had designs on. So the Florentine government signed a treaty with him, offering him a *condotta*—that is, taking him for three years as a condottiere at a salary of 30,000 ducats a year, with Cesare supplying 300 cavalry squadrons. These troops would join the army Florence had promised Louis for his Neapolitan expedition.

Conquest of Elba and Piombino

As it happened, the Florentines had signed the agreement without the slightest intention of sticking to it. They wanted to get rid of this formidable army, which included their worst enemies, Vitellozzo and the Orsinis. Knowing he was in a strong position, Il Valentino tried to exploit the situation. He demanded that one quarter of his condottiere's salary be paid in advance and that half the Florentine artillery be handed over to him, as he wanted to use it against Piombino.

This time Florence said no. Feeling that he had wasted enough time, on May 25 Cesare began marching west to the coast, picking up the siege artillery he needed at Pisa on the way. A papal fleet of six galleys, three brigantines, and six galiots was waiting for him, and Cesare used it to seize the island of Elba and the smaller one of Pianosa. When he laid siege to Piombino, on the Ligurian coast, its despairing lord rushed to Lyon and begged Louis—in vain—to dissuade Cesare from his designs. The siege lasted two months. Cesare did not wait to see the surrender, however; in mid-June he left for Rome on one of the papal galleys to join the French army on its southward march to Naples. Now he had to serve the king of France and repay him for the military and diplomatic aid he had benefited from in the Romagnas.

The march on Naples
Massacre of Capua and abdication of King Federigo

Louis had stacked the deck so as to avoid making the same mistake as his predecessor, Charles, who had allowed the House of Aragon to hound the French out of their kingdom. On November 11, 1500, he signed a treaty of alliance with the Aragonese king of Spain, Ferdinand, dividing up the kingdom between them. Louis would take the Terra di Lavoro and the Abruzzi, along with the title of king of Naples, while Ferdinand would have Apulia and the title of duke. In June the next year Alexander gave the treaty his blessing. He pronounced Federigo of Naples deposed, on the pretext that he was conspiring with the sultan, and shortly afterward announced the creation of a papal league with France and Spain. The Franco-Spanish expedition was touted as the first stage of a Crusade against the Turkish Infidel.

Alexander viewed the march-past from his balcony on the roof of the Castel Sant'Angelo. With Cesare, attired as gonfalonier of the Church, at his side, he watched as 12,000 foot soldiers and 2,000 cavalrymen marched over the bridge below in neat array. Next came 4,000 infantrymen, most of them Spaniards, their yellow-and-scarlet uniforms marking them out as Cesare's own troops.

The Naples campaign was swift and brutal. Aided by his allies the Colonnas, King Federigo was counting on making a firm stand at Capua, but on July 24 the city gates were opened, by treachery, and appalling carnage ensued. The dead amounted to over 4,000. Women were seen throwing themselves from the battlements to avoid being raped. The historian Guicciardini, writing long after the event, says that Cesare chose the most beautiful women and had them kept out of the soldiers' reach and led away for his later enjoyment. This was no doubt an infamous anti-Cesare rumor, spread abroad to make him solely responsible for the Capuan massacre, when in fact the troop commander San Severino was the culprit.

All thought of resistance disappeared in face of the terror. King Federigo, betrayed by his cousin on the Spanish throne, accepted Louis's offer and in return for his throne received a pension and the title of duke of Anjou in France. For his part, Cesare gleaned rich revenues in the Franco-Aragonese kingdom and, notably, the title of duke of Andria, conferred on him by Ferdinand of Aragon.

Ruin of the Colonnas
Lucrezia as governor of the Church

Among the vanquished in the campaign were Federigo's allies, the Colonnas. Since the start of the Naples expedition, Alexander had been carrying out a campaign against their castles near Rome, which fell easily into his hands. For four days he went around visiting his new acquisitions with an escort of cavalry and footsoldiers, going first to Sermoneta then to Castelgandolfo, where he stayed. After dining there, he took a boat trip on the Albano Lake, while people on the bank shouted "Borgia! Borgia!" and shots were fired in his honor.

He had left the administration of the Vatican and the everyday running of Church affairs to none other than his daughter Lucrezia, who now occupied his apartments. She opened the letters addressed to the Holy Father and before answering them sought the advice of one of the Curia cardinals. Burckard describes how she consulted the cardinal of Lisbon, who told her, "When the pope brings up a matter in consistory, the vice-chancellor or another cardinal takes down the proposed solutions in writing. That means that someone should be here to record our conversation!" Lucrezia answered that she was quite capable of writing, whereupon the cardinal asked her, "*Ubi est penna vestra?*" ("Where is your pen?")

Lucrezia immediately grasped the bawdy play on words, *penna* having the second meaning of penis. She burst out laughing and gave up her task. Burckard, who was totally devoid of a sense of humor, noted bitterly that Lucrezia never once deigned to consult him about her duties.

On two other occasions Lucrezia took the pope's place while her father again went the rounds of the confiscated fiefs. The extraordinary spectacle of a young woman of twenty-one acting as the head of Christendom hardly shocked those at the Vatican, inured as they were to many other liberties. For example, Burckard notes the parody of the Mass that the pope's jester, Gabrieletto, acted out at Easter, and the time when, in an excess of devotion at Pentecost, priests and monks prostrated themselves before the pope, kissing the ground in Turkish fashion.

Money problems
Lucrezia's marriage to Alfonso d'Este

These parodies and grotesque shows of piety Alexander left to those in Rome. He preferred to concentrate on the money coming into the papal coffers from confiscated lands and inheritances. He dispatched the governor of Rome to seize Ascanio Sforza's treasures, which he had hidden in a monastery. Burckard notes that it took four hours to trundle them to the Vatican. The pope also canceled the will of Cardinal Zeno, who had died in Padua, leaving Venice more than 100,000 ducats for the Crusade. When Venice refused to hand over the money, Alexander threatened an interdict but only managed to get his hands on two coffers. Fortunately, one contained 20,000 ducats.

The reason for this ruthless amassing of monies was the ever heavier expenses the pope had to meet to help his children—Cesare, always short of funds for his grandiose expeditions, and Lucrezia, for whom her father had in mind a new, royal marriage. It was Cesare who chose the husband-to-be—now that he was settled in the Romagna, he needed a trustworthy neighbor, in particular to deflect any attacks by Venice. It so happened that the prince and heir to the duchy of Ferrara, Alfonso d'Este, son of Ercole I, was a widower. He was twenty-four years old, childless, and would suit Lucrezia to perfection now that she had just turned twenty-one.

Overtures were first made to the Ferrara court in early 1501, but Alfonso, who was considering marrying Louise of Savoie, the duke of Angoulême's widow, slipped out of Cesare's grasp. At first, neither his sister, Isabella d'Este, the marchioness of Mantua, nor her sister-in-law, Elisabetta da Gonzaga, the duchess of Urbino, nor Alfonso's father, Duke Ercole of Ferrara, would have anything to do with the idea of a union with the Borgias, whom they considered upstarts. But Alexander was determined to surmount the difficulties. Louis of France, although at first unforthcoming, also lent a hand. The pope had made Louis's prime minister, Georges d'Amboise, legate *a latere* for France. He was granted wide-ranging powers giving him access to all ecclesiastical establishments with a view to carrying out religious reform.

This satisfied Louis, who then intervened with Duke Ercole and advised him to give in. First, though, he should insist on a larger dowry. The duke demanded that Alexander double the proposed sum (100,000 ducats) and scrap the tax Ferrara paid the papacy each year, and asked for a considerable number of benefices for his friends and relations. These demands did not put Alexander off the project and, ever optimistic, in May 1501 he declared in full consistory that the marriage was a fact. He did have a problem, however, in canceling Ferrara's tax—the cardinals would certainly oppose such a transfer of Church rights merely to benefit the pope's private interests. The whole marriage plan was in danger of collapsing. Lucrezia, realizing that the marriage would be a personal triumph for her, persuaded her father to accept Ercole's tough conditions. The pope gave the groom's brother, Cardinal Ippolito d'Este, the extremely wealthy post of archpriest of St. Peter's of the Vatican. On August 26 the marriage contract was signed in Rome and six days later a proxy ceremony was held in Ferrara, at the Castle of Belfiore.

When the pope heard the news, the cannons of the Castel Sant'Angelo thundered till nightfall. The next day Lucrezia went to give thanks to the Virgin at Sta. Marìa del Popolo. She wore a sumptuous gown of plush brocade, and was accompanied by the French and Spanish ambassadors, four bishops, and 300 riders. Even her jesters were there, in their brightly colored costumes. After the ceremony, as a token of her happiness the pope's daughter presented her gown— which Burckard sized up as worth 300 ducats—to one of her jesters, who put it on and ran through the streets shouting, "Long life to the great duchess of Ferrara! Long live Pope Alexander!" The pope held a consistory where he gave an apologia for the House of Este. Meanwhile the Castel Sant'Angelo and the streets of Rome were illumined and the great Campidoglio bell pealed without stopping. At the banquets, Lucrezia was served from silver platters—a privilege reserved for married women. She appreciated the honor warmly, having had to use only earthenware dishes while she was widowed.

Licentious entertainments at the Vatican
The feast of the courtesans and episode of the stallions

On September 15 two envoys from Ferrara, Gerardo Saraceni and Ettore Bellingeri, both experienced jurists and diplomats, turned up at the Vatican to pay their respects to the future duchess. They were to write a dispatch about her for Duke Ercole. The pope's daughter looked tired, they said, and often sent Francesco Borgia, the cardinal of Cosenza, to audiences in her place. The reason for this was, quite simply, that she spent most of the night dancing until the small hours with her brother Cesare, the new duke of Romagna. Occasionally, these nocturnal entertainments took on the bawdiness of Boccaccio's tales.

One evening in late October Cesare invited his father and Lucrezia to his apartments at the Vatican to a dinner at which fifty of the most famous courtesans of Rome also were present. "After dinner," writes Burckard, "the gallant ladies danced with the servants and others who were there, first clothed, then naked. When the meal was over, the lighted candelabra which had been on the table were placed on the floor and chestnuts were thrown among them which the courtesans had to pick up, crawling between the candles. At the end prizes were displayed—silk mantles, boots, caps, and other objects—which were promised to any man who made love to those courtesans the greatest number of times. The coupling took place in front of everyone present, the prizes being given to the winners according to the arbitration of the onlookers."

Although Burckard took obvious, smug pleasure in relating the episode, he did not make it up. The prostitutes were invited and lascivious dances did take place, as historians of the papacy acknowledge. The only point of dispute in his account could possibly be that Lucrezia and the pope stayed on right through the orgy. It was not in Lucrezia's interest that news should be leaked to the Ferrara court, which knew of her every move, that she had witnessed such a spectacle. In general, Ercole's envoys at the Vatican lauded her reserve and piety.

The pope caught a chill the night of the wild party and next day, All Saints', was not well enough to celebrate High Mass at St. Peter's and proclaim the customary papal indulgences for the living and the dead. The day after, All Souls', the pope still had not recovered, and again a cardinal took his place in the basilica. But ten days later he was up again and arranged an amusing diversion for Lucrezia. Burckard once more takes up his pen: "On Thursday a peasant entered the City by the Porto Viridaria [near the Vatican] leading two mares with loads of wood on their backs. When the animals reached St. Peter's piazza some of the pope's servants came up, cut through the straps, threw off the saddles and led the mares to the courtyard inside the palace gate. Four stallions from the palace stables were then let out, freed from their harness and reins. They immediately ran to the mares, fighting furiously with great whinnying among themselves, biting and kicking in their efforts to mount them, and seriously wounding them with their hooves. The pope and Donna Lucrezia, laughing heartily and with evident pleasure, watched the sight from a window over the palace gate."

Endowments of Lucrezia's children
Last papal concessions
The bride's wardrobe

The pope seemed to be using every possible means to make Lucrezia gay and carefree just before her wedding. He also was eager to spare her any worry about her two small children. Giovanni, the so-called *infans Romanus*, whom Lucrezia most probably had with Perotto Caldes, had already been legitimized, so his inheritance was assured. That November, Alexander bestowed on his two grandsons some lands confiscated from the Roman barons. Giovanni received the duchy of Nepi, while Rodrigo, Lucrezia's legitimate son by Alfonso of Bisceglie, was given the duchy of Sermoneta. To make these transfers irrevocable, Alexander put up for sale the Gaetanis' estates, which had been confiscated as a penalty for lèse majesté, then had them bought back fraudulently by Lucrezia for 80,000 pounds. The money was paid to the Apostolic Chamber by the papal treasury. Then he visited the lands that were to fall into his grandsons' hands: first Nepi, then the fiefs of the Colonnas. In a final act of foresight, he made the cardinals of Alessandria and Cosenza and four other prelates the boys' guardians.

All that was left now was to make ready for Lucrezia's trip to her future home. The question of who should go with her called for lengthy discussions between Alexander and Ercole d'Este's envoys.

The duke wanted the cortege to be headed by a cardinal, but the pope felt that would be asking too much of the Sacred College. Instead he suggested that the cardinal of Salerno, who was also legate of the Marches, join Lucrezia when she was crossing the Romagna, and celebrate the nuptial Mass. But, for the ceremony to take place he had to get Cesare's assent—an impossibility, as it turned out, since Cesare, who was in Rome, thought the marriage was all settled and was plunged in some other mysterious business of his own, closeted night and day in his apartment. Irritated by this attitude, Alexander had to deal with the matter by himself. He confided to the Ferrarese ambassadors that, compared with her brother, Lucrezia was admirable: she had remarkable tact, was always ready to grant audiences and to give them with a pleasant manner. She also had proved her abilities as governor of Spoleto. The pope was sure that if she had to negotiate with him he would lose hands down.

All these compliments were, of course, destined eventually for the ears of Lucrezia's future father-in-law and husband. But Ercole was losing patience. He said he would not send an escort for Lucrezia until he had seen the bull dispensing Ferrara from its annual 4,000-ducat tax to the Apostolic Chamber.

What especially upset Ercole was the time taken to pay the promised dowry of 100,000 ducats. While he waited, he instructed his envoys to check the bride's trousseau: he had insisted that it be worth the same as the dowry, 100,000 ducats. Among other marvels in Lucrezia's wardrobe, the Ferrarese saw one dress worth 15,000, and 200 Spanish-style blouses, many costing 100 ducats apiece, with richly embroidered sleeves fringed with gold. Besides these sumptuous clothes, Lucrezia was taking along fabulous jewels, a table service of silver and gold, and costly furniture.

Satisfied with their inspection, the diplomats then turned their attention to the matter of recording the pope's promises. Ferrara was to be given the towns of Cento and Pieve di Cento, snatched from the diocese of Bologna; Giulio, Ercole's handsome illegitimate son, was to receive several ecclesiastical benefices; and the Tuscan Gianluca Castellini de Pontremoli, the duke's private counselor, who had worked hard at the marriage negotiations, would receive a cardinal's hat. The greed of Ercole, whom the pope called "the shopkeeper of Ferrara," knew no bounds, but finally the matter was settled.

The Ferrarese in Rome

On December 9, a cortege 500 strong left Ferrara for Rome where it was to pick up Lucrezia. Heading the delegation was a good-looking young man of twenty-five, Cardinal Ippolito, the future bridegroom's brother. Accompanying him were his two legitimate brothers, Ferrante and Sigismondo. Two bishops and some vassals of the Estes—the lords of Correggio and Mirandola and Annibale Bentivoglio of Bologna— were there with their magnificent retinues. The treasurer Francesco Bagnacavallo bore the family's hereditary jewels, freshly mounted for the young bride.

Because of the winter weather, progress was slow, and the procession made stops at Bologna, Florence, Poggibonsi, and Siena. When they finally reached the outskirts of Rome after days of rain and sleet, the cold tramontane wind suddenly cleared the sky and the walls of the Eternal City loomed on the horizon. The cortege came to a halt, damages suffered en route were quickly repaired, and all the travelers put on their ceremonial garb so as to look their best. By now the nineteen cardinals appointed to welcome the Ferrara delegation were waiting at the Porta del Popolo along with the Roman authorities and members of the pope's household. There, too, was the duke of Romagna, flanked by eighty halberdiers. Glittering with gold and jewels, he rode a horse whose trappings of pearls and precious stones were worth 10,000 ducats, according to the Venetian Sanudo. Near the Ponte Molle, 4,000 infantry and cavalry were drawn up, all wearing his personal livery.

After the welcoming speeches, which lasted a full two hours, the pope's son embraced Ippolito and conducted him to the Vatican. As they crossed the Sant'Angelo Bridge, so many bombards were fired from the castle that the terrified horses reared and nearly threw their riders.

As usual, the pope peered down on the procession from one of his palace windows. He greeted Ippolito and the Este princes warmly, then sent them off to pay their respects to Lucrezia at the Palace of Sta. Maria in Portico. They found her posed, a dazzling figure, on the great stairway on the arm of an elderly cavalier. She offered them refreshments as well as little gifts of silver gilt, goblets, ewers, and dishes of silver. A friend of Niccolò da Correggio's who went by the name of Il Prete (the Priest) passed on intimate details to Alfonso's sister, Isabella d'Este, so that she could form an opinion of her new sister-in-law and future rival in matters of dress and finery. He noted that Ippolito's eyes glowed with pleasure at the sight of this "charming and most gracious lady." Describing her dress, he wrote that she wore her hair in a simple style, without curls, her bosom being covered up to the neck like those of the other ladies. That day she had on a dress of dark brocade shot with violet, her shoulders covered with a mantle embroidered with gold and lined with sable. Her hair was caught up in a bejeweled net of green silk, and around her throat she wore great strings of pearls and rubies. Gianluca Castellini asserted that she possessed an "undeniable beauty, which is enhanced by her manner, and, in short, appeared so gentle that one cannot, nay should not suspect her of any sinister deeds. . . . Your Highness and lord Alfonso will be perfectly satisfied with her for, besides her perfect grace, her modesty, affability and courtesy, she appears to be God-fearing and a fervent Catholic."

Another Roman wedding

The two families spent Christmas together, with the Este princes serving the midnight Mass, magnificently celebrated by the pope. Next day Lucrezia gave a party in her palace, which was attended by some fifty noble ladies, coiffed in the Roman fashion with a flat square of material on their heads. As Lucrezia danced with Ferrante d'Este everyone again admired her radiant beauty as well as that of one of her cousins, Angela Borgia. Barely fifteen, she was already betrothed to Francesco Maria della Rovere, Cardinal Giuliano's nephew.

The pope had decided to throw the festivities open to the citizens of Rome. Every day the area around St. Peter's was filled with races in which everyone took part—young men, twelve-year-old children, Jews, old men, buffaloes ridden bareback, even courtesans.

On December 30 the marriage ceremony took place in the Sala Paulina at the Vatican, the pope, Cesare, and thirteen cardinals being present at the ceremony. Don Ferrante, acting as his brother's proxy, gave Lucrezia a gold wedding ring set with precious stones, after which

Cardinal Ippolito presented her with the family jewels. As he did so, he recited a little speech written by Ercole's counselor, pointing out discreetly that if Lucrezia were unfaithful to her husband, he would be allowed to take back the jewels. The staggering display included four wedding rings with a diamond, a ruby, an emerald, and a turquoise, all specially crafted for the bride-to-be. The other jewels came from the ducal treasury. The admiring Burckard saw the cardinal take out a hair ornament with sixteen diamonds, as many rubies, and about 150 pearls as well as four collars, the whole probably worth 8,000 ducats. More gifts were in store for the bride when she reached Ferrara, the cardinal promised.

In the afternoon Cesare staged a mock siege of a wooden castle on the piazza of St. Peter's, after which a ball was given in the papal apartments. Lucrezia and Cesare danced together in the Sala del Papagallo, with a beaming Alexander looking on from his throne. The company then applauded a classical comedy and a pastoral poem, after which the Estes and the Borgias sat down to an intimate dinner. Everyone—powerful lord or humble citizen—ended the day with the memory of royal prodigality.

The next day, another of Ercole's counselors saw the pope to check that the bulls regarding the promised concessions to Ferrara had been duly drawn up. They agreed that Lucrezia's dowry—100,000 ducats— would be counted next day. So the year 1502 dawned with a seemingly endless counting of piles of gold coins behind the Vatican walls, while the people continued their celebration down below. Thirteen triumphal chariots went by, symbolizing the thirteen Roman districts. Allegories were staged of the grandeur of Rome, of Julius Caesar, and indirectly the duke of Valentinois and the Romagnas. Once more pastoral comedies were staged and a dance given in the evening, in the Sala dei Pontifici. Here a masked Cesare performed a Moorish dance, while at her father's request Lucrezia danced with a young girl from Valencia. On January 2 Cesare mounted a horse and fought bulls in a makeshift bullring in front of St. Peter's, aided by eight Spaniards with spears. As usual, his skill won universal admiration. One bull was killed by a blow he aimed precisely between its horns. In the next fight, which was on foot, Cesare slew another bull with the help of a dozen companions armed with pikes. Altogether eight bulls and two buffaloes were killed, but one man also met his death.

That evening another play—Plautus's *Menaechmi*—was given in the papal apartments for the Ferrarese guests. Before it, the guests watched an allegorical pantomime full of political allusions. First Juno promised Cesare and Ercole happy marriages, then Rome and Ferrara argued over Lucrezia until Mercury—the god of money—reconciled them. All the while the Ferrarese representatives went on painstakingly counting the dowry money in a back room of the Vatican. By January 2 they had counted 25,000 ducats, having discovered several worn pieces. Finally, on the 5th, Ferrante removed the pile of ducats that was left, promising himself to do a further check when he reached Ferrara.

Lucrezia's enchanted journey

The day of Lucrezia's departure dawned with the north wind blowing gustily and snowflakes, rare in Rome, swirling in the air. Dressed snugly in a lined gown, Lucrezia came to take leave of her father and brother in the Sala del Papagallo, while on the piazza escort of a large lords and ladies, dwarfs and jesters awaited her. Together with 200 horsemen that Cesare had provided, in all there were 1,000 in Lucrezia's retinue. Riding next to her litter were over three bishops, the faithful Cardinal Francesco Borgia, and Cardinal Ippolito, along with the princes of Este and their suite. The chests carrying Lucrezia's baggage were strapped to the backs of 150 mules and borne in wagons covered with stuffs and velvet in her colors of brown and yellow.

One can only guess what were the last words that father and daughter exchanged, but the pope's anxiety is apparent in the orders he gave his subjects, urging them to give Lucrezia a fitting welcome on her long northward journey up the Via Flaminia. The first stops were at Nepi and Spoleto, where the people remembered Lucrezia's time there with affection; then, at Urbino, Duke Guidobaldo of Montefeltro and his wife, Elisabetta da Gonzaga—who was Isabella d'Este's sister-in-law—put their fine palace at her disposal. The duchess rode with Lucrezia along the hilly road leading to Pesaro. As they neared the gates of the city Lucrezia had ruled in her first marriage, scores of children dressed in Cesare's colors of red and yellow ran up to her waving olive branches and shouting, "The duke! The duke! Lucrezia! Lucrezia!" With their mistress's permission, the citizens danced with her ladies-in-waiting. Lucrezia herself retired to the palace to rest and to wash her hair—either to avoid a migraine or out of vanity, for she used bleaches to keep the bright gold of her hair.

At Rimini, the governor of the Romagna, Ramiro de Lorca, offered her three companies of crossbowmen to defend the cortege against Caracciolo. The Venetian commander was lurking nearby, intent on wreaking vengeance on Lucrezia for his wife's abduction, which he blamed on Cesare. So the cavalcade quickened its pace: Cesena, Forlì, Faenza—all cities of Cesare's new domain—gave their duke's sister a frenzied welcome. The next city on the long, straight Roman road was Imola, its streets hung with Lucrezia's colors. Complimentary speeches and chariot parades showed that the pope's daughter had replaced their former lady, the virago Caterina Sforza, in the citizens' hearts. Here Lucrezia again washed her hair and picked out the clothes she would wear for her arrival in Ferrara.

Next day she stopped in Bologna, paying a visit to Giovanni Bentivoglio and his sons. She met the lord of Bologna's wife, Ginevra Sforza Bentivoglio. Since that lady was also the aunt of Lucrezia's repudiated husband, Giovanni, it was a potentially embarrassing encounter which both women handled discreetly, no doubt aided by the splendor of the reception, banquet, and ball.

January 30 found the future lady of Ferrara at Castel Bolognese, on the Ferrarese frontier. Here her bridegroom came to meet her, for the first time, disguised with a mask. Alfonso was impatient to set eyes on his bride. His first marriage, to Anna Sforza, had not been a happy one; she was a cold woman with mannish ways who spent her nights with a black slavegirl, forcing her husband to seek solace in brothels. The reports he had received about Lucrezia, the unanimous praises of her beauty—even the racy gossip about her—piqued his curiosity and desire. Lucrezia received her burly, dark husband-to-be with courtesy and respect, and they spent two hours together. Alfonso left her, happy and optimistic, and went on ahead to Ferrara for the official reception. This romantic meeting, quite exceptional in Renaissance court life, seemed to augur well for the marriage.

From Bologna to Ferrara the party traveled by canal. People along the banks were treated to the magical sight of the royal barge looming out of the pale February mist, bearing the pope's daughter wrapped in a great ermine-lined cloak of dark-brown satin over a dress of crimson and gold. Beside her sat the duchess of Urbino, whose cape of black velvet was embroidered with gold numbers and the signs of the zodiac. Jewels gleamed at the ladies' throats and on their heads.

At Malalbergo, in the duchy of Ferrara, another boat appeared, bringing Isabella d'Este from Mantua to welcome her new sister-in-law. Over her costly green velvet gown and magnificent jewels she wore a black-velvet cloak lined with pale lynx fur. The two women scrutinized and sized each other up under the impassive gaze of Elisabetta da Gonzaga. This meeting of three of the most famous women of the Renaissance was the first of several courtly battles that they would engage in during the protracted wedding celebrations.

A little farther on, at Torre della Fossa, Ercole d'Este was waiting, along with seventy-five mounted archers in red and white livery who were lined up along the canal against the backdrop of the gray winter sky. Alighting from her barge, Lucrezia bowed to her father-in-law for the kissing of hands and stepped on board the huge ducal vessel, hung with cloth of gold, that was to bear her to her new capital. Alfonso had stayed behind with his father, laughing at the antics and jokes of Lucrezia's Spanish-speaking clowns. Once at Ferrara, the young bride-to-be was taken to the palace of Alberto d'Este, Ercole's illegitimate brother, to rest and refresh herself.

Wedding celebrations at Ferrara

The entrance of the future bride and groom into the city of Ferrara heralded the beginning of the marriage festivities the next day. First to march were the ducal archers, followed by eighty trumpeters and twenty-four bagpipe players and drummers. Next came the Ferrarese nobles, each man wearing a gold chain around his neck. Alfonso, in gray and white, rode a bay horse caparisoned in purple and gold, with his brother-in-law Annibale Bentivoglio trotting alongside. Then, behind a group of Roman and Spanish nobles, ambassadors, and bishops came the bride, riding a roan mule whose harness was studded with gold and with a canopy over her head. Gasps of admiration greeted her appearance. She wore a gown of striped cloth of gold and dark silk, with full sleeves in the French style, and over her shoulders a mantle of spun gold lined with ermine and slashed at the sides. The ruby-and-diamond necklace around her graceful neck had belonged to Duke Ercole's late wife, the duchess of Este. On her head was a cap that sparkled with precious stones. Six of her husband's grooms escorted her, with the French ambassador riding at her side followed by the duchess of Urbino, Duke Ercole, Geronima Borgia, Fabio Orsini's wife, and the faithful Adriana da Mila. The glittering group made its way under triumphal arches decorated with allegorical scenes, one of which showed a flock of nymphs crowding around their queen, who was seated on the back of a red bull. As the cortege came up to the palace gates, two acrobats swung down from the top of the towers to compliment the bride. Then Lucrezia alighted—a signal for the archers to fight over the canopy and the bride's mule, as was the custom.

At the palace, Isabella of Mantua, in a magnificent gold gown embroidered with musical notes, stood ready to greet the pope's daughter at the top of a marble flight of stairs. In the great hall, on two thrones that had been specially set up, the bride and bridegroom listened to verses recited in Latin praising Lucrezia's beauty and Alfonso's virtues. One aged humanist, Pellegrino Prisciano, waxed eloquent over the Borgia family, comparing Alexander to St. Peter: "Peter had a most beautiful daughter, Petronilla; Alexander has Lucrezia, altogether resplendent in beauty and virtue. O mysteries of all-powerful God! O fortunate humanity!"

And Ludovico Ariosto, a young and as yet unknown poet of twenty-seven, sang the praises of the new star in the Ferrara firmament, but since he was in the service of Ippolito d'Este, the poems showing his ardent admiration of Lucrezia were not printed until later. These lines from canto XIII of *Orlando Furioso* are typical:

> *I admire the one compared to whom*
> *Other women are as tin to silver,*
> *Copper to gold, the sober peony to the rose,*
> *The pale willow to the green laurel tree*
> *And painted glass to the gems of the East!*

Ariosto was not the only one to fall under the golden-haired Lucrezia's spell. "She is full of charm and grace," Il Prete, Isabella d'Este's secret agent, wrote from Rome. The marchioness of Cotrone, one of Isabella's ladies-in-waiting, wrote more critically, "If the bride is not noticeably beautiful, she stands out thanks to the sweetness of her expression." Lucrezia had the advantage of youth: not yet twenty-two, she was six years younger than her sister-in-law. And to her physical charm she added that of her character: "She is full of tact, prudent, intelligent, animated, pleasing, very amiable," wrote one of those who saw her arrive, the chronicler Zambotto. "Her quick mind makes her eyes sparkle." Gaiety was the quality most often singled out. One of the best descriptions of her came from Niccolò Cagnolo of Parma:

"She is of middle height and graceful of form; her face is rather long, as is her nose; her hair is golden, her eyes gray, her mouth rather large, the teeth brilliantly white, her bosom smooth and white and admirably proportioned. Her whole being exudes good humor and gaiety." Love of life and laughter were the secrets of Lucrezia's charm, as they were of her father's and brother's. Alfonso d'Este—a strong, silent, often withdrawn man who spent his time indulging his passions for artillery, music, and pottery and his appetites in brothels—was soon captivated by his young wife's charms.

When dusk fell, Lucrezia withdrew to the nuptial bedchamber where her ladies-in-waiting removed her golden gown under the supervision of the faithful Adriana da Mila. Then the womenfolk, as well as the Spanish prelates and the pope's relatives and intimates, eavesdropped in the antechamber, ears cocked for echoes of the wedding night. By morning everyone knew that Alfonso had proved he was a gallant and lusty husband, even though his ardor—expressed three times—was no more than average.

On the morning of February 3 the young bride lay long abed and dressed slowly, taking a light breakfast and chatting in Spanish with her cousins. But toward midday it was time to receive the Este family, the eagle-eyed Isabella of Mantua, and the lord and envoys at the Ferrara court. The festivities opened with a ball, where Lucrezia, who adored dancing, was duly admired. A performance of Plautus's comedy, *Epidicus*, followed, the first of a series of five plays given in the great hall of the Palazzo della Raggione. The interludes of Moorish dances and allegorical tableaux intrigued the spectators at least as much as Plautus's plot.

Every day the entertainments became more and more refined, up to Sunday when all the wedding guests gathered in the cathedral and the archbishop gave Alfonso a cap and sword blessd by his father-in-law, the pope. At a ball that followed, Lucrezia, resplendent in a violet dress covered all over with gold fish scales, performed a French dance with one of her ladies. Then the French ambassador presented his gifts: medals of gold for Ercole and Alfonso and, for Lucrezia, a gold rosary whose hollow beads were filled with heady musk, a mingling of devotion and pleasure.

The ambassadors of the Italian states brought their presents next day, Shrove Tuesday. Two large velvet cloaks lined with ermine, which the Venetian envoys spread out at the bride's feet, were particularly admired. Finally, during the intermission of the last play, Alfonso took part in a concert of viol music, playing the instrument with skill. Then a huge gold globe burst in the air, and four Venuses stepped out and proceeded to sing divinely.

Ash Wednesday signaled the departure of the ambassadors and princes. Up to the last minute Charlotte d'Albret, Cesare's wife, had been expected to attend, but only her brother, Cardinal Amanieu, showed up, and then only for the last moments of the festivities. Nonetheless, five days after the end of Carnival, the two Borgia cousins and Adriana da Mila, together with their enormous train of 450 people and 350 horses, were still staying on in Ferrara, at Ercole's expense. The duke complained roundly to his envoy in Rome of having to go on paying for the wedding, which had already cost him 25,000 ducats. Yet at least he had no regrets about the actual marriage. As he wrote in all sincerity to Alexander: "Before the most illustrious duchess, our common daughter, arrived, it was my firm intention to love and honor her. . . . Now that Her Highness is here, the satisfaction she has given me by her virtues and talents is so great that my will and desire are all the greater. . . . I consider Her Highness as the dearest possession I have in this world."

Alexander immediately took advantage of this confession to ask Ercole to raise Lucrezia's allowance from 6,000 to 12,000 ducats. This would allow the young woman to do honor to her rank as princess and keep her reputation as one of the best-dressed ladies in all Italy. For the time being, he got only 10,000 ducats. In front of the Ferrarese ambassador, the pope expressed his pleasure that Alfonso had acquired the habit of sleeping with the duchess each night and was not doing what most young men did, namely finding enjoyment elsewhere during the day. Yet, added Alexander, no doubt thinking of his own youth and of Cesare's conduct beneath his very eyes, "the practice, one must recognize, does do them good!"

Papal visit to Piombino

In Rome, the pope decided to make a journey, officially taking possession of the last fortresses that had fallen to the duke of Romagna— Piombino and the island of Elba. He left surrounded by all the appurtenances of his high office—the sedia gestoria, the golden canopy, his chapel choir, and Burckard's colleague, who was to organize the ceremonies. Six cardinals went along, as well as the duke himself. At

Corneto, on the coast north of Rome, they set sail on six galleys, landing at Piombino on February 21, where they stayed four days. Next, the pope and Cesare sailed for Elba, where they wanted to inspect two fortresses that were being built under the supervision of Leonardo da Vinci, who now served as military engineer for the duke of Romagna. After inspecting the coasts of the island, Alexander sailed back to Piombino, where his son put on a sumptuous ballet entertainment for him, with superb male and female dancers in gold-spangled costumes who paid him homage as though he was an emperor.

On their homeward journey a violent storm arose, and for five days the frail vessels were buffeted perilously. Everyone got seasick and feared for his safety—all save Alexander, who sat on deck and merely cried "Jesus!" at each shuddering whack of the waves, never complaining except to say that he was hungry and call out for some fried fish. When at last they landed at Porto Ercole, the cardinals declared they were quite incapable of going on to Rome and should be allowed to rest before joining the remainder of the papal cavalcade at Civitavecchia. Finally the pope returned to the Vatican with the cardinals, many still green about the gills. Despite his seventy-one years, Alexander had stood the exhausting and terrifying trip amazingly well. "He came back to Rome," wrote the Florentine secretary, "in the best of health and in the most cheerful frame of mind."

His optimism was justified, for he had seen for himself that Cesare would be able to resume his campaigns and march on Tuscany whenever he chose. Alexander had also heard about Lucrezia's social triumph at Ferrara. For two years his children had held paramount positions on the world stage. France and Venice were constantly giving proof of their benevolence toward the pope's family. The newly conquered territories were calm under the iron rule of Michelotto Corella at Piombino and Ramiro de Lorca in the Romagna. Cesare Borgia, the papacy's temporal arm, stood poised as the sovereign arbiter of Italy's princes and republics.

6

Appointments with the Devil

A model for Machiavelli

From that time on, the eyes of all Italy were fixed on Cesare Borgia, noting the least of his gestures with terror or admiration. It was in this period of heady success that fate put in his path the man who would make him the stuff of legend: Niccolò Machiavelli, secretary of the second chancellory of the Florentine republic. Machiavelli would take Il Valentino as his model for the prince who promotes himself solely through the strength of his own will:

"Whoever judges it necessary in his new principality to secure himself against enemies, to gain friends to himself, to conquer either by force or by fraud, to make himself loved and feared by the people, and followed and revered by the soldiers, to eliminate those who can or might offend you, to renew old orders through new modes, to be severe and pleasant, magnanimous and liberal, to eliminate an unfaithful military, to create a new one, to maintain friendships with kings and princes so that they must either benefit you with favor or be hesitant to offend you—you can find no fresher examples than the actions of the duke of Valentino."

Maintaining order in Rome

What strikes the observer, at first glance, is indeed how supremely efficient the duke was in everything he undertook. He knew how to delegate power and at the same time keep total control of it. He retained the option of taking it back and wielding it absolutely whenever he chose. One example is an episode during Cesare's government of the Romagna. His lieutenant general, Don Ramiro de Lorca, a violent, domineering man, ruthlessly put down revolts in the territory, ignoring the traditional right of asylum of churches and consecrated places as he hunted down criminals and troublemakers. Once, at Faenza, it happened that a miscreant miraculously escaped death by hanging when the rope around his neck snapped. Abetted by the crowd, he ran off and took shelter in a church. Ramiro, who had been warned, rushed to the church, forcing the prior to give up the fugitive, and had the wretched man hanged once again, from one of the windows of the mayor's palace. Not content with setting this example, Lorca held the citizens of Faenza responsible for the incident and quite arbitrarily fined them 10,000 ducats. The citizens then sent a delegation to Rome and submitted the matter to the pope and the duke of Romagna. Cesare actually profited from the situation. Without disowning his lieutenant, he canceled the fine, which not only increased his popularity but ensured that in future people would think twice before disobeying his deputies.

The way the Romagna was governed served as a lesson in administration. The province changed from an arena of dissension, robbery, and crimes aggravated by the wars of rival baronial clans to a peaceful state where lives and property were protected by the prince, who also encouraged public prosperity. The protector of da Vinci, who besides being a painter of genius was also a great engineer, Cesare was unendingly curious about innovations and started scores of public-works projects in the cities and ports of the Romagna.

External dangers
Florence and Vitelli's seizure of Arezzo

With peace reigning in his duchy, Cesare was now forced to attack the root of the disorders, namely the enclaves that offered a haven to those who rejected him as their overlord. He also had to be wary of the neighboring states, which out of a desire to defend their independence tended to take an ambiguous and at times sulkily hostile attitude, as did Florence. In each case, however, Cesare could not start any action without the permission of the great powers theoretically allied to him, Venice and France.

Like the Venetians, Louis felt that his Borgia ally had benefited enough from the alliance, but in the spring of 1502 an unexpected crisis weakened the king's position in Italy, forcing him to take a conciliatory attitude. In the kingdom of Naples, tension had flared up between the French and Spanish. The Treaty of Granada had not spelled out clearly enough each ally's lands and rights, and a dispute had arisen over the customs at Foggia, which brought in a lot of money from the levying of transhumance rights. The French viceroy of Naples, Louis d'Armagnac, had come to blows with the great Spanish captain, Gonsalvo de Cordoba.

Cesare was sorely tempted to take advantage of the situation, first of all by avenging himself on the Florentines, who had not honored the treaty he had signed with them which, among other things, promised him a comfortable condottiere's allowance. But out of prudence, he was loath to intervene openly. It so happened that one of his captains, Vitellozzo Vitelli, was eager to act in his place. In the autumn of 1501, Cesare had stopped him in the nick of time as he was invading Florentine territory to avenge his brother's execution, Paolo Vitelli having been sentenced to death for treason. This time Cesare let Vitelli collaborate with Piero de' Medici in stirring up the citizens of Arezzo.

All went according to plan. On June 4 the little town took up arms and flung open its gates to Vitelli. Soon other troops joined him, led by his brother Giulio and Baglioni, the lord of Perugia, and in a few days Vitelli had seized all the fortresses of the Val di Chiana. Caught unawares, the Florentines sent envoys to Rome demanding the pope's explanation. The Pisans, who were bitter enemies of the Florentines, chose that moment to offer Cesare the keys of their city. By June 10 they could tell him that his standard was waving on their walls.

The news was music to Cesare's ears. Yet he knew that France would not allow him to establish his dominion in Tuscany. In agreement with his son, therefore, the pope told the Pisan envoys that neither he nor Cesare could accept their offer. At the same time he assured the Florentine ambassadors that his son had had nothing to do with Vitelli's venture. It was true that while Cesare did allow his captain to act, he gave him nothing in the way of men or arms—he needed them for the campaign he was plotting in the Romagna.

Preparing for the third Romagna campaign
Execution of Astorre Manfredi

On the eve of his new campaign, on June 2, Il Valentino received the Venetian envoy, Giustiniani, who brought him friendly greetings from the doge. Cesare resolved to put this friendship to the test at once. He had the young deposed lord of Faenza, Astorre Manfredi—a longtime client of Venice—put to death.

On June 6 Giustiniani wrote to his government that Astorre and his brother had been drowned in the Tiber with their majordomo. Before their death, he wrote, the young men had been tortured. Burckard describes in his journal for June 9 how the bodies were fished out of the river: "The lord of Faenza, a young man of around eighteen, so fine in physique and stature that not one in a thousand was his equal, was taken out of the Tiber, with a stone fastened around his neck. Two young men found near him were tied together by their arms, one being fifteen years old, the other about twenty-five. The body of an unknown female was also found."

Young Astorre's assassination aroused not a murmur of protest from Venice, leaving Cesare reassured that the doge would not interfere with his coming moves in the Romagna. Moreover, the young man's cruel fate gave all his opponents something to think about and served as a timely warning to anyone thinking of putting up a show of resistance in the province. At Spoleto, Il Valentino had concentrated 6,000 infantrymen and 700 men-at-arms, each one having about three gunners. Besides this roughly 10,000-strong army, 2,000 armed men were spread throughout the Romagna. A thousand of these, under counts Montevecchio and San Lorenzo, were encamped between Urbino and Sinigaglia, while another 1,000, under Dionigi di Naldo, were lying at Verucchio, about 12 miles from Rimini. Cesare left Rome on June 12, reaching Spoleto three days later. Here he put out an edict ordering every Romagnol family to provide him with one soldier—enough to give him a reserve army.

The siege of Camerino

Officially, Cesare was aiming his next thrust at Camerino. This little stronghold, perched high on the eastern foothills of the Apennines, was ruled by the iron hand of a tyrant who had come to power over the dead body of his brother. He was Giulio Cesare Varano, a seasoned warrior of seventy who ruled together with his four sons, Venanzio, Annibale, Piero, and Gianmaria. By refusing to pay the tribute due to the Holy See, he had laid himself open to the censures meted out to rebellious vassals. Already, Cesare had sent one army against him, commanded by Francesco Orsini, the duke of Gravina, and Oliveretto Eufreducci, who had just seized the stronghold of Fermi, having first killed his own uncle and all his family. Gravina and Oliveretto da Fermo now needed reinforcements to ring the fortress.

Hearing of the threatened attack, Varano hoped to get help from Guidobaldo da Montefeltro, the duke of Urbino: this information was relayed to Cesare by the chancellor of Camerino, who was captured at Foligno by Cesare's men. He also said that the duke of Urbino was arming soldiers and raising taxes to come to Camerino's aid. Shortly afterward, a messenger captured leaving Urbino disclosed that Montefeltro was preparing a raid against Cesare's artillery at Gubbio. This news was the pretext Cesare needed to attack Montefeltro: because of the promises he had made to Varano, was he not guilty of treachery against the Holy See?

Surprise attack and conquest of the duchy of Urbino

Cesare hid his plan with diabolical skill, paying Guidobaldo da Montefeltro the compliment of informing him of his march on Camerino. The duke of Urbino suspected nothing. He felt no enmity toward Cesare: a peace-loving ruler and patron of arts and letters, he was quite the antithesis of the petty tyrants of the Romagna. He lived in his palace surrounded by the affection of his subjects and his family, which included his adopted heir, his thirteen-year-old nephew, Francesco Maria della Rovere, the lord of Sinigaglia. Pope Alexander had given the youth his father's title of prefect of Rome and marked him out for marriage to his niece, Angela Borgia. Guidobaldo himself had always been loyal to the pope, honorably carrying out his duties as captain general of the Church whenever the pope asked him. With his wife, Elisabetta da Gonzaga, he had given Lucrezia a warm welcome six months before.

In light of these good relations with the pope and his family, Guidobaldo was not surprised when Cesare announced his plan of campaign and asked him to help by transporting provisions to Gubbio. When Il Valentino said he would take the Sassoferrata road to reach Camerino, Guidobaldo gave orders for the roads to be cleared and sent oxen for pulling the artillery. Cesare persisted: would the duke furnish him with 1,000 men, to be passed on to Vitelli, in Tuscany? Here Guidobaldo, not wanting to cross Louis of France, refused to help until he had received a papal brief about it. Nonetheless, he did suggest that he would let Vitelli recruit soldiers in his duchy and offered to pay up to 1,000 ducats toward the levy. He was obligingness itself.

Under cover of these peaceable dealings, Cesare took the offensive. Leaving all his baggage at Nocera, he led his troops on a forced march up the Via Flaminia 43 miles north to Cagli, just below the fort on the frontier of the duchy of Urbino. Caught unawares, the garrison surrendered on June 20. Guidobaldo received the news that very evening while he was dining alfresco in a monastery garden about a mile from Urbino. To his horror, he heard that his duchy was being invaded from two other directions as well. Montevecchio and San Lorenzo were pressing westward toward Urbino from Fano, on the Adriatic coast, while Dionigi di Naldo was coming from Verucchio, on Guidobaldo's northern frontier, by way of the Marecchia gorges. This meant that three of Cesare's armies were converging on his capital. For a moment he considered fleeing northwest to his fortress of San Leo, but the road was blocked. He then sent his young nephew to Bagno di Romagna while he himself, in spite of his gout, fled disguised as a peasant into the hills as far as Ravenna. From there he made for Mantua, where his wife was visiting Isabella.

Cesare rode into the city of Urbino as a conqueror, lance at rest, just a few hours after Guidobaldo had taken off. Following their lord's advice, the inhabitants had put up no resistance to avoid damage and suffering. Il Valentino settled into the palace, having first forbidden his men to do any pillaging. Without firing a shot he now found himself master of Urbino—a duchy that covered a large part of the Romagna and the Marches, stretching 62 miles from north to south, from San Marino to Gubbio, and some 30 to 35 miles west to east, from the Luna Mountains to Fossombrone.

At Urbino itself Cesare had an inventory made of the Montefeltro works of art, planning to have most of them sent to his palace at Cesena along with the duke's library. When Isabella of Mantua heard of this she tried to take advantage of Cesare's plundering, even as the unfortunate Guidobaldo was a refugee at her own court. On June 30 she wrote to her brother, Cardinal Ippolito d'Este, asking him to arrange for a small ancient statue of Venus to be sent her, also a Cupid "which the duke of Romagna had once given the duke of Urbino." Cesare, pleased to gain his Mantuan neighbors' goodwill at so small a price, dispatched one of his chamberlains to take the statue to Isabella. He pointed out, however, that the Cupid was not classical but the work of Michelangelo.

Soderini and Machiavelli's mission to Cesare

Scarcely had he entered Urbino when Cesare proposed to the Florentines that they come to an understanding. At once they sent Francesco Soderini, the bishop of Volterra, along with a formidable negotiator by the name of Niccolò Machiavelli who, at thirty-three, had already gained considerable experience in diplomatic dealings, notably at the court of Florence and with Caterina Sforza, the fiery lady of Imola and Forlì.

The two Florentines reached Urbino in the evening of June 24. Although Cesare had been there only a day, he behaved as though he had ruled there all his life. When he received the envoys, shortly before midnight, he was studying a plan of campaign with Ramiro de Lorca. He did not talk much, merely pointing out that he was not in position of strength vis-à-vis Florence. He demanded that Florence pay him the money due him as condottiere, for if he received the promised sum—40,000 ducats for a *condotta* of three years—he would not take any action against the republic. His intentions were peaceful, he said. While assuring the envoys that he was not responsible for Vitelli's action against Arezzo, he pointed out that the attack showed the risks anyone took who broke his word to a soldier. As for himself, he claimed that his aim in his campaigns was not to tyrannize the country but to crush tyrants—which naturally excluded the Florentines.

Soderini and Machiavelli were impressed by Cesare's extraordinary vitality. "This lord is splendid and magnificent. To acquire fame or increase his power, he never takes any rest and knows neither fatigue nor danger. No sooner has he arrived in a place than word goes out that he has left. He knows how to be respected by his men, and has succeeded in mustering the best troops in Italy. All these things, together with his extraordinary good fortune, bring him victory and make him universally feared. Moreover, he guides argument in such a masterly way that one needs plenty of time to be able to gain any point in a discussion with him. He knows, too, how to use threat to back up his eloquence. 'Make up your minds fast,' he tells diplomats. 'I cannot keep my army unoccupied in this mountainous area. There can be no half-measures between you and me: you are either my friends or my enemies.' "

When Soderini reminded him that Florence was under the protection of the king of France, he retorted that he did not need to be told about French politics by anyone in Italy.

When he thought the envoys had run out of arguments, he gave them four days to reply. Machiavelli rode off to get his instructions from Florence. The Signoria, however, was in a quandary. The councillors simply wanted to gain time, hoping against hope that Louis would come out in Florence's favor. The French king was rumored to be moving south to Naples with 20,000 men to settle his difference with Spain.

Louis did in fact reach Asti on July 7. He sent a messenger to Cesare urging him not to take any action against Florence. At the same time, however, Cardinal d'Amboise was pressing the Florentine government to reach an accommodation with Cesare. Accordingly, the Signoria asked Soderini to suggest paying him a six-months' *condotta* salary, in exchange for which Cesare would order Vitelli to withdraw from Arezzo and the other strongholds he was occupying.

Cesare was scornful, saying he would not agree to any such action until the agreement was signed. This proved a good move, since on the 19th the Signoria, hearing that the French had entered Italy, instructed Soderini to break off his talks with Cesare. While the roughly sketched treaty remained a dead letter, its contents were relayed to Vitelli and Baglioni. Warned of this volte-face, the two condottieri conceived a violent distrust of their employer.

Surrender of Camerino

While these fruitless negotiations were going on with Florence, Cesare was happily planning the siege of Camerino, which was to be carried out by two other condottieri of his, Francesco Orsini and Oliveretto da Fermo. The old tyrant of the city, Giulio Cesare Varano, had sent two of his sons, Piero and Gianmaria, to plead for help from Venice. As he waited for it to arrive, Giulio and his other sons made some successful sorties against the attackers. But then one of the Varanos' enemies, a young aristocrat called Gianantonio Ferracioli, staged a revolt and opened the gates to Cesare's troops. On July 19, the same day the agreement between Il Valentino and Florence was broken, Camerino surrendered. Varano was taken prisoner and shut up in the castle of Pergola, where, according to the historian Guicciardini, he was found strangled not long afterward. His sons Venanzio and Annibale were clapped into prison at the fortress of Cattolica, between Rimini and Pesaro.

Rome greeted the capture with terrific enthusiasm. For three days all the church bells pealed and the city was lit up while a huge crowd hailed Cesare, shouting "Il duca! Il duca!" Besides the Camerino coup, the pope wanted to celebrate Cesare's entry into Urbino, even if that exploit smacked somewhat of treachery. In an audience with Giustiniani, the Venetian ambassador, Alexander insisted over and over again on his son's honor. To clear him of any taint of unscrupulousness, he stressed that "no one ever kept his word more faithfully than he; nor has he ever broken a promise."

At the same time that he broke the news to his father, Cesare wrote about his success to Lucrezia, who was then lying dangerously ill at Ferrara after giving birth to a stillborn child. His letter was gentle and affectionate: "Most noble and excellent lady, our very dear sister. Persuaded that there could be no more efficacious or health-giving medicine for your present indisposition than the reception of good and happy news, we would inform you that we have just learned the news of the capture of Camerino. We beg you to greet this message at once by recovering your health since, tormented as we are to know that you are ill, nothing, not even this happy event, can give us any pleasure." Not content with kind words, he sent his sister his personal doctor, Gaspare Torrella, as well as another famous physician from Cesena, Niccolò Masini. Apart from his personal grief, Lucrezia's death would be a political catastrophe for him since it would deprive him, at a crucial time, of the alliance with Ferrara. To be reassured, he decided to go and see his sister for himself at the Ferrara court before joining the king of France in Milan.

Intrigues surrounding the French king
Cesare's journey to Ferrara and Milan

Cesare urgently needed to curry favor with Louis of France. He had been warned by the pope's secretary, Francesco Troches, that Louis was furious because of Vitelli's and Baglioni's moves against Florence, his protégé. Troches had been keeping his eyes and ears open assiduously for two months. In June he had left Rome with Cardinal Amanieu d'Albret, Cesare's brother-in-law, accompanied by two pretty courtesans. The group made for Savona, staying with Cardinal Giuliano della Rovere, then for Lombardy, where he saw the French king.

Thus warned, Cesare ordered his two condottieri to leave Arezzo and Tuscany. He set off immediately, with typical speed and secretiveness, leaving Urbino masked and disguised as a Knight of St. John of Jerusalem, only four men traveling with him. After a brief stop at Forlì to change horses, he reached Ferrara, staying only two hours— enough to see Lucrezia, whom he was pleased to find on the road to recovery. He and his brother-in-law Alfonso, whom he had persuaded to visit Louis with him, then rode posthaste to Milan by way of Modena. They found the king's entourage transformed into a sort of council of Cesare's enemies. Guidobaldo da Montefeltro, the deposed duke of Urbino, was there; also Piero Varano, son of the strangled tyrant of Camerino; Giovanni Sforza da Pesaro; and Francesco da Gonzaga of Mantua, a relative and ally of Cesare's opponents even though, like his wife, Isabella, he was apt to change his mind like a weathervane. Throughout Italy, there were renewed attacks against the Borgias, sparked by Cesare's fresh triumphs. Louis of France could not ignore the pamphlets that were being circulated everywhere, such as the famous Savelli Letter.

The pamphlet war against the Borgias
The Savelli Letter

According to Burckard, who gives the text in his diary, the Savelli Letter was printed in Germany and passed on to him by his crony Giambattista Ferrari, the cardinal of Modena. Included in Burckard's diary for the end of 1501, the letter is dated November 25 of that year. Purportedly, it was sent from Gonsalvo de Cordoba's camp in Taranto to a Roman nobleman who had taken refuge at the court of Emperor Maximilian. The writer, as some historians surmise, may have been a member of the Colonna family. Couched in a vehement style, the text lists most of the grievances and slanders that had been the stuff of Roman gossip for years, and attempts to dissuade Savelli from demanding reparations for the damages he has suffered. There is no use turning to the pope, the writer says, a man "whose life, soiled with rape and robbery, has been spent in duping mankind."

Savelli's correspondent is convinced the emperor should be warned of these abominable crimes. The time of the Antichrist has come: "It is impossible to imagine a more avowed enemy of God than this pope. The least of his faults is that of trafficking in Church possessions; in this he is aided by the cardinal of Modena who, like Cerberus at the gate of Hell, barks at all comers and asks them shamelessly how much money they have." Alexander has besmirched the Vatican with blood, especially through the murders of Alfonso of Aragon and the chamberlain Perotto Caldes. The papal palace has been the scene of rape, incest, and the infamous treatment of adolescents and young girls. For good measure, the writer throws in the tale of the chestnut supper and the rutting stallions. Astonishingly, he goes on to describe Lucrezia's departure for Ferrara (which happened a month after the date given on the letter) as well as Cesare's latest campaigns in the Romagna (including the capture of Urbino and that of Camerino, which took place on July 19, 1502). The attacks on Cesare are as barbed as those directed to his father: "He has the same perversity, the same cruelty." He is blamed for having put an entire country to fire and the sword, with the blessing of the pope, who then parceled out the confiscated lands to his incestuous children and grandchildren. "Cesare is absolute master. He can assuage his passions as he wills. He lives surrounded by prostitutes, like the Turks, and guarded by his armed soldiers. At his orders men are killed, maimed, thrown into the Tiber, poisoned, despoiled of their possessions. These people thirst for human blood." The letter ends with a fervent plea to Maximilian: "If the emperor does not remedy the situation, Rome will become a desert. Everyone will be forced to flee in order to survive. Let the princes therefore come to the rescue of religion in distress! Let them save Peter's bark from the storm and guide it safely to port! Through them may justice and peace once more flourish under Rome!"

This letter-cum-pamphlet raises several problems. A comparison of its purported date with some of the incidents reported in it shows that the document, believed to have been written on November 25, 1501, refers to events that took place in July 1502. Burckard claims to have seen the letter after Cardinal Ferrari handed it to the pope. True, the cardinal could have shown it to him in November or December 1501, but it is unlikely he did so in July 1502: Burckard himself says that Ferrari fell seriously ill on July 3 and died, after a brief recovery, on the 20th—the day after the capture of Camerino described in the Savelli Letter.

It is disconcerting to see Cardinal Ferrari just as badly treated in the Savelli Letter as in the twenty-eight epigrams Burckard reproduces in his diary. That Ferrari got rich at Church expense was common knowledge, and Alexander profited from this wealth. At the cardinal's death he confiscated his possessions, which amounted to at least 14,000 ducats in cash. He availed himself, as was his right, of the rich benefices the cardinal left behind, notably the archbishopric of Capua and the see of Modena. Several wealthy prebendaries had been conferred on Ferrari's secretary and favorite, Sebastiano Pinzon. Later, under Pope Julius II, this unsavory character would be accused of having poisoned his master.

In attacking Cardinal Ferrari and accusing him of complicity with the pope, the Savelli Letter is in line with the pamphlet campaign carried out in July 1502 against Alexander's old crony, which indirectly sullied the pope.

It may be that a first letter, addressed, through Savelli, to the emperor and the Christian princes—and no doubt written in Italian, to make it look like a private latter—was circulated clandestinely during the winter of 1501. But this would not be the letter Burckard copied out in his diary, which was written in Latin and included elements that were added in the early summer of 1502.

The lampoons against the Borgias were based on the same accusations as those in the letter, rehashed as news. No amount of coercion could silence the pamphleteers. In December 1501 a Neapolitan called Manciano who had been going about Rome masked and uttering scurrilous language against Il Valentino was arrested on the orders of the duke, who, unlike his father, reacted swiftly and ruthlessly to criticism. The man's tongue was cut out and his right hand cut off and exposed, with the tongue hanging from the little finger, at one of the windows of the Church of Sta. Croce.

Not long after that a Venetian was arrested for translating another lampoon against the pope and his son into Greek and Latin. Despite the intervention of the Venetian ambassador, he was put to death that very evening. Alexander confided to Costabili, the Ferrarese envoy, "The duke is good-hearted but he has not yet learned how to tolerate insults."

Cesare welcomed in Milan
Renewal of his alliance with Louis XII

The French king was not oblivious to the hatred that had been building up against the Borgias. Nonetheless, when Cesare reached Milan on the morning of August 5 he gave him an effusive welcome, riding to meet him and calling him "my cousin" and "my dear relative," so much so that the disgruntled Italian lords began to regret that they had expressed their feelings about their enemy so openly. The king himself escorted Cesare into the apartments prepared for him in the castle of Milan, and invited him to use his clothes and horses as he wished. Next day saw a banquet and various festivities, where Cesare and the king sat side by side, with the powerful Cardinal d'Amboise behaving as cordially as his monarch. The lesson in all this was plain: Louis needed the pope's and his son's support in his campaign against Ferdinand of Aragon. For his part, d'Amboise was counting on Cesare's aid at the next conclave so that the pro-Borgia cardinals would vote for him as a candidate to the papal throne.

At this juncture, neither the complaints of the despoiled Italian lords nor the venemous pamphlet attacks found a ready audience with the French king. The Savelli Letter can be explained in this context. On October 13, 1501, at Trento, Louis had signed an agreement with Emperor Maximilian, who promised him the investiture of Milan. The emperor's son, Archduke Philip of Austria, had come to Blois with his wife Juana, the daughter of Ferdinand and Isabella. The archduke promised to arrange for their son and heir Charles—the future Emperor Charles V—to marry the French king's eldest daughter, Claude. Shortly thereafter a treaty signed at Lyon stated that Louis would hand over to Claude his possessions in the kingdom of Naples, while Ferdinand and Isabella would do likewise in favor of their grandson Charles.

This play of treaties seemed to ensure peace in southern Italy. But not long afterward a crisis arose between France and the Catholic Kings in the kingdom of Naples, compromising the agreement between the two dynasties. The anonymous writer of the Savelli Letter—who wrote from the Taranto camp of Gonsalvo de Cordoba, Ferdinand's general—had as his aim to break up the present agreement between France and the house of Austria, by encouraging Maximilian to condemn Alexander, and especially Cesare, Louis's main ally in Italy.

This and other equally virulent attacks did in fact achieve their purpose. The Austrians kept their distance from France and its Borgia ally. Archduke Philip, busy with preparations for his dynastic alliance with the French king, tried to intervene between Ferdinand and Louis but could do nothing to prevent confrontation in the kingdom of Naples. War was inevitable, and Cesare would side with France. So it was that in spite of hostile rumors and the grudges he might have had against Il Valentino, Louis behaved as the most cordial of hosts. The dispossessed Italian lords could only champ at the bit. Francesco da Gonzaga, for his part, made a shrewd about-face and proposed that his son be betrothed to Louise, the daughter of Cesare and Charlotte d'Albret. Given Mantua's situation—it was surrounded on all sides by territories held by France or its allies, Venice and Cesare Borgia—this matrimonial arrangement was a clever way to ensure peace in the duchy. When told of her husband's choice of future daughter-in-law, Isabella d'Este agreed, but not without a mental reservation. She hoped that the pope's death would bring about the ruin of the invading duke and cause the agreement binding her son to be annulled. In Milan, Cesare, reassured as to the king's good intentions, renewed his alliance with France, promising to fight at Louis's side for three years. For his part, the king would provide Il Valentino with 300 lances, which he could use as he wished against the Bentivoglios of Bologna and the condottieri Baglioni, Orsini, and Vitellozzo Vitelli if they refused to stop their attacks on Florence.

Louis invited his new ally to accompany him to Genoa, where he was to make a ceremonial entrance on August 26, and they left together, Cesare riding with him as far as Asti. When he took his leave, a royal guard of honor escorted the duke to the gates. September 7 found him back in Ferrara, where he once more saw Lucrezia, still on her sickbed. Again he came to his brother-in-law's aid, holding his sister's foot while she was being bled. But other, political matters also took up his time. Ercole d'Este and his son, who were closely linked like Cesare to the crown of France, discussed with him their plans for forcing Bologna to surrender.

Revolt of Bologna and rebellion of the condottieri
The Diet of Magione

Having secured Louis's agreement, Il Valentino was eager to go to Bologna and establish papal authority there. But Louis had asked him not to touch the lands of the Bentivoglios, the lords of Bologna. He had sent an envoy to Giovanni Bentivoglio to assure him personally of his protection, a rather irksome move for Cesare and Alexander.

The measures Rome was taking did not in fact augur a friendly alliance. On September 2 the pope published a brief summoning Bentivoglio and his two sons to appear in Rome within fifteen days to discuss ways of setting up a better government in Bologna. The Bentivoglios got out of this, supported by the Bolognese, who rallied around them, friends and enemies of the family alike.

While the entire city was declaring itself against Rome, Cesare returned to his domains at Imola to prepare a possible punitive raid. Cardinal Borgia, the bishop of Elna, and his lieutenant Ramiro de Lorca greeted him on his arrival. He also met once more his "excellent and most beloved engineer," Leonardo da Vinci, who had been inspecting the Romagnol forts during his absence. Leonardo's itinerary was full: July 30, Urbino; August 1, Pesaro, where he dreamed up new machines and made working drawings; August 8, Rimini, where he made notes about the music of one of the fountains; August 11, Cesena, the capital of the new duchy, where Cesare had asked him to erect a university building and appeals court, or Rota, where a "president of the Romagna," an administrative and judiciary head, would be headquartered. Cesare had already picked the man for this position, the wise Antonio del Monte San Savino, who would later strip the ruthless Ramiro de Lorca of all his old privileges. The president was solemnly installed in June 1503, the ceremony marking the crowning point of a masterly administrative organization.

As a result of the decree by which every household had to provide Cesare with one soldier, the Romagnol towns were beginning to look like recruiting centers. The town of Fano lined up 1,200 new soldiers, while at Imola, Cesare ordered two regiments, each consisting of 500 pikemen, to wear his colors of red and yellow. Michele Corella was put at the head of this militia, which saved the duke the trouble of using mercenaries or condottieri.

In September 1502 Il Valentino was still a long way from his goal of military independence, as the Bologna drama showed. On the 17th, after the pope's fifteen-day time limit had elapsed, the brief was read out a second time in the Reggimento palace, and the citizens, who had taken up arms, shouted that they would not let Bentivoglio leave for Rome. This rebellion against the pope and his son called for swift reprisals, yet Cesare could not carry them out as his condottieri were far away, 90 miles to the south, near Perugia. As soon as the condottieri heard of the Borgias' designs on the Bentivoglios, they registered their disapproval. Such a plan, they pointed out, violated the treaty between Cesare and the Bentivoglios drawn up at the surrender of Castel Bolognese. Since Vitellozzo Vitelli and the Orsinis had vouched for that treaty, they could not possibly take part in any action against Bologna. If they allowed Cesare to bring down the Bentivoglios of Bologna— like the Riarios of Imola, the Malatestas of Rimini, the Sforzas of Pesaro, the Manfredis of Faenza, the Appianos of Piombino, the Montefeltros of Urbino, and the Varanos of Camerino—they feared they would be hounded out of their own lands and exterminated.

The first condottieri to rise up against Cesare were Vitellozzo Vitelli and the two Baglionis of Perugia, Gentile and Giampaolo. Meeting at Todi on the 25th, they decided to refuse to attack Bologna if ordered to do so. They appealed to the other condottieri in Cesare's employ. Five days later a plenary meeting took place at Magione, a stronghold that belonged to Cardinal Orsini, situated on a hill above Lake Trasimeno, about 12 miles west of Perugia. The Orsinis had joined the conspiracy because Louis had told their cardinal in Milan that the pope intended to crush their family.

Several fierce warriors stood out in the motley group. Besides the Baglionis and Vitelli, who was in the throes of syphilis and had to be carried about in a litter, there were the Orsinis, as well as Pandolfo Petrucci of Siena, whom Cesare considered the prime mover of the conspiracy, and the sinister Oliveretto da Fermo. Joining them was Hermes Bentivoglio, who had the reputation of being an assassin, having rid Bologna of the Marescottis, his family's enemies. All the participants resolved to rally around the Bentivoglios if Cesare persisted in his plan. They would not remain inactive in the face of aggression: before the French lances arrived, they vowed to raise an army of 700 armed men and 9,000 footsoldiers. They also invited Florence and Venice to join them against Cesare. Only Venice agreed, ordering its condottiere Bartolomeo Alviano to restore Guidobaldo, who had fled to the Adriatic coast, to his duchy of Urbino. The conspirators' plan of action called for Bentivoglio to march on Imola while his allies seized Urbino and Pesaro.

This was a formidable threat, which could have been fatal to Cesare, who at that time had no more than 2,500 foot and 400 horse. Luckily for him, however, the conspirators distrusted one another. When the Diet ended, Pandolfo Petrucci sent word to Cesare that he would not take any action against him. The Orsinis, for their part, were negotiating with the pope in Rome, Paolo Orsini toying with the idea of going to Imola to assure Il Valentino of his family's loyalty. Finally, the slippery Giovanni Bentivoglio tried to start negotiations with Cesare through Ercole d'Este.

Machiavelli's second mission
The duchy of Urbino slips out of Cesare's grasp

Still fearing Cesare, the republic of Florence was even more fearful of Vitellozzo Vitelli and the Orsinis, whom it suspected of trying to restore their relatives the Medicis to power. The Florentines therefore felt they should warn Il Valentino of the plot against him, protesting that the republic could not approve of a plan which, through Cesare, was also directed against the king of France. On October 5 the secretary Niccolò Machiavelli was entrusted with the mission.

For the next three months, Machiavelli—who was not well off, suffered from poor health, and hated being away from his young wife, Marietta—would be forced to live in Cesare's entourage amid the hardships of the Romagnol camps. The duke's character and the extraordinary events he witnessed would relegate Machiavelli's personal problems to the background, and his letters very quickly took on a passionately excited tone. Out of his memories he would create an immortal work.

Riding post so as to reach Imola as quickly as he could, the secretary arrived on October 7 to be ushered, still in his traveling garb, into Cesare's presence. He thanked the duke for giving the Florentine merchants back the cloth that had been confiscated from them at Urbino and then mentioned the Diet of Magione. In reply Cesare assured him that he had never approved of the actions of those condottieri who were Florence's enemies—Vitellozzo Vitelli and the Orsinis—and claimed he was strong enough to stand up to the rebels.

He did not believe the group had any strength, and he confided in Machiavelli that the Orsinis and Petruccis were already making overtures to him. The only thing worrying him was a troublesome incident that had happened that very day. While work was being done on the San Leo fortress, some villagers who favored the duke of Urbino had seized the place, even though its entrance was barred with beams. As they did so, he added, "some say they shouted St. Mark's name, others, the Orsinis' and Vitellis'."

The fall of San Leo, the historic capital of the Montefeltro dynasty, was of some consequence. The news, relayed from one mountain to the next, started a sort of chain reaction as one stronghold after another rose up in revolt. After three days the whole duchy was handed over to its former lord, Guidobaldo. The castle of Urbino was captured by the peasants who, with the help of the townsfolk, fired at it with cannons that had been left behind in the stronghold. The governor just managed to escape and flee to Forlì with a convoy of fifteen mules loaded with treasure.

Cesare took this frontal blow bravely. He showed Machiavelli a dispatch from France dated October 4 informing him that Louis and Cardinal d'Amboise had ordered the governor of the Milanese, Chaumont d'Amboise, to send Il Valentino 300 lances at once to help him in his plans against Bologna. If Cesare so desired, the governor would come to Parma himself with 300 more. "If they acted in this way when I asked for troops to attack Bologna," added Cesare, "they will act quite differently when I request them for use against those who, being mostly sworn enemies of the king, have always tried to do him harm in Italy. . . . Their plans will turn to my advantage. Nothing could be more useful to me in order to fortify my states. Now I'll be able to tell who my friends are and whom I should distrust. If the Venetians side with my enemies, which I doubt, they will fulfill all my wishes and those of His Majesty." The audience ended with a plea to Florence to form an alliance—an appeal that the Signoria would contrive, with Machiavelli's help, to leave unanswered.

Armed struggle between Cesare and the rebel condottieri

As soon as he arrived, Machiavelli began trying to size up Cesare's forces. After the fall of Urbino, Michelotto Corella was given orders to regroup them at Rimini, and Ramiro de Lorca was told to reinforce the Romagna garrisons. In early October, Il Valentino had 2,500 footsoldiers, plus 800 men enlisted in the Val da Lamona and 1,000 mercenaries that Michelotto was to recruit—in all, 4,300 infantry. He had 1,000 mercenaries raised, Gascons in Lombardy as well as Swiss. Supporting these offensive forces would be a reserve army of 5,000 Romagnols. As for the cavalry, it was based on Cesare's company of 100 lances and three 50-lance companies under the command of three Spanish captains. Leading the light horse was Gaspare San Severino, better known as Captain Fracassa, and Ludovico Pico della Mirandola.

By the end of the month, according to the figures Machiavelli sent Florence, Cesare's army totaled 5,350 footsoldiers, including 600 Gascons and Germans. It would later gain 3,000 Swiss. The men-at-arms numbered 340 (or around 1,300 including the gunners). With the addition of the five French companies—some 2,000 men in all—promised by Louis, which had just begun to march into Faenzan territory, that made 840 units of heavy cavalry (3,300 men) already raised. According to Machiavelli, they would be joined by at least 150 more men-at-arms raised in Lombardy, along with further cavalry units, some 500 light horse and detached lances. The fire power was good, Machiavelli judging Cesare's artillery to be as great as that of all the other Italian states combined.

Cesare's situation vis-à-vis the rebel condottieri was therefore not as bad as they thought. It was, however, compromised by an ill-timed move on the part of Michelotto Corella and Ugo de Moncada, another Spanish captain. On the Rimini road they went to the aid of the commanders of Pergola and Fossombrone, which were being besieged by the inhabitants. As a reprisal they then massacred the population, women and children included. A delighted Il Valentino told Machiavelli: "This year the stars do not seem to favor the rebels." But he soon had to swallow his words. Having decided to help Guidobaldo, Vitelli and the Orsinis advanced toward Urbino, skirmishing with Corella and Moncada at Calmazzo, near Fossombrone. Even with their 100 lances and 200 light horse, Cesare's captains were defeated and de Moncada was taken prisoner. That same day, the rebel condottieri reached Urbino, triumphant. Paolo Orsini wrote to Venice telling the exiled duke the good news, and Guidobaldo made for his capital once again, entering Urbino shortly afterward amid general rejoicing.

Vitellozzo Vitelli offered to recapture Guidobaldo's Urbino strongholds for him, while Oliveretto da Fermo invested Camerino. Giampaolo Baglioni marched up to Fano, where he besieged Michelotto. After some hesitation, Giovanni Bentivoglio threw the hostility of the Bolognese in the Borgias' face, ordering the university's professors of canon law to tell the people, from the church pulpits, to ignore the interdict the pope had placed on the city.

The conspiracy crumbles

Venice, which had been supporting the conspirators, now left them in the lurch, prompted by a letter from Louis threatening to treat the doge as an enemy if he opposed "the Church's enterprise." The withdrawal of Venetian support gave some of the rebels food for thought. Pandolfo Petrucci sent his secretary to Cesare to negotiate an agreement. Paolo Orsini came in person to Imola on October 25, leaving a few days later with the text of a treaty in his hands, according to which Cesare promised to protect the estates of any condottiere who became his ally and vowed to serve him and Mother Church. As for the Bentivoglios' fate, it would be debated in a small committee made up of Cesare, Cardinal Orsini, and Pandolfo Petrucci. Any decision it reached would have to be accepted unanimously.

Machiavelli, at first surprised by this apparent capitulation, was told confidentially by Cesare that he had nothing but scorn for this "rabble of bankrupts." "I am biding my time," muttered the duke.

There was in fact some merit in biding time. During the long waiting period Cesare had to go on paying his troops, though he forbade them to do their usual pillaging of towns. Up until December, Alexander forked out 6,000 ducats to pay for his son's army, while in consistories and at ambassadors' receptions he condemned the condottieri's action and lauded Louis of France, who was supporting Cesare. To emphasize his hostility to Ferdinand of Aragon, then fighting France in the kingdom of Naples, he imprisoned his daughter-in-law Sancia in the Castel Sant'Angelo—ostensibly because of her loose morals. Her young husband, Jofré, was proving less than impressive: when the pope asked him to review a company of 100 men-at-arms, he proved incapable of equipping them. Nonetheless, despite these domestic problems, the aging pope thought only of flattering Florence, Ferrara, and Mantua, the states capable of coming to Cesare's aid. He paid Francesco da Gonzaga 40,000 ducats out of the dowry set aside for Cesare's infant daughter and gave the marquess's brother the promise of a cardinal's hat.

As time passed, the condottieri were just as much hated by the people as their adversaries, for their actions were equally violent. When Oliveretto Eufreducci took Camerino, along with Gianmaria Varano, he massacred all the Spaniards he found there. Michele Corella's revenge was cruel and swift. Having captured young Piero Varano at Pesaro, en route to Camerino, he had him strangled in the public square. The young man was carried into the nearby church, where he recovered, but a Spanish monk guarding him noticed it and called some soldiers to finish the deed. Recognized later at Cagli, the monk was torn limb from limb by the enraged crowd.

The rebels negotiate with Cesare

Returning to his cronies with the draft of Cesare's proposed treaty in his hands, Paolo Orsini called a meeting in the little village church of Cortocetto, near Fano. He pointed out that the duke was offering them a reasonable way to settle their differences, but some of the others objected to the idea of entering Cesare's service and undoing what they had just achieved. They drew the line at hounding Guidobaldo out of Urbino a second time. This was Vitelli's reason for turning down the agreement, which also put an end to his plans of revenge on Florence. It was, however, Baglioni who most strongly opposed it. He refused to study Cesare's conditions and urged his fellow condottieri to remember what a devilish character they were dealing with. If they were not completely mad, he said, they should realize that their only hope lay in their weapons.

Paolo Orsini, who was a smooth speaker, managed to rally all the others by showing them that if they went on opposing Cesare they would soon be completely and dangerously isolated. Indeed, by early November Il Valentino had already made separate deals with the Orsinis and Pandolfo Petrucci. He received Antonio Galeazzo Bentivoglio, sent as a negotiator by his father at the urging of Ercole d'Este, and a treaty guaranteeing the Borgias and Bentivoglios was drawn up and signed at the Vatican on November 23, with the king of France and Florence and Ferrara as guarantors. Bologna would provide Cesare with 100 lances and 200 light horse for one or two campaigns a year. The city would pay him 12,000 ducats in return for a *condotta* of 100 lances that the duke promised to put at Bologna's disposal for five years. This Borgia-Bentivoglio alliance eliminated the grievance that had provoked the condottieri's rebellion in the first place. In theory there was nothing to stop them from signing a treaty that reconciled the other condottieri with Cesare as well.

On November 27 Paolo Orsini entered Imola bearing the document, now signed by all the rebels, including Vittellozzo Vitelli. Two days later, to fulfill the promises in the treaty, he reached Urbino, together with the president of the Romagna tribunal, ready to retake possession in Cesare's name. Guidobaldo watched in anguish as his subjects ran up to offer him jewels and gold and silver to enable him to make a last stand. But he realized his means were limited. He agreed to withdraw, in return for a promise that he would be allowed to keep the Montefeltro fortresses of San Leo, Majuolo, Sant'Agata, and San Marino. Amidst general weeping, he left his little capital and went to Città di Castello to stay with his friend Bishop Vitelli, the first stop in his exile.

Once again Cesare was duke of Urbino. He ordered the reconciled condottieri to help him reconquer a number of small towns, the first being Sinigaglia, which Giovanna da Montefeltro held in the name of her young son Francesco Maria della Rovere, Guidobaldo's nephew. As they were making their way there, on December 10, Cesare turned off on the road leading to Cesena. He divided his troops among the Romagnol garrisons so as to lessen the burden of maintaining soldiers in each stronghold, "which," wrote Machiavelli, "did not prevent the country from suffering severely that winter." To avoid shortages, Cesare had bought 30,000 bushels of wheat in Venice, which were rapidly consumed. He had to fall back on private stocks of grain in Cesena. These acute food-supply problems served as an excuse for disbanding three companies of French troops, which took off for Lombardy, leaving Cesare with just two companies of fifty men each.

The apparent reduction in the forces surrounding the duke soothed the fears Vitelli and the other conspirators still harbored concerning Cesare, oblivious as they were to the fact that 1,000 Swiss mercenaries had just turned up in strictest secrecy. In reality, Cesare could at any moment have gathered around him an army of 13,000, a huge figure which was hidden from the conspirators' spies by the scattering of troops in the garrisons. From this point on, Cesare had it within his power to entice the former rebels into a trap and exterminate them.

Execution of Ramiro de Lorca

On December 22 a ball was held at Cesena for the departing French. At the same time people celebrated an unforeseen event, the arrest of the hated and ruthless Ramiro de Lorca, Cesare's lieutenant general of the Romagna. He had been seized on his return from Pesaro, where he had gone on official business to get grain. After three days in prison, he was condemned to death for embezzlement, accused of exporting huge quantities of the wheat he was supposed to bring back. What really earned him the death penalty was that he had treacherously plotted with the condottieri to trap Il Valentino. At dawn on December 26 the people of Cesena found his headless body lying in the middle of the piazza. He was dressed in his rich suit and purple mantle. His head, with its black beard, was impaled on a pike, while beside the corpse lay the bloodstained execution block and blade.

The execution of one of Cesare's most loyal servants caught everyone's imagination. Machiavelli drew a moral from it: "The reason for his death is not known, save that the prince willed it so, which shows that he can make and unmake men at his will, according to their merits." Later, in Chapter VII of *The Prince*, the Florentine secretary would give another explanation:

"The tyranny of his servant Ramiro had been necessary to ensure Cesare's dominion. Then, as time passed, because he knew that past rigors had generated some hatred for Ramiro, to purge the spirits of that people and to gain them entirely to himself, he wished to show that if any cruelty had been committed, this had not come from him but from the harsh nature of his minister."

The trap at Sinigaglia

On the day Ramiro was executed, Cesare quit Cesena, leaving the mutilated body on the town square, and marched south on the Via Emilia. Three days later he arrived at Fano, where he received the envoys of the city of Ancona, who assured him of their loyalty. A messenger from Vitellozzo Vitelli announced that the little Adriatic port of Sinigaglia had surrendered to the condottieri and that Giovanna da Montefeltro, the regent, had set sail for Venice. Only the citadel, in charge of the Genoese Andrea Doria, still held out, and Doria refused to hand it over to anyone except Cesare himself.

The duke sent word that he would arrive the next day, which was just what the condottieri wanted to hear. Once he reached Sinigaglia, Cesare would be an easy prey, caught between the citadel and their forces ringing the town. To gain their trust, he told them he wanted to set himself up in the town. He asked Vitelli to clear it of all troops. Oliveretto Eufreducci moved his small following to quarters on the outskirts of the town, while Vitellozzo and the Orsinis camped in nearby villages. The condottieri were sure they had military superiority, believing that the departure of the French troops had left Cesare with only a small force.

In fact, according to Machiavelli, Il Valentino had left Cesena with 10,000 infantrymen and 3,000 horse, taking pains to split up his men so that they would march along parallel routes before converging on Sinigaglia. The reason for such a large force was that he knew, from a confession extracted from Ramiro de Lorca, what the condottieri had up their sleeve. He therefore decided to turn their own trap against them. This was the masterpiece of trickery that the historian Paolo Giovio later called *"il bellissimo inganno,"* "the magnificent deceit."

At dawn on December 31, Cesare reached the outskirts of Sinigaglia—the new town, or Borgo, which was separated from the old town by a canal linked to the little River Misa. He noted that only Oliveretto's soldiers (1,000 foot and 150 cavalry) were billeted there. Led by Michelotto Corella, Cesare's advance guard of 200 lances took up its position on the canal bridge, in two lines facing each other to allow the infantry and most of the duke's cavalry to pass through to the town. This control of the bridge effectively prevented the conspirators' troops from withdrawing to the town. Cesare was wearing a breastplate instead of his usual doublet, as a protection against any shots that might be fired at him. Surprised by all these precautions, which were ruining their plan, Francesco Orsini, Paolo Orsini, and his son moved forward unarmed. Glumly, Vitellozzo Vitelli followed them on his mule, wearing a black cape lined with green. He had come against his better judgment, having an intuition of the pending disaster, and had not had time to arm himself or make ready his horse.

Cesare greeted the condottieri effusively and invited them to join him. On the town piazza Oliveretto was parading at the head of a contingent, but at a sign from Cesare, Michelotto asked him to send his soldiers back to their billets and join his companions, who were trotting along with the duke.

Michelotto had prepared the Palazzo Bernardino for Cesare's use, and the duke invited the condottieri inside. The building had one door at the front and another in back. Once indoors the men were quietly arrested by guards who crept up from the rear. Going outside the palace, the duke calmly gave instructions for the escort to disperse— his guests had no need of it now. Then he gave orders for an attack on Vitelli's and the Orsinis' soldiers in the outlying areas. Oliveretto's forces were to be hunted down in the Sinigaglia Borgo and sacked. That night, while their troops were being crushed, Michelotto throttled Oliveretto and Vitelli in the Bernardino palace after a cursory trial. Oliveretto had made a clumsy attempt to escape this ignominious death by plunging a dagger into his heart. Vitellozzo had simply begged Cesare to ask the pope to grant him a plenary indulgence for the salvation of his soul. At daybreak the bodies were carried to the nearby church of the Misericordia hospital. Against the Orsinis, who were being kept under arrest, Cesare would do nothing until he knew if his father had managed to arrest Giulio Orsini and Cardinal Giambattista in Rome. The two men were, therefore, led behind him in chains.

"An act worthy of a Roman"

At one fell swoop, Il Valentino had got rid of his former generals and worst enemies. To Machiavelli he said he rejoiced because "these men were also avowed enemies of Florence." The next day, the citadel having surrendered after Andrea Doria's flight, Cesare sent word to the various Italian rulers explaining what he had done. He had been forced, he asserted, to forestall the conspirators' treacherous actions, and he asked each ruler to give thanks to God that he had been able to put an end to the disasters Italy had suffered because of the evildoers.

No doubt there was much truth in this judgment on the conspirators, who were out-and-out ruffians, with the possible exception of Vitellozzo, whose only motive at the outset was to avenge his father's death. So it is not surprising that the Sinigaglia affair provoked almost universal admiration. In France, Charlotte d'Albret was shocked at what her husband had done, but Louis considered it an exalted deed "worthy of a Roman." Cesare's success was generally attributed to his good luck. But Machiavelli, whose mission was drawing to a close and who lived through all the vicissitudes before the coup at Cesare's side, showed in his perspicacious reflection on the Sinigaglia trap that it was the end result of some extremely shrewd calculations. The whole exploit bore the stamp of Il Valentino's genius, his *virtù*, which was made up of intuition, reasoning, and bravery, never hampered by vulgar scruples. The conspirators' execution crowned a career where crime was carried out only for highly political ends, for a higher good. When Isabella da Gonzaga received Cesare's message, she at once wrote back congratulating him, adding that "because we think that after the strains and fatigues you have undergone in this glorious enterprise you might perhaps wish to have some diversion, I had the idea of sending you a hundred masks, by my messenger Giovanni."

Occupation of the rebels' lands

Yet, for Cesare, the time for rejoicing had not yet come. The condottieri now out of the way, his next task was to seize their possessions. Swiftly he made for Città di Castello and there reestablished the power of the Church of Rome. Then he pushed on to Perugia, where Giampaolo Baglioni had gathered together Guidobaldo of Urbino, Fabio Orsini, Annibale and Venanzio Varano, and Vitelli's nephew—all of whom scattered as quickly as they could when they heard the duke was coming. Perugia swore obedience to him, and Cesare set up his secretary Agapito Gherardi as his representative while another of his trusted followers was sent to Fermo, now rid of its tyrant, Oliveretto.

Not far from Perugia the duke's men captured Penthesilea Baglioni, the wife of the famous Venetian condottiere Bartolomeo Alviano, and imprisoned her in the fortress of Todi with her children and women as a potential hostage. After several protests by the Venetian ambassador, however, Cesare had her freed. The incident shows his extraordinary ability to size up the risk and merits of a situation and the extreme care he always took to choose the best moment in which to act. Another example is in his treatment of the two members of the Orsini family taken prisoner at Sinigaglia. As Cesare made his way from Perugia to Siena, from which he intended to oust Petrucci, the duke of Gravina and Paolo Orsini were dragged along in chains in his train. Their fate was trickier to settle than Oliveretto's or Vitellozzo's: they could not be punished while the head of their clan, Cardinal

Giambattista, was at liberty, and the pope was taking his time about laying hands on him.

Arrest of Cardinal Orsini
Execution of his relatives

The pope was playing his role to perfection. He invited Cardinal Orsini to the New Year celebrations—lavish banquets in the company of beautiful women and fancy dress parades, at one of which a row of thirty transvestites sauntered past wearing false noses "in the shape of a priapus," that is, male genitals. Thus entertained, Giambattista felt reassured about his fate and thought it would be a good move to congratulate the pope on the capture of Sinigaglia. As he was on his way to the Vatican to wait for Alexander in the Sala del Pappagallo, he was promptly arrested and taken prisoner to the Castel Sant'Angelo. Incarcerated with him were Rinaldo Orsini, the archbishop of Florence, Bernardino Alviano, brother of the condottiere Bartolomeo, and Giacomo Santa Croce, a friend of the Orsinis, who was soon let out on bail. The cardinal's estates were seized and his eighty-year-old mother hounded out of her house and thrown into the street, with nothing but the clothes on her back and two servant women, as no one would risk taking her in. All these moves threw Rome into a panic; the bishop of Chiusi actually died of fright.

On hearing of the cardinal's arrest, Cesare had his relatives, Paolo Orsini and the duke of Gravina, strangled on the spot. The executions took place on January 18 at Sartiano, near Castel della Pieve. That done, Cesare pushed deep into Sienese territory, laying waste the little towns of Pienza, Chiusi, and San Quirico. On January 27 he gave the Sienese an ultimatum, leaving them twenty-four hours to expel Petrucci from the city. He won his case, then set out down the long road to Rome, passing Acquapendente, Montefiascone, and Viterbo, which he pillaged. He had no respect for Church property and preferred to give his old troopers pleasure rather than provoke mutiny in their ranks.

Campaign against the Orsinis

Meanwhile, in Rome, Alexander had sent Jofré off to the Orsinis' lands, a mission that turned out to be beyond the young man's capabilities. Now the pope turned to Cesare, urging him to destroy the various members of that powerful clan and their friends, especially the Savellis—including Silvio Savelli, the addressee of the mysterious anti-Borgia diatribe. The most powerful of these lords was Giangiordano Orsini, entrenched behind the stout walls of his Bracciano castle, so he had to be the first to go. Cesare, however, refused to obey his father's orders. Was not Giangiordano in the pay of the king of France? Further, Cesare pointed out that he was bound by his oath as a knight of the Order of St. Michael not to attack a fellow knight. He balked again when Alexander asked him to lay siege to Pitigliano, a fief of the famous condottiere Niccolò Orsini, a former captain general of the Church and now a general in the Venetian army. He knew that from now on he had to be especially careful, as Louis had just formed an alliance between Siena, Lucca, Florence, and Bologna to put a curb on Cesare's activities. Confining his energies to what he considered possible, he decided to besiege the fortress of Ceri, on a small hill east of Cerveteri, which was being defended by the cardinal's brother Giulio Orsini, in place of its lord, Giovanni.

Tragic death of Cardinal Orsini

To this dawdling on the part of his son the pope reacted by treating his prisoner, the cardinal, even more harshly. In the midst of the Carnival celebrations Orsini's old mother came to see the pope and begged him to let her prepare her son's food and bring it to him herself in the dungeon of the Castel Sant'Angelo. Without mentioning her fears that he was being poisoned, she tried to buy her way by having a gift of 2,000 ducats and a beautiful pearl handed to the pope by one of her son's mistresses, who came to the Vatican disguised as a horseman. But it was too late. The cardinal died on February 22 and, as rumors of poisoning spread, Alexander ordered the body to be carried to the burial place in an open coffin so everyone could see it was not covered in blotches, as was commonly thought to happen in cases of poisoning. Yet neither this gesture nor doctors' testimony affected public opinion in the least. People recalled that the Borgias believed the cardinal, along with Pandolfo Petrucci, was at the heart of the condottiere conspiracy. His disappearance was therefore a necessary political act. Burckard's diary stops at the cardinal's dramatic death, not resuming until six months later, on August 12. Fortunately, envoys' dispatches and chronicles make it possible to fill the gap, which was probably caused by a trip of Burckard's to Strasbourg. Indeed, history continued its ineluctable course in the Eternal City.

Final aftereffects of the condottiere revolt

The siege of Ceri gave Cesare a chance to deploy new weapons, in particular several sophisticated machines that came from the fertile brain of Leonardo da Vinci—ballistas, dummy guns, and catapults, as well as a huge sloping platform that allowed soldiers to attack ramparts without risk. On April 6, after a month-long siege, the stronghold surrendered, with Giulio Orsini receiving a pass allowing him to withdraw to Pitigliano with his sons.

To the north of Rome, meanwhile, the papal troops were seizing Savelli possessions. The biggest coup was the capture of Palombara Sabina, near the frontier of the kingdom of Naples. Thus Silvio Savelli was rendered harmless. To mark the end of hostilities Alexander behaved generously, receiving Giulio Orsini, who had come to visit him with Cesare, and treating him like a gentleman. In spite of all the bloodshed, the reconciliation would serve Cesare's interests in time to come.

While the fate of the Orsinis and their allies was being weighed, the pope's son was able to consolidate his hold over the Romagna, even in absentia, thanks to the special commissioners he set up in each town. The duchy of Urbino, where scattered revolts were flaring up, was put under the iron hand of Pedro Ramirez, a Spanish officer. Cesare took advantage of the confusion and postponed the agreement he had made with Guidobaldo, ordering his men to attack the forts the deposed duke still had under his control. Ottaviano Fregoso and Palmerio Tiberti besieged Majuolo and San Leo, while Ugo de Moncada camped before Cagli and a watchful eye was kept on Camerino. Annibale and Venanzio Varano, who might one day escape and try to retake their father's estates, were strangled in Cattolica by one of Michelotto Corella's nephews.

Cesare prepares to intervene in the Neapolitan war
Suspicious death of Cardinal Michieli
Creation of new cardinals

Cesare's resounding victory left him in a good position to respond to the call of his ally, Louis of France, who was suffering severe reverses in the kingdom of Naples. Stuart d'Aubigny, defeated in Calabria, had been captured by the Spanish, and the duke of Nemours, after fighting at Cerignola, had withdrawn to the Castel Nuovo in Naples, which underwent a long siege before surrendering on June 12. A little farther north, the French were holding their own at Gaeta. Louis sent the marquess of Saluces to Naples to relieve the forts. In the meantime he made ready to attack Fuenterrabia, and even Barcelona and Valencia. Realizing that he would need the support of all his allies in Italy, Louis begged them to join the new army he was sending out under the command of La Trémoille. At once, Florence, Ferrara, and Mantua agreed. Alexander and his son hesitated, however, even though all was in order for Cesare to take part in the new Neapolitan campaign.

It was thanks to his father that Cesare's army was in this state of readiness. The pope had got hold of the necessary funds by his usual methods. In March he had created eight new posts at the Vatican which called for a payment of 760 ducats per candidate. Michelotto had registered several supposed Marranos, or Christian converts, liable to be heavily taxed, and on the death of the Venetian cardinal Giovanni Michieli, Alexander had had his whole fortune seized, all 150,000 ducats of it, as well as some priceless articles, including a fine silver dinner service. The death was at once deemed suspicious, since the cardinal had been sick only two days, during which he had vomited violently. The ambassador Giustiniani wrote to the Council of Ten in Venice, "The pope has the habit of fattening his cardinals before poisoning them, the better to inherit their wealth."

More than in the case of other quick deaths that were useful to the pope, there is some evidence that Michieli's death was indeed caused by poisoning. In 1504, under Pope Julius, the cardinal's secretary, Asquinio da Collorado, who was condemned to death, made a last-minute confession that he had administered poison to Michieli on Alexander's and Cesare's orders. But these declarations, extracted by torture or false promises, have to be treated with caution. Poisoning was at that time a very inexact science. When poisonous substances were mixed together, after being steeped a long time or brought to their boiling point, they often lost their noxious properties. While it is certainly not impossible that the Borgias used "the green powder" (cantarella) or "the white powder" (arsenic), administered either by a strong dose or as a slow poison, the number of cases in which they succeeded must have been minuscule. A surer way to get rid of someone was by strangulation or repeated stabbing with a dagger.

The rich Venetian cardinal's money proving insufficient, the pope appointed nine new cardinals in May. They included four of his friends, all Spaniards. Two of the men were related to the pope, one was a boyhood friend of Cesare's, and the others came from powers friendly to the Borgias. Each new prince of the Church paid an estimated 120,000 to 130,000 ducats for their red hats.

What could be done with all that money? Raise fresh troops, outfit them in red-and-yellow uniforms with Cesare's name embroidered front and back, and have them parade before the pope. In this way Cesare delighted his father in April when 500 men of his elite corps marched past under the Vatican windows. Still, Cesare was not prepared to send them off to fight alongside the French. He considered Louis to be in a bad position at this point and was preparing a rapprochement with Aragon by way of secret conversations with Captain Gonsalvo de Cordoba. The pope's private secretary, Francesco Troches, who was privy to these negotiations—and furious at not being raised to the purple—fled from Rome in mid-May, most likely to relay these secrets to the king of France. Seized on a ship bound for Corsica, he was brought back to Rome and secretly strangled, having first talked for an hour with Cesare in a Trastevere prison.

It did not take long for rumors to fly concerning Il Valentino's treachery vis-à-vis France. But Alexander quashed them roundly by announcing in consistory at the end of July that Cesare was about to join the French army in Naples with 500 horse and 2,000 footsoldiers.

Dinner in Cardinal da Corneto's vineyard
The pope's illness and death

On the eve of Cesare's planned departure for Naples (August 6), father and son went to dine in the vineyard of Adriano Castellesi da Corneto, a scholar and humanist who had recently been made cardinal. They lingered on into the night, enjoying the cool air—imprudently, since Rome was in the grip of malaria, and already several of the pope's intimates had fallen victim to the disease. Rodrigo, his grand-nephew, an extremely stout man who commanded the pope's guard, was one; another was Juan Borgia, the cardinal-archbishop of Monreale, who was obese. Watching the funeral corteges gloomily from his window, Alexander had confided to Giustiniani that "this month is bad for those who are fat"—an allusion to himself. Just then an owl flew in and flopped down at his feet, and with a cry of "Bad omen! It's a bad omen!" Alexander hastily retreated to his room.

The omen was in fact about to be fulfilled. In the week following the dinner, Alexander and Cesare both felt ill. On August 11, at the service celebrating the anniversary of his election, all the envoys noticed how agitated the pope looked. Cesare delayed his departure. Next day the pope became violently feverish and coughed up bile. The doctors bled him on the 15th, Burckard noting that 13 ounces of blood were taken from him—a considerable amount for a man seventy-two years old. Feeling slightly better, he asked a few cardinals to come to his bedside and play cards with him. His faithful doctor, the bishop of Venosa, watched over him day and night.

On his own sickbed, Cesare had the same severe feverish attacks, suffering terrible stomach pains and vomiting. To get rid of the fever his doctors plunged him in a great oil jar filled with ice water, which made the skin peel over his entire body. While he seemed to be recovering, the pope's condition deteriorated on the 17th. The next day all hope was lost. The old man confessed to the bishop of Carinola, a fellow Valencian, and received extreme unction. Burckard noted that he never once asked to see either Cesare, Lucrezia, or Jofré. Perhaps, on his deathbed, he was striving, out of piety or fear of Eternal Judgment, to clear his mind of all thoughts of the ones to whom he had so passionately devoted his energies, setting their welfare above that of Christianity. . . . Toward vespers, Alexander VI drew his last breath.

On receiving the news of his father's death, Cesare, still on his sickbed, gave orders to the faithful Michelotto, who forced Cardinal-Chamberlain Casanova to hand over the keys to the pope's closets, under threat of death. There, Michelotto seized 200,000 ducats' worth of silver and jewels and two chests containing 100,000 gold coins. Following the strange but hallowed tradition, the palace servants then proceeded to ransack the papal apartments.

A diabolical sight

While the pillaging raged, Burckard dressed the body and had it borne into the Vatican's Sala del Papagallo, where it remained all night in solitary state, as no one could be found to watch over it and recite the Office for the Dead. The next day the corpse was placed on a bier behind the railings of the high altar in St. Peter's. The face rapidly became black and swollen, the tongue doubling in size and hanging grotesquely out of the mouth. "It was a hideous sight," wrote Burckard. "He seemed monstrous and horrible, black as the Devil," added Giustiniani. Dreadful tales began to be whispered. According to one, a demon had entered the funerary chamber in the shape of a monkey, seeking the pope's soul.

Francesco da Gonzaga, writing to his wife from the French camp in Viterbo, described the weirdest of the rumors: "While the pope was sick, he began to speak in such a strange way that people thought he was delirious, even though he was quite lucid. He called out, 'I am coming, I am coming, but wait a little more!' Those who were privy to the secret said that after Innocent's death during the conclave, he made a pact with the Devil, buying the papacy in exchange for his soul. Among other conditions it was stipulated that he would live and profit from the throne of St. Peter for twelve years, which indeed he did, with the addition of four days. They said he saw seven devils in the room when he was on the point of dying. When he died, the body began to boil and the mouth to foam like a cauldron on the fire, and that lasted as long as he was above ground. He also swelled up in extraordinary fashion, ceasing to have human form, and there was no difference between the length and the width of the body."

In the August heat, the body decomposed rapidly, and in the evening of the 19th it was buried provisionally in the Capello delle Febbre. Six porters carried the corpse, trying unceremoniously to stuff it into a coffin that was obviously too small. Then, with the help of two carpenters, they threw aside the pope's miter, covered the body with an old cloth, and pummeled it into the coffin with their fists. Not a candle was lit; no priest was present at the barbaric interment. Writing to Isabella, Gonzaga said that even the dwarf wife of a cripple in Mantua had had a more honorable burial.

The different phases of Alexander's illness and the hideous appearance of his corpse pointed to poisoning, and very soon Rome was seething with rumors. It was noted that Adriano da Corneto and the pope's other guests, three of them cardinals, had also fallen sick. Had they, too, ingested poison? Pietro Martire d'Anghiera, who was visiting Spain, recounted the scene of the fatal banquet and the macabre remedy the doctor had prescribed for Cesare—being plunged into the palpitating entrails of a disemboweled mule. The sixteenth-century historian Paolo Giovio repeats the banquet scene, simply changing the remedy to immersion in ice water. Guiccardini and most later historians relay the same legend: in agreement with the pope, Cesare had sent Cardinal da Corneto some poisoned wine that was to be served only to their host but which, through carelessness, was poured out to everyone present. According to another version, Adriano da Corneto himself poisoned the pope. In the twentieth century, Portigliotti again takes up the poisoning theory. The substance responsible for the pope's death, he says, was cantarella, which he identifies as arsenic. Arsenic, however, keeps corpses from decomposing; thus the rapid decomposition of the pope's body would prove that the poison (if in fact poison had been present) was not the notorious potion of the Borgias. A more plausible explanation of Alexander's sickness and that of most of the guests at the famous banquet seems to be a hypothetical epidemic of malaria, probably combined with faulty digestion of some badly prepared dishes.

Fate had suddenly struck Cesare a severe blow. Deprived of the pope's support, surrounded on all sides by his enemies, powerless through sickness to take any action, he saw his most cherished hopes vanish into thin air. The good luck that had hoisted him to a sovereign's rank now plunged him into the abyss. His proud device, *Aut Caesar, aut nihil* (Either Caesar or nothing), now more than ever seemed to prefigure his destiny.

PART THREE

Rays of the Setting Sun

1

The Lone Wolf

Disorder in Rome

In his Vatican rooms above the now deserted papal apartments, the duke of Valentinois and the Romagnas lay wretchedly on his sickbed, wracked by fever and a gnawing despair in the wake of the unexpected catastrophe. Not that he had neglected to face his father's inevitable death: on the contrary, he had taken it into consideration and built his future plans upon it, as he confided to Machiavelli a month later. Only, he had not foreseen that the day his father in fact died, he himself would also be on the brink of death.

What were Cesare's plans at this point? There is no clear evidence. Perhaps he had in mind a hereditary title for himself, in the form of some kind of lay vicariate of the Holy See such as a feudal kingship, similar to that of Naples, embracing the Romagna, the Marches, and the recently conquered duchy of Urbino. This plan would have been unrealistic, for opposing him were not only the dispossessed lords, seething with resentment, but the great states—Florence, Venice, and France—who were hardly eager to perpetuate the power of a restless, expansionist new prince.

At the moment, the news of Alexander's death was spreading havoc among the Roman populace, who circulated insulting anti-Borgia pamphlets and scurrilous lampoons throughout the city. Far from Rome, cities such as Città di Castello, Perugia, Urbino, Camerino, and Piombino were rocked by revolts against Cesare's representatives, but it was mainly in the Romagna that violent opposition arose, incited by the Orsinis and the Colonnas. From all sides, the Orsinis were rushing back to reoccupy their lands. Silvio Savelli retook his Roman palace, opened up the jails, and released all the Borgias' prisoners. Prospero Colonna meanwhile was making a forced march north from Naples.

To control the situation, Il Valentino used his customary ploy of trying to sow the seeds of discord among his enemies. On his secretary Agapito's advice, he reminded Prospero Colonna that an agreement had been signed linking Lucrezia's son, Rodrigo Borgia, with a Colonna. On the other hand, any agreement with the rabble-rousing Orsinis was out of the question. Michelotto Corella set fire to their Monte Giordano palace as a warning. As captain general of the Church, Cesare had an army of 12,000 men at his bidding in the Borgo, so he could take action if he so desired. Yet now that the Holy See was vacant, power was automatically transferred to the Sacred College of Cardinals.

The day after Alexander's death, nineteen cardinals met with the governor of the Castel Sant'Angelo, a Spaniard, Francisco de Roccamura, bishop of Nicastro, who assured them of his loyalty and even had the cannon fired over the Sant'Angelo Bridge to disperse the Spanish soldiers occupying it. Nevertheless, a majority of the cardinals favored Cesare, and on August 22 he was confirmed in his offices and made responsible for public security until a new pope was elected. As was the custom, messages were sent out to the Roman barons asking them to leave Rome while the next conclave was being held, but events had already caught up with them. That same day, Prospero Colonna entered Rome and took possession of the palace from which he had so long been banished. That night the Capitol was lit up by Colonna supporters while pro-Colonna areas of the city resounded with exuberant shouts. Meanwhile the Orsinis were zeroing in on the pro-Orsini quarter and soon held the area around the Porta San Pancrazio with 2,000 men. From there they roughed up Borgia supporters and set fire to some 100 Spaniards' homes.

Happily, by September 1, the opposing factions had seen fit to obey the Sacred College—doubtless because they saw their forces were equally matched—and the armies retreated some 12 miles from the city gates. For its part, the French army, bound for Naples, undertook not to come down from the hills it was occupying.

Cesare's retreat
First conclave of 1503
Election of Pius III

Cesare had tried to stay on in Rome on the pretext of his poor health, but to avoid upsetting the cardinals, he resigned himself to leaving on September 2. He did so in his usual dramatic manner: thirteen chariots trundled his artillery; a hundred wagons were loaded with his baggage. He was escorted by his cavalry and twelve halberdiers and borne in a stretcher covered with crimson damask. Weak and emaciated, his face purple and covered with pustules, he was barely recognizable from the handsome blond athlete who not so long ago used to brave bulls and wrestlers in the Romagna. At least he kept up his old pomp and dignity—behind him, led by a page, came his charger in black-velvet trappings with the ducal coronet and insignia. The French and Spanish envoys also rode in the procession, and Cesare was accompanied by his mother, Vannozza, and his brother Jofré. Sancia, Jofré's wife, had meanwhile been released from the Castel Sant'Angelo and handed over to the care of Prospero Colonna, who was to see her safely conveyed to Naples.

Having haughtily refused to grant Cardinal Cesarini an audience at the city gates, Cesare made for his family fief of Nepi, where he kept closely informed of happenings in Rome. He had made the eleven Spanish cardinals swear to vote in the next papal election according to his bidding. The princes of the Church flocked to Rome in early September for Alexander's obsequies, which by custom lasted nine days. Last to arrive were Georges d'Amboise, Ascanio Sforza, who had been freed by Louis in return for a promise to vote for d'Amboise, and Louis of Aragon, a close friend of Sforza's. The king of France had made a secret agreement with Cesare by which Cesare would pledge to serve the king against any powers save the Church and obey him like a vassal. In return, Louis vowed to help Il Valentino recover the possessions he might lose following Alexander's death. Thus the French felt sure they could count on the eleven Spanish cardinals' votes. This was forgetting the quasi-unanimity of the twenty-two Italian cardinals—an unprecedented proportion out of thirty-seven participants—who were eager to elect one of their countrymen. Nevertheless, they were split by factions. This prejudiced the chances of Giuliano della Rovere, Cesare's most dangerous enemy, who was returning to Rome after ten years' exile with high hopes of benefiting from the present situation "for the good of religion and for peace in Italy," as he confided to the Venetian ambassador.

With Cesare far away, the Spanish cardinals appointed a new leader, Bernardino de Carvajal. It now looked very unlikely they would vote for d'Amboise. This became clear in the first ballot, when Carvajal received twelve votes and d'Amboise thirteen, as against Giuliano's fifteen, Carafa's fourteen, and Riario's eight. D'Amboise realized that his chances of being elected were nil. That evening, with Ascanio Sforza and the cardinals of the French connection—and with the Spanish cardinals' agreement—he put forward the name of Cardinal Francesco Piccolomini, a feeble octogenarian who seemed not long for this world. This interim pope was unanimously elected the next day, September 22. In memory of his uncle, he took the name Pius III.

A pontificate of twenty-seven days

That the new pope owed his election indirectly to Il Valentino, he acknowledged by coming to Cesare's aid when his possessions were everywhere being overrun by his enemies. During Alexander's obsequies and the laborious conclave, the Venetians had provided Guidobaldo of Urbino with troops and allowed him to take over the fortress of San Leo. This done, the next move was to oust Pedro Ramirez from Urbino. The Florentines, for their part, had helped Giampaolo Baglioni clear Cesare's partisans out of Magione and Giacomo Appiano to return to his fief of Piombino. Baglioni was advancing on Camerino, accompanied by the last surviving member of the Varano family. The Vitellis, now once more ensconced in Città di Castello, were celebrating their homecoming by triumphantly carrying a golden calf through the streets to erase the memory of the red Borgia bull. On the Adriatic coast, Bartolomeo Alviano had set Pandolfo Malatesta up once again in Rimini, and Giovanni Sforza in Pesaro. Luckily for Cesare, his capital of Cesena, with its solid fortifications, could hold fast, protected by Dionigi di Naldo's tough force of 1,000 veterans.

In this sorry context Pius III, at the Spanish cardinals' urging, gave Cesare permission to return to Rome. On October 3 the duke was greeted by cardinals d'Amboise, d'Albret, Sforza, and San Severino.

Only 500 foot soldiers and 150 cavalry were with him, the rest of his men having been sent to Louis to take part in the Naples campaign. Still undermined by fever, he received the Venetian ambassador Giustiniani in his palace of San Clemente in the Borgo where, despite his weak condition, he proved to be more optimistic than ever, spoke arrogantly, and was confident he would recover all his lands and dignities. Shortly afterward, in fact, a papal bull confirmed that he was vicar and gonfalonier of the Church. On the 12th, the various Romagnol towns again swore their oath of allegiance to him. The following day, Pius sent Florence a brief requesting a safe-conduct for Il Valentino so that he could chase the tyrants out of his possessions.

On October 14 Cesare's luck turned. In Rome, to a blast of trumpets, Gonsalvo de Cordoba had an edict proclaimed which forbade Spanish captains to serve under Cesare's banner, calling on them instead to rally to his side to halt Louis's march on Naples. Many of Cesare's men left him, among them Ugo de Moncada, who later became one of Charles V's best generals. A secret agreement was drawn up by Spain with Alviano, Baglioni, and the Orsinis to capture the duke in person or to pursue him "to the death." Alerted, Cesare tried to flee Rome. Two of his companions having deserted him, he hurled his meager seventy-two light horse against the Orsinis, who held the Borgo gate, then was pursued right up to the Vatican. Here, threatened with a siege, he fled through the covered way to the Castel Sant'Angelo, taking with him the two "infantes Romani," Rodrigo and Giovanni, and his own illegitimate children, Girolamo and Camilla. The Orsinis and Alvianos stormed off to sack his palace, which fortunately no longer held Cesare's treasures, recently entrusted to Cardinal d'Este for Ferrara. With so many enemy troops surrounding the Castel Sant'Angelo, he sent Michelotto and Taddeo della Volpe, the head of the contingent he had sent to the French, into action. Taddeo managed to cross the Sant'Angelo Bridge, driving back the Orsinis, and rejoined his master. All, it seemed, was not lost.

But just at this crucial moment Cesare's main buttress collapsed. The pope's surgeon had made painful incisions in Pius's leg without knowing that the pope was suffering from an ulcer in the left tibia, and the resulting fever had raged unabated. Pope Pius, whose health had been rapidly declining, received extreme unction during the night of October 17 and died the next day. He had been pope for twenty-seven days.

Second conclave of 1503
Election of Julius II

Immediately following Pius's death the wheeling and dealing began afresh. This time Giuliano della Rovere was well and truly determined to win. For a moment Cesare believed he could stop him. On October 26 he received Machiavelli in the Castel Sant'Angelo, the Florentine having been sent on a mission to observe the situation in Rome at the time of the new conclave. Here Cesare told him that, armed with the Spanish vote, he was going to try to get Georges d'Amboise elected. This was no more than bluster for d'Amboise himself realized that there was too much Italian and Spanish opposition against him. He therefore rallied to the side of Giuliano della Rovere, who had spent a long exile in France and might as a result find favor with the French. On October 29 Giuliano signed a treaty with Cesare and the Spaniards, promising when elected to confirm Il Valentino as gonfalonier and captain-general of the Church, to favor him and confirm him in the possession of his lands, on condition that Cesare put himself completely at his disposal. Machiavelli was flabbergasted to learn that Cesare had, in return for mere promises, ensured Giuliano the votes of the cardinals on his side. From that moment on, della Rovere's election seemed certain.

On October 31 the conclave opened. Each of the thirty-eight cardinals swore, if elected, to respect the terms of a "capitulation" submitting the actions of a future pope to the sanction of the majority of the cardinals. Giuliano told the Venetian ambassador what he thought of this forced commitment: "You see the wretched state to which we have been reduced by Alexander's rotting carcass, thanks to the number of cardinals. Necessity constrains men to do that which they hate when they depend on others; but once free, they act in a different manner."

In the first hour of the night, most of the cardinals came to Cardinal della Rovere's chamber to greet him as the new pope. Burckard reveals at this point in his diary how closely he was linked with Giuliano della Rovere: he paid homage to the man whose interests he had always secretly supported against those of the Borgias. As a reward he was promised the see of Orta as well as a harnessed mule, a cloak, and a surplice, so he could carry out his bishop's duties with due dignity. The cardinal of San Pietro in Vincoli—Giuliano della Rovere—was elected on the first ballot. He took the name Julius II, an echo more of Julius Caesar than of the obscure pope Julius I. It was obvious he had been preparing for his pontificate for a long time. Hardly was he installed on his throne when he had the papal ring of the Fisherman brought to him, already engraved with his name. The next morning his arms, already painted, were posted throughout the city. He distributed the promised favors, created four new cardinals—men devoted to him—and made Burckard's cup run over by granting him another bishop's seat, that of Città Castellana, while at the same time letting him keep his position and copious benefices. Il Valentino was to find a tough adversary in this pope—a man in his early seventies who had surmounted many trials, including attacks of gout and the "French disease"—whom history would dub with the epithet "the Terrible."

Julius's deceptions
Capture of Romagna strongholds
Cesare is arrested

At first, nothing pointed to future conflicts of any kind between the two men. Cesare trusted the pope's promises, believing, as an astonished Machiavelli noted, "that another man will keep his word better than one will one's own." In early November, at Julius's invitation, he left the Castel Sant'Angelo and took up residence in spacious apartments the pope had put at his disposal above the audience chamber. Every evening the duke and the pope chatted together amicably. They discussed a marriage link between the families: Cesare's daughter, Louise, would not marry the marquess of Mantua's son but the pope's nephew, Francesco Maria della Rovere, the young lord of Sinigaglia. Il Valentino believed the pope was sincere, since only one of his illegitimate children had survived—a daughter, Felicia della Rovere. The last of the boys died a year before, and Julius devoted all his paternal affection to his nephew.

As a surety, the duke was given the town of Ostia, where galleys were tied up in the harbor. He was waiting to be named gonfalonier of the Church before setting off for Genoa where he would get his hands on 200,000 ducats the bankers were holding for him. The money would be used to raise mercenaries in Lombardy so that Cesare could regain power in his duchy of Romagna.

The international situation augured well for such an intervention. French and Spanish troops were clashing at Garigliano, on the Gulf of Gaeta north of Naples, leaving the field clear for Cesare to stop the Venetians from advancing into the Romagna. Early in November Julius ordered the Romagnol towns to pledge allegiance once more to the pope. He asked the Florentines to give Cesare a safe-conduct through Tuscany with his army. Superficially, he seemed to be sticking to his promise to set up Il Valentino again in his possessions, but the truth was quite otherwise, as Julius bluntly told Machiavelli. The important thing for the pope was to eliminate the Venetians. This could be done only with Cesare's troops, but he intended to get rid of him when the field was clear. He wanted to install the papacy as sole ruler of the Romagna. Apprised of the pope's plans, Machiavelli advised the Signoria of Florence to delay Cesare's safe-conduct pass. Moreover, the pope had indicated that he might possibly use the services of Cesare's captain, Dionigi di Naldo, who had stayed behind in the Romagna and whom he was trying to tempt into his service.

On November 10 the pope confided much the same thing to Giustiniani, the Venetian envoy. If he wanted the doge to give up attacking the Romagna, it was to reestablish the power of Rome, never Cesare's. Firmly, he stated what he intended to do about Il Valentino: "Even though we made certain promises to him, we do not consider that our promise should go beyond the security of his life and the money and goods which he has stolen, most of which has been dissipated. We intend that his states should return to the Church and we hope to have the honor of recovering what our predecessors did ill to relinquish."

The doge, however, paid no heed to these warnings. His troops continued their march toward Faenza, and Machiavelli, much alarmed, pointed out to Julius that if he did not act at once he would be reduced to nothing more than "the Venetians' chaplain." Julius slyly took advantage of the situation to disorient Cesare. As the situation in the Romagna went from bad to worse, the duke was left without any directives from the pope. First idle, then increasingly worried, he waited for a sign that did not come. He who was usually resoluteness itself seemed to have lost his head. "He no longer knows his mind," said his cousin the cardinal-bishop of Elna. Soderini, the Florentine cardinal, found him "irresolute, hesitant, and suspicious, not standing firm in any decision." The fact is that, unlike the time when his father was pope, he now was quite unconscious of the inside story. Actually, the pope was trying to tire him out and break down his moral resistance, at the same time publicly showing him favor and affection. The text of his briefs advised the Romagnols to remain loyal to him and love him, as he did himself, "because of his distinguished qualities and exceptional merit."

Although he was trying hard to be patient, the refusal of his safe-conduct pass galvanized Cesare into action. Still confident of the pope's support, he asked Julius to let him leave. He planned to use five galleys tied up at Ostia to sail with his staff to Genoa, proceeding from there to the Romagna by way of Ferrara. On November 19 he left Rome, not realizing that Julius had just sent Romagna a series of briefs quite different from the earlier ones. Now showing his hand quite openly, he stated that he disapproved of the way Alexander had made his son the papal vicar, and exhorted the whole population to rally to the standard of the Church.

A few days later, just as he was getting ready to embark at Ostia, Cesare was approached by two cardinals, Remolines and Soderini, who ordered him in the pope's name to give them the passwords for the Romagnol forts. These were needed, they said, so that some resistance could be organized against the Venetians before Cesare arrived. Miffed, since he saw his expedition was about to be ruined in advance, Cesare refused, whereupon the captain of the papal fleet immediately arrested him, obeying some secret orders from Julius. On November 24, the pope broke the last of the promises in his treaty with Cesare when he appointed a trusted crony, Giovanni Sacchi, archbishop of Ragusa, governor of the Romagna. This authoritarian step finished off the existence of the Romagna as an independent duchy. The people of Cesena, Cesare's capital, were not taken in, however, and when the act was read out they rose up in revolt, demanding loudly that their duke be returned to them.

Cesare a prisoner in Rome

Still refusing to give the password, on November 29 Il Valentino was brought back to Rome a prisoner and shut up in his old Vatican apartments, now taken over by Cardinal d'Amboise. That same day, at the pope's orders, Michelotto Corella, Taddeo della Volpe, and other officers of the duke's were arrested in Tuscany. Their troops were disarmed, and Julius had Michelotto tortured "to find out all the

cruelties, robberies, murders, and other crimes which over the past
ten years have been done in Rome against God and man." Cesare's
strongman, however, divulged nothing of any value. Sentenced to
imprisonment, he left the Torre di Nona dungeon in 1506 and on
Machiavelli's recommendation was engaged by Florence to recruit a
militia similar to that of the Romagna.

When he heard of his confidant's torture and interrogation, Cesare
felt sure that he had been betrayed and all was lost. Forced to yield
to the inevitable, he gave the pope the required password. One of his
men, Pedro de Oviedo, set out for the Romagna together with Carlo
de Moncalieri, the pope's secret chamberlain, who was to take possession of the fortresses. The city of Forlì, fearing that the Riarios
would come back, refused to see the envoys. At Cesena, where the
two men could hardly make their way in the snowy weather, Pedro
Ramirez, governor of the Rocca fortress, seized the wretched Oviedo
and, without allowing him to confess, hanged him from the castle
walls as a traitor and disloyal servant.

The news made Julius fly into a rage. He ordered two of his cardinals
to seize Cesare and imprison him in the dungeon of the Castel
Sant'Angelo. Thanks to the intervention of two Spanish cardinals, he
was moved instead to the Borgia Tower at the Vatican, where he was
given the two rooms that Bisceglie, his brother-in-law, occupied when
Cesare had had him strangled. According to the envoy Cattaneo,
Cesare wept when he was brought to the place.

Meanwhile, two close associates of Cesare's, cardinals Francisco
Remolines and Luís Borgia, archbishop of Valencia, took off for Naples
with the two "infantes Romani" and Cesare's illegitimate children.
Their task was to ask Gonsalvo de Cordoba for a safe-conduct for
Cesare in the name of the Catholic King, Ferdinand of Spain.

While this was going on, Pope Julius was confiscating all the duke's
possessions, proclaiming that he was going to use them to compensate
those people who had a grievance against him. Guidobaldo of Urbino
demanded an indemnity of 200,000 ducats, Florence the same sum,
and the Riarios, the pope's nephews, 50,000 ducats. Clearly, this
spelled Cesare's financial ruin. The duke of Urbino, who was a passionate collector, clung especially to the hope of recovering his fine
library. Meeting him at the Vatican, flanked by the papal guard, Cesare
begged his victim's forgiveness. According to a witness, one Ugolini,
"he made two extremely deep bows and laid the blame on his youth,
the bad advice he had been given, the wicked deeds and totally per-

verted charcter of the pope, and all those who had encouraged him in the venture. He cursed his father's memory. He promised to give back everything he had taken at Urbino, except for the tapestries of the history of Troy, which he had given the cardinal of Rouen." This was a strange sight for those who had known the arrogant Cesare in his time of triumph. But it is readily understood when one recalls how wily and unscrupulous Il Valentino was: he was preparing for the future, believing that fickle fate would allow him to return to power, perhaps with his former victim's help. This time he was mistaken: no one took him seriously.

It may well have been someone who was present at that humiliating session at the Vatican who put on a stage show of the history of the Borgias not long afterward. The show—a truly topical revue glorifying Guidobaldo—took place in the Urbino palace. According to Ugolini's account, there were scenes showing the conquest of the duchy of Urbino, the courteous welcome given Lucrezia on her journey to Ferrara, then Guidobaldo's sudden attack and forced retreat. Next came a gloomy tableau showing the execution of the condottieri at Sinigaglia, and finally divine vengeance—Alexander's death and Guidobaldo's triumphant return to his lands. This unsparing tragicomedy is one of the first literary expressions of the black legend of the Borgias. It belongs to the genre of the cruel lampoons that were turned out repeatedly throughout Alexander's papacy, but with the difference that this time there is a desire to stigmatize the memory of the pope and his family forever.

In his gloom, Il Valentino nevertheless had the satisfaction of recognizing some old friends. When Machiavelli came to visit he found him lying on his bed, silently watching people around him playing chess—much as Alexander on his deathbed had watched the cardinals playing cards. From time to time some Spanish cardinal would come and talk with him. Giovanni Vera, his old tutor, was one of the most faithful. Cesare commented on the current happenings, railed at his enemies sarcastically, and laughed at those who feared him while he was sick and in chains. Many of his far-off partisans were still loyal to him: his captain Taddeo della Volpe, who was imprisoned in Florence, refused to trade his freedom for a pledge to serve the republic, while Cesare's treasurer, Alessandro Francio, still kept for him the 300,000 ducats he had deposited in Florence and Genoa banks. Nonetheless, incapable as he was of moving or communicating with the outside world, he who was once so active began to fade. "Little by little," Machiavelli wrote to the Signoria after his last visit, "he is slipping down to the grave."

A liberating compromise

Fate had not played her last card. On January 3, 1504, news reached the Vatican of Gonsalvo de Cordoba's great victory: he had forced the French to retreat at the mouth of the Garigliano, between Rome and Naples. On the first day of the new year, Gaeta, the port they had fled to, surrendered. Several days later Rome heard that the French were fleeing in disarray and that Piero de' Medici had drowned crossing the river at the boundary. These events meant that the Catholic Kings now held sway over Naples and the influence of the Spaniards in Rome was much stronger. Diego de Mendoza, the Spanish ambassador, interceded for the imprisoned duke, and a compromise was reached. Cesare would give up his claims to the duchy in exchange for his freedom and within forty days would surrender those Romagnol strongholds still held by his castellans.

On the 29th Pope Julius signed the agreement. In February Cesare was allowed to leave for Ostia, where he was to stay until Bernardino Carvajal had put the finishing touches to the agreement. At the last moment a problem arose at the fortress of Forlì, where its commander, Gonsalvo da Miramonte, was asking for a 15,000-ducat compensation. Cesare promised to fork out the money himself, asserting that nothing would stand in the way of his liberation and departure for France on the papal galleys, which were already waiting at the jetty. But no orders came from Rome. Anxious about secret plans the pope might be harboring concerning the duke, Carvajal took it upon himself to free Cesare on April 26 after making him sign a pledge that he would never bear arms against Pope Julius.

Cesare in Naples
A prisoner once more in the Castel Nuovo

Gonsalvo de Cordoba had sent four ships to Ostia with a safe-conduct for Cesare for the kingdom of Naples. Il Valentino lost no time in embarking, reaching Naples quickly by way of nearby Ardea, then on horseback along the strand. His friends and relations gave him a tumultuous welcome. Cardinals Borgia and Loriz were there, as well as his brother Jofré and Jofré's wife, Sancia—who now lived in her palace, separated from her husband. (Cesare would later try in vain to reconcile her with his brother.) Gonsalvo was waiting for the duke at the Castel Nuovo, where he told him of a plan he and the late Piero de' Medici had concocted against Florence. Could Cesare perhaps take part in the expedition, giving it the benefit of his contacts and influence at Pisa, Siena, and Piombino? Il Valentino readily agreed: this could be a way of avenging himself on the Florentines, who he now realized had constantly deceived him. He even sent off his captain, Baldassare da Scipione, to raise men-at-arms in Rome. He decided to go from Tuscany to the Romagna, thereby breaking the promise Carvajal had encouraged him to make at Ostia. Julius, however, was on the lookout. Apprised of Cesare's plans, he complained to Ferdinand of Spain that the duke had not kept his word—the fortress of Forlì had still not surrendered as promised. Eager to remain on good terms with the pope, Ferdinand then gave Gonsalvo orders to arrest the man he had just invited to be his guest.

Caught between his word—he had given Cesare a safe-conduct pass—and his duty to his sovereign, the Great Captain chose his duty. In the evening of May 26, the day before the expedition was due to leave—the troops were ready, meeting points arranged, the artillery loaded on the galleys—Cesare came to the Castel Nuovo to take his leave of Gonsalvo. Then he went to his quarters and said goodbye to Pedro Navarro, his aide-de-camp. "But I am here, Monsignore, to keep you company tonight and I have been told not to sleep!" said Navarro. Seeing in a flash that he was under arrest, Cesare cried out, "Santa Maria, I am betrayed! How cruelly Gonsalvo has dealt with me!"

One of the fortress guards, Nuñez de Ocampo, asked him to surrender his sword and set a sentinel at his door. Once again Cesare was a prisoner. This caused a great scandal among the champions of the chivalric tradition. Captain Scipione, to whom Cesare had given his pass for safekeeping, challenged any man who would deny the felony of King Ferdinand of Aragon and Queen Isabella of Castile, but no one could be found to take up the challenge. Cesare had been paid back in his own coinage. In his maximum-security prison, known ominously as "the Oven," behind its double row of bars he could, bitterly, recall his maxim: "It is good to deceive those who are past masters in perfidy."

For almost three months Cesare was under constant pressure to make his castellans surrender the last remaining Romagnol forts. At Forlì, Gonsalvo da Miramonte still held out. Not until August 10, after taking hostages and being told that the promised 15,000 ducats were waiting for him in a Venetian bank, did he march defiantly out of the fortress, lance held high, leading his 200 archers in full armor. Cesare Borgia's banner fluttered in the wind. Cries of "Duca! Duca!" broke out on all sides. The papal governor and a gentleman sent by Lucrezia took part in the surrender ceremony. Such was the final act of Cesare's dominion over the Romagna. Cruel vendettas burst out in many places, especially at Camerino and Pesaro. Cesare's partisans were slaughtered. The duke, helpless, heard the news from far away. At twenty-nine, his career seemed forever ruined.

Il Valentino and the Catholic Kings

Cesare's fate was now in the hands of the Catholic Kings of Spain, and their feelings toward him were hostile in the extreme. They knew that he was allied to the king of France, their enemy, and that the pope, with whom they were eager to curry favor, detested him. As soon as they heard of Cesare's flight to Naples they had given their ambassadors instructions: "We regard the duke's arrival with profound displeasure, but not for political reasons alone. For, as you know, we hold this man in horror because of the gravity of his crimes; nor do we wish such a man to be considered as being in our service, even if he came to us laden with fortresses, soldiers, and money. We have written to Gonsalvo de Cordoba, the duke of Terranova, instructing him to send the duke to us, and have given him two galleys for the voyage, so that he cannot flee anywhere else. Gonsalvo could either send him to the Holy Roman emperor or to France, to join his wife. We would have you explain to the pope how bitterly we resent the insult to His Holiness if the duke of Valentinois were to be received in Naples; assure him that he will find no shelter here, nor will he be permitted to go to other provinces where he might prove harmful to His Holiness's security."

In Spain's eyes, the violation of Cesare's safe-conduct, and his arrest, were justified because not all the Romagnol forts had been given back to the pope. Once that lacuna was filled, they had to find another pretext for keeping him behind bars. This time they found it in their own lands: the duchess of Gandia, Cesare's brother's widow, instituted proceedings against her brother-in-law, accusing him of murdering both her husband and Lucrezia's, the duke of Bisceglie. Cesare must therefore appear before the Spanish court. On August 20 he was moved from the Castel Nuovo to Ischia, where he was put aboard a galley under the watchful eye of his personal enemy, Prospero Colonna. A whole fleet surrounded the ship to provide maximum security.

Rome breathed a huge sigh of relief. France's reaction, however, was one of shock. Wasn't it agreed that Cesare would be set free when Forlì surrendered? "The king of Spain's word is as worthless as the Punic faith!" cried Louis XII, but words were useless.

The Chinchilla prison

In September 1504 Cesare disembarked at Villanueva del Grao—the very same Valencian port from which Alonso Borja, the founder of his family's greatness, had departed some sixty years before. No triumphant crowds greeted the former cardinal of Valencia, who merely passed through the ancient cathedral like a stranger. He was clapped into the fortress of Chinchilla, perched high in the mountains about 12 miles southeast of Albacete. At first he was kept in strict confinement, with only one of his squires to attend him. Then, as time passed, by royal decree he was given eight servants. More and more people were interceding in his favor—the Spanish cardinals in Rome, his brother-in-law Jean de Navarre, and especially Lucrezia, who bombarded the pope and the marquess of Mantua with letters from Ferrara, begging them to ask the Catholic Kings to release the captive.

Cesare's case was long in coming to court, possibly because of the death on November 26 of Queen Isabella of Spain, who was more eager than her husband to avenge the duchess of Gandia. Eight months dragged by. In May 1505, short of funds, Cesare asked Jean of Navarre to request that Louis pay him the 100,000-pound dowry that had been promised to Charlotte but never actually handed over. But the king, angry with Cesare, decided to deprive him of the advantages he had given him in his kingdom. All avenues of hope around him seemed closed, yet Cesare refused to give in. In fact, during his imprisonment the aftereffects of his illness had disappeared and he had recovered much of his old strength. He resolved to escape.

From his prison in the tallest of the castle towers, he could look down on the roofs of the little town of Chinchilla. Making some pretext or other, he invited Gabriel Guzman, the castle governor, to join him on the ramparts and point out the various buildings below. At one point Guzman had his back to Cesare and was leaning out over the battlements. Cesare attacked him, tackled him to the ground, and tried to toss him over the wall. Guzman, however, was the stronger of the two and managed to tear himself free. To justify himself, Cesare claimed he merely wanted to test his strength, as he used to do when he wrestled the Romagnol peasants, but this explanation convinced no one, and he was transferred to the castle of La Mota in Medina del Campo, in the heart of Castile.

Long captivity and escape from Medina

This castle was the home of the titular queen of Castile, Juana la Loca. Mentally unstable and melancholic, she lived in one of the lower rooms, never stirring from the fireside. Her mother, Queen Isabella, aware that her daughter would probably be incapable of ruling, had decided in her will that her husband, Ferdinand, would rule after her, on condition that he did not remarry.

The fifty-four-year-old Ferdinand decided to draw closer to France by marrying an eighteen-year-old princess, the beautiful Germaine de Foix, who was Louis's niece. Her dowry would be half the kingdom of Naples, ceded to France under the Treaty of Granada. Louis further recognized Ferdinand's right to the kingdom of Navarre, which on his death would go to the French crown through Gaston de Foix, Germaine's brother. The treaty linking France and Spain was duly signed at Blois on October 12, 1505, and the wedding set for March 18, 1506, at Duenas, near the royal capital of Valladolid. Before that, however, the ticklish question of the Spanish regency came up once again. A majority of the Cortes, the Spanish parliament, decided that Ferdinand should be regent of Castile, but a strong minority, under Count Benavente, declared for Philip, archduke of Austria, who was Juana la Loca's husband and a Habsburg. Philip had now left Flanders and with the support of his father, the emperor Maximilian, was sailing to Spain to reclaim the regency, basing his claim on Isabella's will.

From his prison Cesare followed these goings-on with the keenest interest. He would, in fact, find a part to play in them—and hoped for another chance to retrieve his fortune. In October, Ferdinand, having greeted his new bride at Saragossa, left for Naples. His presence there was now urgently required owing to his viceroy Gonsalvo's behavior, which was growing increasingly suspicious. He thought of replacing Gonsalvo with his son Alfonso of Aragon, the archbishop of Saragossa, but Gonsalvo managed to delay the transfer of power. Deciding to fight him, Ferdinand hit upon the idea of using Cesare Borgia against Gonsalvo if need arose. To this end he sent an aide to demand that his son-in-law, Philip, hand Cesare over to him.

It so happened that Philip had every intention of using Cesare himself if Ferdinand failed to recognize his rights to the Castilian regency. His answer was to refer the matter to the Council of Castile, which decided that Cesare should remain in Castile until the duchess of Gandia's process was settled. No decision had been reached about Cesare's future role when Philip suddenly died, at the age of twenty-eight. This put the commander of Medina, Bernardino de Cardenas, in a tricky spot. He knew that Ferdinand, who was then at Naples, would become regent and might well want to have his revenge on the governor for refusing to hand over Cesare. So Cardenas told the king's envoy he was now willing to hand over Cesare Borgia.

Warned by Cardenas, Cesare had no desire to be a mere plaything in Ferdinand's hands. On October 25, 1506, when the guard was being changed, he made a spectacular escape. As at Chinchilla, he was being held at the top of a tall tower overlooking the deep castle moat. His chaplain acted as go-between for Cesare while Count Benavente, his partisan at the Cortes, plotted the escape. Ropes were smuggled into the keep—they could still be seen a century later, hanging down from the window of the tall tower. One of Cesare's servants was first down the rope, but it was too short for the great height and he fell, breaking several bones. Later the wretched man was apprehended and put to death. Cesare was luckier. He came down, but before he could land the alarm had been given and the rope cut, hurling him down onto the moat. It was a brutal fall. Awaiting him were his chaplain, his majordomo, and an accomplice, Don Jaime. Badly injured and with his hands covered with blood, Cesare nevertheless managed to mount the horse they had ready for him and galloped off into the night to Villalon, in the lands of his ally Benavente.

Flight to Navarre

A month went by before Cesare's wounds healed. His friends guarded him closely, since orders had been given out for his arrest, and Queen Juana la Loca had put a 10,000-ducat price on his head. With two guides, he headed north. Questioned along the way, they said they were grain merchants returning from Medina, where they had collected money, and were now going back up to the coast to meet another shipment. This story, rehearsed with Benavente, was intended to explain away the large sums of money they were carrying. Cesare wanted to reach his brother-in-law Jean's court at Pamplona as quickly as he could. For safety's sake, however, he avoided the direct route from Burgos and made instead for Santander where, riding their horses to death, they arrived on November 29.

While supper was being prepared at their inn, Cesare went to look for a ship they could rent to go to Bernico, whence they could take the road to Navarre. To the captain he explained that he had to go to the little port and meet one of their ships loaded with grain from France. The money he was offered aroused the man's suspicions, and he warned the chief of police, who came and questioned the strangers at the inn. The record includes the tiniest details. The three men were sitting at a meal of three fowls and a large dish of roast meat. On being questioned separately, each man repeated the same story of the ship and its cargo of grain. As they suggested leaving 50 gold crowns as surety, and even that one of them should stay as hostage, they were let go. All these details and witnesses' testimony are contained in the report drawn up by the corregidor Cristobal Vasquez de Acuña, whose job it was to investigate Il Valentino's escape. An inhabitant of Castres who saw the three men described one of them as "doubled up, with a very ugly face, a big nose and dark complexion." The innkeeper noticed that one of the three kept to himself, wrapped in his cloak, that he was heavy and of medium height, with flaring nostrils and big eyes, and that his hands were bandaged. These sketched portraits are precious in their naïveté, showing us as they do how Cesare struck simple villagers.

The interrogation over, the travelers wolfed down their meal and went to haggle with Francisco Gonzalez, the captain of their ship, persuading him to bring down his price from 50 to 26 ducats. After a stormy crossing they were forced to land at a small, out-of-the-way fishing village called Castro Urdiales, near Bilbao, normally only reachable by sea. There they had to spend two days in a posada before finding mules at the nearby monastery of Santa Clara. The exhausting journey—all recounted in the report of the corregidor who ferreted out the witnesses—continued from Durango, where they changed mules, to the last of the Basque towns of Guipuzcoa. When they finally reached the boundary, a man was waiting for Cesare. He guided him across Navarre to Pamplona, where he arrived on December 3.

Means for a new career

Was this the dawn of a new career? Cesare apparently had agreed with Benavente that he would proceed from Navarre to Flanders, where he would meet the emperor Maximilian. In the euphoria of his successsful escapade he wrote to his family, to Lucrezia and Alfonso d'Este, and to the marquess of Mantua, one of his frequent correspondents. Cesare's letter of January 7 to the marquess bore a seal with the double arms of France and the Borgias, inscribed "César Borgia of France, duke of Romagna." Another letter, to Cardinal Ippolito d'Este, inquired after the fate of Cesare's treasures. In December 1503, at the time of his downfall, he had entrusted the cardinal with all the weapons, precious stones, and works of art from his palace. However, when the treasures were moved to Ferrara, the Florentines had seized them, agreeing to give them back that summer only in return for a large ransom. Giovanni Bentivoglio of Bologna had also confiscated some of the treasures, which had duly been moved to Ferrara. As Pope Julius had instructed Bentivoglio to restore "those possessions stolen from the Church," these must have been the silver-gilt pieces that Cesare's strongman, Michelotto, had seized at Alexander's death. Cesare had no hope of recovering the other treasures he had stored in Cardinal Remolines's palace in Rome; when Remolines died in 1507, Julius confiscated twelve chests and ninety-four bales containing oriental carpets, Flemish tapestries, furniture, and statues.

Cesare's secretary, Federigo, who had been delivering his letters in Italy in December 1506, had orders to observe the situation there with an eagle eye. Gonzaga of Mantua, now roped into the pope's service, had just succeeded in ousting Bentivoglio from Bologna. But the people of the Romagna had not forgotten their duke, and it looked as though Cesare would find his duchy a more fertile field of action than Flanders.

He was never to know this, however, for the pope had Federigo arrested in Bologna.

Unable to dispose of his treasures, or to get his hands on the large deposits he had made in Genoese banks (since Julius had seized them), Cesare then remembered he was a French prince, the duke of Valence and lord of Issoudun. The revenues from his lands were still owing to him. Nor had any action been taken on his claim to his wife's dowry. In early 1507, therefore, he sent his majordomo, Requesenz, to Louis to claim his due and ask permission to come to his court and take up arms in the king's service. Louis's answer was to take Issoudun firmly away from Cesare. He wanted to punish him for threatening his ally, Florence, accepting the protectorate of Pisa, and trying to oust his protégé Bentivoglio from Bologna. Especially, he blamed Cesare for not helping him recover the kingdom of Naples and for having, on the contrary, aided Louis's enemies. Because of all Cesare's "nasty tricks" and "great ingratitude," Louis ordered all the profits and revenues formerly conferred on Il Valentino to revert to the French crown.

It was a harsh settling of accounts as well as a painful insult for Cesare. Feeling all his old pugnacity, and still possessing the ardor of young manhood, the thirty-one-year-old Cesare itched to fight all those who had done him wrong—Ferdinand of Spain, Pope Julius, and finally Louis of France. His brother-in-law's tiny kingdom of Navarre was the arena where he could contrive to wreak vengeance on his enemies. On one side Navarre was threatened by Ferdinand, on the French side by Louis, a situation resulting from the rival claims to the throne by the houses of Aragon and de Foix. Cesare's brother-in-law, Jean d'Albret, who had succeeded François Phoebus de Foix, faced a powerful opposition. At its head was one Luís de Beaumonte, count of Lerins and constable of Navarre, who was fighting to win the kingdom for Ferdinand of Aragon.

Cesare at the siege of Viana

King Jean of Navarre appointed Cesare captain-general of the royal troops and sent him off to do battle with the count of Beaumonte. In Luís de Beaumonte, Cesare had a formidable adversary. Though a tiny man, he was renowned for his ferocity—his epitaph at the monastery of Veruela reads, "In so small a body was never seen such strength." He was as unscrupulous as he was fiery: to satisfy his ambitions he had started three wars in Navarre, one after another. Three times King Jean had summoned him to appear in court, and when after the third appeal he still remained adamant, condemned him for the crime of lèse majesté and sentenced him to death. For the moment, Beaumonte was holding fast in the castle of Viana. He had to be dislodged from it once and for all. Jean and Cesare led their men to the fort. They were relying on the little town, which was loyal to the king. They planned to besiege Beaumonte's castle, which was separated from the honey-colored houses of the little hilltop town by a barren, ravine-cut stretch of country.

Under Cesare's command were 1,000 knights, 200 men-at-arms, 5,000 infantry, and some siege and field artillery. He invested the castle, which was short of provisions. Meanwhile the count of Beaumonte was encamped some distance away, at Mendavia, on the Logroño road. He had an army of 200 lances and 600 footsoldiers to harass the enemy. During the night of March 11 a violent storm broke out, causing Cesare's sentinels to withdraw. Beaumonte seized the opportunity to lead a convoy of sixty mules laden with flour down into a hollow close by the town and sneak the provisions inside the fortress through a gate (known from then on as Puerta del Socorro, or Gate of Help). Twice more he went back and forth, bringing supplies unobserved. At dawn, when he was returning from the castle with a strong escort, he ran right into a reinforcement of Castilians coming from Logroño. They had been sent to the king of Navarre by his ally the duke of Najera, a friend of Count Benavente's.

At once the alarm was sounded in the town. Cesare, who was sleeping, hurriedly put on his armor and leaped on his horse, without waiting to see if anyone followed him.

A heroic, lone death

Swearing and blaspheming, Il Valentino headed straight for the enemy, galloping through the Solana gate, which had just been opened for him, and killing three men. Turning around, Beaumonte observed the lone, furious figure—like some solitary wolf—and sent forward twenty of his knights. Their leaders, Luís Garcia de Agredo and Pedro de Allo, drew him into a narrow ravine, out of sight of the Viana garrison and Beaumonte's troops. Alone against these men, Cesare fought like a hero. Wounded by a spear thrust into his armpit, he was unhorsed, then stabbed at from all sides and started to bleed profusely. His attackers stripped him of his weapons and shining armor, seized his horse, and galloped off to their leader, leaving the body naked under a large rock.

As soon as he glimpsed the magnificent breastplate in his knights' hands, Beaumonte realized that the victim was a great prince, and at once gave orders for the body to be found and brought to his tent at Mendavia. Before they reached the scene of the fighting, his men heard shouts coming from the king of Navarre's army. They hastily retreated, taking with them a young squire they had found wandering desolately in the plain. Brought to Beaumonte, the youth burst into tears when he saw Cesare's armor: he confessed that he had handed it that very morning to his master, Monseigneur César Borgia of France, duke of Romagna.

In the meantime Jean of Navarre had found his brother-in-law's naked, bleeding body. He had it covered with a cloak and carried to Viana. Cesare's remains were buried with magnificent obsequies that contrasted vividly with the simple parish church, that of Sta. Maria.

That same year, 1507, an elaborate marble tomb was erected, carved with bas-reliefs representing the biblical kings in attitudes of grief. The tomb's pompous epitaph, which was written by the poet Soria, was published four years later in the *Romancero español*, a book of Castilian poetry. The words celebrate the illustrious memory of the son of Pope Alexander VI:

> *Aquí yace en poca tierra*
> *El que toda le temía,*
> *El que la paz y la guerra*
> *En la su mano tenía.*
> *O tu, que vas a buscar*
> *Cosas dignas de loar,*
> *Si tu loas lo más digno*
> *Aquí pare tu camino;*
> *No cures de más andar.*

> *Here in a scant spot of earth*
> *Lies he whom all the earth once feared,*
> *He who in his hand once bore*
> *Mankind's fate of peace or war.*

O you who now would wander wide
Seeking things that merit praise,
Here you may your journey stay:
Never farther seek to stray!

But today the Church of Viana is empty. Toward the end of the seventeenth century a bishop of Calahorra had the tomb destroyed so as to efface the memory of a man to whom legend had given a sulfurous halo. This profanation is the counterpart of a crime perpetrated two centuries earlier when another bishop of Calahorra was incarcerated in the Castel Sant'Angelo until he rotted to death.

A few bones buried below the church steps and a couple of gracefully carved pilasters from the tomb that are now part of the high altar— that is all that is left on Spanish soil of the one who for so many years made the world tremble at his name.

CHAPTER

2

The Beautiful Lady of Ferrara

Cesare's violently adventurous life tends to eclipse his sister's. Yet Lucrezia's story provides a calm and pleasing counterpoint to her brother's heroic theme.

The men of the Este family

Though Lucrezia's marriage led to a geographical separation from her father and brother, the bonds of affection linking them were unbroken. Envoys and messengers were exchanged in a constant stream from one point to the other. Every day, Beltrando Costabili, the envoy of Lucrezia's father-in-law, Ercole d'Este, gave the pope news of the young couple. In return, he brought back word of Rome's financial commitments.

After the glittering marriage celebrations, the Este court quickly went back to its parsimonious ways in the forbidding, stout-walled castle with its rings of dark, dank moats. True, Lucrezia seems to have been treated well by her father-in-law, who presented her with his late wife Eleonora's jewels, and by her husband, Alfonso, who must in many ways have reminded her of Cesare. He was a broad-shouldered, dark-haired man with sensual lips and a gaze that could be both tender and hard. He had a passion for artillery, tournaments, dogs, and horses. He also liked to play the viol and was skilled at making and decorating pottery, but there his artistic tastes ended. From the Estes and his grandfather, the terrible Ferrante of Naples, he had inherited a tendency toward eccentricity and cruelty that sometimes erupted in shocking fashion. Before the death of his first wife, Anna Sforza, he had been known to walk naked through the streets of Ferrara, creating a scandal among his subjects. On another occasion he had let loose a raging bull on the crowded cathedral square, causing several fatal accidents, which he observed amusedly from his palace balcony.

His brother, Cardinal Ippolito, who was notorious for his amorous escapades, was just as cruel. But for the time being at least, Lucrezia hardly had a chance to get to know him better. Ippolito lived in Rome, where he had just begun a love affair with the tempestuous Sancia of Aragon. She was his cousin "on the wrong side of the blanket," since King Alfonso, her natural father, was the brother of Eleonora of Aragon, Ippolito's mother. Ercole's other children, princes Sigismondo and Ferrante and the bastard Giulio, were just as impassioned as their brothers.

Such was the family that Lucrezia had married into. Compared with the princes and clerics she had rubbed shoulders with in Rome and her other homes, there was nothing exceptional about her new in-laws. Yet a certain lassitude, combined with Duke Ercole's stinginess—he had not added one ducat to the 10,000 proposed for Lucrezia's allowance—made her withdrawn and ill-humored. The only people she felt at ease with were a few members of the aristocracy who shared her passion for literature. She had brought with her from Rome a little personal library which boasted, besides the Gospels and the letters of Catherine of Siena, the works of Dante and Petrarch. The first privileged souls to be admitted to her private apartments—three rooms decorated with light-blue and gold hangings, overlooking a melancholy garden—were some refugees from the court of Isabella d'Este, her new sister-in-law, who was married to the marquess of Mantua, Francesco da Gonzaga.

A select coterie of poets

Niccolò da Correggio, Ercole's illegitimate nephew, had been Isabella's arbiter of taste. A poet, songwriter, and stage manager of classical comedies, he remained a member of Lucrezia's circle until his death, in 1508, and his son would pay her homage in his last book of poems. Tito Vespasiano Strozzi, of the famous Florentine family of that name, was one of the respected elder statesmen in Ferrara. A holder of high office—he was one of the Twelve Judges of the supreme court—he was also one of the celebrated Latin poets in the duchy. His son Ercole, a cripple from birth, made up for his disability with his elegant, melancholy poetry, much appreciated by the ladies. One day Lucrezia gave him a rose she had just kissed as a tribute to his verse, and young Strozzi at once improvised a famous quatrain:

Abloom on the soil of joy, O rose plucked by her hand,
Why are your scarlet petals filled with light?
Has Venus tinted them, or Lucrezia's lips
Whose kiss has thereby made you blush anew?

Such goings-on made Ercole grumpier than ever, and he grew even more irritated on hearing that Lucrezia had sent Strozzi off to Venice, where he bought, on credit, masses of precious stuffs—satins of white, cream, fawn, and rose, taffetas, gold brocade, velvets, muslin—and even ordered a cradle for her future baby.

Another member of Lucrezia's little court was Isabella's former master of rhyme, Antonio Tebaldeo, a savant who had studied medicine at Bologna before coming to Mantua, where he corrected Isabella's poems and composed sonnets for the marquess to sign. Lucrezia had no difficulty in roping him into her circle. The poet, who complained that at Mantua he had been served rotten meat and vile wine and been treated wretchedly, had entered the service of Ippolito d'Este, who bequeathed him to his sister-in-law when he left for Rome.

Intimate scenes: the bath and the banquet

Lucrezia saw to it that the pleasures of the mind alternated with those of the body. The night belonged to her lord and master, Alfonso, who never shirked his conjugal duty. In the daytime, after poetry recitals and hunting parties with old Duke Ercole, came the ceremony of the bath. The intimate scene was described for Isabella d'Este by Bernardino Prosperi, who had strict instructions to feed her with every detail of her young sister-in-law's life.

Lucia, her chambermaid, prepared the fires and set out the powders, hairnets, and Moorish peignoirs while the perfumed water was getting hot. When the bath was ready, Lucrezia and her favorite, Nicola, stepped into the huge tub together, with Lucia taking charge of the heat. The young women laughed and joked, enjoying a long soak in their scented bath. Then, naked beneath their brightly colored wraps, with their long tresses held in sparkling gold snoods, they stretched out on plump cushions, enveloped in the fragrance of the perfume-braziers. This way of life, delicate and voluptuous, worked like a charm on Lucrezia's rough-mannered husband, and gradually Alfonso progressed from forced conjugal duty to affection, then finally to love, braving the gossip of those who took pleasure in denigrating his marriage to the pope's daughter.

One evening, Lucrezia decided to confound her envious in-laws and invited the whole Este family to dinner in her apartments. Here she laid out all her gold and silverware—the buffet set given her by Cardinal Ascanio Sforza for her first marriage; silver flasks, a huge gold basin, a box with an intricate leaf pattern, a saltcellar delicately carved with the Aragon coat of arms, and items with the Orsini bear emblem or the arms of Francisco Gacet, the Toledo cleric her father had given her as steward. Her rooms were decorated with the Borgia device: everywhere were bulls of all sizes, sculpted or carved in relief, or else serving as handles and lids on the various vessels. Running around them were the words *Alexander Sextus Pontifex Maximus.*

Worries about politics and health

The idea behind this ostentatious display of wealth was to show up once more the duke of Ferrara's stinginess. How scandalous that a princess who had a style of living like that should have to be content with a measly allowance of 10,000 ducats! But Ercole turned a deaf ear, sticking to his guns until June, when Lucrezia became pregnant. At that time she was allowed to set up house in Belriguardo, the Estes' loveliest country estate. There she learned of Cesare's victorious march on Urbino and Guidobaldo da Montefeltro's flight.

But then, just as she was feeling more a part of the Este household, she was seized with a sudden fear. Was Cesare planning to retrace his steps and attack Ferrara? She felt ashamed, too, when she remembered the warm welcome she had received not long ago from Guidobaldo's wife, Elisabetta. To those around her she therefore said she would willingly give 25,000 ducats not to have made the duchess's acquaintance. She was very upset to hear that the Urbino palace had been pillaged. The capture of Camerino, too, seemed to her to augur ill. Would it not very likely bring Venice into the act? Already, the lords

Cesare had dispossessed were gathering in the Milanese to get help from France. Alfonso and his brother-in-law, Gonzaga, hesitated as to what action to take. Alfonso felt he should go to Milan to find out what the king thought. Gonzaga, urged by Isabella, was willing to come to the defense of Guidobaldo da Montefeltro, who had asked him for refuge at Mantua. His wife, Elisabetta, the marquess's sister, was already there.

Political interests were closely intertwined with family connections. At this crucial juncture Lucrezia could have stepped in and persuaded Alfonso and Ercole to stay by Cesare's side, since he was the privileged ally of the powerful king of France, but her poor state of health prevented her. Coming close to the end of a difficult pregnancy, she had just returned from Ferrara when, in mid-July, she fell victim to an epidemic that was sweeping the whole population. Cesare sent two doctors to tend her, while her father dispatched his personal physician from Rome. Five Ferrarese doctors looked after Lucrezia, and Alfonso, though poised to leave Ferrara and join Louis of France, chose to stay behind at his wife's bedside.

One night Cesare suddenly appeared. For many hours he and Lucrezia talked together, in the Valencian dialect. Perhaps he promised her that his latest conquest, Camerino, would be given in fief to the mysterious "infans Romanus," Giovanni Borgia, who was then being passed off as his own child and was in fact Lucrezia's illegitimate son.

After stopping two days in Ferrara, Cesare rode off with his brother-in-law to meet Louis. While they were away, most of Lucrezia's ladies-in-waiting—from her cousin Angela Borgia to the young African Caterinella—were stricken by the epidemic and had to take to their beds.

By the beginning of September Lucrezia's condition had worsened. One night she started to have convulsions and fell backwards, groaning. She delivered a stillborn baby girl. Puerperal fever set in, and very quickly she was desperately ill and in danger of her life. The alarming news brought the two travelers back, posthaste, to Ferrara. They had moreover got what they wanted—the renewal of the alliance between the French king and Il Valentino. On September 7 Alfonso, Cesare, and his brother-in-law Cardinal d'Albret reached Ferrara late in the night. Cesare managed to cheer his sister up, making her laugh as he held her foot during the prescribed bleeding. The next day, reassured at seeing her recover a little, he abruptly left, worried about the troubles at Urbino. Lucrezia, however, did not make a quick recovery. Sum-

moning her secretary, one of Cesare's trusted followers, and eight
monks, she had a codicil added to the will she had made before leaving
Rome. Ercole's spies found out that it concerned her son, Rodrigo of
Bisceglie. The gesture, coming on the heels of her nocturnal conversation with Cesare about Giovanni Borgia, shows how much she cared
about her children's fate even though she was far removed from them.
It challenges the accusation of frivolity and heartlessness that some
have leveled against the young woman, noting how quickly she recovered from the sudden breakup of her previous marriages.

By late September Lucrezia was finally out of danger. Alexander
was overjoyed, assuring her he approved of Alfonso's and Lucrezia's
joint decision to live apart during her convalescence. In a litter drawn
by two white horses, Lucrezia retired to the convent of the Poor Clares
known as Corpus Domini, while her husband headed for the Holy
House of Loreto to fulfill a vow he had made during his wife's illness.

The calm reigning over the couple and the House of Este was in
marked contrast to the stormy atmosphere surrounding Cesare, now
threatened by his condottieri who had just formed the League of Magione against him. Late autumn, when Il Valentino was setting his
trap at Sinigaglia, found Lucrezia and her husband once more in the
capital. On December 18 Laura da Gonzaga wrote to the ever-nosy
Isabella of Mantua about a visit she had just paid to Lucrezia. The
duchess had received her wearing a rope of the finest pearls about her
neck, her hair dressed in the usual simple way with a magnificent
emerald on her brow and a little green cap, embroidered with gold,
on her head. Lucrezia, she wrote, wanted above all to "hear about
your dress and appearance, especially the way you do your hair." In
exchange, she offered Laura some of her Spanish blouses. But, the
duchess added, Lucrezia also had less frivolous concerns. She was
keenly interested in the details of the agreement between Cesare and
the Mantuan lords regarding his daughter Louise's marriage to the
Mantuan heir.

Money troubles

In fact, Cesare's affairs gave Lucrezia the gravest concern. She tried
desperately to help him pay his soldiers. The money coming from
Rome was not enough to cover his expenses, nor were the treasures
he had seized from the coffers of the unscrupulous Ramiro de Lorca—

jewels, silver and gold objects, even chasubles of gold cloth and the jewel-encrusted miter of the bishop of Fossombrono. The monies she lent him were therefore very welcome. She managed to pass along to him 1,500 ducats, provided by Ercole's secretary Gianluca Castellini, then another 1,000. She now felt well off, since after her terrible illness Ercole had raised her allowance from 10,000 to 12,000 ducats—even though, suspicious as always, he wanted half to be paid in cash and the other half in provisions for the entertainments at his daughter-in-law's little court.

Ercole's parsimoniousness did not prevent Lucrezia from enjoying life. In January 1503 she asked her favorite, Ercole Strozzi, to give a dance in his Ferrara palace. It was a dazzling occasion, with a magnificent banquet following the ball, and all the young members of the House of Este were there—Lucrezia, Alfonso, Ferrante, Giulio, and even the wild prince Sigismondo. Old Duke Ercole, however, turned up his nose at the festivities and left, sulking and in solitary state, for Belriguardo, bearing with him the state account books, which he intended to go over with a fine-tooth comb.

The meeting with Bembo: Platonic sensibilities

It was in the Strozzi household that Lucrezia met the Venetian Pietro Bembo. He had become acquainted with Ercole Strozzi in 1497 when he had accompanied his father, an important official in the Venetian Republic, on a trip to Ferrara. Then twenty-seven, he already enjoyed a reputation as a scholar and prince of humanists and had studied in Venice and Messina. The University of Ferrara had celebrated his arrival, and he made friends with all the young rising stars of literature and science—the Strozzis, the Ciceronian scholar Sadoletto, the poet Ariosto, Celio Calcagnini, and Antonio Tebaldeo.

In mid-October 1502, invited by his friends the Strozzis, Bembo was installed in their beautiful villa of Ostellato with its garden that extended to the edge of the lagoon. He came for a long stay, transporting his library in a large boat. This library was especially rich in the writings of Greek and Latin philosophers and poets. Soon Ostellato became a fashionable center, enlivened by oratorical contests and recitals of poetry, with all the kindred spirits from Ferrara joining him there.

Skilled in the current Neoplatonic philosophy, Bembo believed that a beneficent being was always present to help mankind and presented this optimistic view in his life as well as his writings. In a way similar to Petrarch, he sang of nature and love in his refined Latin and Italian elegies. The ladies in his audience were duly moved by his finesse and charm, and it did not take long for these to have an effect on Lucrezia. To his intellectual grace, the poet added the grace of his handsome person. A fine-looking man, thirty-two years old, open and gallant, Bembo impressed the duchess with his ease of manner and his infectious joy, qualities which indeed he showed to the world at large. He belonged to those happy few indispensable for the success of the many entertainments then being held in glittering succession in Ferrara.

The ball given by Ercole Strozzi was followed by another organized by Bernardino Riccio, one of Alfonso's favorites. Then a ball was held in Diana d'Este's palace, and yet another particularly grand fete ensued at Ercole Strozzi's estate. Duke Ercole, in spite of his avarice, had been compelled to participate in the merrymaking. On his return to Belriguardo he made his customary contribution of having some ancient comedies staged, Plautus's *Menaechmi* and Terence's *The Eunuch*.

From now on, Lucrezia became the moving spirit of these worldly fetes. In April 1503 she herself arranged the welcome for Isabella d'Este, who had come from Mantua on a family visit. She took her about the town, instructed her in Spanish dances to the tambourine, and organized musical contests between the composers of Modena and Ferrara, spending so much money on the visit that she had to borrow against her jewelry. At one time, to meet her expenses she thought of making her father give her the revenues of the vacant see of Ferrara for a whole year. With the passage of time, the Borgia family's position seemed to have stabilized, as though the papacy had become their own property and kingdom.

Lucrezia saw no harm in taking advantage of the exciting life now open to her. She devoted herself to a courtly exchange of letters with Bembo. The Ambrosian Library in Milan has seven of her letters to him, in Italian, and two in Spanish, accompanied by a lock of wonderfully blond tresses. One of these letters, which was stolen in the nineteenth century by a French visitor, is today piously preserved in the manuscript collection of the Bibliothèque Nationale in Paris. But the Frenchman was only imitating Lord Byron who, when he was in Italy meditating over the love letters, appropriated for himself one of these strands of hair, which he thought "the most beautiful and the most golden one can imagine." The lock undoubtedly accompanied a letter which Bembo answered on July 14, 1503: "I am enchanted that you should find each day a new manner of arousing desire as you have done today with that which, just a while ago, adorned your dazzling brow."

To reach this stage of token-giving, the relations between Lucrezia and the poet had gone through a long crescendo. Bembo's first offering was a bit of Latin verse, the medium of the courtly-love tradition, celebrating a handsome bracelet in the shape of a snake which adorned the lady's wrist. Next, as a poetic game, the two correspondents wrote down in verse what each one wished for the other when they gazed into their crystal ball. Bembo was inflamed: his crystal ball was now dearer to him than all the pearls of the Indian Ocean—there he had seen the image of his love. An elegy compares Lucrezia to Helen of Sparta carried off by Paris, but, better than Helen, she does not allow her physical grace to stifle her spirit:

> *If you declaim in a vulgar tongue,*
> *You seem a beauty born in the land of Italy.*
> *If, from your pen, poems proceed,*
> *The Muses, it seems, do not make more beautiful ones.*
> *If, with your ivory hand, you pluck the harp or zither,*
> *You give back life to the music of Thebes.*
> *If you sing the neighboring Po and its waves,*
> *The current conforms to the charm of your notes.*
> *If it delights you to dance with all your agile grace,*
> *O how many times do I dread that a god, seeing you,*
> *May come to carry you off from your abode*
> *And to transport you, divine, with a light flight through the air*
> *To consecrate you as a goddess of a star, new-made and shining*
> *as your own.*

On June 3, while sending Lucrezia two sonnets, Bembo described himself in the midst of writing in the recess of a little window opening on the garden at Ostellato. "I am not able to say anything new," he wrote. "The very most I would be able to write would be about the life I am leading, the solitude, the shady trees, the calm, things which I used to love in other days and which today seem to me tedious and less beautiful. What does this mean? Is it the start of an illness? I should like Your Highness to consult her little book to find out if her sentiments correspond with mine." Doubtless the "little book" was a collection of sayings and prophecies serving, much as a key to dreams, to discover the sense of the poetic vision.

After several months had elapsed, there was no longer any doubt—courtly love had changed to earthly passion. In June, abandoning all prudence, Lucrezia responded with compromising verses, some stanzas of the Spanish poet Lopez de Estuñiga:

> *Yo pienso si me muriese*
> *Y con mis males finase*
> > *Desear,*
> *Tan grande amor fenesciese*
> *Que todo el mundo quedase*
> > *Sin amor.*

> *I think that if I should die*
> *and that with all my sorrows desire should end,*
> *a great love would dim*
> *and the whole world remain*
> *without love.*

This ardent declaration was followed in July by the lock of hair. Lucrezia confided in two of her ladies in whom she had absolute trust, her cousin Angela Borgia and Polissena Malvezzi. They met to adopt a code the lovers would use for their correspondence: the abbreviation F.F. would mark her letters. The only other person privy to the secret was Ercole Strozzi. Lucrezia knew she had to be prudent to avoid Alfonso's jealousy and her father-in-law's suspicions, since there were memories at court of terrible revenge wreaked by wronged husbands in the very bosom of the d'Este family. Bembo, for his part, would address his letters to one of Lucrezia's ladies, called Lisbetta. The poet duly complied with the ritual, devoting much time to the letters when he was composing his celebrated dialogues on love, *Gli Asolani*. But at the beginning of August he fell gravely ill in Ercole Strozzi's home. Throwing caution to the wind, Lucrezia flew to the poet's bedside. The next day the patient believed himself cured by this salutary visit. "I have suddenly recovered health," he wrote, "as if I had drunk a divine elixir. To this kindness you have added those dear, soft words full of love and joy and a comfort that has given me life. . . . I kiss that hand, the sweetest ever kissed by man. I do not say the most beautiful, since nothing more beautiful than Your Grace can ever have been born!"

But Lucrezia did not stay long at the side of "Messer Pietro" in a Ferrara overrun by the plague. She left for Belriguardo, near Ostellato. Meanwhile her joyous court of ladies and gentlemen settled at Medelana where Don Giulio, the duke's handsome bastard, assiduously courted the pretty Angela Borgia.

Death of Alexander
Lucrezia and Cesare in torment

In the midst of her pleasant stay at Medelana, Lucrezia received the shattering news of her father's death. Ippolito brought the news, galloping full tilt from Ferrara under a scorching sun. A fit of violent sobbing seized her as she grieved over the one being who had looked after her since childhood and raised her to the rank of princess. She pushed far from her mind everything that had caused her fear and humiliation—the infamous rumors of crime and vice, her brother's violence, encouraged by the pope's weakness of character. Filial love prevailed. In deep mourning, Lucrezia withdrew into her grief. It was, however, a grief in which none of the members of her adopted family shared. Alfonso, a realistic, totally unintuitive man, paid a brief call on his wife and took off—tears and grief upset him. Duke Ercole, for his part, did not exactly weep, as he was about to pick a quarrel with the pope, Alexander having neglected to include his favorite, Gianluca Castellini, in the list of new cardinals. Writing to his envoy, he said candidly that he was not saddened by the loss. Quite the opposite: "For God's glory and the good of all Christendom, we have many a time wished that Divine Goodness and Providence might send us a good, saintly pastor, one who would erase all scandal from His Church!"

Cardinal Ippolito was hoping that the pope's death would enable him to shine in the coming conclave. He had extracted a last favor from Alexander, the see of Ferrara, on condition that every two years he pay over the revenues to Lucrezia, as she had asked. Although he was gallantry itself in the way he behaved to his sister-in-law—and to her ladies, particularly her flirtatious cousin Angela—he was displeased by the measure.

Lucrezia's most sincere friend, and the one from whom she drew the greatest comfort, was Pietro Bembo. Although still an invalid, he came to visit Lucrezia but could not find the words to express his deep sympathy. He therefore decided to write to her:

"Yesterday I came to Your Highness to tell you how much I sympathized with your unhappiness and to console you as best I could. Yet I could do neither. For when I saw you in that dark room, lying in that black dress, grief-stricken and in tears, I was so seized with emotion that I stood rooted to the spot, unable to speak or find anything to say. I myself needed consolation, whereas I was the one who had come to console you, and I left, touched to the quick by this piteous spectacle, wordless and stammering, as you no doubt noticed, or might have noticed. . . .

"Knowing my devotion and loyalty to you, you must be aware, through your own sorrow, how great my sorrow must be. From your infinite goodness you will draw the consolation so necessary to you, and you will have no need of that of others."

Bembo wrote again, urging Lucrezia to lean on his affection: "These misfortunes have not shaken me nor caused my constant thoughts to burn less brightly; rather, they have given me strength and inflamed me to serve you more each day." At last the poet's constancy was rewarded, and Lucrezia confessed that she loved him. Bembo was beside himself with joy. On October 5 he wrote that he would have sacrificed any treasure to hear the confession she made to him the day before. He regretted that she had not made it earlier. The fire, he went on, into which "F.F." and fate had cast him, was the most ardent and the purest that ever burned in a lover's heart. He hoped that by striving to extinguish this flame in her own heart, Lucrezia would herself be burned by it.

In another letter his exaltation reached a climax: "My sole hope is to be able to contemplate once more my beloved other half without whom I am not only incomplete but reduced to nought."

The frequency of the letters had begun to arouse Alfonso's suspicions, and in October he announced that he was coming to Ostellato to hunt and needed Strozzi's villa to put up his suite. He thus forced Bembo to clear out besides ensuring that he himself would be near Medelena, where Lucrezia was staying, as Ferrara was still in the throes of the plague. In December Bembo was called to Venice, where his young brother Carlo was dangerously ill. Finding him dead on his arrival, he was devastated and sought comfort in Lucrezia's love: "Be assured that in sorrow as in joy, I shall always be the faithful heliotrope, and you will always be my sun." Not long afterward he sent her an Agnus Dei, a wax medal that had been blessed and which he had worn next to his heart. He begged her to wear it around her neck at night for his sake, so that it would take on his presence "on the sweet resting place of your heart." He promised to return after Easter. He did not come back, however, and the love letters ceased, to be replaced by a sober official correspondence—either because the young people's feelings had changed or because Alfonso's jealousy had become too much of a threat. The poet's last token of love would come much later, in 1505, when he had his printer, Aldo Manuco, send Lucrezia a copy of the *Asolani*, his dialogue on love, proudly dedicated to the beautiful Lady of Ferrara.

Thanks to her romantic idyll with Pietro Bembo, Lucrezia has a place of honor in the extremely elegant civilization of her day. Yet the events in Rome served to remind her that violence was in the forefront of the world stage. Her brother Cesare was suffering the consequences since, this time, he was not the one guiding the course of history. Alexander's death, Pius II's short-lived papacy, and the uncertainties of the beginning of Julius's reign had left Cesare helpless and reduced to defending himself against the barons he had despoiled in the Romagna. He could not even look to Louis of France for help, for the king no longer cared a fig for the Borgias. Louis had made his feelings known in no uncertain terms to his ally, the duke of Ferrara, suggesting he get rid of Lucrezia since she had failed so far to give his son an heir. There were, in fact, reasons justifying such a repudiation, including the argument of a prescribed marriage. Nonetheless, neither Ercole nor his son heeded their friend's advice. Aside from the very real affection they both now had for Lucrezia, a divorce would have been a disgrace for the family. It was this consideration that restrained them, as much as the prospect of having to pay back the young woman's huge dowry.

In this atmosphere of hostility, Lucrezia unhesitatingly sided with her brother. She knew that the only thing holding up the greatness of the Borgias was Cesare's conquest, the duchy of Romagna. What was important was to maintain her brother's dominion. Now, however, Venice had entered the scene, supporting the deposed rulers and helping them retake their territories. With very little money at her disposal, Lucrezia nevertheless managed to raise 1,000 infantrymen and 500 archers and sent them to Pedro Ramirez, governor of the fortress of Cesena. These reinforcements worked wonders at Cesena and Imola,

which were now safe from Venetian attack, but Cesare's loyal lieutenant could not prevent Giovanni Sforza from setting himself up
again in Pesaro. To her indignation, Lucrezia learned that her former
husband was indulging in acts of petty revenge and had even executed
the humanist Pandolfo Collenuccio, who had recently brought Ercole's alliance proposals to Cesare.

While the situation was going from bad to worse, and Julius was
trying to take the forts back either by persuasion or intimidation, Lucrezia encouraged resistance to Rome's orders. It may have been she
who advised the commander of Forlìi to insist that the pope pay him
a huge indemnity. In any event, the Lady of Ferrara was represented
when the garrison was allowed to retreat with honor. The support given
these commanders, whom he considered rebels, irritated Julius to
distraction. When he complained about it to Ferrara, Ercole asserted
that he had no part in the matter—his daughter-in-law was paying for
everything. In fact, he turned a blind eye to these goings-on and even
secretly encouraged them since he preferred to see the Romagna dominated by petty lords, whether friends or enemies of Cesare's, rather
than by the pope or Ferrara's redoubtable neighbor, Venice. By aiding
her brother, Lucrezia was unwittingly benefiting her father-in-law and
the duchy of Ferrara.

The fate of the little Roman dukes

Another motive besides concern for Cesare drove Lucrezia to salvage
the last vestiges of the Borgia greatness, and that was concern for her
children's future. The two little Roman dukes, her sons Giovanni and
Rodrigo, found their situation compromised when their grandfather,
Pope Alexander, died. Before the first cardinals' conclave opened, they
were installed in the Castel Sant'Angelo to be near Cesare. Francesco
Borgia, their tutor, hoped to bring them to Ferrara as soon as the
roads, which were clogged with troops pulling out of Rome, were
passable once again. But suddenly young Rodrigo—and possibly the
other children too (Cesare's illegitimate offspring were also staying in
the castle)—came down with malaria in the epidemic then raging in
Rome. Any move was impossible. Moreover, Ercole d'Este had seen
no need for the little princes to come to Ferrara since Alexander's
death. Far better, he thought, to sell all their Italian possessions and
pack them off to be reared in a foreign court—maybe that of Spain,

where their ancestors came from. After that they could settle either in Italy or in Spain. This argument applied particularly to Lucrezia's legitimate child, Rodrigo, who belonged to the House of Aragon through his father's side of the family. Bearing in mind that so far no child had been born of Lucrezia's marriage to his son Alfonso, Ercole feared lest young Rodrigo, the duke of Bisceglie, upset the order of succession to the ducal crown.

Lucrezia was forced to give in, especially as she was now overwhelmed by other worries. After Pope Julius's election, she witnessed her brother's ruin and did her utmost to prevent the Romagna from disintegrating. Nevertheless, she was unable to save Camerino, which she had given to her son Giovanni, lord of Nepi. She agreed to let the boys be taken to Naples, where Cesare met them in April 1504 with a safe-conduct from Gonsalvo de Cordoba and handed them over to be cared for by Sancia, young Rodrigo's aunt. Sancia now lived apart from Jofré, in a handsome palace with a retinue to match. She was on exceedingly good terms with Gonsalvo, and was now his confidante. Cesare hardly had time to spare for the young princes, all his energies being absorbed in preparations for his revenge. When Gonsalvo had him arrested and packed off to prison in Spain, other plans had to be made, with Lucrezia's approval, for their care and upbringing. They were then sent to Bari to be with Isabella of Aragon, the widow of Gian Galeazzo Sforza of Milan, who promised to see to their education.

Lucrezia would never see Rodrigo again. He died of an illness in 1512 when he was only thirteen. Deeply upset, she retreated to the San Bernardino monastery as soon as she received the news. All through the years of separation from her son, she had watched over him tenderly, in spite of the distance dividing them. From Ferrara she had appointed bailiffs for his duchy of Bisceglie, supervising them and quite often penalizing them—in ten years she hired four stewards in succession. Lucrezia's account books list the presents she sent to the people who looked after Rodrigo: embroidered blouses for the governess, little gilded wooden swords for the pages, carnival masks for the duchess of Bari, and a doll for her daughter with a trousseau that was a miniature replica of her own.

When Rodrigo was nine she and Isabella of Aragon had chosen a tutor, Baldassare Bonfiglio, whom she presented with an appropriate suit of clothes with velvet and silk bands, as well as valises stuffed with new books. At various times she nourished hopes of having Rodrigo come north to Ferrara. A pilgrimage to Loreto, which she planned for late August 1506, would have given her an opportunity to meet Isabella of Bari as well as Rodrigo and perhaps bring them back to Ferrara with her. But then it was discovered that Giulio d'Este, Ercole's bastard son, was hatching a plot against Alfonso, and so the trip had to be cancelled.

Now that Rodrigo was dead, Lucrezia had no choice but to liquidate the boy duke's little court. She dispatched two bailiffs to the kingdom of Naples. As the papal lands were now enemy territory, they had to make a detour around them, taking four months to reach Bari. Once there, they paid Bonfiglio, Rodrigo's tutor, handsomely, as well as the page Ferrante, the majordomo Onofrio, the valet Pedro, and two grooms. They also made an inventory of all the tapestries, clothes, silver, and even the horses, prior to shipping them to Ferrara, and before they left had a funeral Mass sung in the St. Nicholas Basilica.

Thus years of vain affection were swallowed up in grief. Happily, the "infans Romanus," Giovanni Borgia, was more fortunate than Rodrigo. When Lucrezia became reigning duchess of Ferrara on Ercole's death, in January 1505, he benefited from the situation, as she persuaded Alfonso that the child needed her and managed to have him brought to Ferrara. Little Giovanni was taken in by Alberto Pio di Carpi, the nephew and pupil of the great scholar Pico della Mirandola, a vassal of the duchy of Ferrara. He wanted to be exonerated for sheltering a chaplain of Giulio d'Este who was being hunted down by Cardinal Ippolito for an unspecified crime, and readily agreed to receive the so-called son of the duke of Valentinois at Carpi. The boy was thus reared in a cultivated, humanist milieu. Later, the good-looking youth was welcomed at the Ferrarese court where, however, he was passed off as Lucrezia's brother, Cesare's shade being reviled at that time. In any case, had not his filiation been established in a perfectly authentic bull of Alexander VI?

Having seen to Giovanni's welfare and schooling, Lucrezia retired and prepared with anticipation for her next confinement. Her hopes were fulfilled when, on September 19, 1505, in Reggio, she gave birth to a boy—an heir to the ducal crown, who was named after the pope, Alexander. But the baby was weak and refused to take food, and died after a little over three weeks. The premature death, coming after a series of miscarriages, might have raised doubts about Lucrezia's ability to give Alfonso an heir, but she would disprove those doubts by providing her husband with a large family.

Cesare's children

Concerned as she was for her own children, Lucrezia did not neglect her brother's family. She kept up a continuous correspondence with Louise, his daughter by Charlotte d'Albret. When the girl's mother died, she was sent to the French court, where she was placed under the guardianship of Louise of Savoie, Francis I's mother. As an infant, she had been betrothed to Federigo, son of the marquess of Mantua, who came to France in 1516 and found a homely-looking little girl with an ugly nose and a birthmark on her forehead. He refused to marry her, claiming that her dowry was not big enough. Her looks did not, however, prevent Louise from making very good marriages— the first with Louis de la Trémoille, and the second, after her husband died at the Battle of Pavia, with Philippe de Bourbon, a distant relative of the French royal family.

Cesare's illegitimate children, whom their father had taken with him to protect them from papal revenge at the beginning of Julius's reign, came to Ferrara at the same time as Lucrezia's son Giovanni. Warmheartedly, Lucrezia strove to give them a position in society that was worthy of their rank. Thanks to her efforts, the boy, Girolamo, married into a noble Ferrarese family. Widowed, he wed Isabella Pio, the lord of Carpi's daughter; their two daughters were given the ducal names of Ippolita and Lucrezia. Very likely, the duchess of Ferrara deplored Girolamo's violent temper, which he had inherited from his father. On the other hand the girl, Camilla, was completely different in character—gentle, extremely pious, and sharing with her aunt a love of art and poetry. Lucrezia placed her in the convent of San Bernardino she had founded in Ferrara, where the girl took the name Sor Lucrezia and was widely respected for her piety and intelligence.

Lucrezia also concerned herself with another illegitimate Borgia offspring, who was legitimized at thirteen under the name Rodrigo, the papal bull describing him as "born of the Roman pontiff and an unmarried woman." An alleged son of Alexander, the child might in fact have been fathered by Francesco Borgia, cardinal of Cosenza, who died in 1511. By seeing to his education, Lucrezia thus repaid a debt of gratitude to her cousin, who had acted as a conscientious tutor to the young duke of Bisceglie. This obscure Rodrigo died in 1527, the abbot of a monastery.

Lucrezia becomes duchess
Her liaison with Francesco da Gonzaga

Lucrezia also had duties at the Ferrara court, where her subjects appreciated her gracious, aristocratic first appearance as duchess on the balcony of the Castello Estense. That happened shortly after the old duke, Ercole, had died on January 23, 1505. In the great hall Alfonso received his duke's sword and scepter from Tito Strozzi, the doyen of the Twelve Judges of Ferrara. Then he rode through the white, snow-covered town before being crowned in the cathedral. Lucrezia, who was greeted by the leading ladies of the aristocracy, watched the celebrations from her vantage point at the castle. She wore a gown of gold and crimson brocade with a floor-length cloak of white moiré silk lined with ermine. On her hair, her forehead, her breast, sparkled the Este jewels. After the reception and the banquet that followed came Ercole's burial Mass, when the court went into mourning. A new life began for the youthful couple, one in which Alfonso immediately made his mark. Suspicious by nature and obsessed with order, he tried to get rid of all the Spaniards in Lucrezia's retinue. Alleging the need for intimacy, he even had an inner passageway built that gave him access, at all hours of the day and night, from the official apartments to the duchess's suite—the three rooms that were her little world.

Now obliged to be perpetually on display, Lucrezia played her new role as best she could. It was around this time that she found support and consolation in the person of her brother-in-law Francesco da Gonzaga, the marquess of Mantua. When he passed through Ferrara in 1504, the marquess had endless talks with her about Cesare's sorry fate. He had promised to act as liaison between her and her brother and, in fact, played an indispensable role during Cesare's long imprisonment in Spain. Lucrezia's passionate concern for her brother's welfare overrode the frictions between the courts of Mantua and Ferrara and at the same time justified in her husband's eyes her intimate friendship with Francesco da Gonzaga.

When, in mid-October 1505, Lucrezia left Reggio, deeply depressed over the death of her newborn baby, Francesco invited her to break her return journey at Borgoforte, where she spent two days in his company. She had known her brother-in-law over the years in the heady glory of his triumphs in the field. A great captain and something of a braggart, the irresistibly attractive Gonzaga now showed himself in quite another guise—as an accomplished courtier, sensitive and full of solicitude for her. Together they wrote a message for the king of Spain asking him yet again to grant Cesare his freedom.

Francesco returned to Mantua with Lucrezia at his side, and she saw the palace loom up out of the gray mist, dominating the lagoons formed by the Mincio River. Isabella Gonzaga met her at the door and led her through her salons, showing off her famous collections of classical statues, medals, and paintings as well as her magnificent library. For two days Lucrezia was subjected to a patronizing survey of her sister-in-law's rich art collections. The somewhat chilly atmosphere contrasted markedly with the marquess's friendliness and generosity, and the two women parted with cold politeness. To send Lucrezia away with a pleasant recollection of her stay, Gonzaga let her use his fastest boat on her return home to Belriguardo.

Ippolito's terrible revenge
Giulio's and Ferrante's plot

In her beautiful Belriguardo palace, Lucrezia found her court in an uproar over a terrible drama of jealousy. It was not Alfonso who was enraged: he had gathered information through his spies and knew of his wife's newfound friendship with Gonzaga, but had been assured he had nothing to fear since, however attractive Gonzaga's physical appearance, the "French evil" had made him impotent.

The jealousy came from another quarter. Giulio d'Este, Ercole's bastard son, had for a long time been in love with Angela Borgia, Lucrezia's cousin and favorite lady-in-waiting. Now, the girl was pregnant, with Giulio's child. But Cardinal Ippolito also courted the flirtatious eighteen-year-old, and Angela had rejected him, even daring to tell him that Giulio's eyes were more handsome than all his person put together. In a fit of jealous rage Ippolito had rushed at Giulio and stabbed at his eyes with his dagger.

Lucrezia had just reached the palace when Giulio was brought in, his face streaming with blood. The doctors at once got to work, and a few days later Alfonso brought him to Ferrara. He was terrible to look at, with his left eye, which had been saved, grotesquely swollen and the right one blinded and lidless. Clearly, Ippolito had to be punished severely, but since only the pope could chastise a prince of the Church, any effort to do so would bring Julius into the Estes' affairs. Alfonso therefore merely demanded that the cardinal apologize to his rival.

Giulio took this as mockery and began to plot appropriate revenge. Meanwhile, he had lost his mistress and the whole family was plotting against him. Angela had her baby on a boat taking her and Lucrezia to Ferrara. The child was spirited away and handed over to an obscure nurse. For consolation, Angela was given several possessions and married off to a petty nobleman, in the Este lands of Modena. Lucrezia, who was always very fond of her cousin, gave her a magnificent wedding, including a superb gown of gold brocade. All Ferrara was invited to the balls and to hear racy comedies inspired by Boccaccio's tales, the wedding taking place at Carnival time.

With the whole town caught up in the festivities, the unfortunate one-eyed Giulio kept in the background, brooding over how to avenge himself on both Ippolito and Alfonso. His brother, Ferrante, who hated his elder brothers, plotted with him. They did not lack henchmen ready to do any dirty deed in return for money. One of these was a blond Gascon giant, a self-confessed priest nicknamed Jean the Cantor. He enjoyed the favor of Ippolito and Alfonso, to whom he acted as go-between for his assignations. One day, at a drunken party, the Gascon managed to rope up the duke, who was naked on a prostitute's couch. It would have been an easy matter to strangle him on the spot, but those were not his orders: a more discreet method of dispatch, like poison, was planned. This perfectionism was fatal to the band of conspirators, whose intrigue came to Ippolito's ears. Under torture, they confessed to plotting to murder the duke, and were at once decapitated and quartered on the grand piazza. Only Giulio and Ferrante, whom their brother spared when they were mounting the scaffold, saw their sentence commuted to imprisonment for life. Shut up in two of the castle dungeons, they stayed there through the reigns of two generations of Estes. Ferrante died at sixty-three after forty-three years of incarceration, while Giulio gained his freedom nineteen years later. Beating the Este longevity record, he died at the ripe age of eighty-three.

Ercole Strozzi as go-between

The uncovering of Giulio's plot and his terrible fate served as a salutary warning to Lucrezia. Prudent by nature, she tried as best she could to keep secret her attraction to her brother-in-law, Gonzaga. To hide her letters from Alfonso's eyes, she once again called on Ercole Strozzi, who wrote to the marquess under the pseudonym Zilio. Every name in the correspondence was disguised: Gonzaga became Guido; Lucrezia, Barbara; Duke Alfonso was Camillo; Ippolito, Tigrino; and Isabella d'Este, Lena. Giving Strozzi courage in his job as go-between was the fact that he bore a grudge against Lucrezia's husband. When his father, Tito Vespasiano Strozzi, died, Alfonso had forced young Ercole to give up the lands his father, an eminent judge, had been given by the first Duke Ercole of Ferrara as a reward for his services.

The secret correspondence had its epilogue at Carnival time in 1507, when Gonzaga visited the Ferrara court. The duchess, as was her duty, received him with full honors, dancing with him so energetically at one of the balls that she had a miscarriage that same evening. But her pleasure at seeing Gonzaga once again helped her recover astonishingly quickly. Very soon after her miscarriage, she gave a reception for five young cardinals who had escaped Pope Julius's siege of Bologna to attend a masquerade ball given by Ippolito. Another dance and banquet followed on February 22, after which Lucrezia gave a private party for her intimates, including Barbara Torelli, Ercole Strozzi's mistress, Giovanna da Rimini, and Lucrezia's favorites, Nicola Trotti and her husband as well as the fair Angela Borgia.

A funeral chant for Cesare

Not long after these festivities, on April 20, an exhausted, dusty rider came to the castle gates. Lucrezia received him, the duke being away. He was Juanito Garcia, Cesare's page. He had witnessed his master's death at Viana and had come to report to Lucrezia.

The terrible news left the young woman petrified with grief. Then she pulled herself together and did her duty of hearing the usual petitions from the townspeople of Ferrara. Her day as duchess ended, she retired to the Corpus Domini monastery. While all the bells of Ferrara tolled in mourning, she contemplated the tragic end of the brother who had guided her destiny throughout her young life. It was thanks to him, to his valor as much as his crimes, that she now sat on a prestigious throne. If she had suffered and at times rebelled, she had always accepted his decisions—indeed, had often played a puppet's role in the making of them—recognizing all the while that they were aimed at a higher good, the greatness and fortune of the Borgia clan. She had accepted that fate. With her father gone, her brother defeated, she had taken up the challenge. She had tried to save the Romagna heritage and used all her powers of persuasion to gain Cesare his freedom, and she had succeeded! Once again, Cesare was on the brink of seizing power; the plan was made, the alliance with the emperor being drawn up, and Navarre seemed a stepping-stone to further glory . . . then, alas, death had entered the scene. Death had cut the thread of this destiny to which she dreamed of linking her own future and that of the duchy of Ferrara, a future where Cesare Borgia would head a federation of Italian princes, setting the people free from local tyrannies and the threats of foreign powers.

A young woman forced too early into maturity by life's trials, inured to making cruel sacrifices and bowing to others' interests, Lucrezia had neither the time nor the opportunity to speak her mind as her brother had to Machiavelli. Rather than criticizing her for being frivolous and weak and confining her in the role of a love object, it is as well to remember the high regard in which her father must have held her to give her several government posts. She was capable of rising to high occasions. Her brother's death gave her just such an opportunity, as is shown in the beautiful funeral chant she ordered Strozzi to compose. Here Il Valentino is depicted as a hero sent by Providence to unite Italy and restore her to the glory of ancient Rome. It was the finest eulogy that could have been made in honor of the mysterious Cesare.

Birth of the heir of Ferrara

The wheel of fortune was turning in Pope Julius's favor. Having set out to destroy the Bentivoglios of Bologna, he succeeded in late 1507, when both Alfonso d'Este and Francesco da Gonzaga, caught up in the whirlwind of events, were forced to bend to the formidable pope's will.

Going into battle in August 1508, the marquess saw Lucrezia once more. Shortly afterward, word went around Ferrara that the young woman was pregnant again. Deeply happy, she set about making prep-

arations for the birth long in advance—the cradle, a layette, a mul-
ticolored canopy for its protection, a confinement bed with an awning
of silver material. The bedroom where she would have the child was
hung with a cloth of her favorite colors of brown and gold, with a
scarlet thread running through it.

Francesco da Gonzaga was kept informed of these preparations by
Ercole Strozzi, who wrote him frequent letters and visited him at
Mantua to give him information at first hand. Alfonso, told of this by
spies in Isabella d'Este's employ, was extremely disturbed. So much
so that when his wife was having her first labor pains, he abruptly
decided to leave for Venice, making the plausible excuse that he did
not want to witness another humiliating, unfortunate birth. But on
the morning of April 4 a perfectly healthy baby was born. He was
named Ercole, after his grandfather, later to become Duke Ercole II.
Immediately, Alfonso rushed back to Ferrara to find, as he had been
told, that although the baby was far from beautiful, with his little
squashed nose, he was a fine, healthy child. So that no one should
be in doubt, he held up the naked newborn for the visiting ambassadors
to see. But politics called, and the elated father had to leave once
again, this time for France—not, it might be added, to Lucrezia's
displeasure.

Strozzi called on Lucrezia to read her the first lines of a little poem
he had written in the newborn baby's honor. He also brought news
from Francesco da Gonzaga. The marquess felt offended because he
had not been officially informed of young Ercole's birth. Only his
wife, Isabella, had received a letter from her brothers Alfonso and
Ippolito. This being so, how could he be expected to come to Ferrara?

The loyal Strozzi, however, pleaded with him on behalf of his
mistress: "If you came it would give her more pleasure than if someone
gave her 25,000 ducats. I cannot express the passion she feels for you."
Another letter pointed out that Barbara (i.e., Lucrezia) would have
liked to write herself but that her eyes could not concentrate on the
page because she was still weak after her delivery. She wished Gonzaga
would be reconciled with Alfonso so that he could come to see her.

The letter must have been intercepted, for soon a mysterious per-
sonage, called "M" in the Strozzi letters, visited Lucrezia and offered
to act as intermediary and go to Mantua to discuss the reconciliation
with Gonzaga. He did in fact go to Mantua, where he presented the
marquess with a little portrait of Lucrezia. It seems, however, that
Lucrezia had given no such instructions. Doubtless the aim was to

attract Gonzaga to Ferrara and to show him up by proving his intimate relationship with Lucrezia. The spy—for the man certainly was one—may have been Masino del Forno, one of Cardinal Ippolito's set. After the incident, Strozzi, Lucrezia, and Gonzaga were doubly cautious, burning their letters after reading them, but their relationship was already out of the bag; moreover, Isabella herself had denounced it to her brother Alfonso. The intrigue was too far gone and the protagonists' passions too intense to avoid ending in an explosive drama.

Murder of Ercole Strozzi

At daybreak on June 6, 1508, the body of Ercole Strozzi was found at a Ferrara crossroads, near the battlemented walls of the Romei palace. It had been stabbed twenty-two times. His cane lay by his side, and he still had his spurs on. There were no bloodstains on the paving stones. No one was in any doubt that this was a case of cold-blooded murder. The corpse had been dragged there from the place of execution.

Everyone expected the duke to order an inquest. Strozzi belonged to one of the leading families of Ferrara, he was a protégé of the duchess, and he had acted as one of Ferrara's Twelve Magistrates. True, Alfonso had made him give back certain lands formerly conferred on his father, but he had not quarreled with the poet over this. No orders, however, came from the ducal palace. Elaborate funeral services were held in the cathedral, attended by all the scholars and artists of Ferrara but by none of the palace officials. Lucrezia did not leave her apartments to honor her friend's memory. It was as though she was paralyzed with fear. Only Strozzi's intimates dared complain, the most vehement being Barbara Torelli, Ercole's mistress. Two weeks before, she had given birth to a little girl, and, lacking Lucrezia's protection, hoped to obtain that of Francesco da Gonzaga. Ercole's brothers wrote to the marquess begging him to help them avenge the hateful crime. Gonzaga offered a 500-ducat reward to anyone who could shed light on the murder, but apparently no one was interested; certainly no one came forward. To console Barbara somewhat, Gonzaga did baptize her daughter by proxy. Everyone in fact was fearful, and Barbara herself panicked and fled Ferrara.

Time passed, but the memory of the mysterious murder did not fade. All sorts of theories were put forward. One of the most likely ones pointed a finger at Barbara's former husband, Ercole Bentivoglio, whom the young woman had left because of his brutality. Furious at being deprived of his wife's dowry and of the possessions reverting to his children, Ercole, the theory went, had urged Gian Galeazzo Sforza, the husband of one of his daughters, to wreak vengeance. Together they decided to attack Barbara through her lover. The assassin himself may have been hired by Alessandro Pio, Angela Borgia's husband. Pio was in touch with Masino del Forno, the spy who shortly before had tried to trap Gonzaga and who may well have been the one who murdered Strozzi.

Yet if Pio were inculpated, then the special services he had rendered Alfonso would come to light. Alfonso had evidently been apprised of Bentivoglio's and Sforza's plan, and had no choice but to agree to it. Strozzi's murder rid him of a spy in the marquess of Mantua's pay and at the same time caused the exchange of love letters between Lucrezia and Gonzaga to stop for lack of a go-between. A few years later, the historian Paolo Giovio wrote that it was common knowledge that "the judge decided to ignore the culprits." Silence had been imposed by terror.

Ferrara and Mantua caught up in war
Pope Julius's ploy

Shaken by her confidant's murder, Lucrezia nevertheless soon came out of her depression and even dared to resume her relationship with Gonzaga. This time she used Lorenzo, one of Ercole Strozzi's brothers. Again, the lovers adopted a code: "falcon" meant love, and "falconer," Lucrezia.

To take her mind off her sorrow the duchess went traveling. In the summer she left for Reggio, where she again met the poet Bernardo Accolti, known as Aretino, who had been her protégé years before in Rome. In the autumn she came back to Ferrara without having seen Gonzaga, who was, like his brother-in-law Alfonso, caught up in the whirlwind of war. The League of Cambrai had united France, England, and the emperor Maximilian against Venice. Pope Julius, who had failed to make the Venetians give back the Romagnol strongholds they had seized after Cesare was defeated, also joined the alliance. Alfonso d'Este had already done so, in the hope of wresting from Venice lands claimed by Ferrara. Francesco da Gonzaga, for his part, was also lined up against Venice, in the hope of regaining lands around Lake Guarda.

The campaign opened under the best auspices. Julius named Alfonso d'Este gonfalonier of the Church to take advantage of the Ferrarese artillery, the best in all Italy. With her husband away fighting, Lucrezia was responsible for governing the duchy along with a council of ten citizens. She followed the armies' movements with passionate interest. Although Venice's huge forces—50,000 men—were routed after a four-day battle, Francesco da Gonzaga, who was in Venetian territory after the victory, was captured and brought in chains to Venice. There the crowd taunted him with "Caged rat! Turco [a rallying cry of the Gonzagas] is taken prisoner! Hang the traitor!"

Overwhelmed by this incident, and fatigued by another pregnancy, Lucrezia tried to help the captive to the best of her ability and managed to get help through to him.

The months that followed were happier. Lucrezia gave birth to another fine baby, destined to be Cardinal Ippolito II d'Este. Toward the end of 1508, she had the satisfaction of seeing her husband and her brother-in-law, Cardinal d'Este, gain a major victory over the Venetians on the River Po, by halting a Venetian fleet that was sailing upriver, devastating the land on both banks as it did so. Eighteen galleys and five ships loaded with 28 heavy cannons and 104 guns were captured in one fell swoop. The victory helped the negotiations that Isabella, the marchioness of Mantua, was carrying out with Venice. She succeeded in freeing her husband by handing over her son Federigo to the pope as a hostage. Julius wanted to be certain that Gonzaga would not turn against him once he had regained his freedom.

The two sister principalities of Ferrara and Mantua were now faced with a situation they had never known before, thanks to the iron-willed Julius. Realizing that the destruction of Venice would be a bad thing for Italy, the pope formed a Holy League that turned the previous alliance upside down. Now, instead of Venice, it was France that had to be booted out of the peninsula. Alfonso d'Este, who refused to betray his friend Louis XII, was relieved of his honor as gonfalonier of the Church—which the pope proceeded to bestow on his brother-in-law Francesco da Gonzaga. In addition, Gonzaga became captain-general of the Venetian army, a post he had held years before when fighting Charles VIII at the Battle of Fornova.

Julius put an interdict on Ferrara and excommunicated its duke.

Lucrezia, still absorbed in her task of governing the state, learned with horror that Francesco da Gonzaga was under the pope's orders to besiege the city. In the end, through an agreement with his wife, Isabella, who never forgot that she was an Este, the marquess found a pretext not to march against Ferrara himself, and feigned a deathly illness. Alfonso fought valiantly, aided by a French contingent that included the Chevalier Bayard. On February 11, 1511, Julius was defeated at La Bastida and Ferrara saved.

A change in fortune
Lucrezia's conversion

The experience of weathering hardships side by side served to reconcile Alfonso and Lucrezia. At Ferrara, the duchess received her victorious defenders with great honors as well as magnificent fetes and banquets. "She is beautiful, good, gentle, and courteous to one and all," wrote Bayard's contemporary biographer, adding, "Nothing is more certain than this, that although her husband is a wise and valiant prince, the above-named lady has by her graciousness been of great service to him."

Louis of France, who eight years before had told the Ferrarese ambassador that "Madame Lucrezia was not the right wife for Don Alfonso," now had to eat his words. Lucrezia was a princess worthy to rival the queen of France. During her husband's absence she had taken his place as governor of the state, at the same time seeing to her responsibilities as mother of a family.

Now, more than ever, she had to be careful to keep what remained of her possessions and those of her two eldest sons. In his hatred of the Borgias, Julius had decreed that the little dukes' lands be completely despoiled. The aging cardinal of Cosenza, Francesco Borgia, was thrown into jail by the pope because he passed the word along to Lucrezia. He managed to escape, however, and with two other cardinals fled to Pisa. There they called a conclave at which they accused Julius of simony and other crimes. Faced with this schismatic assembly, the pope let loose the thunderbolts of the Holy See, excommunicating the rebel cardinals and depriving them of their titles and possessions in two successive bulls.

Death now became the terrible pope's accomplice. Francesco Borgia died of apoplexy in Pisa in 1511. Shortly after that, Julius had the satisfaction of hearing of the death of two other Borgias to whom Lucrezia was particularly attached—Cardinal Pedro Luís and her son Rodrigo. The cardinal, who lived in Naples, where he looked after the boy's interests, had met his death by falling off his mule not long before his ward was stricken with his fatal illness.

Nonetheless, the defeat at La Bastida marked the beginning of Julius's reversal. The Bentivoglios returned to Bologna, where the aroused populace shattered the giant bronze statue of Julius that Michelangelo had carved on the cathedral facade. Alfonso had a cannon made of the fragments, which he proudly christened "La Giuliana." Lucrezia learned with pleasure that Modena had been recaptured along with other places seized from the duchy of Ferrara. At Easter, 1512, success seemed assured with the victory of Gaston de Foix, the French king's young nephew, at Ravenna. He defeated the Spaniards and the papal troops, though with 10,000 dead, the victory was a costly one.

In Ferrara, Lucrezia was more and more taking charge. Her husband left her to supervise city affairs as well as its defense while he went to Rome, where he hoped to have the onerous excommunication edict lifted. The poet Ariosto had intervened on his behalf, as had Fabrizio Colonna, but Julius had set a trap for him. He listed his conditions: Alfonso should give up his sovereignty over Ferrara, renouncing all his rights for himself and Lucrezia's children in favor of the Holy See; finally, he should live in exile in the little town of Asti in Lombardy until the end of his days. While he thought about his answer he would be held prisoner.

Happily, Fabrizio Colonna was able to help the duke escape. Disguised as one of the Colonnas' cooks, Alfonso crossed the hostile papal territory and hurried back as fast as he could to Ferrara. He found his capital besieged by the enemy and the whole of his duchy poised to fall into Venetian hands. Lucrezia, however, was maintaining order and morale in the city, and danger was averted when Alfonso managed to effect a rapprochement with Venice.

Ferrara's great stroke of luck came with Julius's death in February 1513. Now closer than ever before, the duke and duchess gave orders for thanksgiving services to be held in all the churches. Pope Leo X was reconciled with Ferrara and Mantua, his private secretary being Lucrezia's former friend Pietro Bembo, who rumor had it would soon be promoted. He was in fact given the cardinal's hat—which did not prevent him from worshiping Venus. After various love affairs with ladies with poetic names such as Aurora and Topaz, he settled down with a Genoese woman, Morasina, who bore him three sons.

Lucrezia, too, had undergone a great change during those trying years before peace finally returned to Ferrara. She had become very pious, wearing a hairshirt under her embroidered shifts instead of her décolleté gowns. She had works of devotion read to her at mealtimes and took communion three or four times a month in the churches of Ferrara. She joined the third Order of St. Francis and encouraged Francesco da Gonzaga to join as well. Yet the rhythm of her pregnancies had by no means slowed her down. Now thirty-six, she had in fourteen years given Alfonso four sons, one of whom would soon die, and one daughter, and now she was pregnant yet again. Alternating with many miscarriages, these births had weakened her but not altered her looks, if one is to believe the lines Ariosto added to his *Orlando furioso*, published in 1515: "With her singular beauty, her singular prudence, she surpasses all perfection."

Lucrezia had gained emotional serenity. Encouraging her in this was the view of the world, as she saw it from Ferrara. The victorious French king, Francis I, was assuring Ferrara of his protection. When Leo X made hostile moves against the Estes, Alfonso had only to go to Paris to stave them off. Moreover, the pope behaved kindly toward Lucrezia's mother, Vannozza Cattanei, who was still living in Rome.

Death of Vannozza Cattanei

Alexander's onetime mistress was now sixty-two years old. She still watched over her real estate in Rome, where her many rented properties, her three inns—the Lion, the Cow, and the Eagle—in the heart of Rome, and the income from her flocks of sheep on the city outskirts brought in comfortable revenues. She had retained fairly close ties with her children—with Lucrezia, and with Jofré, who at Sancia's death had married one of his cousins, Maria da Mila of Aragon. Illiterate, Vannozza dictated letters to a secretary more used to commerce than diplomatic ways, to judge from the dry style of his missives. Most of them are requests for favors. For example, the old lady would have her daughter ask Cardinal Ippolito to confer benefices in his Capua diocese on nephews of Agapito Gherardi, Cesare's former secretary. To thank the cardinal she was sending him two antique columns that had been unearthed in one of her Roman vineyards. In another letter she asked Lucrezia to have Alfonso intervene with the duke of Milan to make a certain Paolo stop saying bad things about her.

Universally honored as a respectable woman, Vannozza died in 1518, leaving her possessions to pious communities, to the hospital of San Salvatore Laterano, and to orphans. She was buried with solemnity in the Church of Sta. Maria del Popolo, Pope Leo X ordering that she be given the honors normally reserved for cardinals.

Lucrezia's last days

Since Lucrezia was at Ferrara with her youngest children she could not go to Rome for her mother's funeral. Alfonso had left for Paris, taking with him Giovanni, the "infans Romanus." One can only guess at the way Lucrezia took her mother's death, but no doubt it was with noble resignation. Not long after Vannozza, however, Francesco da Gonzaga died of syphilis. Lucrezia wrote a beautiful letter of consolation to Isabella d'Este, proposing faith as a remedy for the grief over a cruel loss: "It is the will of God. Our duty is to bow to his decrees."

When Alfonso returned in the spring of 1519, he found his wife extremely tired, looking gray and drawn and with large rings around her eyes. At that time she was nearing forty and her latest pregnancy, the eleventh counting her several miscarriages, was clearly going to be a difficult one. To comfort her, her husband recounted what the French thought of her: that the good duchess of Ferrara surpassed in virtue the proud duchess of Mantua. But this barely made the invalid smile.

She now spent all her days in bed. To relieve her suffering, her doctors, Palmarino and Bonaciolo, considered bringing on the delivery, and the contractions suddenly started. On June 14 a sickly little girl was born. There was scarcely time to baptize her with the names Isabella Maria when she died. Lucrezia herself went down with puerperal fever. After struggling for several long days and nights, the doctors gave up hope of saving her.

Lucrezia asked those around her to have Pope Leo grant her a plenary indulgence to ensure her eternal salvation. Emotion is palpable in the letter the Ducal Chancellory sent to Rome in her name: "I must pay my debt to nature. Through the great favor of the all-merciful Creator, I know that the end of my life is at hand and that in a few hours I shall be free of it." Death came during the night of June 24, after the duchess had devoutly received the last sacraments. Alfonso was at her side, holding her hand with anguish. After seventeen years of a frequently stormy marriage, he looked the image of a husband mad with grief. To his nephew, the young marquess of Mantua, he confided: "It has pleased our Lord God to call to Himself the soul of the most illustrious duchess, our well-beloved wife. . . . I cannot write these lines without weeping, so hard is it to find myself separated from such a dear and gentle wife, for she was sweet and dear to me by her virtue and the love that united us."

Alfonso led the mourning at the church of the Corpus Domini convent, where Lucrezia was buried in the ducal vault next to Eleonora, Duke Ercole's wife. But it was not in Alfonso's nature to abandon himself to grief. No sooner was the tomb sealed than he found consolation in the arms of his mistress, the fair Laura Dianti, the daughter of a Ferrarese hosier.

Lucrezia's image grew dim, but something of her survived in her children. Duke Ercole II married Renée of France, Louis XII's daughter. Through their daughter, Anna d'Este, he was the grandfather of Henri de Guise, who came within an ace of seizing the French throne from Henri III. Cardinal Ippolito II, who built the famous Villa d'Este at Tivoli, a masterpiece among Italian palaces, was one of the most magnificent patrons of the arts of the Renaissance. Both men would combine, with the touchy arrogance of the Estes, a formidable appetite for enjoying the world's riches and using them to enhance the greatness of their family. In this they followed the shining example set by Lucrezia and the long line of the Borgias.

3

A Triumph in Heaven

While those Estes who were Lucrezia's descendants caused a certain rekindling of the worldly Borgia grandeur, the Spanish branch of the family produced a complete contrast—a Borgia who was the model of Christian virtue, and the story of an exemplary noble family at the dawn of the modern era.

The memory of the murdered duke

After the duke of Gandia's assassination, his widow, Doña Maria Enriquez, immersed herself in piety. At her request her father-in-law, Alexander, raised the huge sanctuary that stood below the ducal palace to the status of a collegiate church, which the duchess then proceeded to transform into a pious memorial to the Borgias. The building was doubled in length, its five extra bays protecting the nave and the canons' choir. The east porch sported the Borgia and Enriquez arms. Inside, each arch's frieze and keystone were adorned with the Borgia bull and the double, five-rayed crown, just like the Vatican apartments. Alexander's crest was topped by the papal tiara.

The pope had endowed the collegiate church with a huge collection of relics. The most distinguished ones were contained in a superb monstrance, a masterpiece wrought in silver gilt and enamel showing cherubs, child musicians, and dolphins at play. One crystal disk showed a thorn from Christ's crown as well as fragments of His tunic and shroud. This was a discreet allusion to the duke's tragic death. Another precious reliquary held a fragment of the True Cross. Other relics included a silver hand of St. Anne, another of St. Martina, a thumb of St. Erasmus, a bust of St. Sebastian, and a silver-gilt diptych with twenty-two compartments containing relics of various saints.

The church also acquired a magnificent altarpiece which the duchess had commissioned for the choir. Around the statue of the Virgin were seven paintings depicting the Seven Joys of Mary. The last Joy, the largest—Death opening the gates of Paradise—was placed above the statue. Among ten large statues crowning the altarpiece were those of St. Sebastian (one of the family's patron saints) and St. Calixtus, a reminder of the first Borgia pope. The duchess had employed the best artists she could find for the work—the Valencian sculptor Damian Forment and the Italian painter Paolo da San Leocadio. The painter alone was paid 60,000 Valencian sous. Two more reredoses were commissioned for the Convent of the Poor Clares, where the duchess looked forward to retiring one day.

Doña Maria also ordered a number of pious canvases for her castle oratory. The painting now in the Patriarch College in Valencia, showing an intercession of the Virgin in favor of an assassin's victim, may be one of them. It shows the Madonna, with St. Dominic and St. Catherine of Siena on either side and, below the group, the three Borgia brothers, Juan, Cesare, and Jofré. The duchess is said to have commissioned the work around the time Cesare was captured, when she was attempting to have him tried for his brother's murder.

The man with a halolike crown of roses kneeling before the Virgin, who holds out to him the red rose of martyrdom, is believed to be the duke of Gandia. Behind him is his fierce-looking assassin, brandishing a cutlass. Juan's ducal beretta lies at his feet. Opposite him is a bearded man in the prime of life—fairly similar in features and profile to the portrait of Cesare in Paolo Giovio's book *Gli Elogi*. He is shown holding his sword tip down, as though he repented of his crime. The young man behind him is, as it were, a witness for the prosecution.

The work probably had just been finished at the time of Cesare's escape. Although she was then only twenty-eight, the duchess gave up what seemed like a wild-goose chase and once again devoted all her energies to religion. Hardly ever did she leave her castle of Gandia, which acted as the capital of a sort of small kingdom between the sierra and the sea. She sold all Juan's Italian estates, purportedly for as much as 82,000 gold ducats. This wealth, along with the revenues from her own lands, admirably cultivated by Mudejar peasants, would one day be passed on to her son. Doña Maria longed to retire to the convent of the Poor Sisters of St. Clare in Gandia, and when her son Juan married she took the veil and the name Sister Maria Gabriela, remaining in the convent until her death in 1537. Her daughter had joined the order shortly before. Promised to the duke of Segovia at eighteen, she broke her engagement to take her vows as Sister Francisca de Jesús.

Juan II, third duke of Gandia

The third duke of Gandia was also very religious. Whenever he met a priest carrying the sacrament to a sick parishioner he would leave whatever he was doing and go with him to assist in the communion and comfort the invalid. True, he had to set an example on his estates, where the peasants were nostalgic for Islam and needed to be convinced of the superiority of the Christian religion. Yet his attitude was sincere. When Juan was fourteen, King Ferdinand, in a move to keep him in the duchy, had arranged for him to marry Doña Juana of Aragon, the daughter of his own illegitimate son Alonso, who had been given the archbishopric of Saragossa. This good-for-nothing prelate had said Mass only once, the day he was ordained. Like the Borgia bishops, he gave himself up to worldly pleasures and his children's future, launching his sons on an ecclesiastical career. Two of them, Juan and Ferdinando, later succeeded him in the see of Saragossa.

The union of Juan of Gandia and Juana of Aragon, Ferdinand's illegitimate granddaughter, was prolific. On October 28, 1510, the first of their offspring was born. He was baptized with the name Francisco, in honor of St. Francis of Assisi, whom his mother had called on in the pangs of childbirth. Six brothers and sisters came next, in such quick succession that the young mother died. Her place was immediately taken by another great lady, Doña Francisca de Castro y Piños. Seven more children came into the world, and Juan had to ask the Church to look after some of his brood. Five of his sons had Church careers, aside from the eldest, who had to succeed his father as duke. Of two other boys, one became viceroy of Catalonia, while the other died young. Two sons became cardinals, one an abbot, another archbishop of Saragossa, and the last grandmaster of the military order of Sta. Maria de Montesa. Four daughters married Spanish grandees and two became abbesses—one went to Madrid to head the royal convent of the Discalced Carmelites, while the other stayed in Gandia to become head of the convent of Poor Sisters of St. Clare, where her grandmother and aunt had retired.

Francis of Gandia's pious youth

When still a child, Francis, the heir to the dukedom, was so precociously pious that his parents, albeit both extremely devout, found his behavior somewhat repellent. Although he had actually set an example for his son, the duke grumbled that his eldest son behaved more like a cleric than a caballero. His mother, the archbishop's daughter, once caught him in a mystical trance and told him reproachfully that she had asked Heaven to send her a duke, not a monk. The boy was almost ten when she died. So grief-stricken was he that he persuaded himself he had caused her death by displeasing God, and he shut himself up in his room and scourged himself.

Not long afterward, other events shattered the calm of Gandia. Charles, the son of Juana la Loca and Philip of Austria, now dead, was linked with the crown of Castile and succeeded his grandfather, Ferdinand of Aragon, who had died in 1516. Elected Holy Roman emperor in 1519, as Charles V, he had to move to Germany, leaving the country in the hands of his Flemish ministers. The Spaniards of Valencia rose up against them in the so-called Revolts of the Germanias. Violent fighting erupted close to Gandia and Játiva, and the duke was forced to leave his castle and escape by sea with his children, landing on the rocky peninsula of Peñiscola. From there they rode on to Saragossa, to be greeted by the duke's brother Juan, who had lately succeeded his father as archbishop.

The widowed duke, who was arranging to take another wife, entrusted the archbishop with the education of his eldest son, and for three years Francis was brought up as a courtier and knight. With a fine house and lots of servants, he lived up to his rank as the sovereign's cousin. To show off his royal connections he paid a visit to his great-grandmother, Maria de Luna, the widow of Enrico Enriquez, grand commander of León. The old lady lived far away in the south of Spain, in the wealthy city of Baeza, one of the cities of the kingdom of Granada. Her palace was thronged with nuns, relatives of hers whom she had offered sanctuary during the Gandia revolts.

No sooner had the youth arrived than he fell dangerously ill. During his illness—which lasted six months, all of which time he was bed-ridden—a series of earth tremors shook the region. Taken to the country, Francis spent forty days lying in a litter set in the fields, which gave him all the time in the world to meditate on the frailty of human life. Yet neither protracted study nor a retreat in the desert was a suitable education for a duke's heir, now thirteen years old. His father decided he had to appear at court, and the way to do this was to be appointed page.

Juan's next move was, accordingly, to the castle of Tordesillas, up north in León. It was here that the unfortunate queen Juana la Loca lived, shut up with the remains of her husband, together with her daughter the Infanta Caterina. Born four months after her father's death, the sixteen-year-old princess had never lived anywhere but with her deranged mother. Francis became particularly attached to her. Contrary to what one might imagine, life in Tordesillas was anything but a penance: court life still revolved around the queen with the usual pomp and royal ceremonies. Nevertheless, rumors of the outside world and news of political intrigue reached the castle as little more than whispers, since Charles V, Queen Juana's son, wielded the real power.

In the calm setting of Tordesillas, with its palace adorned, like Gandia's, with brightly colored tiles and other Moorish decorations, the plash of fountains in flower-filled patios soothed both the mad queen's melancholy and her daughter's carefree mood. For two years Francis forgot his family troubles while his excessive piety mellowed in the young princess's company. In 1525, however, Caterina had to leave León for Portugal, where she was to marry King Juan III.

Her fifteen-year-old page—a solemn-looking youth with olive skin, huge dark eyes, and beautiful hands—would fain have followed his mistress, but his father would not hear of it. He refused to let his heir leave Spanish soil. For some years the duke of Gandia had been on Charles V's list of twenty grandees of the first rank, an honor that conferred the rare privilege of remaining with head covered in the king's presence and conversing with him like a close relative. After the vacationlike episode at Tordesillas, the duke wanted his eldest son to resume his studies with a view to one day taking a high state position. He therefore insisted that the boy come back to Saragossa, under the archbishop's wing. Francis stayed there until he was seventeen, studying rhetoric and philosophy.

Francis de Gandia at court
First meeting with Loyola

By now Francis was an accomplished courtier, an excellent horseman, a skilled hunter and tournament champion, braving the bulls in the arena better than any other. He differed from the youths around him only in his extreme modesty, his shyness in female company, and his horror of debauchery and gambling.

This behavior, so strange in a Borgia, was undoubtedly due not only to his immersion in piety when he was a small child, but also to his embarrassment when conversation turned to the vices practiced at the court of Rome. His patron, Charles V, was then warring with Pope Clement VII, and it was fashionable to express outrage at the Roman excesses and in the same breath recall those of Alexander's day.

Francis was appalled when he learned that divine vengeance had struck the Eternal City through the hand of his own sovereign. In 1527, Charles's soldiers took Rome by storm. Many of them belonged to Luther's new sect and wanted to punish the pope, whom they called the Antichrist. Churches were pillaged, priests slaughtered, nuns raped. The only thing that saved the pope was his swift retreat behind the walls of the Castel Sant'Angelo. These crimes, traumatic for victims and perpetrators alike—the emperor Charles V was supposed to be defender of the faith—deeply disturbed young Francis. In his soul, he was convinced that the root of all the trouble was the sins of the world—and in particular the consequences of the sins of his own family.

Then, by chance, he caught a glimpse of the man who would help him reconcile himself to Heaven. He was riding through the streets of Alcala with some young nobles, on his way to Valladolid, when he caught sight of a man being dragged off to prison by members of the Inquisition. He stopped and stared at the prisoner, marveling at the intense inner glow that lit up his face, and was told his story.

Ignatius de Loyola, a Basque nobleman, had been wounded in 1521 at the siege of Pamplona, after which a painful leg operation had left him crippled. Unable to serve his king, he chose instead to serve his God. During a long retreat at Manresa, in Catalonia, he had written a book of spiritual exercises based on a technique of introspection and analysis that was designed to make men recognize their sins, strengthen their will to resist backsliding, and inculcate in them the desire to grow in divine love. It was this book, and the acts of devotion he encouraged his young students to practice—particularly a Marian ritual set for Saturday which was awkwardly reminiscent of the Jewish sabbath—that had led to his arrest by the Inquisition. Loyola was all the more suspect because, in Spain itself, Luther and several of his imitators were justifying their revolt against the Church by the need to set up a direct dialogue between man and his Creator.

Very possibly, young Francis was troubled when he heard the reason for Loyola's arrest. The sack of Rome inevitably made him sensitive to everything concerning the German reformer, whose followers had served the emperor's cause only too well by taking revenge on the pope. Still, he was too busy at court to worry overmuch about such matters. He lost sight of the ascetic stranger with the burning eyes. In fact, Loyola was freed by the Inquisition at Salamanca soon afterward and went on to France, where he started a movement that eventually gave rise to the powerful Jesuit order.

A young couple finds imperial favor

The Spanish court gained a new queen when Charles V married Isabella of Portugal in 1526. Philip, their first child, was born at the same time as the sack of Rome, and Charles proclaimed his son heir to the kingdoms of Castile and Aragon. Around this time at court, Francis's aristocratic bearing soon attracted the notice of Eleonora de Castro, a lady-in-waiting from a noble Portuguese family. When peace was established between the emperor and the papacy by the Treaty of Barcelona, Charles bade farewell to Isabella, whom he had made regent, and went on to Germany to try to settle the religious conflict. Before he left, the empress suggested that he arrange the marriage of young Borgia and her lady-in-waiting. They were overriding the objections of Francis's father, who disliked the idea of a foreign-born daughter-in-law. On the advice of Francis, who was sincerely in love with Eleonora, the emperor invited the grumpy, pietistic old duke to his court. It was a ruse to get his consent, as his son knew that his father would agree to anything rather than be seen around courtiers. The ruse succeeded, and Francis's father at once gave the marriage his blessing.

Charles himself dowered the bride, making the future bridegroom marquess of Lombay and master of the royal hunt. It was the beginning of a happy, prolific marriage that in eight years would produce five sons and three daughters. The young couple also became on extremely intimate terms with the emperor and empress, to the extent that Isabella had no secrets from the marchioness and her husband. To make his task easier, Francois was given access to the royal apartments at any hour of the day and night.

Yet he did not restrict himself to court and family life. Francis accompanied his master on several campaigns, proving his bravery on more than one occasion. He took part in the conquest of Tunis and La Goulette, where he caught fever and was immobilized for a long time. He accompanied Charles to Provence to fight the French in an expedition that turned out to be a disaster, with the emperor being forced to retreat after two months. In the course of this campaign Francis risked his life to protect the poet Garcilasso de la Vega, who had been mortally wounded in an attack on a fort near Fréjus.

When Charles V traveled around the various states of the empire, as he did frequently, the young marquess and his wife kept the empress company. Francis, who loved music, composed some airs that were widely acclaimed and later performed as motets in church services. The bird hunts he organized let him show off his knowledge of falconry. But he also found time for study. Charles, who in the course of his campaigns had discovered the need for mathematics, astronomy, and cosmography, asked the well-known scholar Alonso de Santa Cruz to teach him those subjects as well as horology, one of Alonso's specialities. But as the emperor had little free time, it was most often Francis who attended the classes for him and repeated them to his employer. He threw himself into the task, but paid the price, suffering from such exhaustion that for some time he lost his voice. Around this time, too, both his grandmother and his brother Rodrigo died. This alternating rhythm of worldly happiness and testing experiences—which seemed like so many warning signs from Heaven—would be the leitmotiv of Francis's life.

Death and burial of the empress Isabella

After the Treaty of Nice and Charles's meeting with Francis I at Aigues-Mortes, the specter of war in Europe seemed to fade, and Charles, eager to raise funds for the fight against the Turks, held a meeting of the Spanish Cortes in Toledo. Never had the Castile court seen so glittering an occasion. Nobles and clergy vied with each other in magnificence during the months-long receptions and spectacular arrivals of the Spanish grandees. The empress, worn down by her fifth pregnancy, took part in the events even though her condition worsened daily. In vain, Eleonora and Francis tried to comfort her: on May 1, 1539, she died after a premature delivery.

Devastated with grief, Charles made a solitary retreat to the monastery of La Sisla near Toledo, having left instructions for Francis and Eleonora to accompany the empress's body to Granada. His wife was to be buried in the royal chapel the Catholic Kings had marked as their ancestral burial place after the Reconquest. With an escort of nobles and prelates the body was duly conveyed from Toledo, having been summarily made ready before it was placed in its leaden casket. Eleonora herself had laid out the body, dressing her mistress in her finest clothes.

The long, slow journey south across more than 200 hot, dusty miles was broken for stops for prayer at various towns along the way. A month after the cortege had set out, it reached Granada. Here a formality had to be carried out by those accompanying the body. Before it was handed over to be placed in the vault, each member of the procession had to inspect the remains and swear that all was in order. Accordingly, the lid was raised in the presence of local notaries. Decay had set in: the empress's classic features were unrecognizable, and all that could be seen was a putrefying mass that gave off a terrible odor. None of those present could vouch that this was in fact the face they had so often admired. Francis was the only one who did actually swear, not because he recognized the empress but because throughout the whole journey he had never once let the coffin out of his sight.

After this appalling vision of death, Francis made a firm resolve. Since no mortal life could escape this terrifying end, he vowed to devote himself on earth to preparing for the life beyond the grave, by serving the only master he could never lose by death—God. He made an oath: *Nunca más servir a señor que se me pueda morir* (Nevermore to serve a lord whom I could lose by death). The day after the burial, he was strengthened in his resolve by the funeral oration given in the solemn cathedral service. The preacher, a mystic by the name of Juan d'Avila, known as the Apostle of Andalusia, used Isabella's example to denounce the vanity of court ceremony and the waywardness of those who lose sight of the goal of earthly life.

Nonetheless, Francis was too much of a realist and too conscious of his family responsibilities to withdraw immediately to a monastery. At most, once back in Toledo he asked Charles to be allowed to return to Gandia, but the emperor would not hear of it. Eager to show Francis how highly he thought of him, he appointed him viceroy and captain general of Catalonia.

The viceroy of Catalonia

The twenty-nine-year-old marquess of Lombay now found himself in a high government post. He would hold it for four years, showing the prudence and energy that his master, who knew him very well, had come to expect of him. Charles desperately needed people he could trust at the head of his government. Now reconciled with Francis I, he asked the king's permission to cross French territory on his way to Flanders. He wished to punish the people of Ghent for rebelling against the regent of the Low Countries, Maria of Hungary. The king acquiesced, and Charles left his kingdom in the charge of a prince regent—young Philip, later Philip II, who was then twelve years old. Francis Borgia, for his part, was to assume the government of the province of Catalonia.

The emperor's departure did not make the new viceroy's task an easy one. The province was swarming with brigands who only needed a sign that the throne was vacant to rise up in revolt. The only way to put them down was to adopt a sort of guerrilla tactic. In order to increase his forces, Charles made Francis a knight of the military Santiago order and a member of the order's council, which consisted of thirteen commanders in chief. Francis thus felt he was serving his God as much as his emperor and conceived of his mission as a sort of Crusade. He hunted the brigands down in their lairs, having them judged extremely harshly and sentencing them to death or the galleys. "The country," he wrote to Charles, "needs punishment more than it does pardon." And in another letter: "I have had six of them, the most notorious, hanged. The others are being tried in the usual way: the best they can expect is to spend the rest of their lives as galley slaves." Nevertheless, before each execution he sent a priest to the condemned man, and after the hanging had thirty Masses said for the dead man's soul. This strict justice was reminiscent of the methods the Inquisition used to crush heresy in Spain.

In private life Francis threw off the ceremonial that was part of his post. He began his day with prayer, took communion once a week, and at the end of the day obeyed the rules of his knightly order of Santiago, withdrawing to the chapel to recite the rosary and meditate. Each night, for hours on end, he would kneel in prayer; he also tried to mortify his flesh by self-inflicted scourgings and fasting. Actually, going without an evening meal was in a way a practical dietary measure, since at the time Francis was enormously and unhealthily fat, so much so that he suffered greatly on his disciplinary rides in the hinterland. Poking fun at himself and referring to the weight of his armor, he wrote to Charles, "Your Majesty can guess what this means for my huge belly!" Nevertheless he did not complain, considering himself, on the contrary, privileged to "go hunting with God's justice on my side." He applied this divine justice in his policing expeditions as well as in acts of pure charity, being always ready to help the poor and suffering. He put down the revolts that flared up when imperial troops set off from Barcelona for Italy and Flanders, he ensured that food supplies reached the province, and he fortified the strongholds when the French were threatening the eastern Pyrenees. In this troubled period he brought the Catalonians the safety they so badly needed.

Rise of the Society of Jesus

While Francis, half layman, half warrior-priest, was establishing order in the province and seeing to the people's material and spiritual needs, the society that Ignatius Loyola had founded in an underground chapel in Montmartre in 1534 had been rising from its humble beginnings. In 1540, Paul III gave it official recognition. Organized like a militia, with a general at its head, the Society of Jesus differed from previous religious orders in its militant goal, which was to win over souls menaced by secular dangers and to spread abroad the new reformed religion. The novices went through a series of tests before they were accepted. Besides the vows of chastity, poverty, and obedience, they could take the vow of absolute obedience to the pope only after extremely difficult tests. Thus the pope had at his disposal an army infinitely more devoted and loyal than any temporal force.

Elected general by his companions in 1541, Loyola sent out the first members of his society to serve the Church. One day Father Antonio Araoz landed at Barcelona. He met Francis Borgia and had no difficulty persuading him to favor the Jesuits' activities in Spain.

By that time the Borgia family's ties with the papacy had been renewed when one of Francis's brothers, Enrico, became cardinal on the premature death of Rodrigo. Paul III, formerly Cardinal Farnese and the brother of Alexander's mistress, Giulia, owed his career to the Borgia pope. Now he united with the Borgias in a more spiritual way.

Meanwhile, the Jesuits were making progress. The king of Portugal gave them decisive support. The founding of the Jesuit college at Coimbra, in Portugal, and Francis Xavier's extraordinary mission in India and China spread the Gospel farther than ever before. Now Germany and Switzerland—open to the influence of the "heretical" Luther, Zwingli, and Calvin—and France became the battleground for the Counter-Reformation. The Jesuits turned up everywhere in the cities of the empire and the universities, finally becoming the pope's spokesmen at the ecumenical Council of Trent.

Francis's religious zeal and his undoubted success as governor won him Charles V's gratitude and confidence. In 1542, at a meeting of the Cortes, the emperor confided that he was disillusioned and exhausted and was thinking of retiring to a monastery. Before he did so, however, he wanted to settle some outstanding matters. That, he told him, was why he had brought along his son, Philip, whom he had proclaimed his heir at Valladolid and was about to present at Saragossa, Barcelona, and Valencia. The prince would act as regent of these kingdoms while his father went first to Italy, then to Germany to attempt to settle the religious conflicts there.

Francis Borgia becomes duke of Gandia

When Charles was about to set off from Barcelona he again saw his friend the viceroy, who had become duke of Gandia. His father had died in December 1542, but Francis had been too busy to take possession of his lands. Delayed in Barcelona because of stormy weather, Charles had long talks with Francis, both men alluding once again to the vanity of worldly goods. When his ship eventually set sail for Italy, Charles took with him a portrait of his "angelic wife" to present to Titian. He wanted the painter to make lifelike copies of it which Charles could always have near him.

Taking advantage of his master's mood, Francis begged to be relieved of his viceregal duties. His presence was needed in Gandia now, he said, where he had to carry out his father's will and settle with his vassals and servants. Charles accepted, on condition that the new duke return to court once he had done what he had to do. To be sure of Francis's return, he made him master of the household of Philip's fiancée, Princess Maria of Portugal. At the same time Francis's wife, Eleonora, was appointed first lady-in-waiting, and two of their daughters Ladies of the Infanta's Palace.

Maria did not arrive for her wedding until late 1543 and when she did, she raised objections to the appointment of Eleonora, whom she disliked. Finally, in mid-1545 Maria died in childbirth, leaving the couple free to shed the burden of service at court.

With pleasure, Francis and Eleonora returned to their lands together with their young children, whom they wanted to rear themselves, far from court intrigue and corruption. There followed three years of serenity, looking after the family estates of Gandia and Lombay. The duke rebuilt and refurnished the Gandia hospital. He fortified the coast, often raided by pirates. With Araoz he discussed setting up a Jesuit mission, in the meantime founding a monastery at Lombay as a training place for taking divine office. And, like his father before him, he made a point of following the priests as they took the last sacrament to the sick.

Death of the duchess
Francis a secret Jesuit

Eleonora, who was an admirable support to her husband in his charitable works as well as a gracious hostess, suddenly came down with a mysterious debilitating disease. Her doctors could do nothing to save her, while Francis prayed that his wife would be spared.

One day while he was praying especially fervently, he had a vision of the Savior and heard these words, later set down when Francis was canonized: "*Si tu quieres que te deje a la Duquesa más tempo en esta vida, yo lo dejo en tu mano. Pero te aviso que a ti no te conviene esto.*" ("If thou desirest to keep the duchess longer in this life, so be it. But I tell thee plainly, it is not the best for thee.") Francis then prayed, "O Lord, the least I can do to repay Thy infinite and gracious generosity is to offer Thee the lives of my wife and my children, as well as my own, and all that I possess in the world. I have received everything from Thy hand. I give it all back to Thee, beseeching Thee to dispose of it according to Thy will."

He recounted his experience to his confessor. Convinced by it that his wife would find eternal life after her death, he was able to comfort her bravely in her last moments, secretly renewing the vow he had made at Granada before the empress's open coffin.

Eleonora died in 1546. At thirty-six, her husband was left with five sons and three daughters. Before becoming a Jesuit, he had to make plans for their future. He confided directly in Ignatius Loyola, with whom he had built up a friendly relationship since meeting Antonio Araoz. Loyola's reply deserves to be quoted. It set up a new form of admission to the Society, that of a secret commitment. Flattered by Francis's request, Loyola at once gave his consent. As to the time and manner in which the young man could become a Jesuit, however, he told Francis:

"So that you can best fulfill all your obligations, it seems to me that this change should come about gradually, and with the utmost care, to the greater glory of Our Lord. Thus you will, little by little, be able to settle your affairs so that, without telling any secular person of your vow, you should shortly be free of anything that might delay the accomplishment of your holy desires.

"To explain further and go into more detail, I think that since your daughters are of marriageable age, you might consider making appropriate provision for them, and that you might arrange a marriage, too, for the marquess, if a suitable partner should arise. For your other sons, it will not be enough for them to have the support of their elder brother, the heir to the dukedom: you should leave them enough for them to complete their studies in one of the principal universities and to live honorable lives in the world. One may suppose that, if they are what they should be and as, I trust, they will be, the emperor will give them benefits befitting your service and in accordance with the goodwill he has always borne you.

"Again, it will be good to proceed with the buildings you have already begun, since I would hope that all your domestic affairs will be behind you when this change in your life is publicly known. Nevertheless, as you are so well versed in letters, I would like you to apply yourself seriously to the study of theology, and I hope that this knowledge will help you in serving God. I would even hope that you could take the degree of doctor in your University of Gandia. But, since the world is not capable of receiving news of that nature, I would wish this to be done quietly, and in secret, until such time when, with God's grace, we can be perfectly free to speak."

Immediately after his wife's death, Francis had secretly taken the vows of chastity and obedience and promised to become a Jesuit. Now, he set to work without delay. His wife's sister was entrusted with the care of the youngest children. In 1548 his eldest son, Carlos, married Maddalena de Centelles, countess of Oliva, and a year later Isabel, the eldest daughter, wed Francisco de Sandoval y Rojas, marquess of Denia and count of Lerma. The other offspring would later do well in the world, with Juan becoming viceroy of Portugal, Alvaro, papal envoy, Fernando, a knight of the Calatrava Order, and Alonso, imperial chamberlain. The second daughter made a good match while the youngest, Dorotea, became a nun of the order of St. Clare.

In the meantime Francis built the first Jesuit university. Annexed to his own castle, it gave scholarships and lodging to poor students, the children of converted Moors and Jews whom he hoped to make into orthodox practicing Catholics.

Francis joins the Society of Jesus
Journey to Rome and ordination

With his plans well launched, on February 1, 1548, Francis Borgia made his solemn profession in the Society of Jesus—but without in the least changing his appearance or way of life. The only difference was that he now devoted more time to studying theology than managing his domains.

In 1550, with an escort of thirty servants, he set off for Rome to obtain the Jubilee Year indulgences together with his second son, Juan. The journey took on the look of a pious procession. Several Jesuit fathers came along, and the duke made confession and took communion every day, still managing to inflict the usual mortifications on his body when the party stopped at inns along the way. Bedded down at his chamber door, his servants heard the cracking of the penitential whip—the discipline—which he used to flagellate himself. Each night, it was said, they counted more than 500.

Francis tried to avoid the honors offered him during the journey. However, when the cortege reached Ferrara, he did stay with his cousin Ercole II, Lucrezia's son, who welcomed him with worldly and religious festivities lasting four days. At Florence, Duke Como de' Medici gave him a similar reception. On arriving in Rome, he found Charles's envoy, Fabrizio Colonna, several cardinals, and former servants of the

Borgias all eagerly waiting to give him a triumphant welcome. This was embarrassing to Francis, who had asked Loyola, who lived in the Society's house, for permission to enter Rome at night. Ignatius had refused, and Francis, who wanted to humble himself, was forced once again to receive worldly honors. He made up for it when he got to the Jesuit house, prostrating himself at Ignatius's feet at the door and devoutly kissing his hand.

In vain, Pope Julius III, who had just succeeded Paul, offered Alexander's descendant an apartment in his palace. Francis refused, explaining that he would rather live among his colleagues. This modesty of personality erased the pride of the former Borgias. On the other hand, one result of the contrast between this attitude of Francis's and people's memories of his ancestors was to thrust him into the limelight. Francis's four-month stay in Rome was tremendously important for the future of the Society. Having a man of his qualities as one of its key members persuaded the hitherto silent Curia that the future of Catholicism depended in large measure on this new foundation, with its ability to mingle intimately with the world. Moreover, Francis helped the order spread worldwide by raising huge funds for the founding of a central Jesuit college, the Collegio Romano, through whose doors hundreds of students would pass and which would become the nursery for the Society's elite troops.

When he left Rome, Francis wrote to Charles asking to be relieved of all his duties so that he could officially enter the religious life. Without waiting for an immediate reply he went back to Spain and visited Loyola's castle in the Basque country, meditating in the room where Ignatius was born. Shortly thereafter, at Oñate, near the Pyrenees, he received a letter from his former patron approving his decision: "It would not be reasonable," Charles wrote, "for me to contend for the person of my servant with the supreme Sovereign to Whom he wishes so ardently to devote himself." Charles thus gave his friend leave from the court and allowed him to resign all his titles in favor of his eldest son. Francis now began his new life with the same determination with which as viceroy he had broached his military campaigns. This time he was setting out on a spiritual reconquest of the world.

On May 23, 1551, he was ordained priest at Oñate, having first laid down his sword and received the tonsure. The duke of Gandia was now Father Francis Borgia. Henceforth he made only the rarest allusions to his ducal rank. For example, when he learned that the

Society was refusing to admit a novice who struck him as a worthy candidate, he announced, "I thank God from the bottom of my heart that he made me duke for, assuredly, there was no other reason why my superiors would have accepted me!"—a statement which, at the very least, showed that beneath the sober black habit he now wore he had not lost his sense of humor.

Francis celebrated his first Mass in the chapel of the Loyola castle, serving communion to his son Juan. Since the pilgrimage to Rome the young man had never left his father's side, and he had thought up a simple way of staying close to him—by marrying Lorenza Oñaz de Loyola, a relative of Ignatius.

Francis's second Mass was said in public, the event being announced far in advance. Julius III had proclaimed a plenary indulgence for all those who attended the "holy duke's" Mass. The little town of Vergara was chosen for the purpose. When the day dawned, so many flocked to hear him that the altar had to be set up in the open country. Starting at nine in the morning, the service did not end until between two and three in the afternoon, so great was the crowd of communicants.

Something inexplicable and wonderful happened on this occasion. Francis was preaching in Spanish, while most of his hearers understood only Basque. Yet people noticed that those members of the crowd who were farthest away from the pulpit were weeping with emotion. Asked why, they said that they "felt inspiration from God had touched their inmost hearts and that in that inspiration they heard certain silent words which told them what the preacher was saying, even though his voice did not reach them."

After this brilliant inauguration of his priesthood—brilliant despite his own wishes—Francis spent some time in a simple hermitage at Oñate, where he carried out the humble tasks of a novice. The outside world had not forgotten him, however: numerous requests for prayers and spiritual counsel came in from former associates at court. Many people believed his place was in Rome, and the pope offered him a cardinal's hat. It was indeed hard to conceive that a secular prince, especially a Borgia, would give up his rank when he took holy orders. Francis spurned the offer. All he aspired to was to be professed, which took place in 1554, when he pronounced the major vow of obedience. From now on he was ready to act, at Ignatius's bidding, on any front where he might be sent to teach or preach, before the people or before the court.

Two of his first missions took Francis to Tordesillas to see Queen

Juana, now more crazed than ever. He helped the aged queen as she lay on her deathbed, his presence even giving her a few gleams of lucidity before she died. During this stay he learned that he had been made commissioner for the provinces of Spain and Portugal. He became more and more active, opening the first novitiate at Simancas and creating twenty colleges in Spain at the request of the cities. He was especially needed in Portugal: in Lisbon he was made court preacher by Juan III and his queen, Caterina, whose page he had been long ago at Tordesillas.

Great changes were afoot in the world. Charles V, discouraged by the failure of his actions against the German reformers and racked by gout, asthma, and other ills, at fifty-four had become prematurely an old man. He decided to abdicate, leaving the throne to his son Philip, who heard the news at the same time he learned that he was to marry Henry VIII's daughter, Mary Tudor.

When Philip set sail for England he left the reins of government in the hands of his sister Juana, widow of the heir to the Portuguese throne. It was Juana, a devoted follower of Francis, who had asked him to go and see her grandmother, Juana la Loca. For many years to come, he was the royal family's spiritual director. It was a difficult assignment, entailing as it did advice on politics and made especially hard because the new pope, Paul IV, to whom the Jesuits owed absolute obedience, declared himself opposed to the Hapsburg hegemony. While Charles was piously preparing to abdicate, Pope Paul had violently taken him and Philip to task, then excommunicated them both and in 1556 declared war on them.

The situation became critical for the Society of Jesus, which was made up for the most part of Charles's subjects. Thus, when Ignatius Loyola died, on July 31, 1556, it was impossible for the electing body to meet in Rome, and Lainez, the vicar general, was not elected until two years later.

Charles V abdicates
Francis Borgia visits Jarandilla

In spite of his clash with the pope, the emperor did not give up a plan he had made Francis privy to years before: to withdraw from the world after giving up the throne. For this purpose he had chosen the mon-

astery of Yuste in Estremadura, run by the Hieronymite order, where
he used to go to meditate and where, on his father's orders, Philip had
built a large house inside the monastery walls.

In 1555, from his palace in Brussels, Charles left his son all his
lands in the Low Countries as well as the kingdoms of Castile, Aragon,
and Sicily. The Treaty of Vaucelles, drawn up with Henri II of France,
gave him Burgundy. Finally Charles set sail for Spain, arriving eventually at Jarandilla, near Yuste, where he waited for his monastery
quarters to be completed.

Jarandilla palace, overlooking the basin of the Tagus and protected
from the north wind by the sierra, was a pleasant residence, bathed
in sunlight in the fine days of late autumn. From its apartments and
gardens the convent of San Jeronimo de Yuste could be seen on the
nearby hills, often swathed in mist. Charles had chosen the place
because of its relative proximity to New Castile and the famous shrine
of Sta. Maria de Guadalupe.

In late 1556 he went to see how work was progressing on his house.
Very simple in plan, the building consisted of four large, light rooms
on two floors. The emperor's bedchamber was connected by a brightly
tiled passageway to the sanctuary choir. The kitchen, with its monumental fireplace, was large enough to hold the fifty-odd domestics
who served the emperor during the day and slept in the village nearby.
With its calm atmosphere, its fountains, and fine garden of orange
and fig trees separated from the fields by a little wood, Jarandilla gave
the emperor, after all his tribulations, a foretaste of the paradise he
hoped to gain.

At Christmastime he invited Francis Borgia to come and see him.
He still remembered their long talks and wanted to persuade his former
duke to leave the Jesuits and act as his spiritual adviser during his last
days. Perhaps he could suggest that Francis join the Hieronymites, or
the Carthusians. Warned in time by Juana, the regent, Francis prepared his and the Society's defense—so well, that after two days' conversation with Charles he was able to convince him of the superiority
of the Jesuit order. Each member, he pointed out, dedicated himself
exclusively to furthering the glory of God; also, the order should not
be criticized merely because of its novelty. The emperor had received
him with exceptional deference, allowing Francis to speak to him with
his head covered, as was fitting for a grandee, and to sleep in the room
next to his at night. These details were enough to disarm the anti-
Jesuit opposition in the highest ranks of government, which was par-

ticularly intense because of the Society's links with Rome. As a result, Juan de La Vega, president of the Council of Castile, became an active protector of the Society.

Francis at Yuste
His mission to Portugal
Death of the emperor

When Charles moved into his house at San Jeronimo de Yuste, he saw only a handful of faithful friends, Francis Borgia being one of them. In 1557 Charles sent him to convey his condolences to his sister Caterina who had lost her husband, King Juan of Portugal.

Welcomed warmly by the dowager queen, Francis stayed with her for several weeks, putting to her a secret proposal from the emperor. The heir to the throne was Sebastiano, who was then only three; if the child should die prematurely, Charles wanted the Portuguese crown to go to his own grandson, Don Carlos, the son of Philip and his first wife, Maria of Portugal. Francis Borgia succeeded in obtaining the queen's consent despite the grumbles of the grandees at court.

His mission to the Portuguese court had important consequences for both the Society and Portugal itself. Francis managed to persuade the queen to entrust the education of the heir to the throne to the Society of Jesus. A Portuguese priest, Luís Gonsalvo de Camara, was appointed the boy's tutor. Unfortunately his influence on the boy, who was weak-minded and quixotic, turned out to be fatal, encouraging the young prince to go on a mad crusade in North Africa about twenty years later. The youth died at the battle of Alcazarquivir, thereby causing a tragic succession crisis which led to Spain's seizing Portugal. Nothing at the time, however, seemed to presage such an outcome: rich from its trade in spices and other colonial products, Portugal was launching its fruitful expeditions on the seas, with the Jesuits joining in the same extraordinary epic.

After touring the wealthy Portuguese colleges and palaces, Francis returned to Spain full of hope but found himself having to contend with a rapidly growing reform movement, flourishing especially at

Sevilla and Valladolid. The Grand Inquisitor, Fernando de Valdes, archbishop of Sevilla, had received denunciations accusing the Jesuits of making accommodations with heresy. The news saddened the aging emperor at Yuste. Once again he summoned his old friend. Charles had caught cold in the late summer of 1558 and was suffering from a violent attack of gout as well. Sensing his end was near, he wanted to have a funeral Mass celebrated with pomp in memory of his father and grandparents. Next, he had a long talk with Francis about eternal life and made him one of the executors of his will.

After calming the emperor, Francis made his way to Valladolid, where he received the news that Charles had died on September 21. Bartolomeo Carranza, the pious archbishop of Toledo, a friend of Francis Borgia's and just as suspect as he was in the Inquisition's eyes, had given Charles the last rites. The emperor's body was temporarily buried in the choir vault of San Jeronimo, under the high altar, until it could be moved to the royal burial ground Philip II had arranged at the Escorial. Above the sepulcher was hung Titian's painting *Gloria*, which, in accordance with his belief and that of his Borgia friend, showed Charles with his empress, at the threshold of paradise, his face serenely triumphant, ready to pass beyond earthly death into eternal life.

Beginning of Philip II's reign
Francis persecuted by the Inquisition
Harassment of his friars

After giving his royal friend's funeral oration before the court, Francis left for another tour of the Jesuit establishments in Spain, in particular those in Granada where the conversion of the former Muslim communities still had high priority. This return to the place where he had first heard the call augured well for future triumphs. On his travels, Francis met ordinary people as well as noblemen, all coming to seek his counsel. He was said to perform miracles. The great mystic St. Teresa of Avila consulted him for guidance of her inner life. Attacks on the Society diminished with the intervention of Francis's friends and supporters. Philip had him draw up a memorandum on the people he thought best fitted to take on state positions. Thus it looked as though Francis would enjoy the same favor under the new reign as he had under that of Charles V.

Then, all of a sudden, the sky clouded over. In August 1559, the Grand Inquisitor published a list of proscribed books. Included in it, along with the works of famous preachers such as Juan of Avila and Luís of Granada, was a book entitled *Obras del Cristiano* (Works of the Christian), whose author was given as Francisco de Borja, duke of Gandia. This was an anthology of pious writings, published in 1550, which included a small devotional treatise the duke had put out earlier, in 1548.

The zeal of the Inquisition knew no bounds. Books were hunted down as well as men suspected of heresy, as was shown in the two great auto-da-fés at Valladolid in 1559. No one, no matter what his rank, could escape persecution. Soon even the archbishop of Toledo was arrested and subjected to a long, painful trial for writing a catechism that seemed to stress the mystical relationship between man and his Creator rather than ritual.

Seeing his reputation suffer and fearful of falling into the hands of the Inquisition just as Ignatius Loyola had years before, Francis fled to Evora, in Portugal, where he became seriously ill. He spent the better part of two years in that country, using his recovery time to preach and carry out his duties as Society Visitor. Philip II had dismissed him not only because of the suspicion of heresy that clung to him but also because he held Francis responsible for his brothers' misdeeds. Pedro Luís Galceran de Borja, grand master of the Montesa order, had renounced his vows in order to marry but had hung on to his order's possessions, causing a rift between himself and the king. Two other brothers of Francis, accused of murdering Diego of Aragon, son of the Catalonian viceroy, had escaped death by going into exile. When Francis himself had fled to Portugal, one of the condemned men, Diego, was hunted down in the monastery where he was hiding and was executed at Játiva. The other, Felipe, was also caught but managed to flee to Africa. These harsh measures dictated from the throne came about just as Francis himself, tired of his long Portuguese exile, had succeeded in escaping. Lainez, the general of the Jesuits, had obtained two briefs from Pius IV summoning his colleague to Rome, and Francis readily obeyed without waiting to ask Philip's permission, saying he had no need of it because he had taken a vow of absolute obedience to the pope. Not the kind of man to take such a snub, Philip wreaked his revenge on Francis's brothers.

Francis becomes vicar general, then general of the Jesuits
A huge missionary effort

When Francis arrived in Rome, in September 1561, Lainez was away in France, defending orthodoxy at the Conference of Poissy. Having tried in vain to set up the Society on French soil, he left for another conference, the Council of Trent. Its final session gave the Catholic Church a weapon with which to oppose the Protestants, in the form of a carefully drawn up body of doctrine.

Now, more than ever, in its general's absence, the Society needed a man at its head who would fend off the attacks against orthodoxy that were breaking out all over Europe. Francis Borgia was just that man: he was made, in turn, vicar general, Italian commissioner, and assistant for Spain and Portugal. Whatever the situation, he always put the interests of the Church first and refused to compromise. For example, he refused to allow his own son Alvaro, a twenty-seven-year-old ambassador to Rome, to marry Francis's fourteen-year-old niece. Alvaro had to ask for a dispensation himself; the pope granted it, at the same time reproaching Francis for being too severe.

With his strictness and authority, Francis was clearly cut out to lead the Society of Jesus. While he was comforting Lainez on his deathbed, the fading leader, by now unable to speak, gave Francis a meaningful look that was interpreted as a signal. Thus, on July 2, 1565, Francis was elected general.

His period of leadership as the Jesuits' third general coincided almost entirely with the reign of the saintly Pius V (January 1566 to May 1572). As Cardinal Ghislieri, very concerned with orthodoxy, Pius had been Grand Inquisitor but, unlike the Spanish members of the Inquisition, had made good use of the Jesuits on becoming pope. Pius now set new rules for them which chimed in with Francis's aspirations, stipulating that the members should have one hour of daily prayer and recite divine office together.

An enormous effort was made to put the teaching in the colleges on firm footing. Two programs were set up defining the primary and secondary curricula. Francis also founded the Collegio Romano, the Jesuit college that was later to become the Gregorian university. He provided funds for the purchase of the site in Rome for the great Roman Jesuit church, known later as the Gesù. Parallel with these efforts, novitiates were set up in each of the Society's provinces, the best-known being that of San Andrea al Quirinale, in Rome, a training ground for some of the most ardent proselytizers. The total number of Jesuits grew by leaps and bounds, from 1,000 at Ignatius's death and 2,800 under Lainez, to 4,000 members scattered among 130 centers and eighteen provinces.

Under Francis's leadership, the huge army fanned out all over the world. Everywhere they went, the Jesuits made themselves available to people, seeing to their spiritual needs, always outside the traditional parochial framework. In Rome, for instance, they worked as papal penitentiaries, hearing confessions in all sorts of languages at St. Peter's. They tended the sick and brought spiritual comfort to the dying. They went along with soldiers as almoners and with explorers as missionaries. From 1566 to 1572, three evangelizing expeditions set out from Spain for Florida, where the Jesuit members were killed by Indians. Three more forays to Peru were more fortunate, as was the Jesuits' first mission to New Spain, which reached Mexico just before Francis Borgia died.

Violent attacks on the Jesuits
The Munich scandal

Often, as though suffering and death were not enough, these missionary efforts were ruined by petty squabbles between religious orders.

Even though protected by Pius V, the Jesuits were under attack from all sides. In the Holy Roman Empire, the most violent one took place in Munich. Determined to ruin the Jesuits' reputation for holiness, founded on chastity, which teachers and students of their colleges fostered, the Lutherans started a rumor that young boys entering the colleges were castrated. The accusation was made when the provincial of the Jesuits, Peter Canisius, was papal legate in the Empire. A public inquiry was therefore set up at which the accuser, a fourteen-year-old boy called Johann Kessel, who had been dismissed from the college for bad conduct, stripped naked in front of the doctors and surgeons drawing up the report. They stated that in fact the boy had no testicles, yet no scar or mark of mutilation was to be seen. The explanation was a simple one, namely that the testicles were folded back inside the boy's belly, and came out again after pressure was applied to the boy's abdomen. Naturally, the accusation fizzled out, but the rumors had been started maliciously and the reformed sectarians kept their argument honed, ready to use another time.

Canisius fought on several different fronts: he had to face the apostasy of the rector of the Jesuit college in Prague; the publication in Magdeburg of a huge antipapal pamphlet, the *Magdeburg Centuries*, edited by Mathias Flach Francovitch, known as Illiricus; and then finally the rumor that he, Canisius, had become a Lutheran. The only way to reply was to found colleges—at Hall in Tyrol, in Poland, and in Transylvania—and to publish the great facts of Church history, as in the remarkable *Annales ecclesiastici*.

The great 1571 confrontation between Turks and Christians
Mission of Francis and Cardinal Alessandrino in Spain and Portugal

The time came when an external danger had to be confronted that was threatening the whole of Christendom. In 1570 Selim II, the new Turkish sultan, launched an all-out destructive expedition against the Christians. Pius V met it with a fierce determination reminiscent of his predecessors' in the previous century. With the aim of uniting all Catholic kingdoms under one banner, legates *a latere* were sent out far and wide, his own nephew Cardinal Alessandrino being assigned Spain, Portugal, and France. When Alessandrino requested that Francis Borgia accompany him as part of the mission, Francis was not only in poor health but overloaded with Society responsibilities. He knew that leaving was tantamount to signing his own death sentence. Yet he had sworn absolute obedience to the pope, and on June 30, 1571, he took off in the cardinal's brilliant cortege.

The old kingdom of Granada was as explosive as a powder keg, with the Mudejars, or Moorish converts, staging periodic revolts against the king's agents. In 1569 the repression had reached a climax. Philip had ordered all the Turkish baths to be destroyed and all traces of the Arabic language and traditional Moorish dress to be done away with. The response was overwhelming: Granada and Almeria were attacked, churches throughout the kingdom profaned, and priests and monks massacred. The king's brother, Juan of Austria, led a powerful army against the rebels, while the Castilian admiral blockaded the coast with his fleet to prevent aid reaching them from North Africa. Finally, in 1571, the Moors were crushed in a decisive battle, whereupon Philip had the survivors dispersed throughout the kingdom. The Moors were wretchedly poor and stricken by plague, and their only source of help in many cases was the Jesuits, who, since the founding of the order, had made it their duty to have compassion on the "new Christians" of Muslim or Jewish origin. Thus Francis Borgia found a divided Spain ruled by the despotic hand of religious persecution—a country galvanized by a constant struggle with the enemy of religion, both within and without.

When Francis and Alessandrino reached Barcelona, the Catalans gave their former viceroy an exultant welcome, recalling his achievements as war leader and governor. In his honor the Inquisition, which had previously condemned his writings, now published them as a homage to his orthodoxy.

In Valencia, Francis was greeted by several of his children, and only just managed to escape the celebration they had planned for him. He had to reach Madrid as quickly as he could, determined as he was to finish his mission with Alessandrino—a purely formal mission, in fact, since Spain had resolved to spearhead the coming Crusade.

Juan of Austria was now in Sicily, in Messina, where a colossal fleet was assembling under the banner of St. Peter and the command of some of the greatest mariners of the day—the Genoan Andrea Doria, the Roman Marcantonio Colonna, the Venetian Barbarigo, and the Castilian Santa Cruz. On October 7 this Christian navy, which had aboard Jesuits and Capucins as spiritual troops, inflicted on Islam the decisive naval defeat of Lepanto.

Francis's embassy with Alessandrino did not end with the victorious Crusade. In Portugal a delicate situation concerning the survival of the royal house awaited them. Under the influence of his Jesuit tutor, the seventeen-year-old king Sebastiano had set up the tutor's brother, Martin de Camara, as his favorite and prime minister. Sebastiano dreamed constantly of victories over the Infidel on foreign soil. His spiritual advisers, on the other hand, felt it was urgent first of all to settle the matter of the dynastic succession. His confessor encouraged the youth to marry, even though it was obvious that he was not cut out for marriage physically, or temperamentally, in view of his intense mysticism. Queen Caterina, the boy's grandmother, preferred one or the other of her grand-nieces, Emperor Maximilian's daughters. That way the Portuguese crown would remain linked with the royal house of Austria. But one of the princesses married Philip II, the other Charles IX of France. The only suitable match left was the French princess, Marguerite of Valois, daughter of Catherine de Médicis and Charles-

IX's sister. Francis pointed out to the young king that Pope Pius had come around to the idea of the match, believing it would bind France to Catholicism. In the end Sebastiano agreed, purely out of Christian resignation.

Fruitless negotiations at the French court

By now it was midwinter. It was clear that the marriage negotiations could be carried out by diplomatic means. Nevertheless, Francis was afraid the papal legation would come up against obstacles in France since, it was said, the princess was promised to the Protestant prince of Navarre. From the Spanish king, Francis obtained a ship to take him back to Italy; Cardinal Alessandrino, on the other hand, was ordered by Rome to proceed with his mission. He therefore continued on his journey on January 2, 1572, bidding Francis join him.

Racked with pain, he had to cross the Pyrenees using roads off the beaten track to avoid crossing the lands of the heretical Jeanne d'Albret, queen of Navarre. He reached the French court at Blois two days after the cardinal, but their mission was too late. In accordance with a secret article of the 1570 treaty of St. Germain-en-Laye which was made with the Protestants, Catherine de Médicis and her son were arranging for Princess Marguerite to marry Henri of Navarre, the youthful leader of the reform party. It was impossible to break off the discussions in Sebastiano's favor. Moreover, there was no likelihood of France's joining the Crusade because, since Francis I's time, France had been closely allied to the Turks; also, there was the striking victory at Lepanto. All in all, Francis's audience with the queen was disappointing in the extreme.

Catherine de Médicis, who claimed to have ancestral rights to Portugal, tried to raise the bidding. She had written to Francis during her stay in Lisbon saying that in order to support Sebastiano's candidacy for Marguerite's hand, she would be prepared for a Spanish Infanta to offer her hand to her own son the duke of Anjou, the future Henri III. But since no such proposal was forthcoming, she left Alessandrino and Francis at Blois and went on to Chenonceaux, where Queen Jeanne of Navarre had just arrived. Together the two women tackled the final phase of their children's marriages. Ten days later the echoes heard in Blois left no doubt: in spite of Queen Jeanne's demands, the union of the young heretic Henri and the princess—a nightmare for the court of Rome—was practically decided.

On February 24 the papal envoys took their leave. Alessandrino made a dignified exit, refusing the royal gifts of gold and silver vases. But just as he was disappearing, Catherine detained Francis and asked him as a grace to leave her the simple rosary that hung from his girdle. The pope's representatives left feeling confused. Although their demands had been politely refused, they saw all too clearly how much the queen mother and some of her counselors mistrusted the Protestants. Perhaps one day things would change in France. . . .

Death at journey's end

At Lyon the cardinal and the Jesuit parted ways. Alessandrino had been urgently recalled to the Vatican, where his uncle, Pope Pius, lay dying. Francis himself could not rush. He had stayed on in Blois after visiting a desecrated, windowless church to say Mass on the Feast of the Purification. It was an extremely cold day; he caught pleurisy, and as he did not look after himself, the sickness got worse. He was then in his sixty-first year, and his body was much weakened by fatigue and fastings. At St.-Jean-de-Maurienne, in Savoie, he had to take to his bed, and the duke had him carried in a litter to Turin. Several receptions had been prepared in his honor, but Francis was too weak to attend. He was taken by boat on the Po and landed near Turin, where he spent Holy Week and celebrated Easter. Then he again went downriver, retracing the route Lucrezia had taken years before, and in four days reached Ferrara.

Alfonso II d'Este, his second cousin, had sent a magnificent brigantine to meet him at his duchy's boundary. In it Francis went to the Jesuit college at Ferrara, but the superficial care he received there was not enough for his condition. Alfonso therefore lodged him in one of his country houses, summoning the most skilled doctors and having prayers said before the Holy Sacrament in all the city churches.

The first months of summer went by without any improvement in Francis's condition. On his bed of pain, he learned that an uprising had broken out in France—doubtless abetted by Catherine de Médicis and finally authorized by the king—at which Catholics confronted Protestants, whom they accused of taking advantage of Henri of Navarre's marriage to Marguerite to try to seize power. The terrible massacre of St. Bartholomew, on August 24, 1572, might possibly have been avoided if Francis had been able to arrange for Sebastiano to marry the French princess. Nonetheless, such speculations of earthly politics were surely far from the sick man's mind at the time.

He knew he was lost and thought only of ensuring his entrance into Heaven. By litter he was brought to Loreto, to the House of Mary (which legend has it was carried there by angels), then returned to Rome and was settled, near death, in the Jesuit house. There, two days later, at midnight on September 30, 1572, he died, comforted by his fellow Jesuits and his brother Tomas, the future archbishop of Saragossa. His humility and self-abasement had given him a power over men such as none of his Borgia ancestors had possessed, a power that set him above the greatest sovereigns of the world. At his death, he was already recognized as a prince in eternity.

His entrance into glory

Francis Borgia's life in glory had barely begun. At his burial all Rome filed through the Jesuit house—cardinals, prelates, lords, and the common people alike. Transferred to the Gesù Church in 1617, his body did not remain there long. At the instigation of the cardinal-duke of Lerma, Francis's grandson, and the request of Cardinal Gaspare de Borja, the Spanish ambassador, the remains (with the exception of one arm, which was left at the Gesù) were transported to Madrid.

Francis was beatified by Pope Urban VIII on November 21, 1624, after which his body was put on display in a magnificent Madrid church built by his grandson, the cardinal-duke. Amid rejoicing, his body was borne in a weeklong procession from one church to another all across the capital. The costly shrine containing it was carried on the shoulders of fourteen grandees of Spain. Several other noblemen held the golden canopy, while others carried the cords of the shrine. Each one was a descendant of Francis—in all, forty-six aristocrats of the highest Spanish nobility, of whom he was grandfather, great-grandfather, or great-great-grandfather. Following the cortege came the knights of Santiago, the Council of the Thirteen Commanders, all the royal councils, the magistrates, and the people. What they were celebrating was, truly, a triumph in Heaven, yet it was also the triumph of a race that was the reflection of proud, Catholic Spain.

Francis still had not been raised to the pinnacle of heavenly honors.

Forty-seven years later, on April 11, 1671, before a crowd of witnesses attesting to miraculous cures through the Blessed Francis, Pope Clement X announced his canonization. According to the *Roman Martyrology*, his feast day, October 3, celebrates "St. Francis Borgia, superior general of the Society of Jesus, memorable for his mortification, his gift of prayer, abandonment of the world, and his refusal of ecclesiastical dignities."

The blood of the Borgias: grandeur and passion

St. Francis Borgia's whole life had been a shining counterpoint to that of his ancestor Alexander. Yet when one studies it closely, one sees that the tapestry is just as lustrous on the right side as the wrong. The same skeins went into the weaving of it; the bright threads of warp and woof represent the same passions—to live in the present, to follow one's own will and desire, to sacrifice everything to an ideal. Each of the Borgias had behaved in a similar fashion, and it was only the goal—God or man—that varied. In each one was an imperious inner voice urging him to go beyond the mediocre. All traveled their roads with the same single-mindedness of purpose, whether their flesh was torn by the thorns of pleasure or mortification. All were explorers of the impossible: for Francis, it was the dawning of a universe built on love; for Cesare, an Italian kingdom. . . .

Whether models or foils for their contemporaries, they were the ones who gave them signposts marking which road to follow, which shoals to avoid. They were the quintessence of the society they lived in, the element that summed up its very nature. In a matchless way they reflected the virtues and vices of their time, accentuating in their personalities what most people strive hypocritically to conceal. They stood out of the common order as liberated beings.

The culmination of the line was superhuman. After the apotheosis came the fall, or rather the dying majesty of a sunset's glow. The line descended from the murdered duke of Gandia shone brightly for some generations in the upper echelons of the laity and the Church. Viceroys and cardinals adorn the long procession of Spanish grandees culminating in Don Mariano Tellez-Giron, who died on June 2, 1882, without heirs. At that time this distinguished nobleman held three principalities, eight duchies, ten marquisates, sixteen counties, a viscounty, and a number of chivalric orders. He himself was ten times over a Spanish grandee of the first class.

Yet a few Borgia patricians, descendants of the collateral branches of the family, still live on in Italy—witnesses to the extraordinary vitality of that handful of ambitious adventurers who left the kingdom of Valencia six centuries ago and made the world resound with the clangor of their deeds.

EPILOGUE

The Borgias Throughout the Ages

The posthumous fate of the Borgias is linked to Niccolò Machiavelli. It is thanks to his treatise *De principatibus* (Of Principalities) that they truly enter immortality. Based on the example of the prestigious actors in the drama of history, this brief twenty-six-chapter memoir, drawn up in a few months between July and December 1513, was written as a guide for political leaders. Next to Alexander VI, the character most often referred to is in fact Cesare Borgia. In his honor posterity would change the book's title to *The Prince*.

A coldly intelligent treatise on the way to seize power and hold on to it, Machiavelli's work has ever since been mandatory reading for all those entertaining ambitions of ruling over their fellow men. It teaches how to go beyond morals, laws, and customs in order to gratify one's own will. Cesare, the great Borgia man raised to superhuman stature, is singled out as exemplar. From the moment it was coined, the term "Machiavellianism" could have been replaced by "Borgianism."

Adding a note of caution to the often incredible account of Cesare's and Alexander's behavior was another book—the *Journal*, also known as the *Liber notarum* or *Diarium* of the papal master of ceremonies, Johannes Burckard. The Vatican archivists carefully preserved this work after its author's death in 1506. It proved to be extremely useful, providing as it did the minutest details of the Roman ritual, the places assigned to dignitaries during holy office, the order of processions, and the papal paraphernalia used for liturgical feasts. Everything was noted painstakingly in this veritable "sacristan's book," but between these descriptions Burckard maliciously sneaked in accounts of the excesses and scandals, the Vatican gossip, and the verses and pamphlets that inundated Rome under Alexander VI.

So valuable a mine of information could not remain secret for long. It was too perfect a contemporary history, and scholars were not slow in putting the material to good use. The *Journal* served as a source for the *History of the Lives of the Pontiffs* published in 1505 as a sequel to the work of Bartolomeo Sacchi, otherwise known as Battista Platina. It stimulated the critical vein of the great writers who were quickly fascinated by the Borgia story. In his *History of Italy*, written between 1537 and 1540, Francesco Guicciardini makes Cesare and his father bear a heavy responsibility for Italy's misfortunes since they welcomed foreign invaders on her soil. This is how he describes the "incredible rejoicing" of the Romans as they viewed Alexander's body in St. Peter's:

> "They could not feast their eyes enough on the sight of the dead serpent who, with his immoderate ambition, his cruelty and avarice, had infected the whole world; this lecherous monster who would indiscriminately sell things sacred or profane. Yet he had been exalted and had enjoyed extraordinary and almost continuous wealth from his earliest youth to the last day of his life, always wanting more and obtaining beyond his wishes. His example may confound those who believe that our weak human eyes can grasp the depth of God's judgment and claim that whatever befalls man, in good or evil, is in accordance with their virtues or vices. It is a misleading concept, for the real punishments or rewards will not be meted out until we reach the world beyond."

Another famous historian, Paolo Giovio, bishop of Nocera, author of the 1550 *History of His Time* and *Lives of Illustrious Men*, relates the most scandalous facts without passing any judgment, as did Onofrio Panvinio in his edition of the *History of the Lives of the Pontiffs* (1557). Geronimo Zurita, author of the *Annals of Aragon* (1590), who recounts several events involving the Borgias in his volume devoted to Ferdinand the Catholic, could do so without embarrassment, since by then the duke of Gandia's descendants were setting an example of worldly success side by side with the most virtuous morality.

The world of the Counter-Reformation, more guilt-conscious and edified by the example of St. Francis Borgia, professed the belief that one generation could atone for another's immorality through penitence. Some writings served this purpose by emphasizing humanity's darker side. One example is *La vita del Duca Valentino* by Tommaso Tomasi, published as late as 1655, a century after it was written, and again in 1670, with interpolations by the adventurer Gregorio Leti.

By this time Burckard's *Journal* was enjoying extraordinary popularity among the intelligentsia and had been printed in a large number of copies. According to Onofrio Panvinio, it was considered a major source of information. In his edition of the *Mémoires de Commines*, published in 1649, the scholar Denys Godefroy reproduced excerpts from the *Diarium* referring to Savonarola. Then in 1684, in a documentary work entitled *Histoire de Charles VIII*, Godefroy's son Théodore published the passages concerning that king's relations with Alexander VI.

From then on, nothing could be written about the Borgias without reference to the "bible" which Burckard's day-to-day jottings had become. When the great history of the Church known as the *Annales ecclesiastici*, begun in the sixteenth century under the Vatican librarian Cardinal Cesare Baronius, reached the Renaissance era, Odorico Rinaldi continued the work, drawing largely on Burckard while taking great pains to cover up the most strident excesses.

In the reign of the Sun King, no one seemed shocked by the society of Alexander's day, which had found an acceptable way to marry faith and licentiousness. Everything changed radically in 1685, however, when Louis XIV revoked the Edict of Nantes. Immediately, a breach was caused within the European scientific community. The universal genius Leibnitz—mathematician, jurist, philosopher, and historian—had believed in a reconciliation between Catholics and Protestants. Disillusioned, he turned to polemics. As librarian to the duke of Brunswick, he had in his collection at Wolfenbüttel a copy of Burckard's *Journal*. Selecting the most scandalous episodes, he published excerpts under the title *Specimen Historiae Arcanae, sive anecdotae de vita Alexandri VI Papae* (Hannover, 1696). This met with huge success and was immediately followed by a second edition. In his commentary, Leibnitz stated that "there has never been a court more contaminated with crime than that of Alexander VI, where shamelessness, treachery, and cruelty were the rule—three capital vices, all three crowned by villainy and covered with the sacred veil of religion." Rome was the school for scandal.

The British historian Alexander Gordon followed in the master's footsteps. His *Lives of Pope Alexander VI and His Son Cesare Borgia* was first published in London in 1729 and reissued in French in 1723 and 1751. This, too, was a bestseller. In a foreword to the French edition, publisher Pierre Mortier of Amsterdam explains his own motivation. The account of the crimes, he writes, was useful to man inasmuch as by inspiring horror of evil it would convey love of virtue. And the horror was all the greater because the one who committed the excesses called himself Head of the Church of Jesus Christ. "The fact that man is subject to the greatest troubles because of the abuse of his reason is a necessary consequence of the constitution of human nature. Yet, if the Spirit of God should choose a villain to govern his Church, one would, whatever one's faith, be hard put not to exclaim, with the Apostle, O altitudo Divitiarum! . . . If the Catholics accuse us Protestants of taking pleasure in publishing the popes' infamies and wickednesses, we shall tell them that, refusing to believe that popes are chosen by the Holy Spirit to be the vicars of Christ on earth, we can, on the basis of the history of their actions, the better justify our reasons for not submitting to their dominion."

The author, for his part, limns his characters in powerful strokes in his Preface: "Lucretia, Alexander's Daughter, . . . as famous for Lewdness, as the Roman Lucretia for Chastity . . . ; a pretended Head of Christ's Flock establishing the Kingdom of Utter Darkness and setting up the Empire of Satan for eclipsing all Goodness . . . ; Caesar Borgia, Duke Valentine, notorious for duplicated Fratricide and Incest with his own Sister, and who by Perjuries, Poison, and Assassinations in destroying his Enemies, shewed himself a Son worthy of such a Father, though at last a memorable Example to the World of the bad Success which attended his Crimes, having before his Death been an Exile, and a Victim to public Vengeance, and forced to renounce all that Tyranny, which was so far from being commendable, that it ought to be utterly detested, let Machiavel's Opinion be what it will; so that what the Ancients feigned about a perfect Tragedy, Divine Providence permitted to be exemplified in him." Contrary to Guicciardini's view, Gordon felt that immanent justice did play a role in the tragedy of the Borgias.

Serious historian as he was, Gordon quotes all his sources, though he puts Burckard on the same level with Machiavelli, Guicciardini together with Tomasi, Panvinio with Pietro Bembo, who became a cardinal and the author of the book A History of His Time. On the other hand, since he did not have intimate details of the pope's love life, Gordon did not hesitate to borrow them from "an authentic copy of a manuscript taken from the original in Rome, said to be in the

Vatican Library." Apart from a few minor points that should be taken with a grain of salt, the documents he used, some of which were published in their entirety in the appendix—twenty-three in all—seem to be trustworthy. Among them are quotations from Machiavelli's *Prince*, an article from Moreri's dictionary on the genealogy of the Borgias, some passages from Guicciardini, particularly about Alexander's death, and a number of excerpts from Burckard. These include the manifestos of Charles VIII and Cardinal Péraud, the signed convention between Alexander VI and the French king, Sultan Bayezid's letters to Alexander and the pope's instructions to Giorgio Buzardo, Cesare's flight to Velletri, the murder of the duke of Gandia, the relationship with Savonarola, Cesare's renunciation of the cardinalate, the pope's accident and the Savelli Letter. The book is thus the first example of a documented study on the Borgias.

In his *Dictionnaire historique et critique,* published in 1697 and reissued in 1702, the French philosopher Pierre Bayle takes the same stand as Gordon, also carefully quoting his sources. The so-called *Supplément* or *Continuation* published in 1758 by Jacques-Georges de Chaufepié cites a larger number of sources and includes Gordon in the earliest ones, among which Tomasi is still recognized as a reliable authority. The same approach is found in the *Annals of Italy* (1744–1749) by Luigi Antonio Muratori, the eminent archivist of the duke of Modena.

If these writers aimed at objectivity in regard to their sources, their story was always told anything but dispassionately. In that philosophers' age, each one was intent on denouncing the Borgias' crimes and their scorn for public and private morality.

In his *Essai sur les moeurs* (1756), Voltaire writes about Alexander with all his native perspicacity. He doubts that the pope was poisoned, even that the Borgias used poison at all. At the same time, however, and without raising an eyebrow, he repeats the accusations of incest against Lucrezia as well as Cesare's crimes. He admits that certain actions which did not shock anyone at the time had a positive impact on history. "Alexander VI left a more heinous image in Europe than did Nero and Caligula, because the holiness of his ministry made him more guilty. Yet it is to him that Rome owed her temporal greatness. . . . His son lost all the fruit of his crimes which the Church had garnered. But, strangely, this sort of religion was never attacked at the time. Since most of the princes, statesmen, and warriors had no religion at all, the popes' crimes did not bother them. The dim-witted common people made pilgrimages; the great went about cutting throats and pillaging. In Alexander VI they merely saw their equal; the seat of all crimes went by the name of the Holy See."

Shortly before ascending the throne in 1740, Frederick II of Prussia, who surely had the same unscrupulous attitude as the princes of the Renaissance, wrote a book called *Anti-Machiavelli*, in which he virtuously rejected the advice given by the Florentine secretary based on Cesare Borgia's example. Jean-Jacques Rousseau, the theoretician of the *Contrat Social*, decries the exploitation of man by his fellow men, but finds that Machiavelli's lengthy account of Cesare's reprehensible feats is useful insofar as, by being informed of these excesses on the part of the great, the people will learn to protect themselves. The history of the Borgias is a warning to citizens to be on their guard.

It is not surprising to find the same point of view among the historians and polemicists of the Revolution. Once the storm had blown over, it became fashionable to meditate on the works of Machiavelli. In his Preface to the great Paris edition of the year VII, the publisher Guiraudet began by expressing some reservations with regard to a writer who "gave the despots lessons on how to oppress the people and how to use their weapons against them." A reading of the book, however, revealed an author who was "inspired by a patriotism as enlightened as it is ardent." In his *Discourses On the First Ten Books of Livy*, Machiavelli does in fact examine different forms of government. He rejects the collusion between religion and power as it existed in the Papal States: "This Rome, once the center of a state whose power and glory once covered the whole world, now found herself at the mercy of old, elective monarchs, none of whom could form a respectable State. . . . Let us imagine the power of a sovereign who was at the same time Vice-God, priest, king, maker of sacred law, and prophet— a ruler who dispensed life and death, tying peoples and individuals into insoluble knots which he alone had the right and the power to untie according to his whim! Let us behold him with the triple crown on his head, with the keys and a God in his hands, with princes and emperors at his feet, his arm and his empire extending almost over the globe, distributing newly discovered worlds to one nation or another—in this, more powerful than the very Romans whose city he was occupying, the city destined to be once more the Capital of the Universe."

Machiavelli, who had dared denounce the power and crimes of the "tyrant of Rome," had been assailed by the international clergy on the papacy's orders. The French Republic would avenge him, since by destroying the power of the popes they also defended Italy's interests. In this they were acting like Machiavelli who, according to Guiraudet, was only seeking the good of his native land by eliminating both national despots and foreign oppressors. The Republic was inspired by Machiavelli's example. The necessity of ensuring safety from foreign attack, wrote the author, "dictated to us the need gradually to seize the Rhine as a border from its source to its mouth and to secure the alliance of Holland and Switzerland and the republican league from Basel to Naples. . . ."

In light of such considerations, the French revised not only their ideas about Machiavelli but also their opinion of Cesare Borgia. They shared the regrets Machiavelli expressed about the "premature deaths of some carefree brigands and the equally unforeseen deaths of Alexander and his dreadful son." Had not Cesare actually sought the downfall of tyrants for the benefit of a lay state where freedom would one day reign?

It was the birth of the precious notion of historical relativity. Machiavelli's intentions and Cesare Borgia's exploits were now better understood. The old view of the terrible family had undergone considerable evolution.

The periods of the French Empire and Restoration did not entirely trust the lessons in liberty as imparted by the Borgias' story. Rather than pondering over the family's political aims, people once again began criticizing their mores—though discreetly. This was to prevent scandal from rebounding on the institutions that had surfaced again after the Revolution, namely the Church and the papacy. Having regained its territories, the Holy See had reverted to its old image of a reactionary monarchy. It would be all too easy to attack its vices by pointing to the Borgias, and the avant-garde poets did not miss the opportunity to do so.

As the Renaissance became more fashionable than ever, Alexander and his family entered a new phase of notoriety. Having cruelly castigated the frivolity of the court of Francis I in *Le Roi s'amuse*, Victor Hugo chose Lucrezia Borgia as the heroine of a drama presented in Paris in February 1833.

To quote Hugo's preface: "Who, actually, is this Lucrezia Borgia? Take the most hideous, the most repulsive, the most complete *moral* deformity; place it where it fits best—in the heart of a woman whose physical beauty and royal grandeur will make the crime stand out all the more strikingly; then add to all that moral deformity the purest feeling a woman can have, that of a mother. . . . Inside our monster put a mother and the monster will interest us and make us weep. And this creature that filled us with fear will inspire pity; that deformed soul will be almost beautiful in our eyes. . . ."

Victor Hugo invented an entirely new "counter-Lucrezia" but attempted to justify himself. "The author will remain silent in the face of criticism. . . . He could, no doubt, answer more than one objection. . . . To those who reproach him for exaggerating Lucrezia Borgia's crimes he will say, 'Go and read Tomasi, read Guicciardini and, above all, read the *Diarium*.' To those who blame him for having accepted certain popular rumors and fables about the death of Lucrezia's husbands, he will say that the people's fables often make up the poet's truth." It is a delicious pirouette, a sort of thumbing one's nose at pedantic historians. And, in conclusion, the poet congratulates himself for having given the monstrous Lucrezia a mother's love. Thus his conscience is appeased and he can rest in peace.

Crime in fantastic abundance runs through the play. "I saw Lucrezia Borgia only from afar . . . , she stood like a terrible phantom over all Italy, like the specter of the whole world," cries Gennaro, Lucrezia's secret son. Needless to say, the poison of the Borgias plays an essential role. "A dreadful poison," says Lucrezia, "a poison, the very thought of which makes every Italian grow pale—everyone who knows the history of these last twenty years. And no one in the world knows the antidote to this terrible concoction, no one save the pope, the duke of Valentinois and myself."

Poison and the dagger are also prominent in Alexandre Dumas, who gives pride of place to the Borgias in the first volume of his series *Les crimes célèbres*. The series was published and republished from 1839 to 1893 without interruption. The renowned Jakob Burckhardt, author of *The Civilization of the Renaissance in Italy*, also firmly believed in the "inexorable poison": "Those who were not slain by the Borgias' dagger perished by their poison." Jules Michelet shared the same opinion: "When the father and son needed money, they used poison to dispose of a cardinal" (*La Renaissance*).

Suddenly it became clear that all this implied too much blood. Some tenacious historians sought to verify the documents on which the accusation was based, and much painstaking research was done in archives and libraries. It caused a craving for public knowledge that profoundly changed the point of view of the age. Encouraged by this reaction and feeling that it was about time for a complete rehabilitation of the Borgias, certain pious souls decided the moment had come to intervene. Cerri in 1858, Abbé Ollivier in 1870, and Father Leonetti in 1880 published some truly hagiographic tales about Alexander VI. Everything that had been written heretofore was untrue. The pope never had any children. Those attributed to him as such were his nephews, sons of a hitherto unknown brother, or else he had been married before taking holy orders. It was Count Henri de L'Epinois, an irreproachable scholar and convinced Catholic, who in the *Revue des questions historiques* finally undertook in 1881 to severely refute all these countertruths, as Father Matagne had done in the same publication in 1873 with reference to Abbé Ollivier and the Jesuits had done in *Civiltà Cattolica*. L'Epinois spoke in the name of historical science but obeyed above all the "most imperious needs of my intelligence, the need to say the truth, the whole truth, at the risk of condemning a pope and an epoch which proved to be among the Church's greatest tribulations."

This was part of a vast movement for documentary rediscovery of the Borgia story. In 1866 Guiseppe Campori devoted a study to Lucrezia under the eloquent title *Una vittima della Storia*, in which he revealed a number of documents taken from the archives of the Este family in Modena. The German scholar Ferdinand Gregorovius, eminently knowledgeable about Roman history, added sixty-five basic documents, including many pieces found in Rome as well as Modena and Mantua. His vast biography of Lucrezia, published in Stuttgart in 1874 and translated into French and Italian in 1876, set a date for the scientific approach to the history of the Borgias.

This work had barely appeared in print when a prodigious scholar, Ludwig von Pastor, undertook to write a *History of the Popes from the Late Middle Ages* on entirely new bases. For three centuries the secret archives of the Vatican had been off-limits to researchers. In 1888 they were finally opened by Pope Leo XIII, who gave Pastor permission to consult the consistorial archives as well as the bulls and briefs of Alexander VI contained in 113 volumes of the Pontifical Chancery. Pastor compared these documents with a multitude of others from nearly eighty libraries and archives in Europe, mainly in Italy. Volume IX about Alexander, published in 1895 and translated and published in France in 1898, was several times reissued and enriched with supplements up to the latest edition, in Italian, by Angelo Mercati and Pio Cenci in 1951.

In this work, which claims to be objective and authentic, none of Alexander's faults is concealed. In his attempt to explain some of the pope's excessive behavior, the author drew on many different, sometimes contradictory documents that had been coming out in scholarly editions. Parallel with this, experts had been busy collating various sources, among them the *Diarii*, a sort of report of daily news put together by the Venetian Marino Sanudo between 1496 and 1523 (published in Venice in fifty-eight large volumes from 1879 to 1902) and again by Priuli from 1494 to 1512 (published from 1912 to 1937). A Flemish scholar, Peter De Roo, compiled a large number of sources about the Borgias, though much of it was already known. This work came out in five volumes, entitled *Material for a History of Pope Alexander VI* (Bruges and New York, 1924, republished in Spain in 1952).

By the beginning of the twentieth century, most of the contemporary testimonies about the Borgias had been published or included as parts of other works. Among the witnesses were diplomats, intelligence officers like the Venetian Giustiniani, the bishop of Modena, Gianandrea Bocciaccio, the Ferrarese Beltrando Costabili, Gerardo Saraceni, and Ettore Bellingeri, and, to a lesser degree, Bernardino de Prosperi and da Correggio, who passed information on to Isabella d'Este, as well as the chroniclers in each Italian city who reported news on the Borgias.

The Borgias' Spanish origins led scholars in that country to study the two popes of the family in particular. Notable are the work of Sanchis Sivera, *El obispo de Valencia, Don Alfonso de Borja* (*Calixtus III*), *1429–1458* (Madrid, 1926) and the fairly recent studies by the Catalan Miquel Batllori, especially *La Correspondencia d'Alexandre VI amb els seus familiars y amb els Reis católicos.*

Alongside these scholarly works, writings about the Borgias mushroomed, reflecting the historical methods and the contemporary concerns that gave rise to them.

Frederick William Rolfe, alias Baron Corvo, published in 1901 a work entitled *Chronicles of the House of Borgia*, recently translated into French. Its inspired style and enthusiasm place it firmly in the rehabilitation movement. The author tries to create a work of historical psychology, as does Emile Gebhart's "Les Borgia," in his book *Moines et Papes* (Paris, 1907). The same concept of relativity is put to use by Louis Gastine, author of a historical novel on Lucrezia and a historical study of Cesare (Paris, 1911). The author uses such tools as "psychological sense" and "the control and purification which emerge from comparative history." To him Cesare is a pure product of his environment.

Somewhat later, the Milanese physician Giuseppe Portigliotti (*I Borgia*, Milan, 1921) offered a psychiatric analysis of the family characters and their behavior. In his book, which is fertile in ideas, the most scandalous hypotheses are held to be the most likely ones. The author at least puts forward different possibilities, in contrast to novelists, who are primarily tempted to give a colorful, dramatic reconstruction, as did Michel Zevaco, author of the swashbuckling story *Borgia* (Bucharest, 1907). But all this is well beyond the limits of historical study.

There is no lack of valuable historical essays in more recent times—as, for instance, those of Franz Funck-Brentano (1932), Rafaele Sabatini (1937), Fred Berence (1937), Gonzague Truc (1939), J. Lucas Dubreton (1952), and Marcel Brion (1979), to name a few of the better known. Some follow the rehabilitation route, either sticking, like Giovanni Soranzo (Milan, 1950) to a middle course, or showing a deplorable partiality, like Oreste Ferrara in his *Il Papa Borgia*, 1938 (new Spanish and Italian editions, 1943 and 1953).

Among the studies devoted to individual members of the family, particular light is shed on the figure of Cesare. After Alvisi, who studies him as duke of Romagna (1878), and Yriarte, who follows him to his grave in Navarre (1889), Woodward gives a precise account of his military campaigns (1913).

Next to Gregorovius, Lucrezia found her best biographer in Maria Bellonci, whose work, constantly reissued from 1939 to 1970, won the widest public acclaim.

The entire family was the subject of study of L. Collison-Morley in his *Story of the Borgias* (London, 1934; French translation, 1951). Their political strategies were described by Gabriele Pepe, *La Politica dei Borgia* (Naples, 1945), and their social milieu by Emmanuele Rodocanachi, *Histoire de Rome, Une cour princière au Vatican pendant la Renaissance, Sixte IV, Innocent VIII, Alexandre VI Borgia 1471–1503* (Paris, 1925).

A story still had to be told, based on an objective sifting of four centuries' worth of literary and scientific material. Its theme: how the Borgias slowly rose in the concatenation of events; how their individual destinies were bound together until a collective goal was reached that each member of the clan accepted; in particular, how their behavior and mentality evolved under the blows of fate and their private passions clashed with the vast changes taking place in society.

Considered as a clan—a perfectly coherent social sample though split up among different classes and nationalities—the Borgias emerge as a remarkable specimen of human solidarity. By observing them together rather than studying one single personality, one finds the key to a whole world in gestation, a world searching for individual and collective values that would in time be those of modern man.

In this immersion in the Borgias' era we can, thanks to historical criticism, throw off the shadowy aura of the centuries, although imagination remains one of the most precious of tools.

A hundred years ago Arthur de Gobineau, the magician of the *Scènes historiques de la Renaissance* (1877), captivated audiences with Alexander's superb speech to Lucrezia: "Do people say that I am both your father and your lover? Let the world, that heap of vermin as ridiculous as they are feebleminded, believe the most absurd tales about the mighty! You must know that for those destined to dominate others, the ordinary rules of life are turned upside down and duty acquires an entirely new meaning. Good and evil are carried off to a higher, different plane. . . . The great law of the world is not to do this or that, to avoid this point or turn to another—it is to live, to grow and develop what is strongest and greatest in us so that if we find ourselves in a mediocre sphere we know how to move on to one that is larger, higher, more open. Remember this. Walk straight ahead. Do only what you like, as long as it is of some use to you. Leave hesitation and scruples to small minds, to plebeians and subordinates. One consideration alone is worthy of you—the elevation of the House of Borgia, the elevation of yourself."

In our own time we can see Lucrezia, Giulia Farnese, Cesare, and Alfonso di Bisceglie before our eyes, more alive than ever, through the magic of cinema. The film *Lucrèce Borgia* by Christian-Jaque (1953) was, like the theater of Gobineau, built on a historical foundation with the help of poetic license. Martine Carol, Pedro Armendariz, Massimo Serato, Valentine Tessier, and Christian Marquand marvelously incarnate the troubled charm of the lords and ladies of the pontifical court.

We are fortunate in our day to live at several speeds and to know how to mix sound and image. Consciously or not, with the aid of scholarship we can evoke the images—questionable, perhaps, but so eloquent—of the centuries-old myth. What if our approach is not entirely innocent? Let us admit it and take advantage of it. For the truth is that, far from fading, the Borgia myth and reality have grown ever more vivid throughout the ages. Long may the Borgias continue to make us reflect—and dream!

Chronology

1377   Pope Gregory XI leaves Avignon and returns to Rome.

1378   Death of Gregory XI. Elections of Urban VI and Clement VII. Beginning of the Great Schism.
Alonso Borja born in Játiva.
Vincent Ferrer begins preaching in the kingdom of Valencia.

1379   Clement VII settles in Avignon.

1380   Death of King Charles V of France. Accession of Charles VI. Clement VII orders Queen Joanna I of Naples to name Louis d'Anjou her heir.

1381   Charles of Durazzo, championed by Urban VI, seizes Naples.

1386   Death of Charles of Durazzo. Ladislas crowned king of Naples.

1387   Louis d'Orléans, brother of Charles VI, weds Valentina Visconti of Milan.

1392   Madness of Charles VI.
Alonso Borja studies at Lerida.

1394   The University of Paris attempts to end the schism. Death of Clement VII. Election of Pedro de Luna, who becomes Pope Benedict XIII of Avignon.

1398   Christian states agree to extract an oath of obedience from the two popes.
With Vincent Ferrer, Alonso Borja campaigns for Benedict XIII.

1403   Benedict XIII flees Avignon.

1404   Innocent VII succeeds Boniface IX of Rome.
Death of Philip the Bold of Burgundy. Accession of John the Fearless.

1406   Gregory XII succeeds Innocent VII in Rome.
Florence seizes Pisa.

1407   Louis d'Orléans assassinated by John the Fearless.
Jan Hus expounds his doctrine in Bohemia.

1408   Oath of obedience again demanded of both popes.
Partisans of Benedict XIII hold Council of Perpignan.

1409   Council of Pisa deposes both popes. Election of Pope Alexander V.

1410   Death of Alexander V. Election of John XXIII. Revolt of the Hussites in Bohemia.
Death of King Martin of Aragon. Appointment of his nephew Ferdinand after two-year interregnum.
From Barcelona, Benedict XIII intervenes in election of the new king of Aragon.
Royal favor granted Alonso Borja.
Sigismond of Hungary becomes Holy Roman Emperor.
First settlement of Benedict XIII on Peñiscola.

1413   John XXIII, hounded from Rome by Ladislas of Naples, signs a treaty with Sigismond and convenes the Council of Constance.

1414   Opening of Council of Constance. Jan Hus arrested and tried before the council.

1415   John XXIII deposed. Gregory XII, pope of Rome, renounces papacy.

Sigismond and the king of Aragon agree to depose Benedict III.
French defeated by English at Agincourt. Formation of the Hussite League in Bohemia. Jan Hus condemned.
Portuguese seize Ceuta in North Africa.

1416   Death of Ferdinand I of Aragon. Accession of Alfonso V.
        Alonso Borja appointed councilor to Alfonso V.
1417   Benedict XIII deposed. The council elects Martin V as next pope.
1418   Massacre of the Armagnacs, partisans of the House of Orléans, by the Burgundians.
        Henry V of England takes Normandy.
        Henry the Navigator of Portugal lands on Madeira.
1419   Hussites seize Prague. End of Council of Constance.
        Benedict XIII settles for last time on Peñiscola.
        Assassination of John the Fearless. His son Philip the Good, duke of Burgundy, forms alliance with Henry V.
        Death of Vincent Ferrer.
1420   Treaty of Troyes: Henry V of England declared regent and heir to the crown of France.
        Martin V preaches crusade against the Hussites.
        Joanna II of Naples names Alfonso V, king of Sicily and Aragon, her heir and appeals for his aid against Louis d'Anjou.
1422   Deaths of Henry V of England and Charles VI of France. They are succeeded by Henry VI and Charles VII.
        Benedict XIII appoints his last cardinal.
1423   First siege of Constantinople by the Turks (Sultan Mourad II).
        Death of Benedict XIII.
        Election of the antipope Clement VIII (Gil Sanchez Muñoz).
1426   Clement VIII crowns himself pope at Peñiscola.
1429   Abdication of Clement VIII. *Alonso Borja's mission to Peñiscola.*
        Alonso Borja nominated Bishop of Valencia.
        Joan of Arc delivers Orléans.
        Coronation of Charles VII.
1430   Mourad II takes Salonica and Janina.
        Convocation of Council of Basel.
        Death of Martin V. Election of Eugenius IV.
        Henry the Navigator occupies the Azores.
        Alonso Borja tutor of Ferrante, bastard son of Alfonso V.
1432   Birth in Játiva of Rodrigo Borja, Alonso's nephew.
1433   Emperor Sigismond crowned in Rome by Eugenius IV. Mantua raised to a marquisate.
1434   Death of Louis III d'Anjou, heir to Naples. Joanna II gives the kingdom to his brother, René d'Anjou.
1435   Death of Joanna II of Naples. Alfonso V of Aragon and René d'Anjou dispute the crown. Peace of Arras between Philip the Good, duke of Burgundy, and Charles VII.
        Mourad II defeated at Belgrade by John Corvinus Hunyade of Transylvania.
1436   Charles VII hounds English out of Paris.
1439   Council of Basel moved to Ferrara, then Florence.
        Union of the Roman and Greek churches.
        Rump council deposes Eugenius IV and elects Amadeus, duke of Savoie, who becomes Felix V.

1440 Frederick of Austria becomes Emperor Frederick III. Discovery of printing.
1442 Alfonso V takes Naples.
 Alonso Borja helps organize the kingdom.
1443 *Alonso Borja negotiates Alfonso V's support of Pope Eugenius IV.*
1444 Christians crushed by the Turks at Varna. Death of Ladislas III Jagellon, king of Hungary.
 Alonso Borja appointed cardinal.
1447 Death of Filippo Maria Visconti, duke of Milan. His son-in-law Francesco Sforza seizes power. Alliance of Rome and Naples against Milan. Death of Eugenius IV. Election of Nicholas V.
1452 *Emperor Frederick II crowned in Rome, proceeds to Naples.*
1453 Porcaro's plot foiled in Rome. Fall of Constantinople to Mahomet II.
1454 Treaty of Lodi: Milan and Venice become allies.
1455 Outbreak of Wars of the Roses. Henry VI deposed.
 Death of Nicholas V. Election of Alonso Borja, who becomes Pope Calixtus III. Organization of crusade against the Turks.
1456 Rehabilitation of Joan of Arc. Calixtus III's first acts of nepotism.
 Rodrigo Borgia becomes cardinal.
 Heroism of John Hunyade. Mahomet II lifts siege of Belgrade.
1458 Mathias Corvinus, son of John Hunyade, elected king of Hungary.
 George Podiebrad proclaimed king of Bohemia.
 Death of Alfonso V. His brother Juan II succeeds him in Aragon, his illegitimate son Ferrante in Naples.
 Death of Calixtus III. Election of Pius II.
1459 Congress of Mantua votes to resume the crusade.
1461 Death of Charles VII of France.
 Accession of Louis XI.
 Discovery of Tolfa alum mines.
1464 *Death of Pius II. Election of Paul II.*
1465 League of the Public Weal in France pits rebel barons against Louis XI at battle of Montlhéry.
1467 Charles the Bold becomes duke of Burgundy.
1467 Castilian nobles set up Isabella as heir to her brother Enrico IV. Treaty of Péronne between Louis XI and Charles the Bold, who takes and burns Liège.
1469 Marriage of Isabella of Castile and Ferdinand of Aragon. Lorenzo the Magnificent comes to power in Florence.
1471 *Death of Paul II. Accession of Sixtus IV.*
 Death of George Podiebrad, king of Bohemia. Henry VI of England defeated by Edward IV of York.
1472 War between Charles the Bold and Louis XI.
 Rodrigo Borgia leaves for Spain as legate a latère.
1475 *Birth of Cesare Borgia, eldest child of Cardinal Rodrigo and Vannozza Cattanei.*
1476 Charles the Bold defeated at Grandson and Morat.
1477 Death of Charles the Bold. His daughter Marie marries Maximilian of Austria, son of Frederick III.
 Legation of Rodrigo Borgia to Naples.
1478 The Pazzi conspiracy. Sixtus IV excommunicates Lorenzo the Magnificent and declares war on him.
1479 Accession of Ferdinand the Catholic as king of Aragon. Ludovico il Moro seizes power in Milan.

1481   Death of Charles of Maine, last Angevin pretender to throne of Naples. War
       resumed between Moslems of Granada and Castilians. The Turks are ousted
       from Otranto. Beginnings of Spanish Inquisition.
1483   Death of Louis XI. Accession of Charles VIII.
1484   Death of Pope Sixtus IV. Election of Innocent VIII.
       Ferrante of Naples refuses oath of obedience.
1486   Massacre of Neapolitan barons. First preachings of Savonarola in Florence.
1489   Innocent VIII orders grand master of the Hospitallers to hand over Prince
       Djem of Turkey. Venetians seize Cyprus.
1491   Charles VIII weds Anne of Brittany. Siege of Granada by Ferdinand of Aragon
       and Isabella of Castile.
1492   Granada seized. Death of Lorenzo the Magnificent.
       *Death of Innocent VIII. Accession of Rodrigo Borgia, who becomes Pope Alex-
       ander VI.*
       Christopher Columbus sails the Atlantic. Discovery of America (the Antilles).
1493   *Marriage of Lucrezia Borgia and Giovanni Sforza.*
       Alexander VI divides territories of the New World between Spain and Portugal.
       Expulsion of Jews from Spain.
       *Juan de Borgia takes possession of the duchy of Gandia in Spain. Marriage of
       Jofré Borgia and Sancia of Aragon negotiated. Cesare nominated cardinal.*
1494   Charles VIII invades Italy. The Medicis fall from power.
       Treaty of Tordesillas seals division of New World between Spain and Portugal.
       Pinturicchio decorates papal apartments.
1495   *Charles VIII passes through Rome. Hostage Djem handed over to Charles.
       Death of Djem.*
       French conquer Naples. Battle of Fornova.
1496   *Campaign of Juan Borgia and Guidobaldo of Urbino against the Orsinis.
       Gonsalvo de Cordoba seizes Ostia.*
       The French viceroy of Naples, Gilbert de Montpensier, surrenders at Atella.
       Giovanni Sforza flees the Vatican.
1497   *Murder of Juan of Gandia.*
       Leonardo da Vinci paints *The Last Supper* in Milan. Vasco da Gama begins
       voyage around the world.
       Marriage of Lucrezia Borgia and Giovanni Sforza dissolved.
1498   *Death of Charles VIII. Louis XII becomes king of France.*
       *Death of Perotto Caldes at the Vatican. Birth of mysterious "infans Romanus,"
       Giovanni Borgia. Trial and death of Savonarola. Lucrezia Borgia marries
       Alfonso of Aragon, duke of Bisceglie. Cesare Borgia, now a layman, becomes
       duke of Valentinois. Divorce of Louis XII.*
1499   Marriages of Louis XII and Anne of Brittany and Cesare Borgia and Charlotte
       d'Albret.
       Louis XII campaigns in Italy. Milan and Genoa seized.
       *Alfonso of Aragon flees Rome. Lucrezia appointed governor of Spoleto. Birth
       of Rodrigo of Aragon.*
       Alexander VI campaigns against the Gaetanis. Capture of Sermoneta.
       Cesare's first Romagna campaign. Capture of Imola and Forli.
1500   *Jubilee Year in Rome.*
       *Cesare Borgia named Gonfalonier of the Church. Murder of Alfonso of Aragon.
       Cesare's second Romagna campaign: capture of Pesaro and Rimini. He is
       defeated at Faenza.*
       Charles of Spain born in Ghent.
       Discovery of Brazil by the Portuguese.

1501 *Cesare takes Faenza, Piombino and Elba. Campaigns with the French in Naples: Capua sacked. Alexander VI seizes the Orsinis' possessions. Marriage of Lucrezia and Alfonso d'Este.*

1502 *Cesare's third Romagna campaign. Conquest of the duchy of Urbino. Capture of Camerino. Alliance between Cesare and Louis XII renewed. Meeting of Lucrezia and Pietro Bembo. Conspiracy of the condottieri. The trap at Sinigaglia.*
Opening of hostilities between French and Spanish in the kingdom of Naples.

1503 French defeated at Seminara and Cerignola in Southern Italy.
Death of Alexander VI. Elections of Pius III, then Julius II.

1504 The French surrender at Gaeta.
The Venetians advance in the Romagna. Cesare Borgia taken prisoner at Ostia, then Naples. He is moved to Spain, imprisoned in Chinchilla.
Death of Isabella of Spain.

1505 *Lucrezia becomes duchess of Ferrara. Cesare transferred to Medina del Campo.*
The emperor invests Louis XII with duchy of Milan.

1506 Genoese rebel against Louis XII.
Giulio d'Este's plot at Ferrara. Death of Philip the Fair, archduke of Austria, husband of Juana la Loca.
Cesare Borgia escapes from Medina del Campo.

1507 *Death of Cesare Borgia at siege of Viana in Navarre.*
Louis XII retakes Genoa. Pope Julius seizes Bologna.

1508 *Birth of heir to duchy of Ferrara, Ercole, son of Alfonso d'Este and Lucrezia Borgia.*
Murder of Ercole Strozzi.

1509 Franco-papal alliance.
Alfonso d'Este made gonfalonier of the Church.
Defeat of Venetians at Agnadello.
Capture of Francesco da Gonzaga.
Julius II retakes the Romagna.

1510 Alliance of Julius and Venice.
Francesco da Gonzaga becomes captain general of the Venetians. Alfonso d'Este excommunicated. Lucrezia acts as governor of Ferrara. Birth of Francis Borgia in Spain.

1511 Council of Pisa opposes Julius II.
Excommunication of rebel cardinals.

1512 Gaston de Foix defeats Spanish and papal forces at Ravenna. The Holy League gains new members. French leave Italy.

1513 *Julius sends ultimatum to duke of Ferrara. Death of Pope Julius.* Accession of Leo X.
The French, beaten at Novara, lose the Milanese.

1515 François I comes to French throne. Victory at Marignan; the Milanese recaptured.

1516 Death of Ferdinand the Catholic. Treaty of Bologna between the Holy See and France.

1517 In Saxony, Martin Luther nails his theses against indulgences.

1519 *Death of Lucrezia Borgia.*
Charles of Spain is elected emperor, becoming Charles V.

1520 Leo X excommunicates Luther.
Revolts in Spain against Charles V's Flemish ministers.

1521 Ferdinand Cortès conquers Mexico.

1522 *Spanish seize duchy of Milan.*

1525 French defeated at Pavia; François I taken prisoner in Madrid.
1526 Treaty of Madrid: François I's sons imprisoned in Spain.
      Charles V weds Isabella of Portugal. Francis Borgia, marquess of Lombay, joins the imperial court.
1527 Charles V's troops sack Rome.
1530 Charles V crowned in Bologna. Marquisate of Mantua made a duchy.
1534 *Ignatius de Loyola founds Society of Jesus in Paris.*
1535 Geneva becomes a reformed republic.
      Expedition of Charles V to Tunis, accompanied by Francis Borgia.
1536 *Charles V invades Provence. Francis Borgia shows his courage.*
1538 Treaty of Nice and meeting at Aigues-Mortes of Charles V and François I.
1539 *Death of Empress Isabella of Portugal, wife of Charles V. Charles appoints Francis Borgia viceroy of Catalonia.* Francis crosses France to put down revolt in Ghent.
1540 Pope Paul III gives Society of Jesus his approval.
      First dealings of Francis Borgia with the order.
1542 First contacts between Portuguese merchants and Japan.
      Francis Borgia attends sessions of the Aragon Cortes at Monzon. Becomes duke of Gandia.
1545 The Jesuit Francisco Xavier lands in Asia.
      Francis Borgia retires to Gandia.
      Start of Council of Trent.
1546 *Death of duchess of Gandia, conversion of Francis Borgia.*
      Death of Luther. The Jesuits land in Brazil.
1547 Deaths of Henry VIII of England and François I of France. Henri II accedes to the French throne. Victory of Charles V at Mühlberg over the League of Smalkaldae.
1548 *Duke Francis Borgia joins Society of Jesus.*
      Jesuits reach Morocco and the Congo.
1550 *Francis Borgia in Rome and Italy.*
      Anglo-French peace. Henri II recaptures Boulogne.
1551 *Francis Borgia takes priestly orders.*
1552 Henri II takes the Three Sees of Lorraine.
1555 *Francis Borgia at Juana la Loca's deathbed.*
      Accession of Pope Paul IV Carafa, enemy of Charles V.
1556 *Abdication of Charles V. His retreat to Yuste.*
      Death of Ignatius de Loyola. Opening of Jesuit colleges in Germany, Bohemia, and Netherlands.
1558 Accession of Sebastiano of Portugal.
      His education by the Jesuits.
1559 *Francis Borgia hounded by the Spanish Inquisition.*
      Death of Henri II of France.
1561 *Francis Borgia retires to Rome.*
      Meeting at Poissy organized by Catherine de Médicis.
1565 Death of Father Lainez, general of the Jesuits.
      Francis Borgia becomes general.
1566 Election of Pope Pius V. Death of Soliman the Magnificent. Mystical writings of St. Theresa of Avila. Beggars' Revolt in the Netherlands.
      Jesuits face setbacks in Germany.
1570 Peace of St.-Germain in France between Catholics and Protestants. Offensive of Selim II against the Christians.

Francis Borgia accompanies Cardinal Alessandrino's legation a latére in Spain, Portugal, and France.

1571 Naval victory of the Christians over the Turks at Lepanto.

Francis Borgia arranges marriage of King Sebastiano of Portugal.

1572 *Francis Borgia at the French court. Last conversation with Catherine de Médicis. His return to Italy and death in Rome.*

Massacre of St. Bartholomew.

Notes

I, Chapter 1. Valencia and Aragon:
The Borgias' Roots in Spain

On the Borgias' roots in the kingdom of Valencia, the main references are in E. Bertaux, *Etudes d'histoire et d'art*, Paris, 1911. On Játiva, see Carlos Sarthou Carreres, *Datos para la Historia de Játiva*, n.p., 1976.

On St. Vincent Ferrer, see his *Life* by Pietro Renzano Panormitano, in Bzovius, *Annales ecclesiastici*, Cologne, 1621–30; Ludwig von Pastor, *Histoire des papes*, Fr. trans., vol. II, Paris, 1888; H. Fages, *Histoire de saint Vincent Ferrier*, Louvain, 1901.

On the Great Schism, L. Gayet, *Le Grand Schisme d'Occident, Les Origines*, Paris, 1889; L. Salembier, *Le Grand Schisme d'Occident*, Paris, 1921; S. Puig y Puig, *Pedro de Luna, ultimo papa de Aviñon*, Barcelona, 1920; article by R. Mols in *Dict. d'hist. et de géogr. eccl.* on the antipope Clement VIII.

On Alonso de Borja (Calixtus III), J. Sanchis Sivera, *El obispo de Valencia Don Alfonso de Borja (1429–58)*, Madrid, 1926; bibliography in *Dict. d'hist. et de géogr. eccl.* (E. Vansteenberghe).

On the Aragonese conquest of Naples: *Estudios sobre Alfonso el Magnánimo con motivo del quinto centenario de su muerte*, Barcelona, 1960; J. Ametler Vinas, *Alfonso V de Aragón en Italia y la crisis religiosa del signo XV*, 3 vols., Gerona, 1903; L. Montalto, *La Corte di Alfonso I di Aragona*, Naples, 1922; Alan Ryder, *The Kingdom of Naples under Alfonso the Magnanimous. The Making of a Modern State*, Oxford, 1976.

I, Chapter 2: The Borgias Arrive in Rome:
Pontificate of Calixtus III

See references above to L. von Pastor and *Dict. d'hist. et de géogr. eccl.*; Ulysse-Chevalier, *Répertoire des sources historiques du Moyen Age. Bio-Bibliographie*, vol. I, Paris, 1905; Alfonso Vila Moreno, *Calixto III: un papa Valenciano*, Saragossa, 1979; J. Rius Serra, *Regesto ibérico de Calixto III*, vol. 1 (1455–56), Barcelona, 1948; vol. 2 (1456–57), Barcelona, 1958; F. Gregorovius, *Geschichte des Stadt Rom im M. A.*, 2nd ed., vol. VII, 1894; Ital. trans., *Storia della città di Roma nel Medio evo*, vol. VII, Venice, 1875.

On the war against the Turks, A. Gegaj, *L'Albanie et l'invasion turque au XVe siècle*, Louvain, 1937; Guglielmotti, *Storia della marina pontificia*, Rome, 1856.

On the arts and literature: E. Muentz, *La Bibliothèque du Vatican au XVe siècle*, Paris, 1887; *Les Arts à la Cour des papes pendant le XVe et le XVIe siècle*, vol. I,

Paris, 1878; J. Heers, *La Vie quotidienne à la Cour pontificale au temps des Borgia et des Médicis*, Paris, 1986.

I, Chapter 3: Cardinal Rodrigo's Charmed Career

On the pontifical chancellery, see A. Giry, *Manuel de diplomatique*, Paris, 1984. Supplementing this are J. Ciampini, *De Sanctae Romanae Ecclesiae Vicecancellario illiusque munere.* . . , Rome, 1697; and *De abbreviatorum de parco majori sive assistentium S.R.E. Vicecancellario . . . antiquo statu . . .*, Rome, 1691; G. Moroni, *Dizionario de erudizione stor. eccl.*, VII, pp. 154–94; Mario Tosi, *Bullaria e Bullatores della Cancelleria Pontificia*, Siena, 1917; J. Le Pelletier, *Instruction . . . pour obtenir en cours de Rome toutes sortes d'expéditions*, Paris, 1686; P. Castel, *Traité de l'usage et pratique de la Cour de Rome*, Paris, 1717; *Taxe de la chancellerie romaine ou la banque du pape*, Rome, 1744 (along with polemical commentaries, publishes a sixteenth-c. tax as well as a list of the chancellery offices, from the datary to the Apostolic Chamber). By way of comparison, see J. Favier, *Les Finances pontificales à l'époque du grand schisme d'Occident*, Paris, 1966.

On the relations between Cardinal Rodrigo and Pius II, see Pastor, *Histoire des papes* . . . , vol. III, Paris, 1892; item *Alexandre VI* by P. Richard in *Dict. hist. et de géogr. eccl.*; Ulysse Chevalier, *Répertoire des sources historiques du Moyen Age, Bio-bibliographie*, vol. I, Paris, 1905. Pius's letter reproving Rodrigo can be found in the register of papal briefs of the *Archivio Segreto Vaticano*: see reference in P. De Roo, *Material for a history of Pope Alexander VI*. See also the *Commentaries* of Pius II: *Pius II pontificis maximi commentarii . . .*, Frankfurt, 1614; J. Cugnoni, *Aeneae Sylvii Piccolomini . . . opera inedita*, Rome, 1883. On the papal resources after the fall of Constantinople, see L. von Pastor for the reigns of Pius II, Paul II, and Sixtus II; add Jean Delumeau, *L'alun de Rome, XVe-XIXe siècle*, Paris, 1962.

On the links between the papacy and Spain, see A. Aguado Bleye, *Manual de Historia de España*, 6th ed., Madrid, 1954; Ballesteros y Beretta, *Historia de España y su influencia en la historia universal*, 3rd ed., 1963; a good summary in French in Albert Mousset, *Histoire d'Espagne*, Paris, 1947; list of documents in Antonio de La Torre, *Documentos sobre las relaciones internacionales de los Reyes Catolicos*, Madrid, 1949–52.

On Rodrigo Borgia's private life: Jacopo Ammanati, *Epistolae et commentarii Jacobi Piccolomini, cardinalis Papiensis*, Milan, 1506. On material conditions, luxurious homes, and Roman courtesans, see L. von Pastor, *Hist. des papes*, vol. V, 1898, and E. Rodocanachi, *Une cour princière au Vatican au temps de la Renaissance*, Paris, 1925.

On Vanozza Cattanei and Rodrigo's illegitimate children, see M. Menotti, *Documenti inediti sulla famiglia e la corte di Alessandro VI*, Rome, 1917; idem, *I Borgia, Storia ed iconografia*, Rome, 1917. Vanoza's funerary inscription, with her children's names, is published in Forcella, *Iscrizioni delle chiese e degli edifici di Roma*, vol. VIII, pp. 136 and 520. On Vanozza's Roman inns, see U. Gnoli, "Alberghi e osterie romane della Rinascenza," in *Pan*, January 1935. An admirable study is that of Léonce Cellier, *Alexandre VI et ses enfants en 1493*, in *Ecole française de Rome, Mélanges d'Archéologie et d'Histoire*, vol. 16 (1906): This gives text of bull of September 19, 1493, establishing Cesare's primogeniture over Juan, future duke of Gandia. The main documents relating to Rodrigo's children and their Spanish endowments are given in L. Thuasne, *Johannis Burcchardi Diarium*, vol. III, Paris, 1885, based on the archives of the dukes of Osuna (now section XI of the *Archivo historico nacional* of Madrid); other documents are given in appendix of C. Yriarte, *César Borgia*, 2nd ed., vol. 2, Paris, 1930.

Regarding Rodrigo's children by unknown women, see F. Gregorovius, *Lucrezia Borgia*, document no. 1, marriage contract of Girolama Borgia (January 24, 1482), which mentions Pier Luigi and Juan Borgia. See also *ibid.*, no. 2, marriage contract between Carlo Canale and Vanozza Cattanei (June 8, 1486); no. 3, marriage contract between Orsino Orsini and Giulia Farnese (May 20, 1489); no. 4, marriage contract between Lucrezia Borgia and Don Cherubino Juan de Centelles (February 26, 1491).

On Innocent VIII, bibliography in L. von Pastor, vol. V; L. Thuasne, *Djem-sultan (1459–95). Etude sur la question d'Orient a la fin au XVe siècle*, Paris, 1892.

On Savonarola, see, among others, P. Villari, *Jérôme Savonarole et son temps . . . suivi d'un choix des lettres et poésies*, vols. I and II, Paris, 1874; Roberto Ridolgi, *Savonarole*, Paris, 1957; Donald Weinstein, *Savonarola and Florence. Prophecy and Patriotism in the Renaissance*, UMI, 1970.

II, Chapter 1: On Olympian Heights

Bibliography in Pastor, vol. V, supplemented by G. B. Picotti, "Nuovi studi documenti intorno a papa Alessandro VI," in *Riv. storia della Chiesa in Italia*, 5 (1951). The essential souce is the *Johannis Burchardi Diarium* (Journal of Burckard), published in its entirety for the first time in 3 vols. by L. Thuasne in 1885 (previously it was known only from extracts): There is a gap, however, in this edition from May 25, 1493 to January 11, 1494. The scholar Enrico Celani, who discovered a complementary manuscript in the Vatican (#5632) that filled the lacuna, published an improved 2-vol. edition in 1907–13. Joseph Turmel translated the text into French and published some extracts, with notes, in Paris in 1932: *Le Journal de Jean Burckard, évèque et cérémoniaire du Vatican.*

On Cardinal Borgia's election see Giovanni Soranzo, *Studi intorno a papa Alessandro VI (Borgia)*, Milan, 1950: *Studio primo*; on the usage of Burckard's journal: *ibid.*, *Studio secondo*.

On Alexander's physical appearance: Sigismondo dei Conti da Foligno, *La storia de suoi tempi*, Rome, 1883; Bernardino de Carvajal, *Oratio de eligendi summo pontifice . . .*, August 6, 1492; Hieronimo Porzio, *Portii Commentarium . . .*, Rome, 1493; on Alexander's portraits, C. Yriarte, *Autour des Borgia*, Paris, 1891, which also examines the portraits of Cesare and Lucrezia.

On the planned marriage between Lucrezia and Gaspare d'Aversa (or de Procida), see Gregorovius, no. 7 (convention of November 8, 1492); see also the annulment (June 10, 1498), no. 15; marriage contract between Lucrezia and Giovanni Sforza da Pesaro (February 2, 1493), *ibid.*, no. 9. Account of the wedding: see letter of Giandrea Bocciaccio to Duke Ercole of Ferrara, Rome, June 13, 1493, *ibid.*, no. 10.

The pope's instructions to the duke of Gandia and Genis Fira, also details of the gifts from the duke to his wife, are given in Sanchis y Sivera, *Algunos documentos y cartas privadas . . .*, Valencia, 1919. Also included is the duke's correspondence with his family, in particular a list of articles Juan purchased in Spain for his sister Lucrezia: shoes, silks, and velvets, cloth of gold, even a hat (*sombrero*) of brown velvet. Details of Cesare's rebuke of his brother are given by Maria Bellonci in the *Archivo Segreto Vaticano*, Archivum Arcis (A. A.), Armadio I–XVIII, 5021, fol. 3 and 4.

On the relationship between Ferrante and Alfonso II of Naples, see F. Trinchera, *Codice Aragonese ossia lettere regie, ordinamenti ed altri atti . . .*, Naples, 1866; on preparations for the French invasion, Ivan Cloulas, *Charles VIII et le mirage italien*,

Paris, 1986. See also a number of documents published by A. Gordon. On the wedding of Jofre Borgia and Sancia, unpublished documents in *Arch. Segr. Vat.*, A.A., Arm. I–XVIII, 5020 and 5024 (list of jewels; program of festivities). Details in Chabas, "Don Jofre de Borja y dona Sancha de Aragon," in *Revue hispanique*, IX (1902).

On the relations between Alexander and Giovanni Sforza, see the brief of September 15, 1493, published by Maria Bellonci, *Lucrezia Borgia*, latest Italian edition, 1970, appendix no. 1. Lorenzo Pucci's letter to his brother Giannozzo (Rome, December 23–24, 1493) is published in Gregorovius, no. 11, based on the *Carte Strozziane*, filza 343, *Arch. de Stato di Firenze*.

On Pinturicchio's decorations in the Borgia apartments, see G. Lafenestre and E. Richtenberger, *Rome, le Vatican, les Eglises*, Paris, 1903 (description and bibliography). On the "totemic" description of the symbols, Francesco Papafava, *Le Vatican*, Paris, 1984. See also D. Redig de Campos, *Architecture, peinture, sculpture du Vatican*, Amsterdam, 1981. On the "rediscovery" of the Borgia Apartments, Evelyn March Philipp, *Pinturicchio*, London, 1901 and C. Yriarte, *Autour des Borgia*, Paris, 1891.

There is ample documentation on Lucrezia's stay in Pesaro and the intimate correspondence between the pope and Giulia Farnese (*Arch. Segr. Vat.*, A.A.; Arm. I–XVIII, 5020–5027): Detailed though biased accounts are given in G. Soranzo, *op cit.*, *Studio terzo: Un prezioso carteggio papale degli anni 1493–94*; *Studio quarto: Il presunto scandalo di Giulia Farnese e Alessandro VI*. See M. Belonci, *op. cit.*, summing up on pp. 69 and 501; 2nd ed., letter from Giacopo Dragozio to Cesare Borgia on the beauty contest between Giulia Farnese and Caterina da Gonzaga.

On the capture and liberation of Giulia Farnese, letter from Galeazzo di San Severino to Alexander (December 1494), published by M. Bellonci, *op. cit.*, no. 3, based on *Arch. Segr. Vat.* A.A., Arm. I–XVIII, 5025; G. Soranzo, *op. cit.*, *Studio quarto*. On Giulia's reception by the pope, L. von Pastor, *op. cit.*, vol. III, German ed., appendix no. 28, and letter from Giorgio Brognolo to the marquess of Mantua (November 29, 1494), original in the *Archivioi Gonzaga*. Giacomo Trotti's dispatch dated December 21, 1494 is cited by Fr. de Navenne, *Rome, le Palais Farnèse et les Farnèse*, Paris, 1914.

II, Chapter 2: The Weapon of Ruse

Bibliography in Pastor, *op. cit.* On Charles VIII's expedition see I. Cloulas, *op. cit.* Burckard gives important testimony (see L. Thuasne ed., with attached documents: ambassadors' dispatches). See documentation in H. F. Delaborde, *L'Expédition de Charles VIII en Italie. Histoire diplomatique et militaire*, Paris, 1888. On the building of fortifications, see E. Rodoconachi, *op. cit.* The manifestos of Cardinal Péraud and treaty of Charles VIII and Alexander have been reproduced in many places since Gordon's work. See French text of treaty in Burckard, ed. Thuasne, vol. II, p. 661, and Latin text in Lunig, *Cod. it. diplomat.*, vol. II, p. 795.

On Cesare's flight to Velletri, see Sigismondo dei Conti, *op. cit.*, vol. II, pp. 101 and 143. On Djem's suspicious death, see L. Thuasne, *Djem-sultan*, Paris, 1892, and I. Cloulas, "Aux origines des guerres d'Italie: les malheurs du prince Zizim," in *Historama*, no. 30 (August 1986), pp. 10–18. On the Italian reaction to the expedition, Anne Denis, *Charles VIII et les Italiens*, Paris, 1979.

On the natural catastrophes of the winter of 1495, see Pastor, *op.cit.*, vol. V, Fr. ed., pp. 455 ff. On the outbreak of syphilis, Hesnaut, *Le "Mal francais" à l'époque de l'expédition de Charles VIII en Italie*, Paris, 1886; Claude Quétel, *Le Mal de Naples. Histoire de la syphilis*, Paris, 1986.

II, Chapter 3: The Enfants Terribles

On the scandals of the Vatican, the essential source is Burckard's Journal. On the Countess of Pesaro's marriage, see B. Feliciangeli, *Il matrimonio di Lucrezia Borgia con Giovanni Sforza, signore di Pesaro*, Turin, 1901. Two briefs from Alexander to Giovanni Sforza and Lucrezia (May 8 and 9, 1495) are published in M. Bellonci, *op. cit.*, nos. 4 and 5. Description of Jofré and Sancia's entry into Rome in Burckard (ed. Turmel, pp. 286–87). Members of the princes of Squillace's suite are listed in the *Arch. Segr. Vat.*, A.A., Arm. I–XVIII, 5024, fol. 127–28; on the budgetary problems of their court see M. Bellonci, p. 504.

On Juan, first duke of Gandia, an admirable summing up is to be found in Miquel Batllori, "La Correspondencia d'Alexandre VI amb els seus familiars i amb els reis catolics," in *Pensamiento politico*, ed. Istituto historico della compagnia de Gesù, Rome, n.d.; introduction to the forthcoming publication of the Borgia letters contained in the *Archivum Arcis*, 5020–5027, examined by Soranzo. On the duke's family, see Chabas and Sanchis Sivera, *Algunos documentos y caras privadas . . .* Valencia, 1919. Noteworthy for information on the capital of the duchy is P. P. Sola and Cervos, *El palacio ducal de Gandia*, Barcelona, 1904 (remarkably well illustrated monograph). On Juan's campaign of 1496–97 against the Orsinis and his march on Ostia with Gonsalvo de Cordoba, biblio. in Pastor, Vol. V, Fr. ed., pp. 468–71. On Giovanni Sforza's flight to Pesaro, see M. Bellonci, *op. cit.*, no. 7 (brief of March 30, 1497). Regarding the Roman barons' estates, note Jean Guiraud's fundamental geopolitical study, *L'Etat pontifical après le grand schisme*, Paris, 1896.

On the Duke of Gandia's assassination, see again biblio. in Pastor, vol. V, pp. 472–86. Account in Burckard. As one of Cesare's possible motives, several authors have cited the jealousy of the two brothers, who purportedly fought for Lucrezia's favors: see Ignazio dell'Oro, *Il segreto dei Borgia*, Milan, 1938, which repeats rumors cited in Sanudo, *Diarii*, pub. 1879, vol. I, 1844–46, and in Malipiero, *Annali Veneti*, pub. 1843, p. 491.

On the duke's funeral and the inquest, letters from the Florentine ambassador Alessandro Braccio, in Thuasne, vol. II, pp. 669 ff., documents 28, 29, and 30 (from *Arch. di Stato* of Florence, *Lettereai X di Balia*, X, 4, no. 54): appointment of the reform commission. See the pope's correspondence with Savonarola in Ridolfi and Villari, *op. cit.*

On the divorce of Lucrezia and Giovanni Sforza, M. Bellonci, *op. cit.*, p. 535, no. 8: brief of Alexander sending him Friar Mariano de Genazzano to handle the divorce (May 26, 1497), from *Arch. de Stato* of Florence, *Diplomatico, Urbino*. On Giovanni Sforza's interventions with Ludovico il Moro, *ibid.*, p. 534, no. 6: letter asking for help in recovering his wife (April 24, 1497) from *Arch. di Stato* of Milan, *Pesaro, Correspondenza*. On the divorce itself, Pastor, *op. cit.*, vol. V, p. 499.

On Perotto Caldès and his murder, see Thuasne, vol. II, p. 433 and note 1. Account of the chamberlain's love affair with Lucrezia and Cesare's anger based on Paolo Capello, Venetian ambassador (*Relazioni degli ambass. Veneti*, 2nd ser., vol. III, pp. 10 and 11), Sanudo, *Diarii*, vol. I, col. 883, and the Bolognese Cristoforo Poggio, used by M. Bellonci, *op. cit.*, pp. 119–121, who suggests that the "infans Romanus," Giovanni Borgia, was born of their liaison. See Sannazaro's epigram in Giacopo Sannazaro, *Le Rime*, Venice, 1538.

The final episode in the struggle between Alexander and Savonarola took the form of a correspondence, inserted in Burckard's Journal (reproduced by Gordon): see works cited on Savonarola and documents of the *Procès de Savonarola*, edited by Robert Klein, with introduction by A. Renaudet, Paris, 1957.

On Lucrezia's marriage to Alfonso of Aragon, see Gregorovius, no. 16 (first contract:

June 20, 1498); marquess de Laurencin, *Relación de los festines que se celebraron en el Vaticano con motivo de las bodas de Lucrecia de Borgia con Don Alonso de Aragon*, Madrid, 1916. Account of Cesare's "laicization" in Burckard.

II, Chapter 4: The Advent of Cesare

For Alexander's and Cesare's political orientations, see G. Pepe, *La politica dei Borgia*, Naples, 1945, and G. Soranzo, *op. cit.*, Studio quinto.

On the relations between Alexander and Louis XII, L. G. Pélissier, *Sopra alcuni documenti relativi all'alleanza tra Alessandro VI e Luigi XII (1498–1499)*, Rome, 1895; "Documents sur les relations de Louis XII, de Ludovic Sforza et du marquis de Mantoue de 1498 a 1500," in *Bull. du comité des trav. hist.* (1893); *Documents relatifs au règne de Louis XII et à sa politique en Italie*, Montpellier, 1912; "Dépêches des ambassadeurs de Ferrare à la cour de Charles VIII et de Louis XII, aux Archives d'Etat de Modène," in *Revue des Bibliothèques*, June–July 1898. See also R. de Maulde La Clavière, "Alexandre VI et le divorce de Louis XII," in *Bibl. Ecole des Chartes*, 1896; B. Quilliet, *Louis XII*, Paris, 1986.

Le Père Anselme, *Histoire généalogique et chronologique de la Maison royale de France*, vol. V, Paris, 1730, pp. 516–20, published the letters patent granting Cesare the counties of Valentinois and Die (given at Etampes, August 1498) and those elevating Valentinois to a duchy (October 1498) together with the decrees of registration in the Grenoble parliament (October 6, 1498 and November 15, 1498, respectively). In April 1499 the king also gave Cesare the revenues of the royal seat of Issoudun and power to appoint officers of the town's salt depot in return for the advance of 50,000 pounds in silver and jewels on the occasion of his marriage (Arch. nat. de Paris X-1A 8610, ordinances of Louis XII).

On Cesare Borgia's itinerary in France and Italy, see C. Yriarte, *César Borgia. Sa vie, sa captivité, sa mort*, 2nd ed., Paris, 1930. Quotation from Brantôme taken from his *Vie des hommes illustres, César Borgia*, ed. L. Lalanne, vol. 2, 1866, pp. 203–19.

On d'Albret's marriage and negotiations, see P. Anselme, *op. cit.*; A. Luchaire, *Alain le Grand, sire d'Albret. L'Administration royale et la féodalité du Midi, 1440–1522*, Paris, 1879. On Charlotte, see E. Bonnafé, *Inventaire de la duchesse de Valentinois, Charlotte d'Albret*, Paris 1878 (marriage contract and inventory of goods according to the Archives of the dukes of La Trémoille). Marriage ceremony and reports on the wedding night in Burckard, vol. II, ed. Thuasne, which quotes Robert de La Mark, lord of Fleurange. Correspondence and marriage deeds of Cesare Borgia with Charlotte d'Albret in the Archives des Pyrénées Atlantiques, at Pau: P. Raymond, *Inventaire-sommaire . . . , Archives civiles*, series E, Paris, 1867. Articles E 104–07 include the letters to Alain d'Albret. Article E 91 contains four parchment and seventeen paper documents and a register referring in particular to Charlotte's marriage contract and trousseau; also the procuration Cesare gave his brother-in-law, Jean d'Albret, king of Navarre, claiming 100,000 pounds from Louis XII (signed Cesare Borgia): most of these documents were published in the *Arch. histor. de la Gironde* (vol. XVIII). See also Jacob, *L'Histoire du XVIe siècle en France*, vol. I, pp. 177–181 and C. Yriarte, *César Borgia*, vol. II, appendix, pp. 324–25.

On the events at the court of Rome, see Burckard, vol. II, ed. Thuasne, pp. 548–52; flight of Alfonso of Aragon, duke of Bisceglie (August 2, 1499); Lucrezia and Jofré's departure from Rome for Spoleto (August 8, 1499). For Lucrezia's brief governorship see Gregorovius, *Lucrezia Borgia*. See also Sanudo, *Diarii*, vol. II. An account of young Rodrigo's baptism is given in Burckard, French ed (J. Turmel), pp.

302 ff. Concerning the ruin of the Gaetanis, see Jacopo Gaetani's protest in Gregorovius, document no. 19 (February 7, 1500).

On Cesare's Romagnol campaigns and itineraries, see Odoardo Alvisi, *Cesare Borgia, duca di Romagna*, Imola, 1878; also Yriarte and Woodward. On Cesare's triumph in Rome (February 1500) see Yriarte, *op. cit.*, p. 210, note 1, criticizing A. Gordon, who followed Tommaso Tomasi too closely.

On the 1500 Jubilee Year see L. von Pastor, *Histoire des papes, Livre IX*, French ed., vol. VI, chapter XI, *Alexandre VI et la religion*, pp. 133 ff.: Most of the details come from Burckard.

On the pope's accident (June 29, 1500) and all the events of that year, see, in the Appendix of vol. II of Burckard, ed. Thuasne, the dispatches of the Florentine secretary Francesco Capello, from the *Archivio di Stato* of Florence; an account of Alfonso of Aragon's murder, complementing Burckard and the Venetian ambassador Paolo Capello. On Lucrezia's retreat to Nepi and her letters signed "La infelicissima," in Gregorovius, *op. cit.*, documents nos. 26–26ter.

On the plans for a crusade, see B. Feliciangeli, "Le proposte par la guerra contro i Turchi presentate da Stefano Taleazzo, vescovo di Torcello, a papa Alessandro VI," in *Archivio Storico italiano*, vol. 40 (1917), p. 12 s 9.

Paolo Capello's evaluation of the pope's physical and moral condition is included in his dispatch to the Venetian senate, ed. E. Alberi, *Relazioni . . .* , 2nd series, vol. 3, p. 11.

II, Chapter 5: Royal Advance

C. Yriarte's *Autour des Borgia*, Paris 1891, contains an important study of Cesare's sword: *L'Epée de César Borgia*, pp. 141–209. This gives an analysis of the decorative themes based on observation of the sword in the Gaetani Palace in Rome (duke of Sermonteta's collection), also a comparison with weapons, particularly short swords or daggers, in various museums. The artist is claimed to be Ercole da Fideli, the Christian name of a converted Jew, Salomone da Sesso, who became a goldsmith at the Ferrara court.

On Cesare's life and entourage in the Romagna, see Andrea Bernardi, *Cronache Forlivese, 1476–1517*, Bologna, 1897; Paolo Bonoli, *Istorie della città di Forli*, Forli, 1661; Biagio Buonaccorsi, *Diario*, Florence, 1518; Cesare Clementini, *Raccolto istorico di Rimini*, Rimini, 1617; Francesco Matarazzo, *Chronaca della città di Perugia, 1492–1503*, ed. F. Bonaini and F. Polidori in *Archivio storico italiano*, Florence, 1852; B. Righi, *Annali di Faenza*, Faenza, 1841. On Pesaro and Pandolfo Collenuccio, see Carlo Cinelli, *Pandolfo Collenuccio e Pesaro a suoi tempi*, Pesaro, 1880; W. M. Tartt, *Pandolfo Collenuccio: Memoirs connected with his Life*, 1868. Study of Italian literature in E. Cecchi and N. Sapegno, *Storia della Letteratura italiana*, 1979 ed., vol. III, *Il Quattrocento* (Boiardo, Sannazaro, and Ariosto), and vol. IV, *Il Cinquecento* (covers Machiavelli, Guicciardini, Bembo, and Baldassare Castiglione).

On the ambiance of the Italian courts and the fashion of courtly love, see Castiglione, *Il Libro del Cortegiani*, ed. A. Quondam and M. Longo, Milan, 1981.

On the poets in Cesare's entourage, see O. Alvisi, *op. cit.*, which quotes poems and epigrams in the Biblioteca Malatestiana of Cesena. The consultation of astrologers reported by Francesco Capello is cited by L. Thuasne, ed. Burckard, vol. III, p. 77, note 1.

On the opponents Cesare attacked, see Pier Desiderio Pasoini, *Caterina Sforza*, Rome, 1893; C. Monteverde, *Astorre Manfredi*, Milan, 1852, and G. Tonducci, *Storia di Faenza*, 1675. On Venice's stance in the siege of Faenza see A. Boanrdi,

"Venezia e Cesare Borgia" in *Nuovo Archivio Veneto*, vol. XX, part II, pp. 10–12 and the *Diarii* of Sanudo and Priuli. The abduction of Dorotea Caracciolo (C. Yriarte, vol. I, pp. 286 ff.) is given much space in Sanudo's *Diarii* (vols. III and VII). The Romagnol campaigns are widely referred to in Machiavelli's *Prince*, in particular chapters VII, XIII, and XX. In Burckard, ed. Thuasne, vol. III, Appendix, pp. 441 and 447, the dispatches of the Florentine envoys Francesco Capello, Luigi de Stufa, and Francesco de Pepis, to Rome.

On the Piombino campaign, see Yriarte, which also covers the Naples campaign. See also A. Q. Pascale, *Raconto del sacco di Capova*, Naples, 1632; F. Granata, *Storia civile di Capua*, 1752.

Account of Lucrezia's "government" of the Church in Burckard. Negotiations and conclusion of Alfonso d'Este's marriage in Maria Bellonci, *op. cit.*: many references and documents are taken from *Archivio di Stato* of Modena, in particular dispatches of Gerardo Saraceni and Ettore Bellingeri; account of the Ferrarese arrival in Rome by Gianluca Castellini de Pontremoli; letters of Beltrando Costabili, Ercole d'Este's ambassador to Rome. The bibliography of L. von Pastor, French ed., vol. VI, pp. 102–03 is also useful.

The courtesans' ball at the Vatican and the episode of the stallions are reported in Burckard, ed. Thuasne and Turmel.

On the endowment of the children, see M. Bellonci, *op. cit.* Both bulls of September 1, 1501 concerning the "infans Romanus" are included in Gregorovius's relevant documents, nos. 29 and 30, based on papers in the *Archivio di Stato* of Modena. See also Burckard, ed. Thuasne, vol. III, supplement to the Appendix, which mentions the copy in the *Archives d'Osuna* in Madrid. Note bibliography in L. von Pastor, French ed., vol. VI, pp. 98–99. Regarding Lucrezia's solicitude for Rodrigo, see letter to the steward Vincente Giordano, Nepi, October 28, 1500, in Gregorovius, document no. 25. On Lucrezia's farewells to her children, M. Bellonci, *op. cit.*, which gives the best account of the journey to Ferrara (document supplementing Gregorovius): see especially the description of Alfonso's impromptu arrival based on an anonymous report that confirms Gianluca Castellini's letters.

On the pope's visit to Piombino, see Burckard, ed. Thuasne, vol. III, pp. 195–97, which quotes Francesco Capello.

II, Chapter 6: Appointments with the Devil

Machiavelli's testimony is fundamental here. Besides works of political thought like *The Prince*, reference has been made to the dispatches of the Romagnol legation and the famous account of the Trap of Sinigaglia (now Senigallia): *Descrizione del modo tenuto dal duca Valentino nello ammazzare Vitellozzo Vitelli, Oliveretto da Fermo, il signor Pagolo e il duca di Gravina Orsini*. Particular use was made of the Italian edition of Niccolo Machiavelli, *Opere*, ed. Ezio Raimondi, Milan, 1969, as well as the French editions by E. Barincou, Oeuvres complètes, coll. La Pléiade, Paris, 1952 and *Toutes les lettres officielles et familières*, Paris, 1955. On Machiavelli, see Christian Bec, *Machiavel* (thematic extracts from the works), Paris, 1985, and J. Heers, *Machiavel*, Paris, 1985 (biography). T. Guiraudet's great edition of Machiavelli, Paris, *an VII*, is interesting for its preface ("Discours sur Machiavel") and notes.

Cesare Borgia's biographers, especially Yriarte, provide the necessary information on the sieges of the Romagnol forts. See also, for Urbino, R. de la Sizeranne, *César Borgia et le duc d'Urbino, 1502–1503*, Paris, 1924 (bibliography), and Sigismondo dci Conti, ed. 1886, for thc sack of Camcrino.

On the Savelli letter, see bibliography in L. von Pastor, French ed., vol. VI, pp. 107–09, which refers to the various anti-Borgia pamphlets and epigrams.

On the plot of the condottieri, their part in the recapture of Urbino, the treaty with Cesare, and the Sinigaglia trap, many books and references are available. See the editions of Machiavelli's works as well as the notes of L. von Pastor, French ed., pp. 114–17. Also the thoughts of G. Pepe, *La politica dei Borgia*, p. 199 ff. and those of G. Soranzo, *op. cit.*, *Studio quinto*, on the development of ties between Cesare and Venice. The dispatches of Giustiniani (or Giustinian), Venetian ambassador to Rome (*Dispacci di A. Giustinian, 1502–1503*, ed. Pasquale Villari, 3 vols., Florence, 1876), and of the ambassador of Mantua, G. L. Cataneo, complement Sigismondo dei Conti for the campaign against the Savellis and Orsinis. See Cesare's letter to Isabella da Gonzaga (February 1, 1503) in Gregorovius, document no. 47, thanking her for her congratulations over the trap of Sinigaglia (reply to Isabella's letter of January 15, 1503, *ibid.*, no. 46). On the death of Cardinal Michieli and suspicion of poisoning, see L. von Pastor, French ed., vol. VI, p. 120, also on Alexander's last promotion to the cardinalate. Burckard's account of the pope's death may be supplemented by Sigismondo dei Conti, vol. II, p. 267, Giustiniani's dispatches, vol. II, pp. 108 and 459, and that of Cataneo (*Archivio Gonzaga* at Mantua). See also the Appendix in Burckard, ed. Thuasne, vol. III, pp. 449–50. Francesco da Gonzaga's letter to his wife Isabella (September 22, 1503) in which he describes the pope's death and obsequies is given in Gregorovius, *op. cit.*, document no. 51. Bibliography in L. von Pastor, French ed., vol. VI, pp. 127–29, with references to works criticizing or accepting the poison hypothesis.

III, Chapter 1: The Lone Wolf

On Pius III's pontificate and the beginnings of that of Julius II, see L. von Pastor, *op. cit.*, vol. VI, pp. 171 ff. (book X). See also E. Rodocanachi, *Une cour princière au Vatican . . .* , and *Le Pontificat de Jules II*, Paris, 1928. Julius's physical appearance and character are described in Sanudo, *Diarii*, vols. XI and XII. His relationship with Cesare Borgia is noted by Machiavelli (*Legations*), also by A. Giustinian of Venice (*Dispacci . . .*), F. Capello of Florence and Costabili of Ferrara. Cesare's anxiety and imprisonment at Ostia, the restoration of the Romagnol forts, and his departure for Naples are described by L. von Pastor, French ed., pp. 216–25, based on ambassadors' dispatches and the Vatican register of briefs. Yriarte, *op. cit.*, relies on the Spanish documents concerning Cesare; some are reproduced in the Appendix. Document no. 6 indexes the documents covering the marriage of Cesare Borgia and Charlotte d'Albret in the Archives des Pyrénées-Atlantiques (Pau): deeds nos. 13 and 14, regarding Cesare's attempts to retrieve the lands previously conferred on him by Louis XII; no. 7, extracts from the chronicle of Don Martin de Cantos regarding the fortress of Chinchilla; no. 8, a list of the furnishings and precious articles entrusted by Cesare to Ippolito d'Este and seized in January 1504 by Giovanni Bentivoglio (based on ms. 1439 of the Biblioteca Universitaria of Bologna); no. 9, letter from King Juan of Navarre to Ferdinand of Spain, December 22, 1505 (Madrid, *Academia de la Historia*, Salazar collection); nos. 10 and 11, dossier of the inquest on Cesare Borgia's escape by Don Pedro de Mendoza, including the report of the corregidor Cristoval Vasquez de Acuña and account of his interrogations (*Archivo general de Simancas, Consejo de Estado* and *Camara de Castilla*).

C. Yriarte relies mainly on the *Annales d'Aragón* of Zurita. Complementing these are: Francisco Javier Ortiz Felipe, *Cesar Borgia y Navarra*, 4th ed., Pamplona, 1983, and Antonio Onieva, *Cesar Borgia, su vida, su muerte y sus restos*, Madrid, 1945.

See, in Gregorovius, *op. cit.*, document no. 56, Cesare's letter to Francesco da Gonzaga (December 7, 1506). Recently the town of Viana has erected a monument with a bust honoring Cesare Borgia.

III, Chapter 2: The Beautiful Lady of Ferrara

Maria Bellonci, *op. cit.*, includes a number of documents referring to this period of Lucrezia's life. Among the most important are:
—Letter from Bernardino de Prosperi to Isabella d'Este on Ercole I's death and accession of Alfonso and Lucrezia (no. 21).
—Correspondence between Lorenzo Strozzi and the marquess of Mantua (no. 22); Gregorovius, *op. cit.*, includes several letters of family interest, in particular one from Isabella of Aragon asking Lucrezia to pay the late duke of Bisceglie's servants (no. 58 bis), as well as letters from Vanozza Cattanei to Lucrezia and Cardinal Ippolito d'Este.
—Two letters of Giovanni Borgia, the "infans Romanus," are given in Gregorovius (nos. 63 and 64).
—M. Bellonci includes two letters on the mysterious bastard Rodrigo Borgia (nos. 23 and 24).
—See also, in M. Bellonci, "Inventaire des joyaux de Lucrèce Borgia," Appendix, pp. 555–78 (435 entries). On the secret information Isabella d'Este received through Il Prete de Correggio and Bernardino de Prosperi about Lucrezia's private life, see A. Luzio, *Isabella d'Este e i Borgia*, Milan, 1908.
—On Ercole Strozzi's role as provider of Lucrezia's wardrobe: I. Polifilo, *La guardaroba di Lucrezia Borgia*, Rome, 1903. On Lucrezia's illnesses: Gagnière, "Le journal des médecins de Lucrèce Borgia," in *La Nouvelle Revue*, 1888.
—On the tragedies of the Este family (Giulio's plot), A. Luzio, *Isabella d'Este nelle tragedie della sua casa*, Mantua, 1912; R. Bacchelli, *La congiura di Don Giulio d'Este*, Milan, 1958.
—Pietro Bembo's letters, *Lettere giovanili di Messer Pietro Bembo*, Milan, 1558, represent only a tiny part of the great writer's oeuvre: see E. Bonara, *Pietro Bembo, La vita e gli studi*, in *Storia della Letteratura Italiana* by E. Cecchi and N. Sapegno, 1979. On his relationship with Lucrezia: B. Gatti, *Lettere di Lucrezia Borgia a Messer Pietro Bembo*, Milan, 1859; B. Morsolin, "Pietro Bembo e Lucrezia Borgia," in *Nuova Antologia*, vol. 52, 1885; P. Rajna, *I versi spagnoli di mano di Pietro Bembo e di Lucrezia Borgia*, Madrid, 1925.
—On Ercole Strozzi, "Ercole Strozzi, poeta ferrarese," in *Attie e Memorie della Deputazione ferrarese di Storia Patria*, XVI, 1906; *Poesie di Ercole Strozzi e di Tito Vespasiano Strozzi*, 1530.
—S. Baruffaldi, *Istoria di Ferrara*, Ferrara, 1700; *Notizie istoriche delle academie letterarie ferraresi*, 1787.

III, Chapter 3: A Triumph in Heaven

On the Spanish branch of the Borgia family, see P. Anselme, *Histoire généalogique et chronologique*, vol. V, pp. 521–26.
On Maria Enriquez, widow of Don Juan I, and on Juan II at Gandia, see E. Bertaux, *Les Borgia dans le royaume de Valence*, Paris, 1911 (bibliography and reproductions of the pious paintings).
Documentation in José Sanchis Sivera, *Algunos documentos y cartas privadas . . .*, Valencia, 1919; Ximo Company, "Un assaig d'historiacó total de l'art: el retaule

de la collegiata de Gandia," in *Debats*, no. 10, December 1984 (*Institucio Alfons el Magnanim*, Valencia); *ibid.*, *Pintura del Renaiximent al Ducat de Gandia*, Valencia, 1985.

On Francis Borgia, see the entry by C. de Dalmasas, in *Dict. hist. et géogr. eccl.* An early, anonymous *Life* was reprinted in Lyon and Paris, 1824. See also P. Ribadeneyra, *Vida del Padre Francisco de Borja*, Madrid, 1592; P. Suau, *Histoire de S. François de Borgia*, Paris, 1910; Adro Xavier, *El duque de Gandia. El noble Santo del Primer Imperior*, Madrid, 1943. Relationship with Charles V: see M. Gachard, *Retraite et mort de Charles Quint au monastère de Yuste. Lettres inédites*, Brussels, 1855. See also the various biographies of Charles V and Philip II. For the Empress Isabella, see Annie Cloulas, "Les portraits de l'impératrice Isabelle de Portugal," in the *Gazette des Beaux-Arts*, 121st year, February 1979, pp. 58–68.

On Francis Borgia's acitivities in Catalonia, see P. J. Blanco, *El virreinato di San Francisco de Borja en Cataluña*, Barcelona, 1921. The banditry that plagued Catalonia in the sixteenth and seventeenth centuries has been studied in depth by P. Vilar, *La Catalogne dans l'Espagne moderne*, vol. I, 1962, pp. 575–84.

On Francis Borgia's last mission to the French court: C. Hirschauer, *La Politique de saint Pie V en France*, Paris, 1922.

On Francis Borgia's work as third general of the Jesuits, see J. Crétineau-Joly, *Histoire religieuse, politique et littéraire de la Compagnie de Jésus*, vols. I and II, Paris, 1844; A. Astrain, *Historia de la Compaña de Jesús en la Assistencia de España*, vol. II, Madrid, 1905; F. Rodrigues, *Historia da Compagnhia de Jesús na Assistencia de Portugal*, vol II, 1–2, Oporto, 1938; H. Fouqueray, *Histoire de la compagnie de Jésus en France*, vol. I, *Les Origines et les premières luttes*, Paris, 1910. On Portugal, see Velloso Queiroz, *Dom Sebastião*, Lisbon, 1945, and F. de S. Loureiro de Mascarengas, *O Po. Luis Goncalves de Câmara e Dom Sebastião*, Coimbra, 1973.

Printed Sources

ADEMOLO (A.), *Alessandro VI, Giulio II e Leone X nel Carnevale di Roma. Documenti inediti (1499–1520)*, Florence, 1886.
AMIANI (M.), *Memorie storiche della città di Fano*, Fano, 1757.
AMMANATI (card.), *Epistolae et Commentarii*, Milan, 1506.
Archivum historicum Societatis Jesu, XLI (Jan.–June, 1972), documents published to commemmorate fourth centenary of death of St. Francis Borgia.
ANSELME (P.), *Histoire généalogique et chronologique de la Maison royale de France*, Vol. V, Paris, 1730, p. 516–26, documents in proof of elevation of duchy of Valentinois; genealogy of Borgias and dukes of Gandia.
AUTON (Jean d'—), *Chronique de Louis XII*, Paris, 1889–1895.

BARONIUS, *Annales ecclesiastici*, Bar-le-Duc, Vol. XXIX, 1876.
BERNARDI (A.), *Cronache forlivesi dal 1476 al 1517*, ed. D. Mazzantini, 2 vols., Bologna, 1895–97.
BORGIA (François de), *Tratados espirituales*, ed. C. de Dalmases, Barcelona, 1964.
BRANTÔME (Pierre de Bourdeille, abbé de), *Œuvres complètes*, ed. L. Lalanne, Paris, 11 vols., 1864–82: vol. II, Paris, 1866, pp. 203–19, *César Borgia*.
BURCKARD (Jean), *Burchardi Johannis diarium sive rerum urbanarum commentarii, 1483–1506*, 3 vols., ed. L. Thuasne, Paris, 1883–85.
—*Liber notarum ab anno 1483 usque ad annum 1506*, ed. E. Celani, Città di Castello, 1910–11.
—*Le journal de Jean Burckard, évêque et cérémoniaire au Vatican*, French trans. with introduction and notes by Joseph Turmel, Paris, 1932.
BURSELLIS, *Annales Bononienses fratris Hieronymi de—*, Milan, 1733.

CAGNOLO (Niccolo), *Lucrezia Borgia in Ferrara. Memorie storiche estratte dalla cronaca ferrarese di N. Cagnolo di Parma*, Ferrara, 1867.
CAMBI (G.), *Istorie in Delizie degli eruditi Toscani*, vols. XXI–XXIII, Florence, 1785.
CAPPELLO (Paolo), *Relazione di Roma* dans Alberi (E.), *Relazioni degli ambasciatori veneti*, 2nd series, vol. 3, Florence, 1846.
CASTIGLIONE (Baldassare), *Il Libro del Cortegiano*, new ed. with introduction by A. Quondam and notes by M. Longo, Milan, 1982.
CIACCONIUS (or CHACON) (Alonso), *Vitae et regestae summorum pontificum*, Rome, 1601; continuation by Oldoini (Agostino), Rome, 1677.
COMMINES (Ph. de), *Mémoires*, ed. M. Dupont, vol. II, Paris, 1843.
—*Lettres et négociations*, ed. J. B. Kervyn de Lettenhove, Brussels, 1867–74.
CONTI (Sigismondo dei—da Foligno), *Le storie dei suoi tempi dal 1475 al 1510*, 2 vols., Rome, 1883.
Cronaca Sublacense del P. D. Cherubino Mirzio da Treveri, Monaco nella protobadia di Subiaco, Rome, 1885.

Cronache della città di Perugia, ed. A. Fabretti, Turin, 1888.
Cronica di Napoli di notar Giacomo, ed. P. Garzilli, Naples, 1845.

DOLFI (Floriano), *Orazione di Fl. Dolfi, bolognese, per la difesa della patria contro Alessandro VI e Cesare Borgia*, Bologna, 1900.
Diario di ser Tommaso di Silvestro Notaro, ed. L. Fumi, Orvieto, 1891–1892.
Diario Ferrarese dall'anno 1409 sino al 1502, Muratori, *Scriptores*, vol. XXIV, Milan, 1738
DU MONT (J.), *Corps universel diplomatique du droit des gens*, Amsterdam, 1726–31.

FORCELLA (V.), *Iscrizione delle chiese e d'altri edifizi di Roma*, 14 vols., Rome, 1869–85.

GACHARD (M.), *Retraite et mort de Charles Quint au monastère de Yuste. Lettres inédites*, vols. I and II, Brussels, 1854.
GASCA QUEIRAZZA (G.), *Scritti autografi di Alessandro VI nell'Archivum Arcis*, 1959.
GATTI (B.), *Lettere di Lucrezia Borgia a M. Pietro Bembo dagli autografi conservati in un codice della Biblioteca Ambrosiana*, Milan, 1859.
GHERARDI (Jacobo) da Volterra, *Diario romano dal 7 settembre 1479 al 12 agosto 1494*, ed. E. Carusi, Città di Castello, 1904.
GIOVIO (Paolo) (Paulus Jovius), *Vitae illustrium virorum*, 2 vols., Basel, 1578.
—*Elogia virorum literis illustrium*, Basel, 1577.
—*Elogia virorum bellica virtate illustriu*, Basel, 1596.
GIUSTINIAN (Antonio), *Dispacci*, ed. P. Villari, Florence, 1886.
GRASSIS (Paris de), *Diarium*, ed. Doellinger, *Beitraege*, vol. III, Vienna, 1882.
GRAZIANI, *Cronaca della città di Perugia secondo un codice appartenente ai Conti Baglioni*, Florence, 1850.
GUICCIARDINI (F.), *Storia d'Italia*, 5 vols., Bari, 1929; new ed., 3 vols., Milan, 1975.
—*Storia fiorentina dal 1378 al 1509*, Bari, 1931.

HURTUBISE (P.), *Correspondance du nonce Antonio Maria Salviati*, vol. I, Rome, 1975.

INFESSURA (Stefano), *Diario della città di Roma*, ed. Oreste Tommasini, Rome, 1890.

LANDUCCI (L.), *Diario fiorentino dal 1450 al 1516*, ed. Jodoco del Badia, Florence, 1883.

MACHIAVELLI (Niccolò), *Lettere famigliari*, ed. E. Alvisi, Florence, 1883.
—*Opere*, ed. E. Raimondi, Milan, 1969.
—*Extraits thématiques*, ed. Ch. Bec, Paris, 1985.
—*Œuvres*, trans. T. Guiraudet, 9 vols., Paris, an VII.
MALIPIERO (D.), *Annali Veneti (1457–1500)*, ed. F. Longo, *Archivio storico italiano*, vol. VII, Florence, 1843.
MARIOTTI, *Saggio di memorie isotoriche della città di Perugia*, Perugia, 1806.
MARTYR (Pietro), *Opus epistolarum*, Amsterdam, 1670.
MATARAZZO (F.), *Cronaca della città di Perugia (1492–1503)*, ed. A. Fabretti, *Archivio storico italiano*, XVI, II, Florence, 1851.
MEDIN (Antonio et Lodovico), *Lamenti storici dei sec. XIV, XV, XVI*, Bologna, 1890.
Monumenta historica Societatis Jesu. Sanctus Franciscus Borgia, 5 vols., Madrid, 1894–1911.

MOREL-FATIO (A.), *Historiographie de Charles Quint. Première partie suivie des Mémoires de Charles Quint*, Paris, 1913.

PELICIER (P.), *Lettres de Charles VIII roi de France*, vols. 1–5, Paris, 1898–1905.
PELISSIER (L. G.), «sopra alcuni documenti relativi all'alleanza tra Allessandro VI e Luigi XII (1498–99),» in Archiv. della Soc. Roman, di storia patria, 18, 1895.
PICCOLOMINI (Aenea), *Alcuni documenti inediti intorno a Pio II e a Pio III*, Siena, 1871.
PLATINA (Battista) (Bartolommeo Sacchi), *Vitae pontificum ad Sixtum IV*, Venice, 1479; et continuation: *Historia de vitis pontificum . . . Sixti IV, Innocentii VIII, Alexandri VI ac Pii III vita annexa*, Paris, 1505; PANVINIO (Onofrio), *Romani pontifices et cardinales S. R. E.*, Venice, 1557.
PRIULI (G.), *I Diarii*, Città di Castello, 1912 and 1919.

RIUS SERRA (J.), *Regesto ibérico de Calixto III*, vol. 1, Barcelona, 1948; vol. 2, Barcelona, 1958.
RONCHINI (A.), «Documenti Borgiani vell' Archivio di Parma», dans *Atti e Memorie della Deput. di Storia per l'Emilia*, 1877.
ROO (Peter de—), *Material for a history of pope Alexandre VI, his relatives and his time*, 5 vols., Bruges and New York, 1924.

SANCHIS SIVERA (José), *Algunos documentos y cartas privadas que pertenecieron al segundo duque de Gandia, Don Juan de Borja*, Valencia, 1919.
SANNAZAR (Jacopo Sannazaro), *Rime*, Venice, 1538.
SANSI (Achille), *Documenti storici inediti tratti dall'Archivio communale di Spoleto*, Foligno, 1861.
SANUDO (Marino), *I Diarii dal 1496 al 1532*, Venice, 1879–1903.
—*La Spedizione di Carlo VIII in Italia*, ed. R. Fulin, Venice, 1873.
STROZZI (Ercole et Tito Vespasiano), *Poesie*, Paris, 1530.

TEDALLINI DI BRANCA (S.), *Diario Romano dal maggio 1485 al giugno 1524*, ed. P. Piccolomini, Città di Castello, 1907.
THEINER (A.), *Codex diplomaticus dominii temporalis Sanctae Sedis. Recueil de documents pour servir à l'histoire du gouvernement temporel des Etats du Saint-Siège, extraits des archives du Vatican*, vol. III (1389–1793), Rome, 1862.
TRINCHERA (F.), *Codice aragonese ossia lettere regie, ordinamenti ed altri atti governativi dei sovrani aragonesi in Napoli*, 2 vols., Naples, 1866.
TUCCIA (Niccolo della), *Chronica di Viterbo*, Florence, 1879.

ZAMBOTTI (B.), *Diario ferrarese dal 1476 al 1504*, ed. G. Pardi, Bologna, 1937.
ZURITA (G.), *Anales de la Corona de Aragón*, vols. IV, and V, Saragossa, 1610.

Bibliography

ADINOLFI (P.), *La Portica di s. Pietro ossia Borgo nell'età di mezzo. Nuovo saggio topogrofico dato sopra pubblichi e privati documenti*, Rome, 1859.
—*Roma nell'età di mezzo*, 2 vols., Rome, 1881.
ALVISI (E.), *Cesare Borgia, duca di Romagna*, Imola, 1878.
AMETLLER VINAS (J.), *Alfonso V de Aragón en Italia y la crisis religiosa del siglo XV*, 3 vols., Gerona, 1903.
ARCO (C. d'), «Notizie su Isabella Estense con documenti,» *Archivio storico italiano*, app. 2, 1845.
ASTRAIN (A.), *Historia de la Compaña de Jesùs en la Asistencia de España*, vol. II, Laínez-Borja, Madrid, 1905.

BACCHELLI (R.), *La congiura di don Giulio d'Este*, Milan, 1958.
BAGLION (Comte L. de la DUFFERIE), *Les Baglioni de Pérouse*, Poitiers, 1907.
BALLESTER JULBE (Constantino), *La Germania de Játiva. Cronicas del siglo SVI*, Murcia, 1920–30.
BATLLORI (Miquel), «La correspondencia d'Alexandre VI amb els seus familars i amb els Reis Catolicos,» in *Actes du Cinquième congrès d'Histoire de la Couronne d'Aragon*, vol. 2, pp. 307–13.
BELLONCI (Maria), *Lucrezia Borgia*, 2nd ed., Milan, 1970; abridged English trans., *Lucrezia Borgia*, London, 1953.
—«La mamma ordina un corredo per Rodrigo», *L'Europeo*, January 10, 1954.
BEMBO (Pietro), *Gli Asolani*, Venice, 1505.
—*Lettere giovanili di Messer Pietro Bembo*, Milan, 1558.
—*Opera historica*, Basel, 1567.
BENDEDEI, *Lettera al pontefice Alessandro VI per gli sponsali di Lucrezia Borgia con Alfonso d'Este*, Ferrara, 1889.
BÉRENCE (Fred), *Lucrèce Borgia*, Paris, 1937.
BERLINER (A.), *Geschichte des Juden in Rom von der aeltesten Zeiten bis zur Gegenwart*, 2 vols., Frankfurt, 1893.
BERNALDEZ (A.), *Historia de los Reyes Católicos don Fernando y doña Isabel*, 2 vols., Seville, 1870–75.
BERTAUX (F.), *Les Borgia dans le royaume de Valence*, Paris, 1911.
BERTONI (G.), *La biblioteca estense e la cultura ferrarese al tempo di Ercole Iº*, Turin, 1903.
—*L'Orlando Furioso e la Rinascenza a Ferrara*, Modena, 1919.
BETHENCOURT (de —), *Historia genealógica y heráldica de la Monarquia Española, Casa Real y Grandes de España*, vol. IV, *Gandia*, Madrid, 1902.
BLANCO (P. G.), *El virreinato di san Francisco de Borja en Cataluña*, Barcelona, 1921.

BOITEUX (M.), «Les Juifs dans le Carnaval de la Rome moderne. XVᵉ–XVIIIᵉ siècle,» in *Mélanges d'archéologie et d'histoire, Ecole française de Rome*, 1976.
BORGATI (M.), *Castel Sant'Angelo in Roma. Storia e descrizione*, Rome, 1890.
BOSCHI (G.), *Lucrezia Borgia*, Bologna, 1923.
BRADFORD (Sarah), *Cesare Borgia, his life and times*, London, 1976.
BRAUDEL (F.), *La Méditerranée et le monde méditerranéen à l'époque de Philippe II*, 2nd ed., Paris, 1966.
BRION (M.), «Lucrèce Borgia, telle qu'elle fut,» *Revue de Paris*, 1954.
—*Les Borgia*, Paris, 1979.
BURCKHARDT (J.), *Die Cultur der Renaissance in Italien*, 3rd ed., 2 vols., Leipzig, 1877–78.

CABANÈS (A.), *Le journal des couches de Lucrèce Borgia*, Paris, 1929 (Dans les coulisses de l'Histoire, 1st series).
CABANÈS (Dr.) et NASS (Dr. L.), *Poisons et sortilèges. Les Césars, envoûteurs et sorciers, les Borgia*, Paris, 1903.
CAMPORI (G.), «Una vittima della storia: Lucrezia Borgia,» *Nuova Antologia*, vol. II, 1866.
CAPPELLETTI (L.), *Lucrezia Borgia e la Storia*, Pisa, 1876.
CARTWRIGHT (J.) *Isabella d'Este, marchioness of Mantua, 1474–1539*, 2 vols., London, 1903.
CATALANO (M.), *Lucrezia Borgia, duchessa di Ferrara. Con nuovi documenti*, Ferrara, n.d.
CÉLIER (L.), «Alexandre VI et ses enfants en 1493,» *Ecole française de Rome. Mélanges d'archéologie et d'histoire*, 1906.
CERRI (D.), *Borgia, ossia Alexandro VI papa, e i suoi contemporanei*, Turin, 1858.
CHABAS (Roque), «Alejandro VI y el duque de Gandia,» *El Archivo*, VII, Valencia, 1893.
—«Don Jofré de Borja y Doña Sancha de Aragón,» *Revue hispanique*, IX, 1902.
CHERRIER (C. de), *Histoire de Charles VIII, roi de France*, 2 vols., Paris, 1868.
CIAN (V.), *Un decennio della vita di Pietro Bembo*, Turin, 1885.
—*Caterina Sforza, a proposito della Caterina Sforza di Pier Desiderio Pasolini*, Turin, 1893.
CIPOLLA (C.), *Storia delle signorie italiane dal 1313 al 1530*, Milan, 1881.
CITTADELLA *(L. N.), Notizie amministrative, storiche, artistiche di Ferrara*, Ferrara, 1868.
—*Saggio di albero genealogico a di memorie su la famiglia Borgia, specialmente in relazione a Ferrara*, Turin, 1872.
CLOULAS (Ivan), *Charles VIII et le mirage italien*, Paris, 1986.
—«Aux origines des guerres d'Italie: les malheurs du prince Zizim,» in *Historama*, n° 30 (August 1986).
CLÉMENT (abbé), *Les Borgia. Histoire du pape Alexandre VI, de César et de Lucrèce Borgia*, Paris, 1882.
COLLISON-MORLEY (L.), The Story of the Borgias, London, 1934.
COMPANY, (Ximo), *Pintura del Renaiximent al Ducat de Gandia*, Valencia, 1985.
CORVO (Frederic ROLFE, "baron"—), *Chronicles of the House of Borgia*, London, 1901.
COULET (N.), «La place des Juifs dans les cérémonies d'entrées solennelles au Moyen Age,» in *Annales, sociétés, civilisations*, 1979.
CROCE (Benedetto), *Versi spagnoli in lode di Lucrezia Borgia, duchessa di Ferrara e delle sue damigelle*, Naples, 1884.
—*La Spagna nella vita italiana durante la Rinascenza*, Bari, 1922.

DAVIDSOHN (R.), «Lucrezia Borgia, suora di penitenza,» *Archivio storico italiano*, 1901.

DELABORDE (H. F.), *L'expédition de Charles VIII en Italie*, Paris, 1888.

DUHR (B.), *Geschichte der Gesellschaft Jesu in den Länder deutscher Zunge*, I, Fribourg, 1907.

EHRELE (F.) and STEVENSON (E.), *Gli affreschi del Pinturicchio nell'Appartemento Borgia*, Rome, 1897.

ESCOLANO (G.), *Decadas de la Historia del Reino de Valencia . . . aumentada y continuada por* D. Juan B. PERALES, Valencia, 1878.

FEDELE (P.), «I gioielli di Vannozza,» dans *Archivio della Società Romana di Storia Patria*, 1905.

FELICIANGELI (B.), *Il matrimonio di Lucrezia Borgia con Giovanni Sforza, signore di Pesaro*, Turin, 1901.

FERRARA (Orestes), *El papa Borgia*, Madrid, 1943.

FORGEOT (H.), *Jean Balue, cardinal d'Angers*, Paris, 1895.

FOUQUERAY (H.), *Histoire de la Compagnie de Jésus en France, des origines à la suppression (1582–1762)*, vol. I, Paris, 1910.

FRIZZI (A.), *Memorie par la storia di Ferrara*, 5 vols., 1791–1800.

FUMI (L.), *Alessandro VI e il Valentino in Orvieto*, Siena, 1877.

FUNCK-BRENTANO (F.), *Lucrèce Borgia*, Paris, 1932.

GAGNIÈRE (A.), «Le journal des médecins de Lucrèce Borgia,» dans *La Nouvelle Revue*, 54, 1888.

GALLIER (A. de—), *César Borgia, duc de Valentinois, et documents inédits sur son séjour en France*, Paris, 1895.

GARNER (J. L.), *Caesar Borgia. A Study of the Renaissance*, London, 1912.

GASTINE (L.), *César Borgia*, Paris, 1911.

GEBHART (F.), «Un problème de morale et d'histoire. Les Borgia,» *Revue des Deux-Mondes*, Paris, 1888–89, article reprinted in *Moines et papes. Essais de psychologie historique*, Paris, 1907.

CHIRARDACCI (C.), *Historia di Bologna*, Città di Castello, 1915.

GIANNONE (P.), *Historia civile del regno di Napoli*, vol. III, Venice, 1766.

GILBERT (W.), *Lucrezia Borgia, duchess of Ferrara*, London, 1869.

GNOLI (U.), *Alberghi ed Osterie in Roma nel Rinascimento*, Rome, 1942.

GORDON (A.), *The Lives of Pope Alexandre VI and Cesar Borgia*, London, 1729.

GORI (F.), «Fortificazioni dei Borgia nella Rocca di Subiaco,» dans *Archivio storico . . . della città e provincia di Roma*, vol. IV, Rome and Spoleto, 1876–83.

GOZZADINI (G.), *Memorie per la vita di Giovanni II Bentivoglio*, Bologna, 1839.

GREGOROVIUS (F.), *Lucrezia Borgia nach Urkunden und Correspondenzen*, Stuttgart, 1874; reed. Dresden, 1952.

—*Storia della città di Roma nel Medio Evo*, Rome, 1910.

GRIMALDI (N.), *Reggio, Lucrezia Borgia e un romanzo d'amore della duchessa di Ferrara*, Reggio Emilia, 1926.

GUERDAN (R.), *César Borgia: «le Prince» de Machiavel*, Paris, 1974.

GUGLIELMOTTI (A.), *Storia della Marina pontificia*, Rome, 1886.

GUIRAUD (J.), *L'Etat pontifical après le Grand Schisme*, Paris, 1896.

HAYWARD (F.), *L'enigme des Borgia*, Paris, 1956 (*Visages de l'Eglise*, 6).

HEERS (J.), *Machiavel*, Paris, 1985.

—*La vie quotidienne à la cour pontificale au temps des Borgia et des Médicis (1420–1520)*, Paris, 1986.

HERMANIN (F.), *L'appartemento Borgia in Vaticano*, Danesi, 1934.

HOEFLER (V. von), *Don Rodrigo de Borja und seine Söhne*, Vienna, 1889.

JAGOT (Dr.), *Le poison des Borgia*, Angers, 1909.

LABANDE-MAILFERT (Y.), *Charles VIII et son milieu (1470–1498). La jeunesse au pouvoir*, Paris, 1975.

LAURENCIN (Marquis de), *Relación de los festines que se celebraron en el Vaticano con motivo de las bodas de Lucrecia Borja con don Alonso de Aragón*, Madrid, 1916.

LEONETTI (A.), *Papa Alessandro VI secondo documenti e carteggi del tempo*, 3 vols., Bologna, 1880.

L'EPINOIS (H. de), «Le pape Alexandre VI,» in *Revue des questions historiques*, 29, 1881.

LETAROUILLY (P.), *Le Vatican et la basilique de Saint-Pierre de Rome*, 3 vols., Paris, 1882.

LITTA (Pompeo), *Famiglie celebri italiane*, 10 vols., Milan, 1819–74; cont., Turin, 1875–86.

LUCAS-DUBRETON (J.), *Les Borgia*, Paris, 1952.

LUZIO (A.), *Federigo Gonzaga, ostaggio alla corte di Giulio II*, Rome, 1887.

—*Isabella d'Este e i Borgia*, Milan, 1916.

—«Isabella d'Este nelle tragedie della sua casa,» in *Atti e Memorie della R. Accademia Virgiliana di Mantova*, new series, V, 1912.

LUZIO (G.) and RENIER (R.), *Mantova e Urbino. Isabella d'Este ed Elisabetta Gonzaga nelle relazioni famigliari e nelle vicende politiche*, Turin and Rome, 1893.

MANCINI (F.), «Lucrezia Borgia governatrice di Spoleto,» in *Archivio storico italiano*, 1957.

MARICOURT (R. de), *Le procès des Borgia considéré au point de vue de l'histoire naturelle et sociale*, Poitiers and Paris, 1883.

MATAGNE (H.), «Une réhabilitation d'Alexandre VI,» *Revue des questions historiques*, 11, p. 466, 1870 and 13, pp. 180, 1872.

MAUGAIN (G.), *Mœurs italiennes de la Renaissance. La Vengeance*, Paris, 1935.

MAULDE LA CLAVIÉRE (R. de), *La diplomatie au temps de Machiavel*, 3 vols., Paris, 1892–93.

—«Alexandre VI et le divorce de Louis XII,» in *Bibliotheque de l'Ecole des Chartes*, 1896.

MENOTTI (M.), *I Borgia. Storia ed iconografia*, Rome, 1917.

—*I Borgia. Documenti inediti sulla famiglia e la corte di Alessandro VI*, Rome, 1917.

MOLLAT (G.), *Les papes d'Avignon (1305–1378)*, Paris, 1964.

MORSOLIN (B.), «Pietro Bembo e Lucrezia Borgia,» in *Nuova Antologia*, 52, 1885.

MÜNTZ (E.), *Les arts à la Cour des papes Innocent VIII, Alexandre VI, Pie III (1484–1503)*, Paris, 1898.

NARBONNE (B.), *La vie privée de Lucrèce Borgia*, Paris, 1953.

NAVENNE (F.), *Rome, le Palais Farnèse et les Farnèse*, Paris, 1914.

NEGRI (P.), «Le missioni di Pandolfo Collenuccio a papa Alessandro VI (1494–98),» in *Archiv. Soc. Rom. di Storia Patria*, vol. 33.

Bibliography

OLIVER Y HURTADO (Manuel), «Don Rodrigo de Borgia: sus hijos y descendientes,» in *Boletin de la Real Academia de la Historia*, December 1886, Madrid.

OLLIVIER (M. J. H.), *Le pape Alexandre VI et les Borgia*, Paris, 1870.

OLMOS Y CANALDA (E.), *Reivindicación de Alejandro VI, el papa Borja*, Valencia, 1954.

ORTIZ FELIPE (Francisco Javier), *Cesar Borgia y Navarra*, Pamplona, 1983.

PALANQUE (J. R.) et CHELINI (J.), *Petite histoire des grands conciles*, Bruges, 1962.

PASCHINI (P.), *Roma nel Rinascimento*, Bologna, 1940.

PASCUAL Y BELTRAN (Buenaventura), *El gran papa español Alejandro VI en sus relaciones con los Reyes Católicos*, Valencia, 1941.

PASINI FRASSONI, «I Borgia in Ferrara,» *Giornale Araldico Genealogico Diplomatico*, Rome, January–February 1880.

PASOLINI (P. D.), *Caterina Sforza*, 2nd ed., Bologna, 1897.

PASTOR (Juan), *Borja espiritu universal. Breve biografia de san Francisco de Borja*, Bilbao, 1970.

PASTOR (Ludwig von), *Geschichte des Päpste seit dem Ausgang des Mittelalters*, Fribourg, vol. I (up to Pius II, 1464), 1901; vol. II (1464–84), 1904; vol. III (1484–1513), 1899; vol. VIII (Pius V, 1566–72), 1920.

PELISSIER (L. G.), *Louis XII et Ludovic Sforza*, 2 vols., Paris, 1896.

PEPE (G.), *La politica dei Borgia*, Naples, 1940.

PERRENS (F. T.), *Histoire de Florence depuis la domination des Médicis jusqu'à la chute de la République (1434–1531)*, vols. I–III, Paris, 1888–90.

PICOTTI (G. B.), *La jeunesse de Léon X*, Paris, 1931.

—«Ancora sul Borgia,» *Rivista di Storia della Chiesa in Italia*, VIII, no. 3, September–December 1954.

—«Nuovi studi e documenti intorno a papa Alessandro VI,» *ibidem*, V, no. 2, 1951.

PISTOFILO BONAVENTURA, *Vita di Alfonso d'Este*, Modena, 1865.

PODESTA (B.), «Intorno alle due statue erette in Bologna a Giulio II,» in *Atti e Memorie Deputaz. storia patria*, vol. VII, Bologna, 1808.

PORTIGLIOTTI (G.), *I. Borgia*, Milan, 1913.

—«Un ritratto tizianesco di Lucrezia Borgia» dans *Rivista d'Italia*, X, 1915.

PORZIO (C.), *La congiura de' Baroni del Regno di Napoli*, Florence, 1884.

QUILLIET (B.), *Louis XII*, Paris, 1986.

RAJNA (P.), «I versi spagnoli di mano di Pietro Bembo e di Lucrezia Borgia, serbati in un codice ambrosiano,» *Homenaje ofrecido a Menendez Pidal*, vol. II, Madrid, 1925.

RENOUARD (Y.), *La Papauté d'Avignon*, Paris, 1962.

RIBADENEYRA (P.), *Vita del Padre Francisco de Borja*, Madrid, 1592.

RICCI (Corrado), *Pinturicchio*, Perugia, 1915.

—*Il figlio di Cesare Borgia (Girolamo)*, Milan, 1918.

RODOCANACHI (Emmanuel), *Histoire de Rome de 1354 à 1471, L'antagonisme entre les Romains et le Saint-Siège*, Paris, 1921.

—*Histoire de Rome. Une cour princière au Vatican pendant la Renaissance. Sixte IV. Innocent VIII. Alexandre VI Borgia (1471–1503)*, Paris, 1925.

RODRIGUES (F.), *História da Companhia de Jesús na Assisténcia de Portugal*, II, 1560–1615, Oporto, 1938.

ROLFE (Frederick-William-Serafino), see CORVO (baron).

RYDER (Alan), *The Kingdom of Naples under Alfonso the Magnanimous. The making of a modern state*, Oxford, 1976.

SABATINI (R.), *The life of Cesare Borgia. A history and some criticism*, London, 1916.
SANCHIS SIVERA (José), *El cardenal Rodrigo de Borja en Valencia*, Madrid, 1924.
—*El obispo de Valencia Don Alfonso de Borja (Calixto III) (1429–1458)*, Madrid, 1926.
SARTHOU CARRES (Carlos), *Datos para la historia de Játiva*, 2nd ed., 1976.
SIZERANNE (R. de La), *César Borgia et le duc d'Urbino*, Paris, n. d., 1924.
SORANZO (G.), *Studi intorno a papa Alessandro VI Borgia*, Milan, 1950.
SUAU (P.), *Histoire de s. François de Borgia*, Paris, 1910.

THUASNE (Louis), *Djem Sultan*, Paris, 1892.
TOMASI (Tommaso), *La vita del duca Valentino*, Montechiaro, 1655.
TOMMASINI (O.), *La vita e gli scritti di N. Machiavelli nelle loro relazioni col Machiavellismo. Storia ed esame critico*, Turin, 1883.
TONINI (L.), *Rimini nella signoria de'Malatesti*, Rimini, 1882.
TRUC (G.), *Rome et les Borgia*, Paris, 1939.

UGHELLI (F.) *Italia sacra, sive de episcopis Italiae*, ed. N. Coletus, 10 vols., Venice, 1717–22.
UGOLINI (Fil.), *Storia dei conti e duchi d'Urbino*, Florence, 1859.

VILA MORENO (Alfonso), *Calixto III: un papa valenciano*, Saragossa, 1979.
VILAR (Pierre), *La Catalogne dans l'Espagne moderne*, 3 vols., Paris, 1962.
VILLARI (Pasquale), *Niccolò Machiavelli e i suoi tempi*, Florence, 1877.
—*Nuovi Studi sui Borgia*, n. d.
—*Jérôme Savonarole et son temps*, Paris, 1874.

WIRTZ (M.), «Ercole Strozzi poeta ferrarese,» in *Atti e Memorie della Deputazione ferrarese di storia patria*, XVI, 1906.
WOODWARD (W. H.), *Cesare Borgia. A biography with documents and illustrations*, London, 1913.

XAVIER (Adro), *El duque de Gandia. El noble santo del Primer Imperio*, 2nd ed., Madrid, 1943.

YRIARTE (Ch.), *César Borgia, Sa vie, sa captivité, sa mort*, 2 vols., Paris, 1889.
—*Autour des Borgia*, Paris, 1891.

INDEX